The Top 20 Things You Need to Know for Top Scores in Biology

1. Characteristics of Cells

Know the form and function of the parts of the cell. Be able to identify:

- the difference between prokaryotic and eukaryotic cells
- the difference between animal and plant cells
- the various organelles on any diagrams provided
- the relationship between the function of each organelle and its role in the cell

See Lesson 6-2.

2. Cellular Processes

Know the details of cellular respiration and photosynthesis along with the reactants and products. Know the specific parts of each process. Understand:

- the relationship between the light and dark reactions of photosynthesis
- glycolysis and the Krebs cycle
- the conditions required for a process to occur
- the materials produced by just a part of the process

See Lesson 6-3.

3. DNA

Know the structure and function of DNA. Know the composition of DNA molecules as well as such processes as:

- replication
- transcription
- translation

Understand the relationship between DNA and RNA. Be able to identify complementary strands of DNA and types of mutations.

See Lesson 6-4.

4. Cell Cycle

Know the parts of the cell cycle. Be able to identify the stages of mitosis (especially on diagrams) and the events that occur during each stage. Be able to compare mitosis with meiosis and to describe the cells produced by each. Know how to:

- calculate the number of chromosomes in a diploid cell given the haploid number
- relate a described event to a stage of mitosis

See Lesson 6-5.

5. Genetics

Be able to recall:

- Mendel's experiment
- the law of segregation
- the law of independent assortment

D1516677

Be able to compare dominant and recessive alleles to describe genotypes and phenotypes. You should also understand technologies relating to genetics, such as:

- DNA sequencing, gel electrophoresis
- recombinant DNA technology
- DNA fingerprinting

See Lessons 7-1 through 7-3.

6. Punnett Squares and Pedigrees

Know how to use a Punnett square provided by the test or to make your own Punnett square to discuss a generation of organisms. Be prepared to make predictions about first and second generations given the genotypes of the organisms involved in a cross.

Be able to examine a provided pedigree and draw conclusions about a genetic trait or the traits of a person on the pedigree.

See Lessons 7-4 and 7-5.

7. Natural Selection

Know the historical development of the theories of Lamarck and Darwin. You will need to understand the factors of natural selection as well as evidence for evolution. Be able to:

- interpret the meaning of fossil or genetic evidence
- define evolution
- evaluate statements about natural selection
- identify examples of evolution

Be comfortable using the Hardy–Weinberg equation and interpreting processes through which new species are formed.

See Lessons 8-1 and 8-2.

8. Origins of Living Things

Be familiar with theories regarding the development of the first living things on Earth and attempts to replicate their formation in the laboratory. Be prepared for questions about fossil evidence and relative or radiometric dating. Review the major events in the development of living things, such as:

- the formation of oxygen in the atmosphere
- the emergence of eukaryotes
- the introduction of multicellular organisms
- the Cambrian explosion
- the mass extinctions that occurred
- the emergence of humans

See Lesson 8-3.

9. Taxonomy

Memorize the modern taxonomic groupings from domain to species. Be able to order the group from the most inclusive to the least inclusive. Know the characteristics of each domain and the kingdoms within them. Be able to identify the kingdom in which an organism should be classified based on its characteristics.

See Lessons 8-3 and 8-4.

10. Skeletal and Muscular Systems

Review the skeletal and muscular systems, and how they relate to one another. Be able to identify types of bones and muscles and know where they might be found.

See Lesson 9-1.

11. Circulatory and Respiratory Systems

Be able to compare open and closed circulatory systems and be familiar with the parts of each. Be able to:

- identify parts of the human heart on a diagram
- trace the flow of blood through the heart

Review the composition of blood and be able to compare the percentages of substances in a sample of blood. Review the parts of the respiratory system and know how it relates to the circulatory system.

See Lesson 9-2.

12. Human Digestive System

Know the parts of the human digestive system. Be able to:

- trace the movement of food through the system
- identify the role of various organs in the digestive process
- describe the role of the human excretory system

See Lesson 9-3.

13. Immune System

Know about the role and layers of the skin. Be able to relate the skin to the immune system. Know the types of cells involved in protecting the body from disease.

See Lesson 9-4.

14. Nervous and Endocrine Systems

Familiarize yourself with the parts of the human nervous system. Be able to identify the parts of a neuron on a diagram, including the dendrite, cell body, and axon. Understand the process that occurs when a neuron is stimulated. Make sure you are able to:

- identify the parts of the brain (such as the cerebellum, cerebrum, medulla oblongata, and hypothamalus) and their functions
- compare the differences between the central and peripheral nervous systems
- compare the differences between the somatic and autonomic nervous systems

Be able to identify each gland of the human body and describe its role. Know that the endocrine system involves chemical messengers as opposed to the electrical messages transmitted in the nervous system.

See Lesson 9-5.

15. Human Reproductive System

Be able to identify and describe the role of the structures of the male and female systems. Understand fertilization and the process of development that occurs afterward. Be prepared to interpret diagrams of a human reproductive system or graphs representing changes in hormone levels during the menstrual cycle.

See Lesson 9-6.

16. Population Growth

Be able to compare exponential and limited population growth. Be prepared to identify the portion of a graph that represents the carrying capacity of a population. Predict how changes in limiting factors will affect the growth of a population.

See Lesson 10-1.

17. Food Chains and Food Webs

Familiarize yourself with the differences between biotic and abiotic factors in an ecosystem. Know how ecosystems, communities, and populations are related. Understand the information represented by:

- food chain diagrams
- food web diagrams
- pyramids of energy or biomass

See Lesson 10-2.

18. Ecological Relationships

Know how an organism's niche is related to its habitat. Be familiar with different types of symbiotic relationships. Be able to classify a relationship between two organisms as:

- mutualism
- commensalism
- parasitism

Recognize interspecific and intraspecific competition.

See Lesson 10-3.

19. Biomes

Review the major biomes on Earth and the factors by which they are classified. Familiarize yourself with the characteristics of aquatic biomes. Study the process of ecological succession. Know the conditions under which it occurs and the types of organisms involved in each stage.

See Lesson 10-4.

20. Nutrient Cycles

Study diagrams of the water, carbon, and nitrogen cycles. Know the processes, such as transpiration, and organisms involved in each.

See Lesson 10-5.

McGRAW-HILL's

SAT
SUBJECT TEST
BIOLOGY E/M

McGRAW-HILL's

SAT
SUBJECT TEST
BIOLOGY E/M

Second Edition

Stephanie M. Zinn, Editor
Nick Tarasen

New York | Chicago | San Francisco | Lisbon | London | Madrid | Mexico City
Milan | New Delhi | San Juan | Seoul | Singapore | Sydney | Toronto

The McGraw·Hill Companies

McGRAW-HILL's SAT Subject Test: Biology E/M

Copyright © 2009, 2006 by The McGraw-Hill Companies, Inc. All rights
reserved. Printed in the United States of America. Except as permitted
under the United States Copyright Act of 1976, no part of this publication
may be reproduced or distributed in any form or by any means, or stored
in a database or retrieval system, without the prior written permission of
the publisher.

1 2 3 4 5 6 7 8 9 0 QPD/QPD 0 1 4 3 2 1 0 9

ISBN 978-0-07-160920-3
MHID 0-07-160920-2

McGraw-Hill books are available at special quantity discounts to use as
premiums and sales promotions, or for use in corporate training pro-
grams. For more information, please write to the Director of Special
Sales, Professional Publishing, McGraw-Hill, Two Penn Plaza, New
York, NY 10121-2298. Or contact your local bookstore.

SAT is a registered trademark of the College Entrance Examination
Board, which was not involved in the production of, and does not
endorse, this product.

The book is printed on acid-free paper.

CONTENTS

PART I

ABOUT THE SAT BIOLOGY E/M TEST

CHAPTER 1

WHAT YOU NEED TO KNOW ABOUT THE SAT BIOLOGY E/M TEST

THE SAT SUBJECT TESTS

What Are the SAT Subject Tests?

The SAT Subject Tests (formerly known as Achievement Tests) are the lesser-known supplements to the SAT, sponsored by the same people—the College Entrance Examination Board. The tests are actually created by the Educational Testing Service, which also creates the SAT. Just as for the SAT, to take the SAT Subject Tests you must sign up for the test(s) in advance, number 2 pencils in hand, and have your results reported to whichever colleges and universities by which you wish to have them considered.

But, whereas the SAT tests general verbal reasoning, mathematical reasoning, and writing skills, the SAT Subject Tests cover specific knowledge in a wide variety of subjects, including English, mathematics, history, science, and foreign languages. SAT Subject Tests are much shorter than the SAT; they're only 1 hour long, so you can take up to three (3) in any one sitting, although you're not required to. You can choose which SAT Subject Tests to take, and how many you'll take on one day. Some students may take the SAT in World History, Math, and Biology in the same sitting, whereas others might choose just Biology and Math on the same day.

Why Should I Take the SAT Subject Tests in Addition to the SAT?

The College Board claims that SAT Subject Tests can help colleges measure your academic performance and predict your future achievement—but they say the same thing about the SAT. The difference is that SAT Subject Tests test your knowledge in specific subjects such as Biology, French, or U.S. History, therefore, they provide colleges and universities with a way to gauge your ability in these subjects, something they cannot get from the SAT. Many colleges and universities now require students to submit scores for SAT Subject Tests as part of their application. Along with your high school transcript, SAT score, letters of recommendation, interview, and essays, these scores provide another way for colleges to weigh your application against those of other applicants.

Although colleges can look at grades to determine how a student is doing in a certain subject, it is often difficult for them to understand if an "A" at one school is equivalent to an "A" at another. If Biology is your strongest subject, then a high SAT Biology score, combined with good grades on your transcript, can convey that strength to a college or university.

How Many SAT Subject Tests Should I Take? And Which Ones Should I Take?

You can take as many SAT Subject Tests as you would like. According to the College Board, in 2007, 41% of SAT Subject Test test-takers took three tests, and 11% took four or more. Remember, though, that you're limited to taking three tests in one sitting; if you want to take more than three, you'll have to sign up for two testing dates. Your first consideration in choosing how many, and which subject tests, to take should be the requirements of the colleges or universities to which you're applying. Many colleges require applicants to take specific tests, or to take a minimum number of tests.

If you can choose, then you should take the SAT Subject Tests for which you're best prepared, and on which you will score highest. If you've taken a class in a specific subject and done well in that class, then you will probably be well prepared to take the test in that subject. When choosing how many to take, remember that taking more tests is not always better. Focusing your preparation on a smaller number of tests will probably leave you better off than taking a larger number for which you are not adequately prepared.

When Should I Take the Subject Tests?

You should take the SAT Subject Tests when you will be most prepared. Ideally, you should take the test as soon as possible after you've finished a course in that subject. So, if you took biology in sophomore year, you may wish to take the SAT Biology test in May or June following that year. Do consider that you may wish to leave yourself time to review for each test properly, especially if some time has passed since you last encountered the material.

THE SAT BIOLOGY E/M TEST

What Is the Format of the SAT Biology-E/M Test? And What Does "E/M" Mean?

The SAT Biology test is a 1-hour test consisting of 80 multiple-choice questions. The SAT Biology test is unique among the SAT Subject Tests in that you have a choice between the "E" version of the test, which focuses more on ecology (subjects such as ecosystems, biomes, food chains and webs, and the water cycle), and the "M" version of the test, which focuses more on molecular biology (subjects such as genetics, inheritance, respiration, and photosynthesis). All test-takers get the same 60 "core" questions, which cover all areas of biology. You can then choose between two 20-questions sections, the ecology section or the molecular section.

What Is Covered on the SAT Biology Test?

Both the Biology-E and the Biology-M tests are designed to cover the material that would be typically taught in a high school biology course and lab. You are also expected to be familiar with algebra and how to use the metric system; some questions will ask you to interpret data as if you had completed a laboratory experiment, and will occasionally require you to do simple mathematical calculations.

The College Board gives an approximate outline of how much of each area of biology the tests cover:

Area	Percentage of Biology-E Devoted to Area	Percentage of Biology-M Devoted to Area
Cellular and Molecular Biology	15	27
Ecology	23	13
Genetics	15	20
Organismal Biology	25	25
Evolution and Diversity	22	15

Although the test may not always be exactly 23% ecology or 27% cellular and molecular biology, you should be aware that the Biology-M test focuses more on cellular and molecular biology and cellular genetics, while the Biology-E test focuses more on ecology and evolution and diversity. Approximately one-fourth of both tests is devoted to organismal biology. This book includes a detailed review of all of the areas covered in both tests.

Does It Matter whether I Take Biology-E or Biology-M? How Do I Choose between Them?

The College Board doesn't care whether you take the Biology-E or the Biology-M test, and almost the same number of students take each test. One is not designed to be harder than the other. You don't even need to indicate which one you're going to be taking until you're actually taking the test. Your test booklet will contain both sets of questions, and instructions on how to answer either the ecology or molecular part.

You should choose whichever test is geared toward your strengths in biology. If your biology course focused more on ecology or evolution, discussing food webs, predator–prey relationships, nutrient cycles, and biomes, then Biology-E is likely to be the test for you. If your biology course focused more on cellular processes and biomolecules, discussing DNA, proteins, chromosomes, mitosis and meiosis, respiration, and photosynthesis, then Biology-M is probably the better test for you.

Colleges care far more about your score on the SAT Biology test than which form of the exam you took—so your first consideration should be choosing the exam with which you're most comfortable. As a guide, however, you may wish to consider the type of biology you might study in the future. If you're applying for or are considering a program in biochemistry, genetics, or microbiology, then Biology-M might be a better choice; if you're applying for or considering a program in environmental studies, ecology, or evolution, then Biology-E might be more suited for you.

What if I Can't Decide between Biology-E and Biology-M?

If you're not sure whether Biology-E or Biology-M is better for you, don't worry! This book is designed to prepare students equally for both tests, and Chapter 2 includes a section on how to use it to help you decide whether to take Biology-E or Biology-M.

Do I Still Have to Study Ecology if I Take Biology-M? Do I Still Have to Study Molecular Biology if I Take Biology-E?

The answer to both of these questions is yes, if you plan to do well. If you're taking Biology-M, you may not be required to know ecology as in-depth as someone taking Biology-E, but you will still be asked some questions on ecology. And if you're taking Biology-E, you shouldn't overlook molecular biology. While you may want to spend more of your energy preparing for the specific test you're taking, reviewing all of the material is your best bet.

TAKING THE TEST

How Do I Register for the SAT Subject Tests?

You can register for the SAT Subject Tests in a number of ways. The easiest and quickest way is through the College Board website, at http://www.college-board.com. Through the website, you can quickly choose the tests you wish to take, choose a date and testing center, and immediately receive a confirmation of your registration. You will need to use a credit card to register online. If you are signing up for Sunday testing for the first time, are younger than 13, or require special testing arrangements, you will need to mail in your registration.

Registering by mail allows you to use a check or money order. Register by mail using the registration form in the SAT *Registration Bulletin*, which should be available in the college counselling office of your high school. The cost is the same as registering by mail.

If you have registered for the SAT or SAT Subject Tests before, you can reregister for the SAT Subject Tests via telephone, by calling (866) 756-7346 from 8 AM to 9 PM, Eastern time. You must pay by credit card, and there is a $12.50 fee for telephone registration.

How Much Does It Cost to Register for the SAT Subject Tests?

Taking the SAT costs $20, plus $9 for each test that you take ($20 for the language tests including listening). Just taking the SAT Biology, then, will cost $29; adding another subject will cost $9 more. Late registration incurs an extra fee of $23.

May I Use a Calculator on the Test?

Although some calculations may be required, **you may not use a calculator on the SAT Biology E/M.** You may use a calculator only on the SAT Math test.

What if I Need to Take the Test Under Special Circumstances?

Students with disabilities or special needs can qualify for testing accommodations or additional time on the through the College Board's Services for Students with Disabilities (SSD). To qualify for a special accommodation because of a physical handicap or learning disability, you will need to apply and support your application with documentation of your disability. Talk to your guidance counselor, and visit the College Board website (http://www.collegeboard.com) for more information on how to register.

How Is the SAT Biology Test Scored?

Your answers for the Biology test will be scored by a machine that reads your answer sheet. Just as in each section of the SAT, your score for each SAT Subject Test will range from 200 to 800. This scaled score is based on your raw score for the test. The raw score is calculated by adding one point for every correct answer, and subtracting 1/4 point for every incorrect answer. This scaled score is then reported to you, your high school, and any colleges and universities you choose.

When Will I Receive My Scores?

You can view your scores by logging into your My SAT account approximately three weeks after the test. Refer to the College Board website to see on what date your score will become available. Scores are also mailed to students approximately 3 weeks after the test. You may also request your scores by telephone for an additional fee.

How Do I Submit My SAT Subject Test Scores to Colleges and Universities?

Once you're ready to submit your scores to colleges and universities, there are a number of ways to do so. When you sign up for the SAT or SAT Subject Tests, your fee includes free reporting of the results to up to four colleges or universities. You can also request that your scores be reported to additional schools for $9.50 per school using the College Board website (http://www.collegeboard.com) or, for a $10 charge, by telephone.

  You should be aware that when you submit scores, all of your past scores—SAT and SAT Subject Tests—will be sent to the colleges or universities you selected. Scores for tests that have not yet taken place or have not yet been scored will not be submitted. Your scores will be sent about 3 weeks after your request; make sure you leave enough time to report your scores before the deadlines sent by the college/university of your choice. Rush reporting is available online or by phone for an additional $27.

CHAPTER 2

HOW TO USE THIS BOOK

STUDYING SMART FOR THE SAT SUBJECT TESTS

Studying hard is an important part of doing well in high school and beyond, and this book provides a comprehensive review of everything you need to know for the SAT Biology-E and Biology-M exams. But with a test that covers a large amount of material, as the Biology E/M test does, it's important to use your studying time wisely—a process we call "studying smart."

Although ideally you would be able to study in depth all of the material presented in this book, we have designed this book with the understanding that you may not have enough time to review all of the material before your test date, and that you may need to spend more time reviewing certain areas of biology than others. This book is organized to allow you to study smart. It helps you:

- Identify the subject matter that need more work
- Strengthen your ability to answer the types of questions that appear on the test
- Focus your studying on the material that's most important for you
- Check your progress with questions at the end of each lesson
- Practice your test-taking skills using sample tests

This chapter explains how to use the features of this book to help you study smart and make the most of your preparation for the SAT Biology E/M test.

Step One: Identify Your Weaknesses

A crucial part of studying smart is knowing how much you need to study and knowing exactly what you need to study. The diagnostic test in Chapter 4 should be your first step in identifying the areas that are most important for you to review before the SAT Biology test. You should take the diagnostic test and score it yourself. Be honest—if you got a question right with a chance guess, then you can mark it right, but you may wish to circle it to indicate that you still might benefit from a review of the material covered in that question.

A detailed explanation of the answer to each question can be found at the end of the diagnostic test. Look for patterns in the question that you're getting wrong or that you had to guess. Are they all in one subject area, such as genetics? Is there one part of ecology that needs a brush up? The diagnostic test should tell you which sections of the book are most important for you to read before the test.

This book also contains, at the beginning of each section, a list of important vocabulary for that section. This vocabulary list provides an important way for you to gauge your ability; you should take some time to consider the words in each list, and ask yourself if you really know the definition and significance of each term. Make a list of sections that include terms with which you are unfamiliar or whose definition you struggle to remember. These sections should be on your list of sections to review before your test day.

Step Two: Strengthen Your Test-Taking Skills

One of the best ways to improve your performance on the SAT Biology test is to familiarize yourself with the most common types of questions asked on the test. The designers of the SAT Biology test don't design the exam randomly. In addition to asking questions that test your knowledge of biology, they specifically emphasize certain skills such as the ability to use collected data to form a conclusion (as one would in a biology lab), solve word problems, or use mathematical approximations such as Punnett squares or the Hardy–Weinberg equation (see Lessons 7.1 and 8.2) to answer questions.

Chapter 5 of this book teaches you how to answer types of questions that are specific to the SAT Biology exam. It will give you important tips on how to strengthen your test-taking skills before the test.

Step Three: Review the Material

This book provides a comprehensive review of all of the material in the five areas of biology covered on the Biology-E and Biology-M tests. Once you have identified the areas that you most need to focus on, you should review the relevant chapters or lessons.

The chapters in this book do not need to be covered in the order in which they appear. If you'd like to focus on Chapter 10 before Chapter 7, you should feel free. Each lesson stands on its own and contains a list of the relevant vocabulary that is covered and a short summary of the most important points.

You should break up your review time over a number of days, if possible. Trying to learn all of the material on the test all at once is not the best way to retain the information you are reviewing. You may wish to develop a schedule for which sections you want to cover, keeping in mind how much time you have before the test, and your preparations for other SAT Subject Tests. Keep in mind that you'll also want to save time to do the practice tests at the end of the book before your test day.

Step Four: Check Your Progress

Each lesson in this book contains review problems that allow you to check your progress as you review the material. You should work these review problems to ensure that you have learned the material that is covered in each section and to accustom yourself to answering the types of questions that will be asked on the test.

The lists of vocabulary at the beginning of each section also provide another way of checking your progress. After reviewing a chapter, go back and look at the vocabulary in each lesson. Are there any terms that you still don't understand? If so, you may want to go back and review them before moving on.

Step Five: Practice, Practice, Practice

The practice tests at the end of this book—two sample Biology-E tests and two sample Biology-M tests—are important tools in your final preparations for the real Biology E/M test. You should take these tests as you might on test day. Sit in a quiet room and time yourself. Practicing using these tests serve a number of functions: first, they allow you to practice answering the type of questions that will appear on the exam. The practice tests have been written to mimic the types of questions found on the actual SAT Biology exam. Second, by timing yourself, you will learn how to pace yourself on the exam and will familiarize yourself with the format of the exam. If you know that you have a tendency to go over time, you'll know that you should maybe circle harder questions and come back to them (see Chapter 3 on Practical Tips for more on this).

Finally, the practice tests provide you with a final chance to review any material that you might not have fully picked up in your review. Each answer is fully explained at the end of each test; if you get a question wrong, you should review the explanation and, if necessary, go back and review the lesson that covers that material. This final check will allow you a final review of the material you most need to cover before your test date.

DECIDING BETWEEN BIOLOGY-E AND BIOLOGY-M

If, after reading Chapter 1, you are still undecided about which version of the SAT Biology test is right for you, this book has a number of features that you might find helpful to figure out on which version you'll do best. The diagnostic test in Chapter 4 is in three parts: Part A is like the portion of the real test that is intended for students who are taking either Biology-E or Biology-M. Part B is like the portion of the test that is intended ONLY for students who are taking Biology-E. Part C is like the portion of the test that is intended ONLY for students who are taking Biology-M. Try answering both parts B and C. Which part were you able to answer more easily? If you're unsure on which test you'll do better, use your results on these parts of the diagnostic test as a rough guide as to whether you're better suited for the E or the M exam.

When you're reviewing the material, pay close attention to those chapters with which you are most comfortable. Did your biology course leave you more familiar with the content in Chapters 6 and 7? If so, Biology-M might be better. If you're more familiar with the material in Chapters 8 and 10, then the Biology-E test is the one that suits you better.

CHAPTER 3

SMART TIPS FOR THE SAT BIOLOGY E/M TEST

PREPARING FOR THE TEST

You've decided you're going to take the test, you've handed over a large sum of money to the College Board to register, and now you need to prepare. Here's how.

Use This Book to Your Advantage

This book has been designed to help you learn the information covered on the SAT Biology test as efficiently as possible. You should look closely at Chapter 2 for suggestions on how to get the most out of its features. Use the diagnostic test to help you find the most important topics for you to review, and use the practice tests at the end to familiarize yourself with the format of the test.

Start Early and Be Realistic

Preparing for the SAT Biology E/M test is probably not the only thing you have to do. You may be filling out college applications, doing homework for classes, participating in extracurricular activities, working at a job, or preparing for the other SAT exams you're taking. Starting as early as you can will help you have enough time to prepare. The more time you have, the more thorough you can be. However, it's important that you be realistic in the amount of time that you'll have to prepare for the test and pace yourself accordingly. Set aside time that you know you'll be able to devote to your test preparation. If you don't have that much time left, then it's important to identify your weaknesses early using the tips in Chapter 2, so that you can make the most out of the time you have.

Know Yourself

The practice tests are important tools in your preparation. Not only do they help you familiarize yourself with the test, they also allow you to figure out your test-taking strengths and weaknesses. Do you have a tendency to lose track when bubbling in answers? Are you constantly fighting against the clock? You will want to know these things before the day of the test, so that you can adjust accordingly and be more careful, so it's important that you take the practice tests seriously. Give yourself a full hour to sit down at a desk in a quiet room and devote your entire attention to the test. Be sure to time yourself (or even ask someone else to time for you), and correct them yourself so that you can gauge your progress.

Learn What to Expect

No one likes surprises at 8 AM on a Saturday morning. The more familiar you are with what you're going to see on the test, the less time you'll have to stare at the test booklet in confusion, trying to figure out what they're asking. The practice questions in this test are written just like the questions on the actual exam. Pay close attention to the forms of questions on the diagnostic and practice tests and the types of questions that are discussed in Chapter 5 so that you know what to expect.

Double-Check Your Admission Ticket

Even the College Board makes mistakes from time to time. You should double-check your admission ticket as soon as possible in case they have, indeed, made a mistake. Minor errors can be handwritten on your admission ticket and handed in on the day of the test, but major errors (say they signed you up for the SAT instead of the SAT Subject Tests) will need some advance notice. So double check that ticket, and be sure to put it in a safe place until the day of the test.

Make Sure You Know Where Your Test Site Is

Knowing in theory how to get to your testing site won't help you if you get lost on the testing day and neither will the added stress of traveling in unfamiliar territory. You need to make sure that you know exactly where your test site is and how long it takes you to get there. Make a practice run so you know how to get to your test site, bearing in mind that traffic conditions and bus and train schedules may be quite different on Saturday morning than at different times.

THE HOME STRETCH

You've reviewed all the material you need to review, and the test is tomorrow. Here's how to make sure that you're not derailed in your quest for SAT Biology success with only 24 hours to go.

Don't Overdo It

Trying to stuff all of those facts into your head the night before isn't an effective studying technique. It's much better to spread your studying out before the exam instead of cramming in one night. Not only are you unlikely to retain much of the information, but you will likely so stress yourself that you'll get a horrible night's sleep. Instead, if you still have things to study, set a realistic time limit for how long you'll spend studying—perhaps a half-hour—and stick to it. Your time is best spent relaxing, not stressing yourself out.

Collect What You'll Need

You're not going to want to run around looking for that admissions ticket on the morning of your test. So be sure that you've set aside everything that you will need to take with you the night before.

- Admission ticket
- Your photo ID

- Directions to the test site
- Car keys or bus/train fare
- Several Number 2 pencils
- Erasers
- Calculator (**only** if you're also taking the SAT Math)
- Tape player (**only** if you're taking an SAT test with Listening)
- Your own timing device
- Sweater/sweatshirt
- Healthy snack

Have Two Alarms

Test sites are rather unforgiving of latecomers, so make sure that you have at least one alarm set before you go to bed. Setting a second alarm clock can't hurt, just in case you ignore the first. Ideally, have someone who will make sure you're awake when you need to be. If you and a friend are both taking the test on the same day, you might agree to call each other to ensure that you're both awake.

Get Your Zs

You've probably heard it before, but it bears repeating that it's important to get a good night's sleep before the test. You don't want to end up being the student with your head on the desk, drooling all over your answer sheet (it does happen!), and taking your test while recovering from a late night out will not help you impress the college or university of your choice. Getting a good night's sleep not only helps you retain the information you've learned, but it also allows you to focus better on the day of the test. So be sure to get enough sleep to leave yourself well rested when you wake up.

Wake Up Early

Accidents happen. Streets can be busy, buses get delayed, and nervous SAT Subject Test takers can make a wrong turn or get on the wrong train. It may be difficult finding your way to your specific testing room, and there may be a long line to register. There are any number of reasons why it's advantageous to leave yourself extra time to get to your testing site. Watching the clock is something you should do during the test, not before, and the added stress won't help you focus on doing your best.

Take It Easy

Don't rush around the morning before your exam. Take the time to get prepared without running around and stressing yourself out. Take 5 or 10 minutes over breakfast to give yourself one last review of some material. And listen to music that calms your nerves while driving or riding to the test site.

Eat Brain Food

A heavy breakfast the morning of your exam will probably leave you tired and struggling to stay awake, and overloading on sugar or caffeine will likely make you jittery before the test and not much more alert for the main event.

Taking the SAT Subject Tests can be an energy-consuming activity, so it's important to have a solid breakfast—try a healthy cereal, oatmeal, or scrambled eggs. Also, consider bringing a snack for the short break you'll have between your subject tests. A piece of fruit or a granola bar will help you keep up your energy for the long haul.

Dress for Success

Unfortunately, the College Board does not give bonus points for looking fashionable. Being comfortable in the room where you're taking the test, however, will likely result in you having a better score. There's no guarantee that your test site will be air-conditioned or that their heaters won't be on overdrive; test sites are often uncomfortably cold or hot. Dress in layers, so that can adjust, no matter what the temperature, and wear comfortable clothing that won't get in the way when you're trying to focus.

Bring a Timer

There's no assurance that your test site will have a clock, and that your desk will be pointed in the direction of a clock. Get a stopwatch, timer, or watch (ideally, one that doesn't make lots of noise) so you can tell how long you have left on your test and pace yourself. Make sure you know how to use your watch beforehand.

DURING THE TEST

Don't Panic!

You're as prepared as you're going to be at this point, so there's no point in doing extra stressing out the morning of the exam. Don't panic over the things you haven't studied—focus on the test at hand. And use your nervousness to make sure you're extra careful and aware while taking your test and filling in your answer sheets.

Focus, Focus, Focus

To do best on the test, you're going to want to give it your best attention. Worrying about your score, thinking about what you're going to do when you finally get done, and paying attention to the other people in the room will only distract you from your goal. You've got 1 hour, and you need to make the best of it—so don't let your attention stray.

Choose the Right Test

The SAT Subject Tests has the added complication that there are a number of tests to choose from, and you must be especially careful on the SAT Biology test to make sure that you're answering the correct subset of questions that you want to answer. You don't want to get halfway through the ecology section when you'd rather be answering questions on molecular biology. So pay close attention to the instructions and the questions that you're answering to make sure that you're answering the right ones and that you're filling in your answers in the right place.

Use Your Test Booklet

They're not going to reuse your test booklet when you're done with it, so feel free to scribble all over it. Writing in the test booklet can be immensely useful. You can cross out answers you know are wrong, underline the answers that you know are right, circle important words in question, do calculations, or draw a large circle around the questions that you've skipped or that you're unsure about and want to double check if you have the time. Writing the correct answer to each question in your test booklet may also be useful should you make a mistake in bubbling in your answers. Don't be afraid to make the test booklet your very own.

Bubble Carefully

Bubbling is full of potential pitfalls. Not only is there the matter of correctly filling in bubbles with the right mark, but there's also the mistake of bubbling in the right answer . . . in the space for the wrong question.

First, it's important to know exactly how to bubble-in the answer sheets. Completely fill in the bubbles as much as possible while minimizing the amount of stray marks on your answer sheet. If you change your mind on a question, then be sure to erase completely, and watch that you haven't erased the answer to more than one question. Do remember, however, that this isn't a competition to see who bubbles the best. Your time is best spent getting to all of the questions rather than making sure that each bubble is exactly filled in.

Second, it's important that you make sure you're always bubbling in the answer to the right question. Every five or ten questions, you should make sure that the number of the question you're answering is the same as the number of the space you're bubbling in.

Everyone has different bubbling techniques. Some people prefer bubbling after every answer, while some prefer doing an entire page of problems, writing the answers in the test booklet, before bubbling in their answers. If you choose the latter, be sure to start filling in your answer sheet more often as you approach the time limit; you don't want to run out of time to bubble-in the answer to a question you spent time on. For the same reason, it's a bad idea to leave all of your bubbling to the end, as you may run out of time to bubble-in all your answers. Whatever method you prefer, make sure that you pay close attention to the questions you're answering.

Skip Around

Each question, easy or difficult, simple or complicated, gets you the same number of points. It would be unfortunate for you never to reach the two really easy questions at the end of the test because you got bogged down on an earlier question. For that reason, it's best for you to leave the questions that are harder for you, that require complicated calculations, or that you're struggling with until later in the test, after you've already collected the points from the easy questions. Mark the questions you're skipping clearly on your test booklet, perhaps by drawing a large circle or question mark, so that you can easily find them later on.

If you do skip around, however, be especially careful that you stay on track in filling out your answer sheet. If you skip question 30, then be sure to skip the answer bubbles for question 30 as well.

Watch the Time

Make sure that you're on track to finish all of the questions on time. With 80 questions in 60 minutes, you may not have a lot of spare time. Check yourself at 10- or 15-minute intervals using your watch or timer.

Make Educated Guesses

The SAT Subject Test has a penalty when you get a question wrong, to discourage random guessing on multiple-choice questions. If you have absolutely no clue as to the right answer to a question, you are better off leaving the question unanswered, because you will not be penalized.

However, studies have shown that test takers that are more comfortable making educated guesses consistently perform better on standardized tests. If you can eliminate one or more of the answers to a question, then it is to your advantage to guess on that question. So if you have an educated guess, then you should be bold and give an answer to the question.

Pay Attention to What the Questions Are Asking

The College Board doesn't make the SAT Biology test an especially tricky exam, but it's important that you look closely at each question to make sure you know what it's asking. If a question asks about bacterial growth when the temperature was increasing, be sure not to look at times when temperature was decreasing. Questions using words such as "except" or "not" can be tricky; it may help to circle or underline these key words so you do not forget.

Look for Hidden Hints

Believe it or not, occasionally the College Board helps you out in answering your questions. Sometimes, question number 75 contains a tidbit of information that helps you answer question number 2, on which you had to guess. So look around for questions that cover material that you've already seen, and if you have extra time, don't be afraid to go back and make a new educated guess.

Don't Panic if Time Runs Out

Ideally, you will not run out of time, because you've been pacing yourself and checking your progress. But, occasionally, it does happen, and it's important for you to know what to do so that you don't panic. The first thing to do if you're running out of time is to make sure that you've bubbled in all of your answers. The time you've spent answering those questions is like an investment—you don't want to waste it by not having bubbled in your answers.

After bubbling in your answers, you should look ahead to the questions that are left. Are any of them especially easy, or in an area that you're especially familiar with? If so, you should answer those first. You'll want to avoid questions that require you to do calculations, or that ask you to interpret a graph carefully—you may not have time for those. Instead, choose questions that ask you to simply recall information. Questions that ask you to identify parts on a diagram, for example, are quicker to answer. Also look for a series of questions that all have the same answer, as for these questions you'll only have to look over one answer set for two or three questions, which may save you precious seconds.

Don't go too fast or try to answer too many questions. It's better to do well on the questions you answer than to go to fast and make random guesses.

Use Extra Time Wisely

If you finish early, you shouldn't just sit at your desk and stare at the clock. There are plenty of things you can do! Your first task should be to go back and review any questions that you skipped. Now, you have the time to seriously consider those harder questions that you skipped before. After that, you may wish to go back and review any questions that you may have guessed on, or that involved a calculation that you may want to double check. Resist the urge to second guess too many of your answers, however, as this may lead you to change an already correct answer to a wrong one. Finally, you're happy with your answers, you may want to spend time cleaning up your answer sheet, erasing any stray marks and making sure that all of your bubbles are filled in.

AFTER THE TEST

Relax!

Congratulations, you've done it! There's no more you can do at this point. Plan an enjoyable activity for the afternoon after your test. After 3 hours inside filling in bubbles, what could be better than an afternoon at the mall, or a bike ride outside? Resist the temptation to chide yourself for any mistakes you may have made. You've done your best, so it's time to focus on the other tasks ahead. And reward yourself—you made it!

Don't Forget to Report Your Scores

Just because you've received your scores doesn't mean that all of the colleges or universities you've applied to have also received them. Make sure that you eventually sent the final version of your scores to all of the colleges and universities you're applying to, especially if you're taking the SAT Subject Tests before you take the SAT, or if you're planning an additional testing date.

CHAPTER 4

DIAGNOSTIC TEST

To prepare most effectively for the SAT Biology test, you should identify the areas in which your skills are weak. Then, focus on improving your skills in these areas. (Of course, also becoming stronger in your strong areas will only help your score!) Use the results of this Diagnostic Test to prioritize areas in which you need further preparation.

The following Diagnostic Test is exactly half the length of the real SAT Biology E/M test. It matches the actual test in content coverage and level of difficulty. As with the actual test, this test is in three parts. Part A (Questions 1–30) is for everyone taking Biology-E or Biology-M. Part B (Questions 31–40) is ONLY for students taking Biology-E. Part C (Questions 41–50) is ONLY for students taking Biology-M.

When you're finished with the test, determine your score and carefully read the answer explanations for the questions you answered incorrectly. Identify your weak areas by determining the areas in which you made the most errors. Review these chapters of the book first. Then, as time permits, go back, and review your stronger areas.

Allow one-half hour to take the diagnostic test. Time yourself and work uninterrupted. If you run out of time, take note of where you ended when time ran out and continue until you have tried all 50 questions. To truly identify your weak areas, you need to complete the test. Remember that you lose $\frac{1}{4}$ of a point for each incorrect answer. Because of this penalty, do not guess on a question unless you can eliminate one or more of the answers. Your score is calculated using the following formula:

$$\text{Number of correct answers} - \frac{1}{4}(\text{Number of incorrect answers})$$

The Diagnostic Test will be an accurate reflection of how you'll do on test day if you treat it as the real examination. Here are some hints on how to take the test under conditions similar to those of the actual exam:

- Complete the test in one sitting.
- Time yourself.
- Tear out your answer key and fill in the ovals just as you would on the actual test day.
- Become familiar with the directions to the test and the reference information provided. You'll save time on the actual test day by already being familiar with this information.

ANSWER SHEET FOR THE DIAGNOSTIC TEST

Tear out this answer sheet and use it to mark your answers. There are 50 lines of numbered ovals on this answer sheet. There are 30 lines for the core Biology Test (Part A, Questions 1–30), 10 lines for the Biology-E section (Part B, Questions 31–40), and 10 lines for the Biology-M section (Part C, Questions 41–50). For Biology-E, use ONLY ovals 1–40 for marking your answers. For Biology-M, use ovals 1–30 PLUS ovals 41–50.

Part A

1. Ⓐ Ⓑ Ⓒ Ⓓ Ⓔ
2. Ⓐ Ⓑ Ⓒ Ⓓ Ⓔ
3. Ⓐ Ⓑ Ⓒ Ⓓ Ⓔ
4. Ⓐ Ⓑ Ⓒ Ⓓ Ⓔ
5. Ⓐ Ⓑ Ⓒ Ⓓ Ⓔ
6. Ⓐ Ⓑ Ⓒ Ⓓ Ⓔ
7. Ⓐ Ⓑ Ⓒ Ⓓ Ⓔ
8. Ⓐ Ⓑ Ⓒ Ⓓ Ⓔ
9. Ⓐ Ⓑ Ⓒ Ⓓ Ⓔ
10. Ⓐ Ⓑ Ⓒ Ⓓ Ⓔ
11. Ⓐ Ⓑ Ⓒ Ⓓ Ⓔ
12. Ⓐ Ⓑ Ⓒ Ⓓ Ⓔ
13. Ⓐ Ⓑ Ⓒ Ⓓ Ⓔ
14. Ⓐ Ⓑ Ⓒ Ⓓ Ⓔ
15. Ⓐ Ⓑ Ⓒ Ⓓ Ⓔ
16. Ⓐ Ⓑ Ⓒ Ⓓ Ⓔ
17. Ⓐ Ⓑ Ⓒ Ⓓ Ⓔ
18. Ⓐ Ⓑ Ⓒ Ⓓ Ⓔ
19. Ⓐ Ⓑ Ⓒ Ⓓ Ⓔ
20. Ⓐ Ⓑ Ⓒ Ⓓ Ⓔ
21. Ⓐ Ⓑ Ⓒ Ⓓ Ⓔ
22. Ⓐ Ⓑ Ⓒ Ⓓ Ⓔ
23. Ⓐ Ⓑ Ⓒ Ⓓ Ⓔ
24. Ⓐ Ⓑ Ⓒ Ⓓ Ⓔ
25. Ⓐ Ⓑ Ⓒ Ⓓ Ⓔ
26. Ⓐ Ⓑ Ⓒ Ⓓ Ⓔ
27. Ⓐ Ⓑ Ⓒ Ⓓ Ⓔ
28. Ⓐ Ⓑ Ⓒ Ⓓ Ⓔ
29. Ⓐ Ⓑ Ⓒ Ⓓ Ⓔ
30. Ⓐ Ⓑ Ⓒ Ⓓ Ⓔ

Part B

31. Ⓐ Ⓑ Ⓒ Ⓓ Ⓔ
32. Ⓐ Ⓑ Ⓒ Ⓓ Ⓔ
33. Ⓐ Ⓑ Ⓒ Ⓓ Ⓔ
34. Ⓐ Ⓑ Ⓒ Ⓓ Ⓔ
35. Ⓐ Ⓑ Ⓒ Ⓓ Ⓔ
36. Ⓐ Ⓑ Ⓒ Ⓓ Ⓔ
37. Ⓐ Ⓑ Ⓒ Ⓓ Ⓔ
38. Ⓐ Ⓑ Ⓒ Ⓓ Ⓔ
39. Ⓐ Ⓑ Ⓒ Ⓓ Ⓔ
40. Ⓐ Ⓑ Ⓒ Ⓓ Ⓔ

Part C

41. Ⓐ Ⓑ Ⓒ Ⓓ Ⓔ
42. Ⓐ Ⓑ Ⓒ Ⓓ Ⓔ
43. Ⓐ Ⓑ Ⓒ Ⓓ Ⓔ
44. Ⓐ Ⓑ Ⓒ Ⓓ Ⓔ
45. Ⓐ Ⓑ Ⓒ Ⓓ Ⓔ
46. Ⓐ Ⓑ Ⓒ Ⓓ Ⓔ
47. Ⓐ Ⓑ Ⓒ Ⓓ Ⓔ
48. Ⓐ Ⓑ Ⓒ Ⓓ Ⓔ
49. Ⓐ Ⓑ Ⓒ Ⓓ Ⓔ
50. Ⓐ Ⓑ Ⓒ Ⓓ Ⓔ

DIAGNOSTIC TEST

Time: 30 Minutes

Part A (Core Questions 1–30—for both Biology-E and Biology-M)

Directions: Determine the BEST answer for each question. Then fill in the corresponding oval on the answer sheet.

1. Which of the following methods of reproduction leads to populations with the greatest genetic diversity?

   (A) binary fission
   (B) sexual reproduction
   (C) asexual reproduction
   (D) alternation of generations
   (E) binary fission and conjugation

2. Which of the following organ systems maintains homeostasis in the human body by removing nitrogenous wastes from the blood?

   (A) urinary system
   (B) lymphatic system
   (C) circulatory system
   (D) respiratory system
   (E) integumentary system

Use the following diagram to answer Question 3.

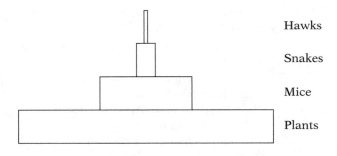

Hawks

Snakes

Mice

Plants

3. The ecological pyramid shows the amount of energy available at each trophic level. Which of the following statements best describes energy flow in this diagram?

   (A) Energy is passed up the pyramid with the least energy at the top.
   (B) Energy is passed up the pyramid with the most energy at the top.
   (C) Energy is passed down the pyramid with the most energy at the top.
   (D) Energy is passed down the pyramid with the most energy at the bottom.
   (E) Energy is a constant in the pyramid.

4. In plant cells, where is sunlight's energy used to build organic chemicals?

   (A) chlorophyll
   (B) leaves
   (C) stomata
   (D) cuticle
   (E) chloroplasts

5. Tay–Sachs disease is a genetic disorder that affects the central nervous system. The condition is lethal at an early age in homozygous recessive individuals (tt). Which statement best explains why a fatal disease can be carried in a population?

   (A) If one parent is heterozygous, the offspring have a 25% chance of being heterozygous.
   (B) If one parent is heterozygous, the offspring have a 75% chance of being heterozygous.
   (C) If one parent is heterozygous, the offspring have a 100% chance of being heterozygous.
   (D) If one parent is heterozygous, all offspring will be carriers.
   (E) If one parent is heterozygous, the offspring have a 50% chance of being heterozygous.

6. Many scientists believe that an asteroid impact on Earth at the end of the Cretaceous Period was responsible for dinosaurs becoming extinct. Which of the following best explains why there are still organisms on Earth?

   (A) The dinosaurs quickly evolved into new organisms when faced with a changed environment.
   (B) The ancestors of organisms living today were able to adapt to the changed environment.
   (C) The ancestors of organisms living today evolved to fill the niches left by the dinosaurs.
   (D) The asteroid brought new organisms that started new lines of organisms leading to those of today.
   (E) The evolutionary process started over and has resulted in the organisms present now.

GO ON TO THE NEXT PAGE

7. Which of the following best describes a biological community?

    (A) a group of individuals of the same species that live together in the same area at the same time
    (B) all populations of different species that live and interact in the same area
    (C) all populations of different species that live and interact in the same area and the abiotic environment
    (D) the part of Earth where life exists
    (E) a group of organisms that share similar ecological niches in different areas

8. Which biome is defined as having dry, hot summers and cold winters?

    (A) taiga
    (B) tropical rainforest
    (C) savannas
    (D) temperate grasslands
    (E) temperate deciduous forests

9. Although mutations in DNA are very common, they are seldom expressed when passed to offspring. Which of the following explanations is correct?

    (A) Many mutations are recessive, and it is unlikely that both parents will have the same recessive mutation.
    (B) Mutations are not passed to offspring because they are lethal to the organism.
    (C) Mutations only occur in body cells and not in the gametes.
    (D) Most mutations are fatal and not passed to offspring.
    (E) Most mutations only occur in body cells and are usually repaired before the cells divide.

10. Which of the following actions causes water to move from the soil into the roots of a plant?

    (A) evaporation of water from the leaves
    (B) capillary action
    (C) hydrophyllic compounds
    (D) osmosis
    (E) active transport

11. The movement of specific materials across a plasma membrane through a transport protein is called

    (A) concentration gradient
    (B) active transport
    (C) osmosis
    (D) facilitated transport
    (E) phagocytosis

12. After meiosis, the number of chromosomes in a gamete is _____ the number of chromosomes than the parent cell.

    (A) twice
    (B) three times
    (C) the same as
    (D) one-half
    (E) one-quarter

Use the diagram below to answer Question 13.

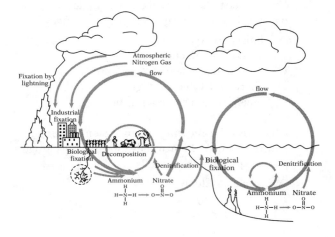

13. The atmosphere is made up of about 78% nitrogen. Nitrogen is very important to plant growth. Nitrogen in soil is often a limiting factor for plants, even though it is common in air. Which statement best describes why it is often limited in soil?

    (A) The nitrogen is quickly removed from the soil and tied up in plants.
    (B) The nitrogen is not being returned to the atmosphere quickly enough.
    (C) The nitrogen compounds are water soluble and quickly washed away.
    (D) The nitrogen-fixing bacteria fix nitrogen in the soil and water at a slow rate.
    (E) The denitrifying bacteria remove nitrogen from the soil too fast.

14. Which plant adaptation would best suit a plant growing on a forest floor?

    (A) has shallow roots
    (B) requires low light
    (C) has a deep tap root
    (D) requires strong light
    (E) requires moist soil

GO ON TO THE NEXT PAGE

15. Place the following stages of mitosis in animal cells in the order in which they occur.

I.

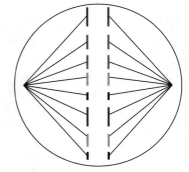

II.

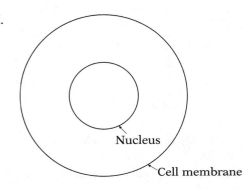

III.

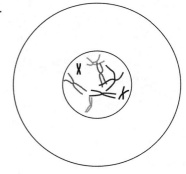

IV.

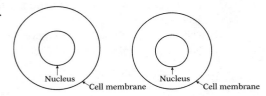

V.

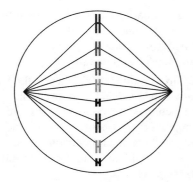

VI.

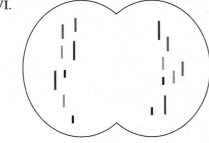

(A) II, IV, VI, I, V, III
(B) II, IV, V, I, VI, III
(C) II, V, IV, VI, I, III
(D) III, VI, V, I, IV, II
(E) III, IV, V, VI, I, II

16. When a human egg is fertilized, the sex of the child is determined by the presence or absence of a Y chromosome. A male child will have an X and a Y chromosome. A female child will have two X chromosomes. Which statement describes the inheritance of sex chromosomes?

(A) The gametes from each parent have either an X or a Y chromosome.
(B) The gamete from the mother has either an X or a Y chromosome.
(C) The gamete from the father has either an X or a Y chromosome.
(D) The gamete from the father only has an X chromosome.
(E) The gamete from the mother only has a Y chromosome.

GO ON TO THE NEXT PAGE

17. According to Charles Darwin's theory of evolution by natural selection, "survival of the fittest" is an important part of natural selection. What is meant by the phrase, "survival of the fittest?"

    (A) The strongest members of a population are those who breed and leave offspring.
    (B) The members of a population that are strongest are the ones that survive the longest.
    (C) The members of a population that are best suited for their environment breed and have offspring.
    (D) The weakest members of a population do not reproduce so their traits are not passed on.
    (E) The members of a population that are least suited die off immediately.

18. Skin protects the body from harmful ultraviolet radiation by producing a dark-colored pigment called melanin. In which layer of skin is melanin produced?

    (A) dead epidermis
    (B) living epidermis
    (C) dermis
    (D) subcutaneous layer
    (E) epithelial

19. How many net ATP molecules are produced during aerobic cellular respiration?

    (A) 2
    (B) 4
    (C) 36
    (D) 38
    (E) 44

20. A plasmid is a small, circular ring of DNA. Plasmids are useful for inserting DNA fragments into cells to produce transgenic organisms. Plasmids are usually found in

    (A) viruses
    (B) bacteria
    (C) fungi
    (D) plant cells
    (E) animal cells

21. Mosses are able to reproduce asexually. Asexual reproduction in mosses is called

    (A) alternation of generations
    (B) sporophyte generation
    (C) vegetative reproduction
    (D) gametophyte reproduction
    (E) binary fission

22. For this segment of DNA, which is the proper sequence in messenger RNA (mRNA)?

    AGTTCG

    (A) TCUUGC
    (B) UCAACG
    (C) AGTTCG
    (D) TCAACG
    (E) UCAAGC

23.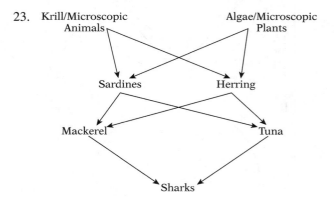

    In this food web, which would likely happen if an oil spill killed all the herring?

    (A) The krill population would decrease.
    (B) The sardine population would increase.
    (C) The mackerel and tuna populations would decrease.
    (D) The shark population would increase.
    (E) The algae population would decrease.

GO ON TO THE NEXT PAGE

24. Which of the following represents an unsaturated fat?

(A)

(B)

(C)

(D)
Phosphate   Base (cytosine)   Sugar (ribose)

(E)

25. When your body temperature begins to drop, one thing that happens is that you shiver. How does shivering help raise your body temperature?

    (A) Shivering dilates blood vessels.
    (B) Shivering constricts blood vessels.
    (C) Shivering increases the heart rate.
    (D) Shivering stimulates rapid muscle action.
    (E) Shivering tightens skin to cause goose bumps.

26. The process where an ancestral species evolves into an array of species that occupy different niches is called

    (A) convergent evolution
    (B) divergent evolution
    (C) adaptive radiation
    (D) gradualism
    (E) directional selection

27. Which equation best represents photosynthesis in plants?

    (A) carbon dioxide + water → starch + oxygen
    (B) carbon dioxide + water → glucose + oxygen
    (C) glucose + oxygen → carbon dioxide + water
    (D) carbon dioxide + glucose → starch + oxygen
    (E) light + carbon dioxide → glucose + oxygen

28. Pea plants may be tall or short. The genetic material received by the offspring from the parent determines this characteristic. This Punnett square shows the possible outcomes of the cross between parents. Which best describes the number of short offspring?

	T	T
T	TT	TT
t	Tt	Tt

    T—tall plant
    t—short plant

    (A) None are short.
    (B) 25% are short.
    (C) 50% are short.
    (D) 75% are short.
    (E) All are short.

29. ATP is the energy storage molecule found in both plants and animals. The energy in ATP is released when it

    (A) passes electrons to NADH
    (B) is split into a phosphate ion and ADP
    (C) loses electrons and becomes ADP
    (D) breaks its bonds and loses all its phosphate ions
    (E) breaks the bonds within one of its phosphate groups

30. Which system in the human body regulates long-term processes, such as fluid balance, growth, and sexual development?

    (A) endocrine system
    (B) reproductive system
    (C) integumentary system
    (D) circulatory system
    (E) lymphatic system

GO ON TO THE NEXT PAGE

Part B (Biology-E Questions 31–40)

31.

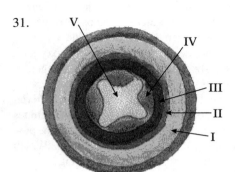

In this diagram, which part of the root carries water up to the rest of the plant?

(A) I
(B) II
(C) III
(D) IV
(E) V

32. In the carbon cycle, where do the producers get their carbon?

(A) the soil
(B) carbohydrates in plants
(C) fossil fuels
(D) the atmosphere
(E) animal remains

33. Mammals who bear young that have a short development period in the mother and then continue their development inside a pouch on the outside of the mother's body are called

(A) marsupials
(B) amniotes
(C) placentals
(D) monotremes
(E) prokaryotes

34.

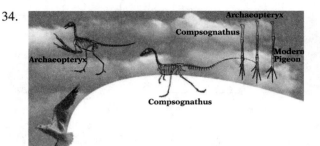

Similarities in structure are often used as evidence of evolution. In this example, the arm of the *Compsognathus* is very similar to the wing of the *Archaeopteryx* and modern bird. These similarities are called

(A) analogous structures
(B) homologous structures
(C) vestigial structures
(D) homogenous structures
(E) embryological structures

35. Endotherms are animals that maintain a constant body temperature. Which of the following animals is an endotherm?

(A) fish
(B) lizard
(C) snake
(D) bird
(E) insect

GO ON TO THE NEXT PAGE

36.

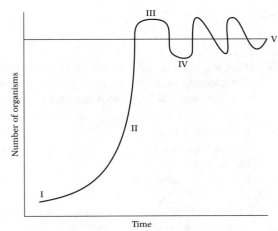

This graph shows population growth over a period of time. Which represents the carrying capacity of an environment on this growth chart?

(A) I
(B) II
(C) III
(D) IV
(E) V

37. The process of speciation can proceed in many different ways. Which describes the process of speciation where rapid speciation takes place followed by long periods of stability?

(A) gradualism
(B) punctuated equilibrium
(C) adaptive radiation
(D) convergent evolution
(E) divergent evolution

38. Which of the following statements about ecological succession is true?

(A) It is a natural progression of plant types that cannot be reversed.
(B) It always occurs over a short period of time.
(C) The rate can be changed by factors such as fire, clear cutting, and lava flows.
(D) It only takes place on freshly cleared or new land such as islands.
(E) The rate is very slow and constant.

39. Vestigial structures often provide clues to the evolutionary past of an organism. Which of the following would be considered a vestigial structure?

(A) gill slits in an embryo
(B) wing of a bat
(C) pelvis in a whale
(D) flippers on a dolphin
(E) fins on a fish

40. Which of the following best describes the niche of an earthworm?

(A) Earthworms are decomposers who live in the soil.
(B) Earthworms eat decaying organic matter.
(C) Earthworms are usually found living in the soil.
(D) Earthworms are used as food by some birds.
(E) Earthworms help the soil by aerating it.

GO ON TO THE NEXT PAGE

Part C (Biology-M Questions 41–50)

41. A plant with a genotype of PP produces purple flowers. A plant with a genotype of pp produces white flowers. If the plants are crossed, which describes the possible genotypes of the offspring?

   (A) 100% are pp
   (B) 100% are Pp
   (C) 100% are PP
   (D) 50% are PP and 50% are pp
   (E) 25% are PP, 50% are Pp, and 25% are pp

42. Muscle cells are a specialized type of cell that must perform great amounts of work. The work requires large amounts of energy. Which of these organelles would be found in large numbers in muscle cells?

   (A) chloroplasts
   (B) ribosomes
   (C) mitochondria
   (D) lysosomes
   (E) vacuoles

43. One method for identifying reaction pathways is by adding reactants that contain radioactive isotopes. The products of the reaction can be checked for the presence of the radioisotope. If the oxygen atoms in water were a radioisotope, where would the oxygen radioisotopes be found in the photosynthesis reaction?

   (A) in glucose molecules
   (B) in water
   (C) in oxygen gas
   (D) in ATP
   (E) in carbon dioxide

44. Genetic drift is the changes in allele frequency by chance processes. On which type of population would genetic drift have the most effect?

   (A) a small, isolated population
   (B) a large, isolated population
   (C) two widespread, interbreeding populations
   (D) two geographically isolated, large populations
   (E) two isolated, interbreeding populations

45. Enzymes act as catalysts to speed up chemical reactions in cells. Enzymes are a kind of

   (A) protein
   (B) nucleic acid
   (C) carbohydrate
   (D) lipid
   (E) steroid

46. DNA is a long, double-stranded molecule made up of nucleotide bases. What kind of chemical bond holds the two strands of DNA together?

   (A) hydrogen bonds
   (B) covalent bonds
   (C) metallic bonds
   (D) ionic bonds
   (E) polar covalent bonds

47. The invertebrates that have spines or bumps on their endoskeletons, radial symmetry, and a water vascular system, belong to the phylum

   (A) Porifera (sponges)
   (B) Annelida (earthworms)
   (C) Arthropoda (insects, crabs, and scorpions)
   (D) Echinodermata (starfishes and sea urchins)
   (E) Mollusca (snails and slugs)

48. The vascular tissue composed of living tubular cells that carry sugars from the leaves to other parts of the plant is called

   (A) phloem
   (B) xylem
   (C) parenchyma
   (D) cambium
   (E) pericycle

GO ON TO THE NEXT PAGE

49. The framework of a membrane consists of two rows of phospholipid molecules. The molecules are arranged with their polar heads to the outside and their nonpolar tails to the inside. With this arrangement in a membrane, where would you expect to find water molecules?

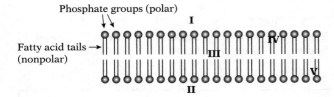

Phosphate groups (polar)

Fatty acid tails → (nonpolar)

I

II

III

IV

V

   (A) I and II
   (B) IV and V
   (C) I, II, and III
   (D) III, IV, and V
   (E) I, II, IV, and V

50. The beak of a bird is adapted to the type of food the bird eats. If a bird has a short, stout beak, it probably uses its beak to
   (A) drink nectar from flowers
   (B) catch fish
   (C) pick up small insects
   (D) tear flesh from animals
   (E) crack seeds

S T O P

IF YOU FINISH BEFORE TIME RUNS OUT, GO BACK AND CHECK YOUR WORK.

SCORE SHEET

Number of questions correct: _____

Less: 0.25 × number of questions wrong: _____

(Remember that omitted questions are not counted as wrong.)

Raw score: _____

Raw Score	Scaled Score	Raw Score	Scaled Score	Raw Score	Scaled Score	Raw Score	Scaled Score	Raw Score	Scaled Score
80	800	57	690	34	520	11	380	−12	250
79	800	56	680	33	520	10	370	−13	240
78	800	55	670	32	510	9	370	−14	240
77	800	54	670	31	510	8	360	−15	230
76	800	53	660	30	500	7	350	−16	230
75	800	52	650	29	500	6	350	−17	230
74	800	51	650	28	490	5	340	−18	220
73	790	50	640	27	490	4	330	−19	220
72	790	49	630	26	480	3	330	−20	220
71	780	48	620	25	480	2	320		
70	780	47	620	24	470	1	320		
69	770	46	610	23	470	0	310		
68	760	45	600	22	460	−1	310		
67	760	44	600	21	450	−2	300		
66	750	43	590	20	440	−3	300		
65	740	42	580	19	440	−4	290		
64	740	41	580	18	430	−5	290		
63	730	40	570	17	420	−6	280		
62	720	39	560	16	420	−7	270		
61	710	38	560	15	410	−8	270		
60	710	37	550	14	400	−9	260		
59	700	36	540	13	400	−10	260		
58	700	35	530	12	390	−11	250		

Note: This is only a sample scoring scale. Scoring scales differ from exam to exam.

ANSWER KEY

Part A

1. B	11. D	21. C
2. A	12. D	22. E
3. A	13. D	23. C
4. E	14. B	24. C
5. E	15. B	25. D
6. B	16. C	26. C
7. B	17. C	27. B
8. D	18. B	28. A
9. A	19. C	29. B
10. D	20. B	30. A

Part B

31. E	36. E
32. D	37. B
33. A	38. C
34. B	39. C
35. D	40. A

Part C

41. B	46. A
42. C	47. D
43. C	48. A
44. A	49. A
45. A	50. E

ANSWERS AND EXPLANATIONS

Part A (Core Questions 1–30)

1. **B** Sexual reproduction results in the greatest genetic diversity of offspring. Organisms that reproduce with asexual methods or a combination of asexual methods do not generate as much genetic diversity.

2. **A** The urinary system includes the kidneys. The kidneys filter nitrogenous wastes from the blood.

3. **A** Energy is transferred up the pyramid because each organism is consumed by the one above it. The amount of energy available decreases at each trophic level because the transfers are not 100% efficient; some energy is used to run other life processes and some energy is converted to heat.

4. **E** Chloroplasts are the plant cell structures where the process of photosynthesis occurs.

5. **E** Carriers in a population are heterozygous. Because they are not affected by having one recessive gene, they are able to reproduce and pass the recessive gene on to their offspring. A cross between a non-Tay–Sachs parent (TT) and someone who is a carrier (Tt) results in offspring having a 50% chance of carrying the trait.

6. **B** Many groups of organisms became extinct at the end of the Cretaceous Period. The organisms that survived were well adapted to the new environment and were able to reproduce.

7. **B** This is the definition of a biological community. A biological community is the collection of organisms that live in the same area and are interdependent on each other.

8. **D** Temperate grasslands are found in the interior of continents. Because they are located in the interior of continents, they have less precipitation than coastal areas and, therefore, fewer trees.

9. **A** Mutations are very common and are usually recessive. When an offspring only has one recessive gene, in most cases, it will not be expressed.

10. **D** When water is more highly concentrated in the soil than in the roots, the water diffuses into the roots. Osmosis is the term that applies to diffusion of water.

11. **D** Facilitated transport is a type of passive transport where only specific molecules are allowed to pass through a membrane without an expense of energy.

12. **D** Meiosis reduces the number of chromosomes by one half. During sexual reproduction, two gametes unite to form a zygote with the correct number of chromosomes.

13. **D** Nitrogen-fixing bacteria convert nitrogen from the atmosphere into a form used by plants. The nitrogen fixation process is much slower than the rate at which plants could use the nitrogen compounds.

14. **B** The tall trees shade plants growing on the forest floor. Successful plants on the forest floor are those adapted to low light conditions.

15. **B** The sequence for mitosis is interphase, prophase, metaphase, anaphase, telophase, and cytokinesis.

16. **C** The father provides the only gamete that has either an X or a Y chromosome. The mother only contributes an X chromosome.

17. **C** In a population, the fittest members are those best adapted to survive under the current conditions. It is more likely that they will reproduce and pass on their genes to their offspring.

18. **B** Melanin production takes place in the living epidermis. The melanin protects the underlying tissues from damage by UV radiation.

19. **C** Two ATPs are produced in glycolysis, and 34 are produced in the Kreb's cycle and electron transport chain for a total of 36 ATPs.

20. **B** Plasmids are circular pieces of DNA found in bacterial cells.

21. **C** Vegetative reproduction is a type of asexual reproduction. During vegetative reproduction, new individual plants are produced without going through alternation of generations.

22. **E** Messenger RNA does not have thymine (T). When messenger RNA copies a DNA segment, uracil (U) is hydrogen-bonded to adenine.

23. **C** The mackerel and tuna depend on herring as a food source. The loss of the herring would cause more competition for the sardines.

24. **C** An unsaturated fat is a long-chain lipid molecule where some of the carbon–carbon bonds are double bonds. They are called unsaturated because the molecule does not have the maximum number of carbon–hydrogen bonds because there are carbon–carbon double bonds present.

25. **D** When cold, the body starts shivering. The shivers stimulate muscle movement, which generates heat, causing the body to warm.

26. **C** Adaptive radiation occurs when an ancestral species moves into a new area and fills unoccupied niches. Over time, speciation occurs as populations evolve to become more specialized in their new niches.

27. **B** Carbon dioxide and water combine during photosynthesis to form glucose and oxygen.

28. **A** Shortness in pea plants is a recessive trait. Because one parent is homozygous for tall and the other heterozygous, all of the offspring are either homozygous for tall or heterozygous resulting in tall plants.

29. **B** An enzyme causes the phosphate group on the end to be split from the ATP molecule. The splitting of ATP releases enough energy to drive an endergonic reaction, therefore, the two reactions are often coupled.

30. **A** The endocrine system regulates the release of hormones. Hormones are used by the body to regulate many different functions.

Part B (Biology-E Questions 31–40)

31. **E** The xylem is composed of hard-sided cells that transport water and nutrients from the soil up to the plant.

32. **D** Plants are the producers in most ecosystems. Plants take in carbon dioxide from the atmosphere and use it along with water and energy from the sun to build glucose molecules.

33. **A** Examples of marsupials are animals such as kangaroos and opossums. They are considered more primitive than most mammals because the young are born very small and finish developing in the pouch.

34. **B** Homologous structures are similar structures in different but related organisms. The structures may not have the same outward appearance or function but they always have a similar internal form.

35. **D** Birds generate their own body heat. As a result, they have high energy requirements and must regularly eat.

36. **E** The carrying capacity is the maximum population an environment can support for an extended period of time. The population grows up to the carrying capacity and usually remains around it.

37. **B** Punctuated equilibrium occurs when the environment is stable for long periods of time, and there is little need for speciation to take place. These periods of stability are punctuated by periods of rapid change when speciation occurs.

38. **C** Succession is a natural progression. Its rate can be changed by many different factors.

39. **C** During their evolutionary history, whales lost their need for legs. As a result, the pelvis on whales is greatly reduced.

40. **A** An organism's niche is the role it plays in its environment. Earthworms breakdown or decompose organic matter in the soil.

Part C (Biology-M Questions 41–50)

41. **B** When the two homozygous plants are crossed, the genotype of all the offspring are heterozygous.

42. **C** Mitochondria are the powerhouse organelles in a cell. The mitochondria produce ATP and make it available to other parts of the cell.

43. **C** Oxygen is a product of photosynthesis. The only way a radioisotope can indicate a reaction pathway is to show up as a product in the reaction. The oxygen gas produced in photosynthesis is a direct result of the splitting of water molecules. Glucose, the other product in photosynthesis, receives its oxygen atoms from the incoming carbon dioxide molecules.

44. **A** Genetic drift is most likely to occur in small populations.

45. **A** Enzymes are protein molecules. An enzyme is a special type of protein that acts as a catalyst to facilitate a biochemical reaction.

46. **A** DNA strands are held together with hydrogen bonds. Hydrogen bonds are easily broken, which is important when DNA unravels for transcription.

47. **D** The phylum Echinodermata has all of these characteristics.

48. **A** The vascular tissue composed of living tubular cells that carry sugars from the leaves to other parts of the plant is called phloem.

49. **A** Water molecules are attracted to the polar ends of the lipid bilayer and repelled by the nonpolar tails. As a result, water molecules will line up on either side of the lipid bilayer. (Water molecules are only able to pass through the lipid bilayer by special protein channels.)

50. **E** A short, stout beak is used to apply great force to crack seeds.

CHAPTER 5

TEST-TAKING SKILLS AND STRATEGIES

GENERAL TEST-TAKING STRATEGIES

The following are some general test-taking strategies that apply to all the question types on the SAT Biology test. These strategies can help you gain valuable points when you take the actual exam.

Take Advantage of the Multiple-Choice Format

All 80 questions on the Biology E/M SAT Subject Test exam are variations on the multiple-choice format, which is the most common structure for a standardized test. That means that for every question, the correct answer is right in front of you. All you have to do is pick it out from among four incorrect answers, called "distracters." Consequently, you can use the process of elimination to rule out incorrect answer choices. The more answers you rule out, the easier it is to make the right choice.

If You Can Eliminate One or More Answer Choices, It's OK to Guess

Recall that on the SAT Biology test you are penalized one-quarter of a point for each incorrect answer. That means that if you do not know the answer to a question and cannot rule out any answer choices, guessing is a bad idea because the risk of incurring the penalty is too great. In such cases, the wisest course is to skip the question and move on. However, if you can rule out at least one incorrect choice, your odds of guessing correctly improve to 1 in 4, so now guessing starts to make sense. If you can rule out two choices, your odds improve to 1 in 3. Rule out three choices and your odds improve to 1 in 2, or 50-50. So in short, if you can rule out one or more incorrect answer choices, go ahead and guess.

Mark Up Your Test Booklet

Only your bubble sheet will be scored. Therefore, you are free to mark up your question booklet as much as you want while you tackle the problems. When you eliminate responses, draw a deliberate line through each choice that you cross out. This should minimize potential careless errors.

Try to Predict the Answer to the Question without First Looking at the Choices

This will save you time because it enables you to hunt for the answer efficiently rather than considering each choice and perhaps dreaming up reasons why it could be correct (a syndrome sometimes called "analysis paralysis"). If you already have an idea of what the correct answer should sound like, you can make a decision quickly and confidently.

Go with Your Gut

Finally, in those cases where you may not be 100% confident of the answer you are providing, it is often best to go with your gut feeling and stick with your first answer rather than change it after rethinking the problem. There is something to be said for trusting your instincts, especially if you are prone to "analysis paralysis." More often than not, if you know something about the subject, your first answer is likely to be the correct one.

General Test-Taking Strategies

1. Answer all questions where you can eliminate at least one answer choice. If you cannot eliminate any choices, skip the question and go on.
2. After reading a question, try to predict the answer without first looking at the choices.
3. Be wary of "analysis paralysis." If you are familiar with the material, stick with your first instinct when choosing an answer.

Now let's look at each of the particular question types that you will encounter on the SAT Biology test. There are strategies you should know for each type. Study the example questions so that you recognize the different question types when you encounter them on the real test. Also, take the time to familiarize yourself with the directions. That way you won't have to spend precious time reading them and thinking about them on test day. The answers to the example questions appear at the end of the chapter.

QUESTION TYPE 1: THE MATCHING GAME

Example Questions

Directions: Each set of lettered choices below refers to the numbered statements immediately following it. Choose the one lettered choice that best fits each statement and then blacken the corresponding oval on the Answer Sheet. A choice may be used once, more than once, or not at all in each set.

Questions 1–3

(A) Natural selection
(B) Passive immunity
(C) Convergent evolution
(D) Vestigial structure
(E) Use and disuse

1. Strains of bacteria that are resistant to antibiotics have appeared in hospitals.
2. Whales possess femur bones.
3. Bats and birds both have wings.

Questions like these test your ability to classify. In this example, choices A through E list five concepts that mostly pertain to evolution. Each "question" is really a specific example highlighting one of the particular concepts listed in the answer choices. To answer questions of this type, first take a very quick glance at the list of choices. Do not spend time thinking about the exact definitions of each term. That is not what you are being tested on. Go right to the questions and see if you can associate each example with its corresponding concept without pondering the list of choices.

For example, consider Question 1. The existence of bacteria that are unaffected by antibiotic medicine is a modern example of natural selection at work. Don't be tempted to classify this phenomenon as "passive immunity" because it "sounds right"; people often (incorrectly) say that they shouldn't inappropriately use antibiotics because the bacteria can become "immune" to them. That idea is not entirely accurate because bacteria lack immune systems and don't get sick and recover from the antibiotic. Instead, those susceptible to the antibiotic die off, and those that aren't affected by the chemical survive and reproduce in greater numbers.

If you are going to use the elimination strategy with this type of question, be careful about marking-up your test booklet. Remember that the same choices are used for several questions, so just because you can eliminate one choice for one question, that doesn't mean that the same choice can't be the correct answer for the next question.

Example Answers

1. (A) Natural selection
2. (D) Vestigial structure
3. (C) Convergent evolution

QUESTION TYPE 2: THE NUMBERED DIAGRAM

Example Questions

Directions: Questions 4 and 5 refer to the following diagram of a mammalian heart.

Cross-section of a mammalian heart.

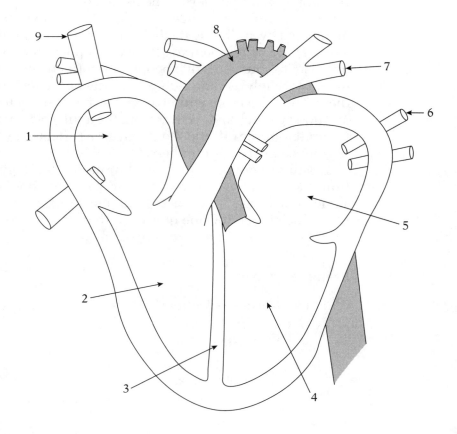

4. Chamber that receives blood from the lungs

    (A) 1
    (B) 2
    (C) 4
    (D) 5
    (E) 6

5. Blood vessel carrying deoxygenated blood

    (A) 3
    (B) 4
    (C) 5
    (D) 8
    (E) 9

Note that you do not need to identify each part of the heart or supply the name of each numbered structure. All you have to know is what the different parts do. Start by reading the description in the question stem. Then, if you can, think of the name the corresponding structure. Find that structure on the diagram and mark the corresponding answer choice. If you cannot recall the exact name of the structure, think of any logical associations that will help you identify it.

Let's use the above example questions to illustrate these strategies. Suppose you read Question 4 and immediately recall that the described structure is the left atrium. Looking at the diagram, you should identify the left atrium as structure number 5. You would then mark D as the correct answer. However, when you go on to Question 5, suppose you do not recall the name of the vessel that carries deoxygenated blood. But you might recall that deoxygenated blood is delivered to the right side of the heart and pumped from there into the lung (where it is oxygenated). Thus, any vessel carrying blood toward or through the right side of the heart—before it goes on to the lungs—would be the correct answer. Scanning the diagram reveals only one such vessel, labeled 9 (and corresponding to choice E). In this way, you can answer the question without even knowing the name of the designated structure (which is the superior vena cava).

Example Answers

4. (D) 5, which points to the left atrium
5. (E) 9, the superior vena cava

QUESTION TYPE 3: THE DIRECT QUESTION

Example Question

Directions: Each of the questions or incomplete statements below is followed by five suggested answers or completions. Choose the one that is BEST in each case and then blacken the corresponding oval on the Answer Sheet.

Question 6

A group of individuals belonging to a single species that live together in a defined area is termed a(n)

(A) population
(B) ecosystem
(C) community
(D) biome
(E) biosphere

Questions of this type simply require a straightforward recall of facts. They are the best type for trying to predict the answer first and then reading through all of the choices. If you are not sure of the answer but can eliminate at least one choice, go ahead and guess. When scanning the answers, be wary of words that look or sound alike. That way you can minimize careless errors.

Example Answer

6. (A) population

QUESTION TYPE 4: THE "PICK THE 'WRONG' ANSWER" QUESTION (A.K.A. "LEAST/EXCEPT/NOT" QUESTIONS)

Example Questions

Directions: Each of the questions or incomplete statements below is followed by five suggested answers or completions. Choose the one that is BEST in each case and then blacken the corresponding oval on the answer sheet.

Question 7

Which of the following processes generates the LEAST amount of energy?

    (A) glycolysis
    (B) lactic acid fermentation
    (C) the Krebs cycle
    (D) oxidative phosphorylation
    (E) aerobic respiration

Question 8

A cell from an *Elodea* plant contains all of the following structures EXCEPT:

    (A) DNA
    (B) Genes
    (C) A cell wall
    (D) A centriole
    (E) A nucleus

Question 9

Which of the following is NOT an organic molecule found in living organisms?

    (A) protein
    (B) nucleic acid
    (C) carbohydrate
    (D) sodium chloride
    (E) lipid

Note that the directions are the same as for the "direct questions." However, be sure to read very carefully. These questions can be tricky. You can still attempt to answer the question before looking at the choices. However, because many choices "may not fit," it is sometimes easier to use more specific strategies.

For the "LEAST" questions, consider making a list from highest to lowest. For example, after reading Question 7, you could rank the choices from highest (most energy generated) to lowest (least energy generated) and indicate your rankings by writing numbers from 1 to 5 next to the choices in your test booklet. Then, choose the highest number (in this case, number 5 corresponding to choice B) because it is the choice that generates the LEAST energy.

(A)	glycolysis	4
(B)	lactic acid fermentation	5
(C)	the Krebs cycle	3
(D)	oxidative phosphorylation	2
(E)	aerobic respiration	1

For the "EXCEPT" and "NOT" questions, consider rephrasing the question into a "direct question" and ruling out answers by the process of elimination. Take Question 8 as an example: You can restate the question "Does a green plant cell contain DNA?" If the answer is "yes" you can cross off choice A. Try this strategy with Questions 8 and 9.

Example Answers

7. (B) lactic acid fermentation (all other choices involve some generation of ATP)
8. (D) a centriole
9. (D) sodium chloride

QUESTION TYPE 5: EASY AS I, II, III

Example Question
Question 10

Which of the following domains includes single-celled organisms?

I.   eukarya
II. archaea
III. bacteria

    (A) I only
    (B) II only
    (C) I and II only
    (D) I and III only
    (E) I, II, and III

This type of question is another opportunity to use the process of elimination. Look at the three Roman numeral items. Start by crossing out any one you know does not apply. Then look in the answer choices and rule out any choice that includes the item you just crossed out. You can also take the opposite tack: Pick a Roman numeral item that you know *does* apply, then rule out any answer choice that does *not* contain that item.

For example, suppose you are sure that Bacteria (III) are composed of single cells, but you are not sure about Eukarya (I) and Archaea (II). Choices A, B, and C are eliminated immediately because you know that because III is correct, the answer must include III. At this point, even if you have to guess, you have a 50–50 chance of picking the correct answer.

Example Answer

10. (E) All domains have single-celled members.

QUESTION TYPE 6: THE LABORATORY QUESTION

Throughout the SAT Biology test you will see questions based on sets of data of the kind usually derived from laboratory experiments. The data will be in the form of tables, graphs, or diagrams. First, you will have to interpret the data. Then, you will have to apply this information to answer the accompanying questions. To answer correctly, you will need not only biology content knowledge (straight recall of facts), but also scientific reasoning/analytic skills.

If You Understand How a Scientific Experiment Is Designed, You Can Answer Many Laboratory Questions Even if You Are Not Familiar with the Subject Matter

For example, you may not have any actual lab experience with genetically mutated strains of *E. coli*, but as long as you are able to make sense of the data presented, you can successfully tackle laboratory questions that deal with this topic. To refresh your understanding of scientific experiments, review the following list of basic terms.

Basic Terminology: Dissecting an Experiment

- *Hypothesis:* A hypothesis is an idea that a scientist investigates in experiments. Experiments are designed to test a specific hypothesis, which will either be supported or negated by data collected.

- *Prediction:* After designing an experiment, a scientist can guess what will happen if the hypothesis is correct or incorrect. This guess is a prediction.

- *Variable:* A variable is the component of an experiment that the scientist manipulates (and, therefore, changes). A well-designed experiment will isolate and test one variable at a time.

- *Constants:* Constants are components of the experiment that are not manipulated (and, therefore, unchanged). A well-designed experiment will hold as many factors constant as possible to ensure a fair test.

- *Experimental sample:* The experimental sample (or experimental group) is the subject of scientific manipulation. More simplistically, the scientist will do something to a thing or organism to test the hypothesis.

- *Control:* The control is the sample (or group) that the scientist does not manipulate and uses instead to compare with the experimental sample.

- *Results:* Results are gathered when the scientist performs an experimental manipulation and observes the outcomes. The scientist will record the findings and organize the information into tables, graphs, and/or drawings.

- *Conclusion:* Once results have been recorded and interpreted, the scientist can determine whether the experiment supports (proves) or fails to support (disproves) the hypothesis.

The following example illustrates how these terms apply to a simple experiment.

Sample Experiment

Dr. Zen notices that his son is hyperactive after eating certain foods but not others. He heard that sugar can wind children up, and he wonders if his son's hyperactivity is caused by eating candy. He designs an experiment by giving half of the children in his son's playgroup a spoonful of sugar. Half the children are given sugar after lunch and allowed to play on the mat until they fall asleep. He then records how long after eating it takes these children to settle into a nap, and how long it takes the other half. The children who eat the sugar take longer to fall asleep. Dr. Zen now thinks that it is the sugar that makes his son hyperactive.

- *What is the hypothesis?* The hypothesis is "sugar intake makes children hyperactive."

- *What is the prediction?* Dr. Zen can make two predictions based on the same hypothesis. Prediction 1: If the hypothesis is true (that sugar intake makes children hyperactive), then children who eat sugar will have more trouble falling asleep than children that do not eat sugar. Prediction 2: Alternatively, if the hypothesis is false, then children who eat sugar will fall asleep at the same time as children who do not.

- *What is the variable?* In this experiment, the only thing that changes is the amount of sugar given to different children.

- *What are the constants?* Dr. Zen keeps as many other factors as possible constant. All of the children are allowed to play on the mat in the same environment at the same time of day.

- *What is the experimental group?* The group of children who receive sugar make up the experimental group and may be called experimental subjects.

- *What is the control group?* Dr. Zen compares the experimental group to the group of children who do not get sugar. Those children make up the control group (and are called control subjects).

- *What is the observation?* Dr. Zen watches all of the children and records when they fall asleep. These records are the results. Another term for this process is the collection of scientific data. Each individual recording is a datapoint. Here is how the data for this experiment may be recorded.

Sugar Group		**No Sugar Group**	
Child 1	15 minutes	Child 6	5 minutes
Child 2	10 minutes	Child 7	1 minute
Child 3	10 minutes	Child 8	2 minutes
Child 4	20 minutes	Child 9	5 minutes
Child 5	15 minutes	Child 10	1 minutes
Average	14 minutes	Average	2.8 minutes

- *What is the conclusion?* Dr. Zen sees that prediction 1 is correct. Therefore, he concludes that sugar makes children hyperactive.

Example Questions

Questions 11–13 refer to the following experiment.

To test the immune response of mice to infection, researchers exposed an experimental group to aerosolized bacteria. The proliferation of blood cell subtypes as a function of time was determined by immunophenotyping blood cells from this experimental group at set intervals after exposure. This was compared with a control group exposed to aerosolized sucrose solution. The amount of antibody produced by the mice groups was also determined at similar time intervals.

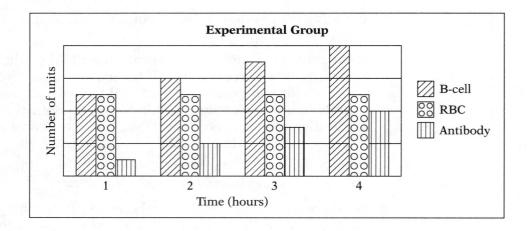

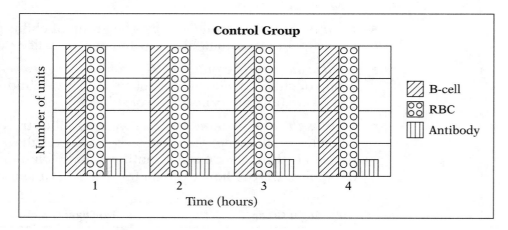

11. Based on the data, which of the following showed an increase after bacterial exposure?

    (A) sucrose levels
    (B) number of B-cells
    (C) number of red blood cells
    (D) type of antibody
    (E) all of the above

12. What is the function of antibodies in an organism's immune system?

    (A) trigger an immune response in the body
    (B) cause an increase in red blood cell number
    (C) act as enzymes, speeding up chemical reactions
    (D) bind to and help destroy pathogens
    (E) prevent bacteria from being harmed

13. Which of the following is the most logical conclusion for the experimental findings?

    (A) B-type immune cells produce antibodies.
    (B) Bacterial exposure inhibits protein synthesis.
    (C) Red blood cells multiply after bacterial exposure.
    (D) B-type cells have a doubling time of approximately 1 hour.
    (E) Sucrose prevents the effects of bacterial infection in mice.

No Matter How Complicated the Question Is, Begin by Dissecting the Experiment into Its Essential Components

In this example you may not know what "immunophenotyping" is, but you should still be able to understand the basics of the experimental design.

Work Backward to Generate a Hypothesis and Prediction; This Will Help You Understand the Graphs (Which Are the Experimental Results)

You should recognize that in this experiment, the scientists compared the "proliferation of blood cell subtypes" after mice were exposed to bacteria (the experimental group) or sucrose (the control group). Now that you recognize what the scientists did, you can generate an appropriate hypothesis and prediction. Let's say you recall that B-cells fight infection. You may hypothesize that "B-type immune cells proliferate (or multiply) after exposure to bacteria." Prediction 1 would be "If the hypothesis is true, the amount of B-type immune cells will be greater in the experimental group than the control group over time." Prediction 2 would be "If the hypothesis is false, the amount of B-type immune cells will be the same in both groups."

Next, Analyze the Graphs and Reach a Conclusion Consistent with Your Predictions

In this example, the first graph shows that in the experimental group, the amount of B-type immune cells increases over time, while the amount of red blood cells remains constant. Alternatively, in graph 2, there is no change in the control group cell amounts. This implies that prediction 1 is correct. Thus, the conclusion is that bacterial infection stimulates B-type immune cell proliferation.

Finally, Ask Yourself whether Any Additional Information Is Available in the Graph

In graph 1, we see that the experimental animals also produce more antibody. Making this observation is important for answering one of the questions.

Example Answers

11. **B** Answering this question is based only on graphic analysis. You may have been tempted to say **D** or **E.** In this case, the *amount* of antibody increases, but the graph says nothing about the *types* of antibodies.

12. **D** This question requires information recall and can be answered without looking at the experimental data. If you said **A,** then you were thinking about the meaning of the term *antigen,* which is what an antibody will bind to and help destroy. There is no immediate relationship between bacterial exposure and red blood cell number **B.**

13. **A** Although prior knowledge will help, this question can be answered based only on the graphic analysis. Out of all the other choices given, this is the most logical conclusion based on the data. You can rule out **B** because protein synthesis was not examined in this experiment, thus, there is no evidence to support that idea. You can rule out **C** because the amount of red blood cells does not change in either group. You should rule out **D** because the graph shows that the height of the B-cells does not actually double, but increases by a lesser amount. Finally, you can rule out **E** because the mice that were given sucrose functioned as the control group. Sucrose was not meant to have any effect on the mice's immune systems. There seems to be a correlation between the elevation of B-cell number and elevation of antibody, so you could suppose that B cells produce the antibodies. *While this is true, it is important to note that this experiment does not actually establish causality. In other words, an unknown third entity may cause both the B-cells and the amount of antibody to increase at the same time.*

PART II

REVIEW OF BIOLOGY TOPICS

CHAPTER 6

UNDERSTANDING MOLECULAR AND CELLULAR BIOLOGY

Lesson 6-1. Molecular Biology

VOCABULARY

- element
- isotopes
- atomic weight
- compounds
- bond
- ionic bond
- ion
- covalent bond
- hydrogen bonds
- hydrophilic
- hydrophobic
- hydrocarbons
- alcohols
- macromolecules
- carbohydrates
- monosaccharides
- glucose
- polymers
- monomers
- dehydration reaction
- hydrolysis
- disaccharides
- isomers
- polysaccharide
- cellulose
- proteins
- amino acids
- peptide bond
- polypeptides
- protein folding
- denaturation
- ribonucleic acid or RNA
- deoxyribonucleic acid or DNA
- nucleotide
- base pairs
- double helix
- lipids
- fats
- steroids
- phospholipids

Although biology is a well-established science in its own right, an understanding of the chemical basis of life is crucial to understanding the mechanisms of cells and organisms. Despite the remarkable diversity and complexity of life, all organisms are made of the same set of chemical compounds, in an almost infinite number of combinations. In this section, we'll review these various compounds and the role they play in living systems.

ELEMENTS, COMPOUNDS, AND BONDS

All of the matter around us is made of atoms, each of which is classified as an element. An **element** is defined as the simplest form of a substance that cannot be broken down any further. Familiar elements include copper, gold, carbon, and oxygen. Under normal circumstances, it is not possible to take an atom of any of these elements and break it down further.

Each atom is composed of a nucleus containing positively charged particles called protons, and uncharged particles called neutrons. The nucleus is orbited by tiny negatively charged particles called electrons. Elements are identified by the number of protons in each of their atoms' nuclei; for example, all carbon atoms have six protons, while all oxygen atoms have eight protons. This number is known as the element's *atomic number;* and elements are arranged in the Periodic Table in the order of increasing atomic number, or number of protons in the nucleus. Each element also has an abbreviation known as its atomic symbol; C stands for carbon, Cl for chlorine, Na for sodium, etc. The atomic number can be written to the lower left of the element (for example, $_6$C, $_{17}$Cl).

Totaling up the number of protons and neutrons in an atom gives its *mass number*. This mass number is indicated to the upper left of the element's atomic symbol (for example, ^{14}N and ^{16}O). Generally, all atoms of a same element have the same mass number; however, occasionally, there are atoms with the same number of protons but a different number of neutrons. Such atoms are known as **isotopes.** For example, while most carbon atoms have six neutrons, giving them a mass number of 12, some carbon molecules have eight neutrons, giving them a mass number of 14. Isotopes are often useful because, as they decay to other elements (for example, when a neutron in ^{14}C converts into a proton, decaying the atom to ^{14}N), they give off radiation that can be detected and used for a variety of purposes, such as carbon dating or molecular tagging.

Because elements vary in the number and frequency of their isotopes, scientists calculate an element's **atomic weight** to take this into account. The atomic weight of an element is the weight of all of its electrons and neutrons in a naturally occurring sample. Because such naturally occurring sample generally contains a number of isotopes of the element, each with different mass numbers, it is generally slightly off from the mass number of the most common isotope. For example, while chlorine is most commonly found as ^{35}Cl, it is also naturally found as ^{37}Cl, so its atomic weight is slightly higher than 35. See Figure 6-1 for the atomic number, mass number, and atomic weight of the first 18 elements.

Hydrogen — Name							Helium
H — Symbol							He
1 — Atomic number							2
1 — Mass number							4
1.00794 — Atomic weight							4.002 602
Lithium	Beryllium	Boron	Carbon	Nitrogen	Oxygen	Fluorine	Neon
Li	Be	B	C	N	O	F	Ne
3	4	5	6	7	8	9	10
7	9	11	12	14	16	19	20
6.941	9.012 182	10.811	12.0107	14.0067	15.9994	18.998 403	20.1797
Sodium	Magnesium	Aluminum	Silicon	Phosphorus	Sulfur	Chlorine	Argon
Na	Mg	Al	Si	P	S	Cl	Ar
11	12	13	14	15	16	17	18
23	24	27	28	31	32	35	40
22.989 770	24.3050	26.981 538	28.0855	30.973 761	32.065	35.453	39.948

Figure 6-1 Periodic table of the first 18 elements with mass number, atomic number, and atomic weight.

Atoms said to be in their *ground state* are electrically neutral, meaning that the number of protons will be equal to the number of electrons. Atoms are most stable, however, when they have enough electrons to complete their outermost orbit level, therefore, they seek to either gain or lose electrons or share them with one another. That is why most elements are often found in **compounds,** which are combinations of atoms of different elements held together by a **bond.** Compounds have specific physical properties that the individual elements do not possess when they are not bound; for example, table salt (sodium chloride, or NaCl), has properties that neither sodium (Na) nor chlorine (Cl) possess independently.

There are two main types of bonds; these bonds largely depend on the fate of the electrons of the participating atoms. Because the electrons orbit far outside the nucleus of protons and neutrons, they are the part of the atom that is involved in interaction with other atoms. An **ionic bond** occurs when one atom "donates" an electron to another. If an atom gains or loses electrons, the atom is no longer neutral, and so it gains an electrical charge. Any atom (or group of atoms bound together) having a positive or negative charge on it is called an **ion.** Such a bond occurs in table salt, when the sodium atom donates an electron to the chlorine atom. Because the chlorine has gained an electron, it takes on a negative charge, and, thus, is a Cl^- ion; because the sodium has lost an electron, it takes on a net positive charge, and thus exists as a Na^+ ion; it is the formation of these ions that characterizes ionic bonds. Because these opposite charges attract, the Na and Cl are held together tightly, becoming a new unit, NaCl (Figure 6-2).

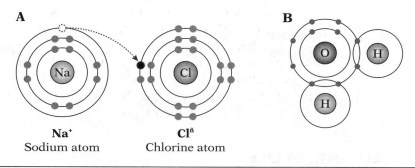

A

Na^+
Sodium atom

Cl^n
Chlorine atom

B

Figure 6-2 A, Ionic bonding in sodium chloride (NaCl). **B,** Covalent bonding in water (H_2O).

A **covalent bond** occurs when two atoms share electrons, creating a molecule. Such a bond occurs, for example, between the atoms that make up the compound methane, which contains four hydrogen atoms and one carbon atom (CH_4). The carbon atom shares electrons with the hydrogen atoms equally. Sometimes, however, the sharing of electrons in a covalent bond is unequal, as in the case of water (H_2O). In water, the oxygen molecule is covalently bonded to each of two hydrogen molecules. However, because the oxygen molecule of water is more attractive to electrons than the hydrogen (a property known as electronegativity), the electrons spend more time around the oxygen molecule than they do the hydrogen molecule. This gives the oxygen part of the molecule a slightly negative charge because of the increased presence of the electrons; the decreased presence of the electrons on the hydrogen side gives it a slight positive charge. Covalent bonds with unequal sharing, such as those found in water, are known as *polar* covalent bonds; covalent bonds with equal sharing, such as that found in methane, are known as *nonpolar* covalent bonds.

Hydrogen bonds, unlike ionic bonds or covalent bonds, do not involve the transfer or sharing of an electron; instead, **hydrogen bonds** are interactions between the positive and negative areas of two polar covalent molecules. Two water molecules, for example, can form a hydrogen bond between the slightly positive end of the hydrogen atoms, and the slightly negative end of the oxygen atom, as shown in Figure 6-3. A hydrogen bond is not as strong as an ionic or a covalent bond, and is much more likely to be broken and reformed between different water molecules. Nevertheless, hydrogen bonds play an

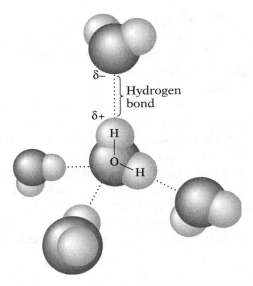

Figure 6-3 Water forms hydrogen bonds because of the partial charges on the oxygen and hydrogen molecules (δ^+ or δ^- indicate a slight positive or negative charge).

important part of the stability of a number of molecules, including DNA and many proteins, as we will see further along.

THE ELEMENTS OF LIFE

There are 92 naturally occurring elements; of these, only 25 are necessary for life. Ninety-six percent of living matter is comprised of only four of these 25 necessary elements: carbon, oxygen, hydrogen, and nitrogen. Most of the others are required only in trace amounts. These elements rarely exist by themselves in the body. More often, they are found in compounds, sometimes forming large molecules that use thousands of atoms.

WATER, WATER, EVERYWHERE

Most of our cells—most of our bodies—are made up of water. Water is an essential precursor for life, and cytosol is made up primarily of water. Oxygen and hydrogen, the elements found in water, are the first and third most common elements in the body, respectively. Oxygen alone accounts for 65% of the human body weight, and most of this oxygen is contained in water.

Recall in our discussion of covalent and hydrogen bonds that the oxygen and hydrogen atoms in a water molecule are linked by a polar covalent bond. Because the slightly positive hydrogen atoms are attracted to the slightly negative oxygen atoms, water molecules are able to form a number of hydrogen bonds. The polarity and hydrogen bonding of water molecules has a number of important consequences that make it crucial for life.

Polar compounds, such as salts, easily dissolve in water because water molecules are polar. When polar molecules—either molecules with a polar covalent bond or with an ionic bond—are placed into water, the positive and negative parts of the water molecules are attracted to the oppositely charged parts of the new molecule. This causes charged substances to dissolve in water easily. Examples of these polar substances include salts, sugars, and alcohols, and parts of some proteins; such polar substances that interact well with water are known as **hydrophilic** substances.

Nonpolar substances, such as oil, however, do not dissolve in water; in fact, they often separate from water. Such substances are said to be **hydrophobic** (easy to remember—just think of these molecules as having a phobia, or fear, of water). Most simple hydrocarbons and lipids are hydrophobic molecules. That hydrophobic molecules avoid water is an important property, because it is the key to many features of biological systems. The plasma membrane of a cell, for example, contains a hydrophobic substance that congregates, and acts as a barrier to prevent the passage of water in and out of the cell.

The hydrogen bonding of water causes it to have specific physical properties that are very favorable to life. Because water molecules attract each other very closely, liquid water has a very high specific heat; this means that increasing or decreasing the temperature of water requires the transfer of a large amount of energy as compared to most other small molecules. Changing the state of water—from gas to liquid, or from liquid to solid, or vice versa—also requires a relatively large input or output of energy. Think of it this way: if you were to put a pot of alcohol next to a pot of water on the stove, and light a burner under the both at the same setting, not only would the pot of alcohol increase its temperature much more quickly, but the amount of energy from the burner required for it to evaporate would be much less. This would be true for almost any other common liquid you could try.

That water requires a lot of energy to change temperature means that it acts as a stabilizing influence on the temperature of cells, organisms, and the Earth itself. Many reactions in organisms are temperature dependent. If it is too warm or too cold, cells cannot carry out all their functions. However, because water does not change its temperature as quickly as the air does, it helps keep the temperature of organisms and cells more constant. Similarly, the large amount of water in the oceans prevents the Earth from cooling or heating up too quickly. Water helps keep the Earth within the range of temperatures that will support life.

THE ROLE OF CARBON

You may have heard at some point that humans, like all organisms on earth, are carbon-based life forms. An entire field of chemistry—organic chemistry—has been developed specifically to study only carbon and compounds containing carbon. Yet only 18.5% of human body weight is carbon. This is a significant portion, but it is less than the amount that is oxygen. How is it then, that we are "carbon-based," and why is carbon so important?

Carbon is the most significant element in the body because carbon atoms are extremely versatile, bonding in a wide variety of conformations. Recall that water is one oxygen atom covalently bonded to two hydrogen atoms. These two bonds (one with each hydrogen atom) are the maximum number of covalent bonds that any oxygen atom can form, under normal circumstances. But a carbon atom can form *four covalent bonds*—more than most any other simple element. This allows carbon atoms to form chains, in which it can bond to other carbon atoms, and still have available bonding sites for other atoms. The ability of carbon to form strong carbon chains is an important property that allows it to form larger molecules that are necessary for life.

Carbon bonds are also extremely flexible. As molecules become more complex, the conformation, or shape, of the molecule becomes an extremely important consideration. Carbon is useful in forming larger biological molecules because it can form a wide variety of stable shapes, allowing a wide variety of molecules to be formed. As in the case of sugars, for example, a chain of five or six carbon atoms can form a carbon ring. Such rings can add additional stability to a large molecule. Carbon atoms are also capable of forming double or triple covalent bonds, which occur when atoms share two or three electrons, instead of just one. These higher-energy bonds increase the variety of bonding possibilities for carbon-based molecules.

The simplest carbon chains are known as **hydrocarbons.** These molecules contain only carbon and hydrogen, and can have one or more carbons in a chain. Examples of such hydrocarbons include methane and propane (with one and four carbons, respectively). But carbons do not just bond with hydrogen. Sometimes, for example, they bond with a hydroxyl group, made up of an oxygen atom bonded to a hydrogen atom. Carbon chains bonded to hydroxyl groups are known as **alcohols.** There are a number of other common groups that are attached to carbon molecules, including carboxyl groups and phosphates. An illustration of these common functional groups that often attach to hydrocarbons is in Figure 6-4. Hydrocarbons are so commonly the base for biological molecules that occasionally, in more complex illustrations, the "C" symbol is omitted; if you see such a diagram on the SAT Subject Test, you should assume the presence of a carbon molecule.

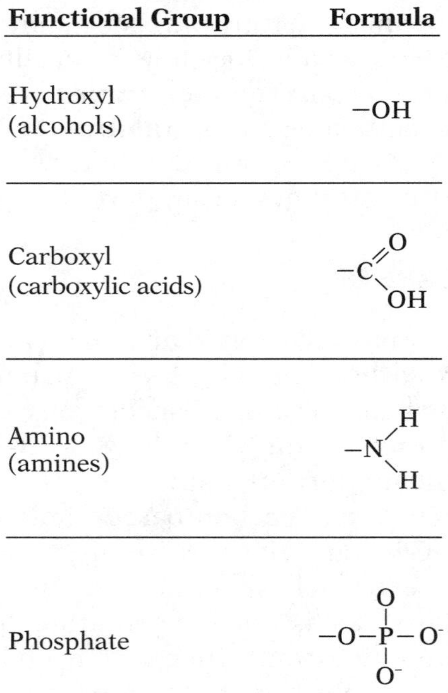

Functional Group	Formula
Hydroxyl (alcohols)	$-OH$
Carboxyl (carboxylic acids)	$-C{\overset{\displaystyle O}{\underset{\displaystyle OH}{}}}$
Amino (amines)	$-N{\overset{\displaystyle H}{\underset{\displaystyle H}{}}}$
Phosphate	$-O-\overset{\displaystyle O}{\underset{\displaystyle O^-}{P}}-O^-$

Figure 6-4 Functional groups commonly found in organic compounds.

Carbon compounds are amazingly diverse; from a simple methane molecule (CH_4) to the most complex of proteins. Yet the same characteristics make them useful as the basis of biological molecules: their ability to form four covalent bonds, their ability to bond with a number of different functional groups, and their ability to form flexible yet sturdy carbon chains. That carbon is so versatile allows it to form the backbone of larger organic molecules, often containing thousands of atoms; these molecules are known as **macromolecules.** The discussion of these macromolecules makes up the remainder of this lesson.

CARBOHYDRATES AND THE DEHYDRATION REACTION

Carbohydrates are an essential macromolecule for life, because they provide the primary source of food for cells. **Carbohydrates** include sugars and the linked chains of sugar molecules that are made from them. They include simple sugars such as glucose and fructose, and larger molecules such as starch and cellulose.

The simplest carbohydrates are the **monosaccharides. Glucose,** which is a six-carbon sugar with the chemical formula $C_6H_{12}O_6$, is the most important monosaccharide because it is the molecule that cells use to derive their energy. Galactose and fructose are monosaccharides with the same chemical formula as glucose, but with slightly different arrangements of atoms. As you can see in Figure 6-5, these monosaccharides are primarily made of a carbon backbone attached to hydroxyl groups and oxygen atoms, most often arranged in a ring (although this is often very difficult to illustrate in books, so they are often drawn in their linear, and not ringed form). Most carbohydrates are very similar, although often with a different number of carbon molecules; they generally have a chemical that is a multiple of the formula CH_2O. For example, five-carbon sugars known as riboses are very important for the structure of DNA, and they have a chemical formula of $C_5H_{10}O_5$.

MONOSACCHARIDES

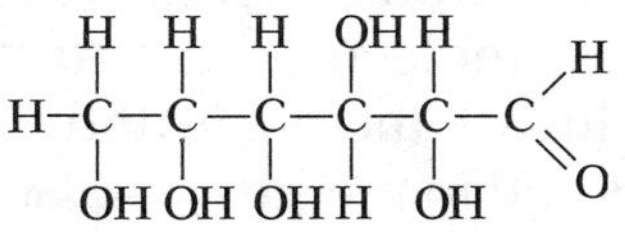

Glucose

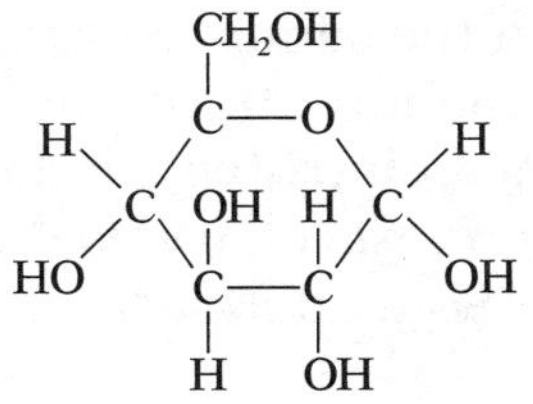

Glucose in ring form

Figure 6-5 Diagram of monosaccharides.

Monosaccharides are able to covalently bond to each other, forming larger molecules containing any number of simple sugars. Larger molecules made up of identical building blocks linked together are known as **polymers,** while the building blocks that are able to covalently bond to make up polymers are known as **monomers.** Imagine, for example, tying a large number of rubber bands together, end-to-end, to form a chain of rubber bands. If you were to do so, the rubber bands would be the monomers, which make up the larger polymer of the chain. Polymers are important in biology because they allow large molecules to be formed with only a few different molecules.

As is the case with many monomers, two monosaccharides can link together using what is known as a **dehydration reaction.** In such a reaction, hydroxyl (–OH) groups in two sugars interact, as in Figure 6-6. A covalent bond is formed between a carbon atom of one sugar and an oxygen atom in the other sugar; in the process, a water molecule is lost from the two sugars (hence, the name, dehydration). Reversing this process to break down a polymer can easily occur with the addition of a water molecule; this process is known as **hydrolysis.**

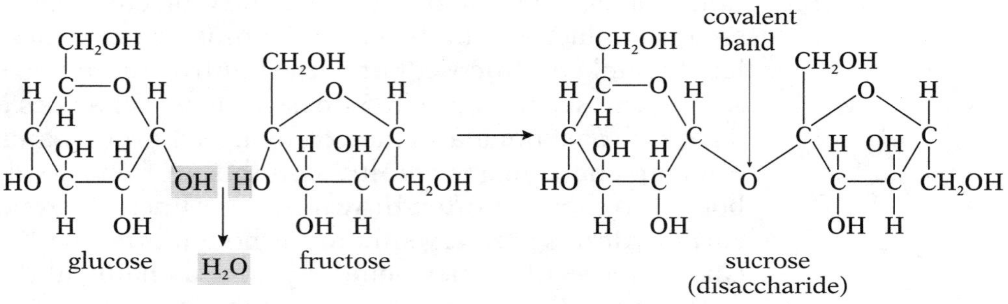

Figure 6-6 Disaccharides and the dehydration reaction.

Disaccharides are carbohydrates formed when two monosaccharides are linked together in a dehydration reaction. Disaccharides are very common. They include maltose (found in chocolate), which is formed by two glucose molecules, and sucrose (table sugar), formed by a glucose molecule and a fructose molecule. Lactose, the sugar found in milk, is formed by the linkage of a glucose molecule and a galactose molecule. (Notice how many carbohydrates end in the suffix "-ose."). Maltose, sucrose, and lactose are also examples of **isomers.** They are different compounds having the same chemical formula, which in this case is $C_{12}H_{22}O_{11}$. Although they are all composed of the same atoms in the same proportions, the three molecules have a different spatial arrangement of the atoms.

Polysaccharides are carbohydrates formed by the linkage of a large number of monosaccharides. Polysaccharides play a variety of essential roles in biology. Some polysaccharides are used to store energy:

- *Starch* is a polysaccharide of glucose monomers found exclusively in plants, although often eaten by humans as a food source. Plants use starch to store energy for use during periods such as winter when they cannot make energy from the sun. The formal name for starch is "amylase," so this is yet another example of a carbohydrate that ends in the suffix "-ose."

- In the liver, humans store glucose in a slightly different type of polymer called *glycogen*. Between meals, when we are not actively ingesting glucose, the glycogen is broken down to ensure a constant energy supply to our cells.

Other polysaccharides serve important structural functions:

- **Cellulose** is the primary component of the cell walls in plants. The strength of the polysaccharide cellulose in plant cell walls is what makes the wood from trees so strong, and allows plants to grow upward and resist the tug of gravity. In fact, the linkages between the monomers in cellulose are so strong it cannot be digested by humans or most organisms.
- *Chitin* is another structural polysaccharide. If you've ever stepped on a large bug only to hear a crunching sound under your shoe, then you've encountered chitin. Chitin is used by insects, spiders, and crustaceans such as shrimp and crabs to form their outer shell, known as the exoskeleton.

AMINO ACIDS, PROTEINS, AND PEPTIDE BONDS

Proteins are another category of essential organic molecules that carry out a wide variety of functions within the cell. They are the workhorses of the cell, carrying out most of the important reactions within the cell. They help assemble, disassemble, and transport molecules. Proteins also often serve structural purposes, making up much of the structure of cells and organisms.

Proteins are made up of molecules known as amino acids. **Amino acids,** or monopeptides, are molecules that contain three functional groups off of the same carbon molecule as shown in Figure 6-7.

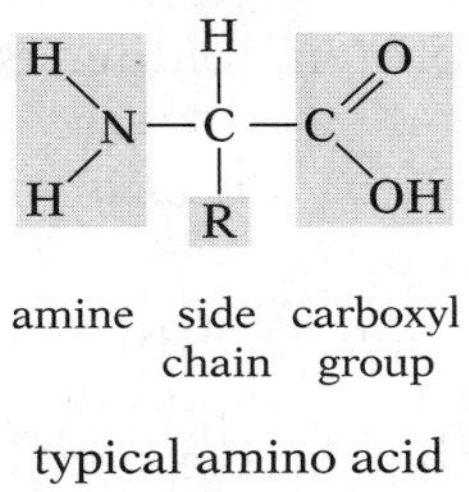

amine side carboxyl
       chain   group

typical amino acid

Figure 6-7 Diagram of an amino acid.

- a carboxyl (–COOH group), which makes the molecule a carboxylic acid
- a amine (–NH_2) group, which gives the word "amino" to the name
- a side chain, also known as an R-group, which can very from just a simply hydrogen molecule to long chains or rings of carbons.

There are 20 different types of amino acids used in proteins. Amino acids can be identified by the type of side chain that is attached to the central carbon. The side chains often give each amino acid distinctive properties that become important when they are combined into a polypeptide.

Despite the differences in their side chains, amino acids all bond in the same way, using a dehydration reaction to create what is known as a **peptide bond.** Chains of amino acids created by peptide bonds are known as **polypeptides.** In a peptide bond, a –OH from the carboxyl side of one amino acid joins with a hydrogen from the amino side of another amino acid, releasing a water molecule and forming a covalent bond between the carbon and nitrogen atoms. Figure 6-8 shows how a peptide bond forms between two amino acids. Note that the peptide bonds do not involve the side chain of amino acids. Instead, a repeating pattern of –N–C–C– forms the backbone of the polypeptide, and the side chains of the amino acids are projected out freely from the backbone of the amino acid chain. A peptide bond always occurs between the C of one amino acid and the N of another.

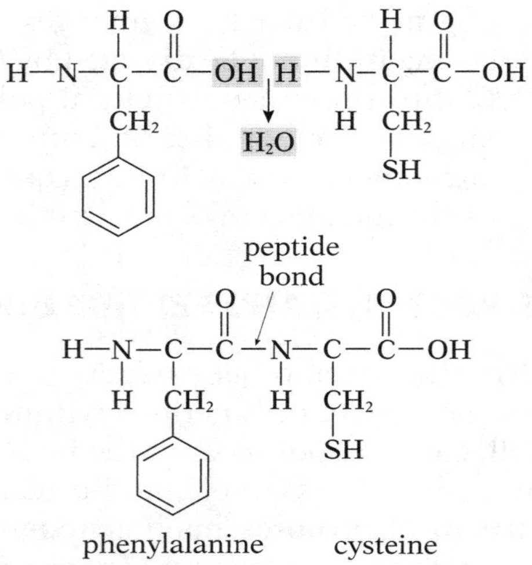

Figure 6-8 Diagram of a peptide bond.

Proteins are highly complex molecules with very specific shapes. These shapes are achieved through what is known as **protein folding.** There are four stages of protein folding, each known as a protein structure.

- The *primary structure* of a protein is simply a chain of amino acids, or the polypeptide.
- The *secondary structure* of proteins is caused by hydrogen bonding of the amino acid backbone. The C=O bond and the N–H bond in amino acids are both polar covalent bonds; this allows a hydrogen bond to form between the oxygen molecule of one peptide and a hydrogen of another peptide. These hydrogen bonds cause certain parts of proteins to take on in a helical shape, known as an α (alpha) helix, or a pleated shape, known as a β sheet.
- Further folding into what is known as the *tertiary structure* of proteins is caused by interactions between the side chains of different peptides in the same polypeptide. Certain amino acid side chains, are polar, and are able to form hydrogen bonds; others are actually able to form ionic bonds between each other. The amino acid cysteine, which contains sulfide (–SH) groups, is able to bond covalently to other cysteine molecules, forming what is known as a disulfide bridge. Finally, because proteins are generally found in the water-filled, and thus polar, cytosol, certain hydrophobic amino acid side chains tend to congregate together, away from water, giving the protein further shape.
- The final structure of proteins, known as its *quaternary structure,* is formed when two or more folded polypeptides join together. Often, there is additional hydrogen bonding between side chains of peptides from different polypeptides. Here again, the specific conformation of the protein is

important, because folded polypeptides must fit together in precise ways in order to form a functional protein.

It's important to note that the types of interactions that will form the tertiary and quaternary structure depend on the side chains that are present, and thus depend on the original amino acid sequence of the polypeptide (which, as we will learn in Lesson 4, is coded for in the DNA). This is a significant property of proteins: *the amino acid sequence of the polypeptide will determine the protein's tertiary structure, and thus its eventual conformation.* Shape, or conformation, is a crucial property of proteins because it is a protein's conformation that determines its ability to function. For example, hemoglobin, the protein that carries oxygen in our red blood cells, is folded to give it a specific pocket to carry the oxygen molecules; if the amino acid sequence were slightly different in the areas of the protein that form the pocket, it might take on a different conformation, and lose its ability to carry an oxygen molecule. For this reason, the amino acid sequences of the essential parts of proteins change very little from species to species.

Proteins are sensitive to their environment. The interactions that form the secondary, tertiary, and quaternary structure of proteins are often dependent on a specific temperature, pH, or salt concentration. Absent the proper conditions, these interactions can no longer take place in the right way, and the protein can lose its shape, a process known as **denaturation.** Proteins that have been denatured no longer have their original conformation, and, therefore, are often no longer able to carry out their original function.

NUCLEOTIDES AND NUCLEIC ACIDS

Nucleic acids carry the instructions for life. There are two main types of nucleic acids in the body: **ribonucleic acid,** or **RNA,** and **deoxyribonucleic acid,** or **DNA.** These important molecules store all of the necessary information for organisms, from the simplest bacteria to the most complex mammal. The information contained in nucleic acids is passed from generation to generation, forming the basis for the inheritance of traits.

Nucleic acids, like the other macromolecules that we have reviewed, are also polymers. The monomer of nucleic acids is known as a **nucleotide.** A nucleotide that makes up DNA or RNA consists of three parts: a pentose (or five-carbon) sugar, a phosphate group, and a nucleotide base, as shown in Figure 6-9.

- The *sugar* in a nucleotide contains five carbons. There are some slight variations in the sugar that is used in the nucleotide. Nucleotides containing a ribose sugar are used in RNA. Other nucleotides have a deoxyribose sugar, which contains one less oxygen atom than a ribose sugar (hence, the prefix, "deoxy"). Deoxyribose sugars are found in DNA.
- The *phosphate group* is covalently bonded to the sugar of the nucleotide (see Figure 6-8). When nucleotides bond together, the phosphate group of one nucleotide binds to the sugar of another nucleotide, in a bond known as a phosphodiester linkage. This is a dehydration reaction. This alternating pattern of sugar–phosphate–sugar–phosphate forms what is known as the sugar–phosphate backbone of the nucleic acid, with the basis sticking out to the side (much like the side group of an amino acid sticks out from the side of a polypeptide).

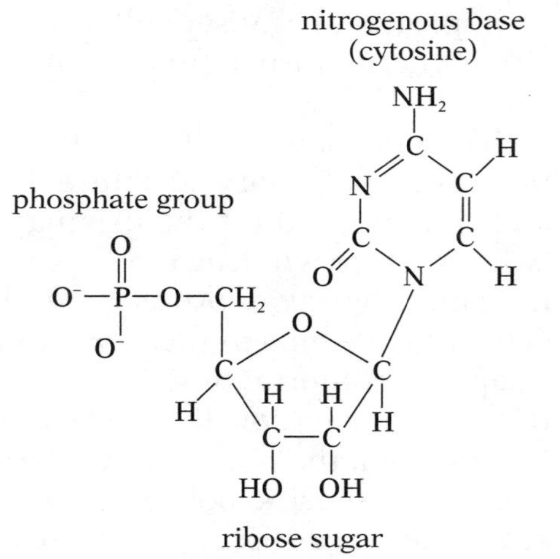

nitrogenous base
(cytosine)

phosphate group

ribose sugar

Figure 6-9 Diagram of a nucleotide.

- The *base* is also covalently bonded to the sugar, opposite the phosphate group. The bases of nucleotides can vary, but all contain nitrogen, giving them the name nitrogenous bases. There are five types of nitrogenous bases (hence, five types of monomers): adenine, cytosine, guanine, thymine, and uracil, each of which is often written simply as its first letter (for example, A for adenine, C for cytosine). Uracil is only found in RNA, and thymine is only found in DNA. The nucleotides are generally identified by the type of nitrogen base that is attached.

Strands of DNA and RNA are said to have a 5′ or a 3′ end. These ends are named for the carbon on the ribose sugar that is closest to that end. As you can see in Figure 6-9, the 5′ carbon is just off the ring, and attaches to the phosphate group of the nucleotide, while the 3′ carbon is the site for attachment to the phosphate group of another nucleotide.

The bases of a nucleotide stick out from the sugar–phosphate backbone, leaving them able to interact with the nitrogenous bases of another DNA strand, like the two DNA strands in Figure 6-10. The bases match up in a very specific pattern: cytosine matches up only with guanine, and adenine matches up only with thymine or uracil. These are known as complementary **base pairs.**

DNA within the cell exists as a double strand. The two complementary strands of DNA will match up in opposite directions. One strand lines up in a 5′ to 3′ direction, while the other strand lines up in a 3′ to 5′ direction. Hydrogen bonds are formed between the complementary base pairs and allow the complementary strands to stick together, although the two strands can easily be separated by a number of proteins. Because the base pairs on the strands are complementary, the sequence of one can be deduced from the sequence of the other. For example, a strand that has the following sequence:

5′ ACCTAAGTTGCAGG 3′

will line up with a strand that has a complementary sequence:

3′ TGGATTCAACGTCC 5′

The two strands of DNA twist into a twisting shape known as a **double helix.** The double-helical structure of DNA was deduced by James Watson and Francis Crick in 1953.

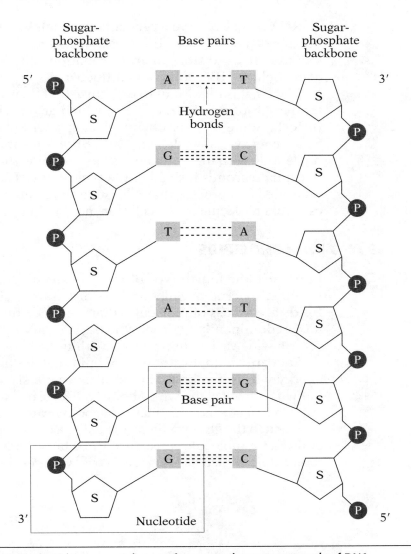

Figure 6-10 Nucleotides can match up to form complementary strands of DNA.

DNA's primary purpose is to store information for the cell. DNA is the cell's genetic material. That is to say, all of the information necessary to make the structures of the cell is contained in its DNA. Each cell has a complete copy of these instructions, and organisms pass on one half of their DNA to their descendants (their mate providing the other half). This accounts for the inheritance of traits across generations.

RNA molecules generally exist in the cell as a single-stranded nucleic acid. There are many types of RNA molecules within the cell.

- Messenger RNA, or mRNA, serves as an intermediary between DNA and the processes that produce proteins.
- Transfer RNA, or tRNA, carries amino acids so they can be linked up during protein synthesis.
- Ribosomal RNA, or rRNA, is an important component of the ribosome that plays a part in producing proteins.
- Other small RNA molecules perform a variety of functions within the cell, acting as mini-enzymes. For more on these, see Lesson 6-4.

RNA can also serve as genetic material. Viruses are not living organisms, but nevertheless store information using nucleic acids. Some use single-stranded RNA to store their information. Viruses with RNA as their genetic code include HIV, polio, and influenza.

Finally, it is important to recognize that there are other types of nucleotides than are found in DNA or RNA, which also perform important functions in the cell. Some serve as chemical signals within the body, while others serve as an energy carrier within the cell. Adenosine triphosphate, or ATP, is a nucleotide with the nitrogenous base adenine that contains three high-energy phosphate groups instead of the typical one. These phosphate groups can be separated in a process that releases a small amount of energy, making ATP an essential molecule in the cell (for more on ATP, see Lesson 6-3).

LIPIDS AND PHOSPHOLIPIDS

Lipids are the fourth type of macromolecule found within the body. Unlike the other macromolecules we have discussed, lipids are not polymers. Instead, **lipids** are a class of molecules that are made up mostly of hydrocarbons and are predominantly hydrophobic. Lipids vary in their size and structure, and serve a wide variety of purposes within the body.

Fats are an important type of lipid that are used to store large amounts of energy within the body. Fat molecules consist of long hydrocarbon chains known as fatty acids with about 16–18 carbons attached to a glycerol molecule. As in amino acids and carbohydrates, the hydrocarbon chains are attached to the glycerol molecule using a dehydration synthesis reaction. Generally, a fat molecule consists of three fatty acids attached to a single glycerol molecule, a molecule known as a triacylglycerol. This is shown in Figure 6-11.

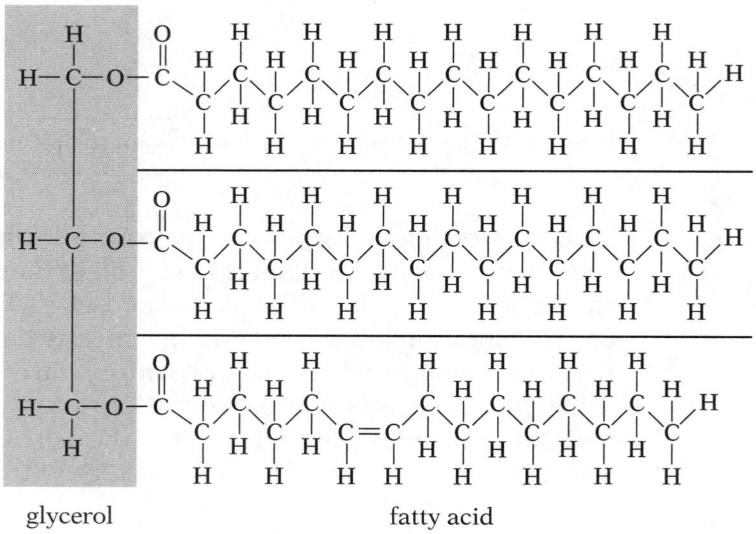

glycerol   fatty acid

Figure 6-11 Diagram of a fat molecule.

The hydrocarbon chains that attach to the glycerol vary in length and in the number of double bonds they contain. Fatty acids that contain one or more double bonds are said to be unsaturated, while fatty acids with no double bonds are said to be saturated. These differences are important because the double bonds change the shape of the fatty acid and change a number of chemical properties of the fatty acids. Unsaturated fats, including many oils such as vegetable oil, are liquid at room temperature. Saturated fats, including most animal fats such as butter and lard, are solid at room temperature.

Fats serve an important function in that they allow for the storage of energy within the body. A number of animals store fats in tissue known as adipose tissue. When fat molecules are broken down, they provide a large amount of energy for the cell. Fat molecules are, thus, useful when animals hibernate during winter, for example. Fat can also serve as insulation from extreme temperatures. Whales, for example, have a layer of fat under their skin which protects them from the cold temperatures of the ocean.

Steroids are another type of lipid that serve an important role in the body. Steroids are made of hydrocarbons arranged into a number of rings. Cholesterol, for example, is a steroid that is found in the plasma membrane of cells, where it helps to add rigidity to the plasma membrane. A number of other steroids serve as hormones, and transmit signals within the body. Testosterone and estrogen, for example, are important steroids that serve as hormones.

Phospholipids, shown in Figure 6-12, are a very widely found type of lipid. As with fat molecules, phospholipids consist of fatty acids attached to a glycerol molecule. Phospholipids, however, are slightly different in that instead of a third fatty acid, a phosphate group with a hydrophilic molecule attaches to the third carbon of the glycerol. This hydrophilic portion near the head of the phospholipids means that unlike most other lipids, phospholipids are not completely hydrophobic. The head of the phospholipids is polar, while the tail of the phospholipids is not.

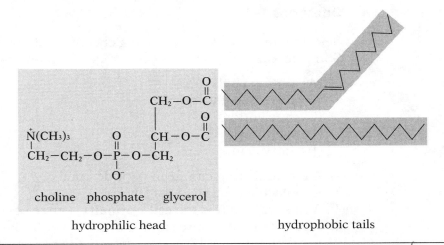

Figure 6-12 Diagram of a phospholipid.

This special property of phospholipids makes them very useful for forming membranes in the cell. Because of their unique structure, the fatty acid tails of phospholipids tend to congregate together with the phosphate head on the outside, forming layers. Often, phospholipids will form a bilayer—two layers of phospholipids with the fatty acid tails on the inside and the glycerol head on the outside. These phospholipids bilayers form the plasma membrane of all cells. They are good membranes because few molecules within the hydrophilic cytosol are able to traverse the hydrophobic area within the phospholipid bilayer.

LESSON SUMMARY

- All matter is made up of atoms of different elements, bonded together to form molecules and compounds.
- There are three types of bonds: ionic, covalent, and hydrogen bonds.
- Compounds of similar polarity will have a tendency to attract each other.
- The hydrogen bonding in water gives it a number of properties that make life possible.
- Carbon's ability to bond to a large number and variety of atoms makes it a good basis for biological compounds.
- Macromolecules are large biological molecules. Many macromolecules are polymers, compounds made from repeating segments called monomers.
- Carbohydrates include simple sugars such as glucose. They can polymerize to form complex polysaccharides such as cellulose, starch, and chitin.
- Proteins are important macromolecules made up of amino acids, joined by peptide bonds. Polypeptides are sequences of amino acids that will fold, depending on the polypeptide sequence, into a protein of a specific shape.
- DNA and RNA are the nucleic acids. Nucleotides, the monomer of the nucleic acids, form base pairs when matched with a complementary nucleic acid.
- Lipids are macromolecules made mostly of hydrocarbons. They include fats, steroids, and phospholipids.

REVIEW QUESTIONS

Questions 1–3

Select which one of the following choices best matches the statement below. Some choices may be used once, more than once, or not at all.

(A) amino acids
(B) monosaccharides
(C) nucleotides
(D) cellulose
(E) fatty acids

1. A molecule that can form peptide bonds
2. A molecule used to make DNA
3. A molecule that is the cell's primary source of food
4. A scientist has a pure sample of some sort of large molecule. After breaking down this molecule, he detects the presence of the nucleotide uracil. Which of the following is NOT true about the large molecule that this scientist had?

(A) It is a nucleic acid.
(B) It was formed using a dehydration reaction.
(C) It contains a sugar–phosphate backbone.
(D) It generally exists as a double helix.
(E) It is used to store information.

5. Which of the following is a polymer?

   I. hemoglobin
   II. polysaccharide
   III. steroids

   (A) I only
   (B) III only
   (C) I and II only
   (D) II and III only
   (E) I, II, and III

6. A student pours an unknown substance into water. The substance does not mix in the water. True statements about the unknown substance include which of the following?

   (A) It must have been a solid.
   (B) It is capable of forming hydrogen bonds.
   (C) It cannot be a compound.
   (D) It cannot be a hydrocarbon.
   (E) It cannot be hydrophilic.

Questions 7 and 8 refer to the following diagram.

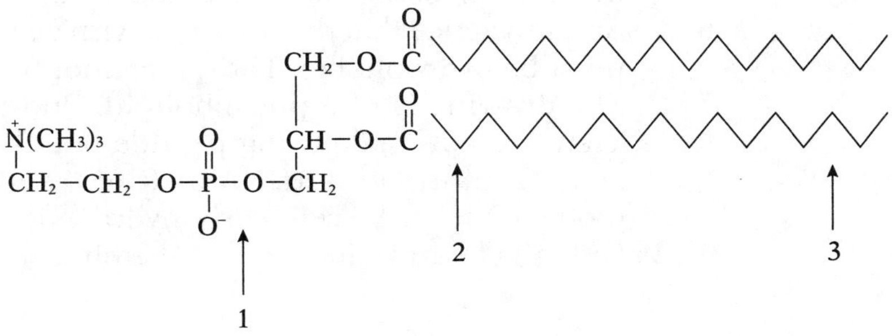

Figure 6-A Diagram of a phospholipid, with arrows pointing to specific parts.

7. Which of the following describes the molecule above?

   (A) It is made using a peptide bond.
   (B) It is a type of lipid.
   (C) It stores genetic information.
   (D) It is often used as a food source in the cell.
   (E) None of the above

8. Which part(s) of the molecule above are attracted to water?

   (A) 1
   (B) 2
   (C) 3
   (D) 1 and 2
   (E) 1 and 3

ANSWERS

1. **A** A peptide bond is simply a specific result from a dehydration synthesis reaction involving amino acids. (amino acids, monosaccharides, nucleotides, cellulose, and fatty acids can all undergo dehydration synthesis, but only amino acids can form peptide bonds from this reaction)

2. **C** Nucleotides, the monomer of DNA. Note that (B) monosaccharides is also technically correct, because deoxyribose is the sugar used to make DNA; however, choice (C) is the best choice out of the alternatives provided.

3. **B** Monosaccharides—specifically glucose—are the cell's primary source of food. Amino acids, fatty acids, nucleotides can be used to derive energy, but they are not the cell's primary source of food. Cellulose cannot be digested by most organisms, and so cannot serve as food.

4. **D** The presence of uracil indicates that the molecule that the scientist discovered was RNA, because only RNA is capable of using the nucleotide uracil. RNA is a nucleic acid formed by a dehydration reaction, with a sugar-phosphate backbone, and is used to store information. Only DNA can exist as a double helix, and DNA does not contain uracil.

5. **C** Hemoglobin is a protein. Proteins are polymers of amino acids. Polysaccharides are polymers of the monosaccharide glucose. Steroids are not polymers; they are multiringed carbon molecules.

6. **E** Any substance that does not mix with water—such as oil, for example—must be hydrophobic. Thus, it cannot be hydrophilic.

7. **B** The drawing is of a phospholipid. Phospholipids are a type of lipid. They are not made using peptide bonds (proteins), they do not store genetic information (DNA or RNA), and are not generally used as a food source in the cell (carbohydrates).

8. **A** Only the hydrophilic head of the phospholipid is attracted to water.

Lesson 6-2. Cells

VOCABULARY

- cells
- metabolism
- plasma membrane
- cytoplasm
- prokaryotic
- eukaryotic
- organelles
- nucleus
- nucleoid
- cytoskeleton
- centrioles
- cilia
- flagella

- nucleolus
- nuclear envelope
- chromatin
- endoplasmic reticulum (ER)
- ribosomes
- Golgi apparatus
- vesicles
- vacuoles
- lysosomes
- mitochondria
- chloroplasts
- plastids
- endosymbiosis

- peroxisomes
- cytoskeleton
- transmembrane proteins
- fluid-mosaic model
- endomembrane system
- cell wall
- diffusion
- concentration gradient
- passive transport
- osmosis
- transport proteins
- active transport

Understanding how cells work is the first step to understanding how organisms work. This section covers the basic features of cells, including cell structure, the different types of cells, the major features of eukaryotic cells, and the movement of molecules in and out of cells. After reading this section, you should have a clear idea of how many of the important processes within cells' work.

CHARACTERISTICS OF CELLS

All living organisms—from bacteria to animals—are made up of **cells.** Many organisms exist only as one cell, while others have millions, if not billions of cells. Cells are known as the fundamental units of life, because it is within cells that the necessary reactions for life take place. Cells possess all of the machinery that allows living organisms to live, grow, and reproduce. Cells require a lot of specialized machinery. They need a way to intake energy, a way to convert energy into a usable form, and a way to produce the necessary products for cell growth and reproduction. The total activity that a cell is undergoing at once is known as its **metabolism.**

All cells share some features; they are all surrounded by a **plasma membrane,** which prevents the contents of the cell from leaking out. Inside the plasma membrane is the **cytoplasm,** the area in which the contents of the cell are suspended. The cytoplasm is filled with a watery liquid known as the cytosol, which takes up any empty spaces within the cell.

There are two major types of cells: prokaryotic cells, and eukaryotic cells. **Prokaryotic** cells are single-celled organisms like bacteria and archaea. Prokaryotic cells are thought to be the evolutionary precursors to **eukaryotic** cells (or "true" cells), which are found in protists, plants, fungi, and animals. Organisms with prokaryotic cells are known as prokaryotes; organisms with eukaryotic cells as eukaryotes.

The main difference between prokaryotic and eukaryotic cells is that eukaryotic cells are larger, more complex, and contain more specialized parts than prokaryotic cells. Eukaryotic cells have specialized compartments known as **organelles** for specific cellular functions. Eukaryotic cells also have a specialized compartment, the **nucleus,** which contains the cell's DNA. Both the organelles and the nucleus are bound by a membrane, which allows them to carry out complex activities such as DNA replication or respiration in a small, contained space.

Prokaryotic cells do not have membrane-bound organelles, or a nucleus; they are not complex enough to have specialized compartments for their cellular functions. Instead, there is a region of the cell, the **nucleoid** that contains the DNA in prokaryotes, but is not separated by a membrane from the rest of the cell. Eukaryotes also have a **cytoskeleton,** a network of microfilaments and microtubules in the cytosol that help give the cell structure and aid in distributing the organelles during division. Prokaryotes undergo cell division, but because they do not have a nucleus or a cytoskeleton, they cannot undergo the process of mitosis. A summary of the differences between prokaryotes and eukaryotes is shown in Table 6-1.

Table 6-1. Differences between Prokaryotic and Eukaryotic Cells

	Prokaryotic Cells	Eukaryotic Cells
Membrane-bound nucleus	No	Yes
Membrane-bound organelles	No	Yes
Cytoskeleton	No	Yes

FEATURES OF EUKARYOTIC CELLS

Figure 6-13 contains a picture of an idealized eukaryotic cell. Note the membrane-bound nucleus in the center, surrounded by the cytoplasm, which mark this as a eukaryotic cell. Within the cytoplasm, there are a number of membrane-bound structures, known as organelles, each of which has a specific function.

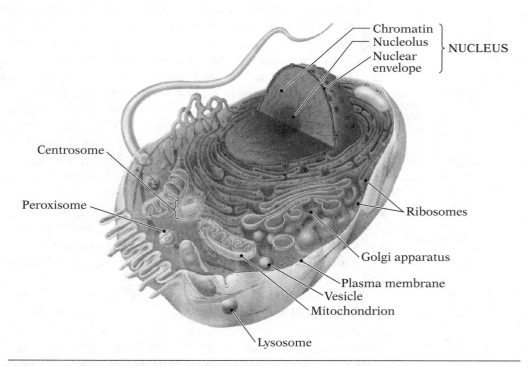

Figure 6-13 Diagram of a eukaryotic cell, with major organelles.

It is important to remember that the separation of all of these functions into discrete areas of the cell is advantageous for a number of reasons; not only does it allow all of the enzymes and compounds necessary for certain reactions to be stored in one place, but it allows for certain harmful waste products to be segregated from the rest of the cytosol. As you read through these organelles, try to think not just in terms of memorizing the function of these organelles, but try instead to understand how the structure and function of these organelles work together to perform an important function within the cell.

Nucleus

The nucleus is generally the largest organelle within the cell. It is a dense, spherical area that contains all of the cell's hereditary material. At the center of the nucleus is the small, dense **nucleolus,** which is where ribosome assembly begins. The nucleolus is surrounded by the nucleoplasm, which contains the DNA. The nucleus is surrounded by a double-membrane, known as the **nuclear envelope,** which is joined with the endoplasmic reticulum. Within the nucleoplasm, DNA is combined with a number of proteins, forming a complex known as **chromatin.**

The nucleus contains all of the machinery necessary to read and copy DNA. When a cell gets ready to divide, proteins within the nucleus copy the cell's DNA in a process known as replication. Eventually, the chromatin within the nucleoplasm forms densely packed structures known as chromosomes, which are then distributed to the daughter cells. At other times, DNA can be copied to make RNA, so that proteins can be made. The process of copying DNA to RNA, known as transcription, also occurs within the nucleus.

Endoplasmic Reticulum and Ribosomes

The **endoplasmic reticulum,** or ER, is a network of membranes that extend from the nucleus and branch throughout the cytoplasm of the cell. It resembles a number of flattened sacs that have been squeezed together on one side of the nucleus. The ER is essential for the production of proteins in eukaryotic cells; it has so many flattened areas to increase its surface area, which allows a greater area for protein synthesis and processing to take place. There are two regions of the ER, known as rough ER and smooth ER.

The rough endoplasmic reticulum is located closer to the nucleus and contains a number of small granules (which appear as dots) along most of its membranes. These granules are **ribosomes,** complexes of RNA and proteins that function as the site where proteins are synthesized using RNA as a template, a process known as translation. Rough ER receives the RNA from the nucleus, and, thus, serves as the major site of protein synthesis for the cell.

The location of the rough ER is ideal for its function. Because the rough ER is close to the nucleus, RNA leaving the nucleus can be directly used for the translation process. However, because it is outside the nuclear envelope, proteins synthesized in the rough ER do not have to be transported through any membranes for use inside the rest of the cell.

The smooth endoplasmic reticulum is located farther from the nucleus than the rough ER, and its membranes are formed more into circular sacs than the flattened rough ER (see Figure 6-13). Unlike the rough ER, smooth

ER does not have ribosomes, so it cannot function as the site of protein synthesis. Instead, smooth ER contains a variety of enzymes that are used for a number of the cell's metabolic functions. Smooth ER is the site where lipids, including oils, phospholipids, and steroids, are produced; many of these steroids produced in the smooth ER function as hormones in the body. A number of molecules within the cell, such as fatty acids, are processed at the smooth ER for later use.

Golgi Apparatus

Many of the products of the rough and smooth endoplasmic reticulum need to be processed before they are useful. These packaging functions take place in the **Golgi apparatus,** which is often known as the manufacturing warehouse of the cell. The Golgi apparatus looks much like the rough ER; it is a series of long, parallel membranes that form sacs, except the Golgi apparatus is farther from the nuclear envelope. The golgi apparatus takes in products from the endoplasmic reticulum, modifies them—perhaps adding a sugar molecule to a protein, for example—and then sorts them according to where they should go: sometimes, another part of the cell, sometimes, to another cell altogether. Having packaged and sorted the proteins for delivery, the Golgi apparatus secretes them in vesicles.

The "outer" side of the Golgi apparatus—the side closer to the cellular membrane and the outside of the cell—contains a number of small, circular membrane-bound sacs known as **vesicles.** These vesicles are made of the membrane of the Golgi apparatus. As products are readied for secretion, portions of the Golgi apparatus bud off to form vesicles, which then travel to the plasma membrane and join with it. The products contained within the vesicles are then released, or secreted, outside the cell.

Vacuoles

Vacuoles are membrane-bound areas for storage within a cell. The most important type of vacuole is the central vacuole, which is found exclusively in plant cells. This large feature of plant cells can make up almost 80% of the volume of a plant cell and is filled with a liquid known as the cell sap. The central vacuole serves a number of functions; cells store necessary proteins and ions in vacuoles and dispose of many harmful waste products there. But the central vacuole is also important for the structure of the plant cell. As it absorbs water, the central vacuole allows the cell retain its shape and grow, minimizing the amount of energy the cell needs for growth.

Lysosomes

Like vacuoles and vesicles, **lysosomes** are membrane-bound sacs found within the cell. But unlike vesicles, whose primary function is transport, and vacuoles, whose primary function is storage, the primary function of lysosomes is the digestion and breakdown of large molecules. Lysosomes, which contain enzymes, join with food vesicles in order to break down the proteins, large sugars, fats, and even DNA. Once these are broken down, they travel through the membrane of the lysosome into the cytosol, where they can be used by the cell for energy or other functions. Lysosomes serve as the mechanism for apoptosis, or programmed cell death. If a cell recognizes that it needs to be destroyed, it starts a series of chemical reactions using "suicide" proteins that allows the lysosome to release its digestive enzymes destroying the cell.

Mitochondria

Mitochondria (singular, mitochondrion) are commonly described as the powerhouses of the cell. They are small, oval-shaped, and contain two membranes. The outer membrane wraps around the mitochondrion and forms the outer shell; the inner membrane folds inward, crisscrossing the inner area of mitochondria in folds known as cristae.

It is in mitochondria that the majority of the cell's energy is produced. Mitochondria are the site of cellular respiration, the process of converting glucose molecules into usable energy for the cell (discussed in Lesson 3). Like the folds in the rough ER, which provide a large surface area for translation, the cristae within the mitochondria provide a large surface area for the multitude of enzymes that are required for cellular respiration. Cells that use a large amount of energy, such as muscle cells, often have hundreds, if not thousands, of mitochondria to serve their energy needs.

Chloroplasts

Mitochondria break down glucose, but chloroplasts help create it. **Chloroplasts** are the site of photosynthesis, the process through which the cell stores energy (in the form of sunlight) by making glucose. Chloroplasts have a round, somewhat flattened shape, like a ball of dough that has been slightly flattened. Like mitochondria, chloroplasts have an outer and inner membrane, but in chloroplasts, the membrane is not folded. Instead, the inside of the chloroplast contains flat, coin-like sacs known as thylakoids. These thylakoids are often stacked to form granum, with thin tubules often connecting these stacks. A specialized fluid known as stroma fills the space between the granum and the inner membrane.

Chloroplasts convert energy into glucose with help of the pigment chlorophyll, which is abundant in all chloroplasts. There are other organelles that capture sunlight using different pigments. With chloroplasts, they constitute a family of plant organelles known as **plastids.**

Endosymbiosis: The Origins of Mitochondria and Chloroplasts

Mitochondria and chloroplasts are unique among the organelles in many ways. Unlike other organelles, which are built by the cells, mitochondria and chloroplasts reproduce themselves, dividing independently of the cell. They are not coded for in the cell's DNA; instead, they have their own DNA, which codes for all the necessary parts of the mitochondrion or chloroplast.

If you suspect that, in many ways, mitochondria and chloroplasts act as self-sufficient entities much like cells, you're right. In fact, it is believed that at some point, cells that evolved the ability to undergo respiration or photosynthesis were swallowed up by other cells, which used them for their energy-producing functions. Over time, these swallowed cells lost some of their unnecessary functions and became the specialized organelles—mitochondria and chloroplasts—that are so essential for cells today. This process is known as **endosymbiosis.**

Peroxisomes

Peroxisomes are another membrane-bound compartment within the cell. They are important in a number of metabolic processes. Primarily, peroxisomes are used to produce hydrogen peroxide (H_2O_2), which, although harmful found within the cytoplasm, can be useful within the peroxisome: H_2O_2 can detoxify other harmful compounds that enter the cell, such as alcohols. Peroxisomes also contain enzymes to break down hydrogen peroxide into water, so that it does not harm the cell.

Cytoskeleton

The **cytoskeleton** is a network of fibers that crisscross the cytoplasm from one end of the cell to the other. The cytoskeleton is made of three types of protein fibers: thick microtubules, thin microfilaments, and intermediate filaments. These fibers are crucial for a number of reasons. First, the cytoskeleton provides an important function in that it helps the cell to retain its shape. Second, the cytoskeleton helps anchor the organelles into place, and also helps to move the contents of the cell when necessary, as is the case when cells need to segregate organelles and chromosomes into daughter cells during cell division. Cilia and flagella, which are *external* features of some cells that are useful for cell movement, are also considered part of the cytoskeleton.

The cytoskeleton provides the mechanism for the contraction of muscle cells. The microfilaments of the cytoskeleton are made of a protein called actin, and are lined up in parallel with filaments of another protein known as myosin. As actin proteins slide along myosin proteins, the cell contracts, creating a muscle contraction. Cells such as amoeba and white blood cells, which change their shape to engulf food or foreign invaders, use this actin–myosin mechanism to create this contraction.

CELL MEMBRANES AND CELL WALLS

We have already discussed the large variety of organelles within the cell and that an important characteristic of each of these specialized cell parts is the membrane that separates them from the rest of the cell. Membranes serve a number of useful functions.

Not only do they serve to segregate environments—inside and outside the organelle, inside and outside the cell—but they often serve as mechanisms for transportation, and as reaction sites for a number of cellular reactions. Last, but not least, these membranes keep the contents of the cell together, providing structure to the cell.

The Plasma Membrane

All cells are surrounded by a plasma membrane that is made up of a phospholipid bilayer. We saw in Lesson 1 that phospholipid bilayers are good barriers because they have a hydrophilic head and a hydrophobic tail so that few molecules can pass through. All of the organelles we discussed in this section contain a membrane made of phospholipid bilayers. The nucleus even has a double bilayer, made of two phospholipid bilayers.

The plasma membrane isn't exclusively made up of just phospholipids, however. There are a number of other large molecules that are part of the plasma membrane.

- **Transmembrane proteins** are special types of protein that are able to insert themselves into the plasma membrane because they have both hydrophobic and hydrophilic regions. The hydrophobic regions of transmembrane proteins are attracted to the hydrophobic fatty acid tails of the bilayer, while the hydrophilic regions are attracted to the cytosol and the polar head of the bilayer. As we will see in the next section, transmembrane proteins play an important part in transporting large molecules into and out of the cell. Transmembrane proteins also help to relay signals across the membrane. Finally, they may also join two cells together.

- The plasma membrane also contains a number of *glycoproteins* and *glycolipids*. Glycoproteins and glycolipids are proteins and lipids that have a small polysaccharide chain, known as an oligosaccharide, attached to them. These oligosaccharides stick out of the cell and can act as cellular signals. The oligosaccharides found on the outside of the cell vary from person to person, and from species to species. Using the oligosaccharide, the body can identify which cells are foreign, and which are not; this is an important part of the immune system.

- *Cholesterol* is a steroid that is very commonly found in the plasma membrane. Cholesterol is a useful component of the plasma membrane. At normal temperatures, cholesterol helps the plasma membrane retain its structure. Cholesterol prevents the plasma membrane from becoming too soft or fluid by making it more rigid. At cold temperatures, though, phospholipids have a tendency to become more solid. At low temperatures, cholesterol helps the phospholipids retain their fluidity.

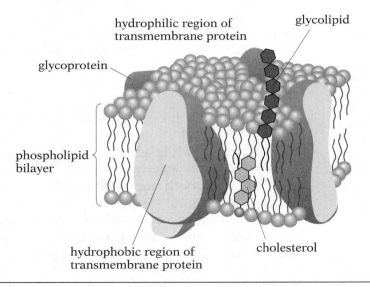

Figure 6-14 The fluid-mosaic model of plasma membranes.

How exactly are all of these various molecules arranged within the plasma membrane? The model that is used to describe the structure of the plasma membrane is known as the **fluid-mosaic model** and is shown in Figure 6-14. The plasma membrane is known as a mosaic because within the sea of phospholipids there are a number of other molecules, as we have just seen. What is fluid about the plasma membrane is that the phospholipids and these molecules can move around within the layer. Molecules do not often "flip flop" from one side of the layer to the other. They can, however, move laterally—sideways—within the layer. This means that proteins and other molecules within the layer can drift around the membrane of a cell, unless they are anchored to something else inside or outside the cell. In this way, the plasma membrane is a fluid mosaic: phospholipids and other molecules constantly in motion.

Sharing Membranes: The Endomembrane System

The endoplasmic reticulum, the Golgi apparatus, and vesicles of the cell are all made up of membranes very similar to that of the plasma membrane. Because of this, and because of the fluidity of the phospholipid bilayer, each of these organelles is capable of transferring or joining a part of its own membranes to the other, or to the plasma membrane. Because the phospholipid bilayer is fluid, the cell is able to pinch off part of the membrane of one organelle to form a vesicle, with the desired product inside. This vesicle can then be transported to the next organelle, or to the plasma membrane of the cell, where it attaches, and whatever is contained within is transported along with the vesicle.

The parts of the cell that exchange membranes are known as the **endomembrane system.** The endomembrane system is useful because it allows these organelles to transport molecules in a simple, efficient way. The endomembrane system allows for the transport of a protein produced in the endoplasmic reticulum to the Golgi apparatus where it is processed. The Golgi apparatus can then form a vesicle, which is transported to and joins the plasma membrane. The finished protein is then released.

An opposite process can occur when a pit in the plasma membrane closes off, forming a vesicle. This allows for the transport of a molecule into the cell. Transport of molecules into and out of the cell are discussed later in this lesson.

Cell Walls

A number of cells have a cell wall in addition to the plasma membrane. The **cell wall** is an additional structure that surrounds the cell and its plasma membrane, providing additional support and structure for the cell.

All bacterial cells have a cell wall. There are two types of cell walls in bacterial cells, but both are made up of a protein called peptidoglycan, which forms a coat around the plasma membrane.

Plant cells have a cell wall that serves a number of crucial functions. The cell wall of plants is made up of the polysaccharide cellulose, other polysaccharides, and protein. A plant's cell wall surrounds each cell in the plant, and is necessary to help the cells maintain their shape. The cell walls provide the rigidity needed for plants to grow upright, and also help to protect plant cells from any mechanical damage.

CELLULAR TRANSPORT

In the last section, we saw that an important property of cells is that they have membranes that separate the cytoplasm of the cell from the areas outside the cell. However, cells still need a mechanism by which important molecules—such as oxygen and food—can enter the cell. And other molecules—proteins that the cell produces, and waste products—need to leave the cell. In this section, we'll discuss the mechanisms by which these processes happen.

Passive Transport

One important principle that dictates the movement of molecules across a membrane is the natural diffusion of a substance across that membrane. All substances have a natural tendency to spread themselves out evenly within a given area. Spray perfume in one area of a room, for example, and the smell (embodied in tiny chemicals) will eventually spread throughout the entire room. **Diffusion** is the tendency of molecules to spread from an area of high concentration to low concentration.

A **concentration gradient** is the difference in concentration of a substance dissolved in a solvent. If, inside the cell, there is a high amount of a certain molecule compared to the outside of the cell, the difference in concentration between the inside (high concentration) and the outside (low concentration) makes up the concentration gradient. Because of the natural tendency of molecules to diffuse, they will move across the membrane (if they are able), from the area of high concentration to low concentration. This is illustrated in Figure 6-15.

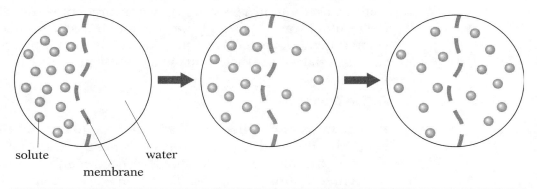

solute

membrane

water

Figure 6-15 Molecules will tend to move from an area of high concentration to an area of low concentration.

This natural diffusion of molecules from an area of high concentration to an area of low concentration—movement termed to be "with" the concentration gradient—occurs naturally, and does not require any investment of energy from the cell. Because it does not require any energy, such a method of transport is known as **passive transport.** Passive transport is always *with* the concentration gradient, never against it. In passive transport, molecules always move from high concentration to low concentration.

Sometimes, however, the molecule that is dissolved in a solution cannot move across a membrane. Consider, for example, a cell membrane that allowed water to pass through but not starch (because of starch's large size). If, on the inside of the cell, the starch concentration is higher, we would expect starch to diffuse across the membrane. In this case, however, the starch cannot move across the membrane. So, instead, the water moves from an area of higher water concentration to an area of lower water concentration—and would move inside the cell. The movement of water to correct a concentration gradient is known as **osmosis.**

When thinking about diffusion and osmosis, it's often difficult to think about where the molecules are moving. What's always important to remember is that chemistry is always trying to reach equilibrium—to reach a point where the concentrations of all of the molecules are equal on both sides. In passive transport—diffusion and osmosis—movement from areas of high concentration to low concentration will always be the tendency.

Cells can use a concentration gradient to their advantage, to facilitate the transportation of molecules into a cell. Consider glucose, a molecule capable of moving freely across the membrane. According to diffusion, we would expect equal concentrations of glucose on both sides of the membrane. But cells need much more than this equal concentration because cells need to consume glucose. So, as glucose enters the cell, it is changed into a different form (glucose-6-phosphate) by the first step in glycolysis (see Lesson 6-3). This form cannot escape the membrane, and so does not diffuse freely. In this way, the cell harnesses passive transport to facilitate the movement of molecules into the cell.

In plant cells, osmosis is used for structural purposes. Because most of the molecules in a plant cell are in the cytosol, and many of these molecules cannot move across the membrane, the tendency is for water to move inside the cell. Plant cells store much of this water in their large central vacuole. So much water enters the cell that it causes the cell to expand and push up against its cell walls—this results in a pressure known as turgor pressure. This turgor pressure, the result of water constantly moving into the cell, is what helps green plants stand upright. As plants run out of water, the turgor pressure decreases—this results in the wilting that occurs when house plants are not watered.

Active Transport

Passive transport is effective when cells need to transport molecules with the concentration gradient. But often, cells need to transport molecules *against* a concentration gradient. Cells often need high concentrations of certain molecules that they consume. Diffusion works against the accumulation of high concentration of molecules on one side of the membrane. We saw above that one way of allowing this accumulation of molecules on one side of the membrane is by modifying the molecules as they enter.

When the cell is trying to move molecules against the gradient, however, energy is required. Molecules cannot freely move through the cell membrane against the concentration gradient. Instead, transportation of molecules across the membranes requires energy, because the cell is moving the molecules from an area of low concentration to an area of high concentration. Such transport that requires energy is known as **active transport.**

An important mechanism that cells use to transport molecules against a concentration gradient is the use of transport proteins. Transport proteins are proteins that are embedded in the membranes of cells that allow the transport of molecules across the membrane. Sometimes, transport proteins allow molecules to move with a gradient. In this case, transport with the use of these proteins occurs naturally, as in passive transport.

A good example of active transport is found in nerve cells, which have a number of transport proteins involved in what is known as the sodium–potassium (Na^+-K^+) pump. Nerve cells expend large amounts of energy transporting sodium ions out of the cell, and potassium ions into the cell, until there are high concentrations of each molecule on either side of the cell. This active transport of ions requires a large amount of energy. When an impulse travels across the nerve cell, the transport proteins open up, allowing sodium ions to rush into the cell, and potassium ions to rush out. This is what carries nerve impulses in the body.

Active transport can also be used to transport other ions across a membrane, as well. The link between active transport and the use of energy will come into play in the next lesson, when we discuss oxidative phosphorylation during respiration.

PLANT AND ANIMAL CELLS

There are a number of significant differences between plant and animal cells. As an end to our discussion of cells, we should review these important differences.

- *Cell walls:* All plant cells are surrounded by cell walls, while animal cells do not have them. The cell wall adds additional support and structure to plant cells, and allows them to resist osmotic pressure. Animal cells, lacking a cell wall, can lyse (burst) if osmotic pressure is too high.
- *Vacuoles:* Plant cells have a much larger central vacuole than animal cells. This vacuole expands and fills up space, creating turgor pressure that helps the plant to stay upright.
- *Chloroplasts:* Plant cells contain chloroplasts and other plastids, organelles capable of carrying out photosynthesis. Animal cells do not have chloroplasts, plastids, or chlorophyll, the pigment that makes plants green.

LESSON SUMMARY

- Cells can be divided into two types: prokaryotic and eukaryotic.
- All cells have DNA, proteins, and a plasma membrane.
- Eukaryotic cells have a number of membrane-bound areas known as organelles.
- The nucleus is a membrane-bound compartment for the cell's DNA.
- The endoplasmic reticulum and Golgi apparatus are involved in the production and packaging of the cell's products.
- Vacuoles, vesicles, lysosomes, and peroxisomes are specialized compartments within the cell.
- Mitochondria and chloroplasts are organelles involved in producing energy for the cell. They are thought to have evolved from organisms that were swallowed up by another.
- The cytoskeleton helps give the cell support and structure.
- Cells are surrounded by a plasma membrane made of phospholipids, proteins, glycolipids, and glycoproteins. Some cells have a cell wall that provides additional support.
- Passive transport is the diffusion of molecules with a concentration gradient. Osmosis is the diffusion of water in response to a concentration gradient.
- Active transport is the movement of molecules against a concentration gradient. Active transport requires energy expenditure by the cell.
- Plant and animal cells differ in a number of important ways.

REVIEW QUESTIONS

The concentration of a certain molecule inside and outside the plasma membrane of a cell was measured over time. The data are shown in the graph below.

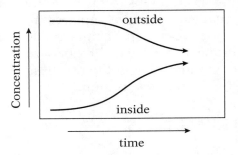

1. True statements about this molecule include which of the following?

   (A) This molecule is hydrophobic.
   (B) This molecule is necessary for cellular function.
   (C) This molecule required the expenditure of energy to enter the cell.
   (D) This molecule entered the cell using diffusion.
   (E) This molecule is embedded into the plasma membrane.

Questions 2–4

Select which one of the following choices best matches the statement below. Some choices may be used once, more than once, or not at all.

   (A) mitochondria
   (B) rough endoplasmic reticulum
   (C) plasma membrane
   (D) vacuole
   (E) nucleus

2. Site of the production of proteins
3. Used to produce energy for the cell
4. Contains the cell's DNA

5. Which of the following cells has a cell wall?

   (I)   plant cells
   (II) animal cells
   (III) bacterial cells

   (A) I only
   (B) II only
   (C) III only
   (D) I and II only
   (E) I and III only

6. Which of the following is present in both prokaryotic and eukaryotic cells?

   (A) nucleus
   (B) nucleoid
   (C) mitochondria
   (D) plasma membrane
   (E) lysosome

7. Phospholipids are NOT necessary for which of the following?

    (A) cell walls
    (B) Golgi apparatus
    (C) plasma membrane
    (D) mitochondria
    (E) endoplasmic reticulum

8. A student investigating an unknown organelle finds that it is capable of using sunlight to build sugars. Which organelle is it?

    (A) Golgi apparatus
    (B) vacuole
    (C) chloroplast
    (D) lysosome
    (E) nucleus

ANSWERS

1. **D** As shown in the graph, the initial concentration is much higher outside the cell than inside the cell. As time passes, the concentration equalizes, and continues to equalize until the concentration gradient—the difference in concentration between the inside and outside—is zero. It does not move against the gradient. All of this indicates that the molecule is being transported using diffusion.

2. **B** The rough endoplasmic reticulum is the site of protein synthesis (because of the presence of ribosomes)

3. **A** The mitochondria produce most of the usable energy for the cell.

4. **E** The nucleus is where the cell's DNA is located.

5. **E** Both plant and bacterial cells have a cell wall. Animal cells do not.

6. **D** The nucleus, mitochondria, and lysosome are membrane-bound organelles found only in eukaryotic cells. The nucleoid is found only in prokaryotic cells. Both types of cells have a plasma membrane.

7. **A** Cell walls are made of cellulose in plants and peptidoglycan in bacteria. All of the other items listed are made of phospholipid bilayers.

8. **C** Chloroplasts contain chlorophyll, which allows them to convert sunlight to chemical energy (complex organic molecules built from simple ones) using the process known as photosynthesis.

Lesson 6-3. Energy in the Cell: Enzymes, Respiration, and Photosynthesis

VOCABULARY

- enzymes
- substrate
- catalysis
- reaction coupling
- energy carrier
- respiration
- glycolysis
- pyruvate
- citric acid cycle
- coenzyme
- oxidative phosphorylation
- electron-transport chain

- fermentation
- photosynthesis
- autotrophs
- heterotrophs
- light reactions
- chlorophyll
- photosystems
- dark reactions
- Calvin cycle
- rubisco
- CAM plants
- anaerobic

Look at a living cell under a microscope, and you'll see a miniature world teeming with activity. But in order for all that activity to take place, the cell requires energy in some usable form. In this section, we'll review the specialized processes that cells use to take in food from their environment and make it available where it is needed within the cell. And we'll review how certain cells are able to transfer the energy of the sun into usable energy for the cell.

ENZYMES AND ENERGY CARRIERS

Before we dive fully into the complex processes of respiration and photosynthesis, it's important to understand how energy in the cell works, and why the processes involving energy breakdown are so complex. To do so, we'll examine the role of enzymes within the cell, and how enzymes use energy in small bundles to do work within the cell. And then we'll look at the molecules that cells use to carry energy to where it's needed in the cell.

How Enzymes Work

Recall from Lesson 6-1 that proteins serve a number of different purposes. Some proteins provide structure. Keratin, for example, is a rigid protein that makes up the hair and nails of humans. The major function of proteins, however, is to carry out the reactions of the cell. Cells carry out thousands of different chemical reactions, and it is proteins, in their role as **enzymes,** that allow these reactions to take place.

The molecule that an enzyme acts upon is known as a **substrate.** Substrates fit into an area on the enzyme known as its *active site*, which is shaped to match a particular substrate specifically. Enzymes take in substrates, change them in some way, and then release them as a finished product, as shown in Figure 6-16. In some cases, enzymes can break up a molecule, forming two products. In other cases, an enzyme can take two substrates and form them into one product. Sometimes, however, an enzyme can do both things at the same time, as we will see. It is important to note that the enzyme itself

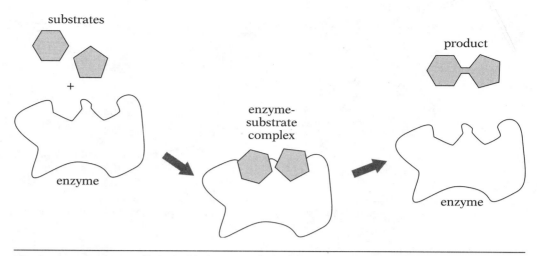

Figure 6-16 Enzymes take in products and make them into substrates.

does not get changed in the process; it is only a catalyst, in that it causes the reaction to occur much more quickly.

Many of the chemical reactions in the cell could take place naturally, without the aid of an enzyme. For example, the breakdown of disaccharides into two monosaccharides can occur naturally. However, without help, these reactions would proceed far too slowly to sustain the level of activity needed for life. Cells need reactions to happen more quickly than they would naturally occur. Enzymes are crucial because they speed up reactions, allowing them to take place much more quickly than they otherwise would. This process of speeding up reactions is known as **catalysis.** Catalyzing reactions is an important function of enzymes within the cell.

Enzymes are able to speed up reactions because they lower the amount of energy that is needed for a reaction to take place. This is known as the *activation energy* of a reaction. Often, the reason a reaction does not take place at a useful pace is because its activation energy is too high, and the cell cannot overcome this barrier to allow the reaction to take place. When enzymes lower that activation energy, the reaction can take place and the substrate transformed into the product. It is important to note that enzymes do not *create* energy—they simply lower the energy barrier that is needed for a reaction.

Reaction Coupling

Certain reactions within the cell are energetically unfavorable. They cannot occur spontaneously because in order to occur, they require energy. Enzymes are crucial for these reactions because they are able to couple these energetically unfavorable reactions with another reaction that is energetically favorable. This is known as **reaction coupling.**

To understand this, think of a waterfall, as shown in Figure 6-17. Water falling down over a waterfall does so because gravity spontaneously pulls it down. This is an energetically favorable reaction, occurring naturally. Now, if you could channel the water so that it turned the turbine of a generator, for example, then you would be capturing some of the energy of the waterfall for use in other places—perhaps to power a light bulb.

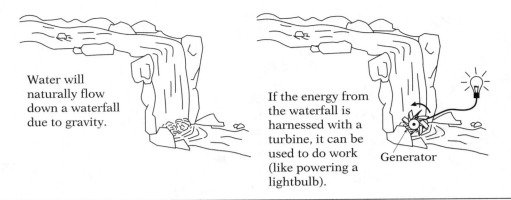

Water will naturally flow down a waterfall due to gravity.

If the energy from the waterfall is harnessed with a turbine, it can be used to do work (like powering a lightbulb).

Generator

Figure 6-17 Enzymes are capable of coupling less favorable reactions with reactions that provide energy.

Enzymes often use reaction coupling to carry out a variety of energetically unfavorable reactions within the cell. In some cases, reaction coupling can be used to create complex molecules. In other cases, reaction coupling can be used to transport molecules across a barrier, and against the concentration gradient. This is how active transport, described in Lesson 6-2, takes place.

Energy Carriers

Glucose is the primary source of the energy that is used to drive reactions within the cell. But a glucose molecule contains too much energy to be released all at once. First, such a process would require too large an activation energy. That is, the amount of energy necessary to initiate such a reaction would be too high for the cell to overcome. And even if the cell could overcome that activation energy, much of the energy contained in the glucose molecule would be lost. There's no reaction in the cell that could harness all of the energy at once.

To solve this problem, cells break down glucose using a step-by-step process. Instead of releasing all of the energy in a glucose molecule at once, cells release this energy slowly, over a number of reactions. It is for this reason that the breakdown of glucose in respiration requires so many complex steps. To carry off the small bits of energy, the cell utilizes reaction coupling. As it breaks down a small part of the glucose molecule, and releases the energy contained in it, it uses that energy to drive another reaction, which stores part of that energy in another molecule known as an **energy carrier.**

Adenosine triphosphate, or ATP, is the most important energy carrier in the cell. As we learned in Lesson 6-1, ATP is made of an adenine nucleotide attached to three phosphate groups. The covalent bonds that hold these phosphate groups together contain a large amount of energy. When one of these bonds is broken, forming adenosine diphosphate, or ADP, it releases energy, as shown in Figure 6-18. The release of this energy can be coupled with a reaction that requires energy to take place. In this way, the energy from the food we consume (glucose) flows through an energy carrier (ATP) before helping enzymes carry out their work within the cell. GTP, or guanosine triphosphate, is a molecule that, as with ATP, contains three phosphate molecules and can be used to carry energy as well.

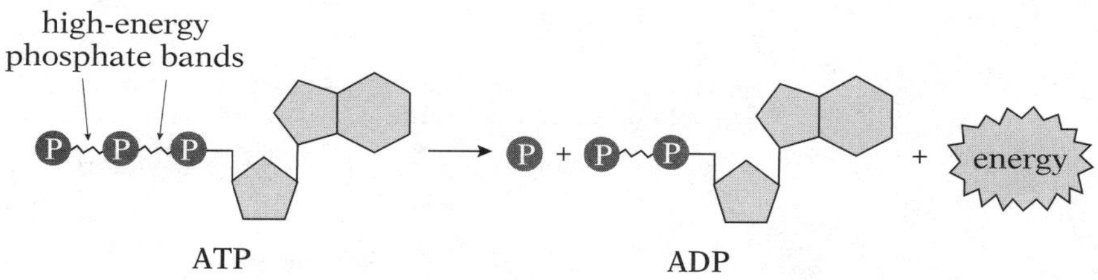

Figure 6-18 ATP acts as an energy carrier.

There are other energy carriers in the cell as well. Instead of storing their energy in a phosphate bond, as ATP does, these molecules carry their energy in an extra electron. NAD+ (nicotinamide adenine dinucleotide) and NADP+ (nicotinamide adenine dinucleotide phosphate) are two such energy carriers that are crucial for respiration and photosynthesis. When these molecules are joined with a hydrogen atom, to form NADH or NADPH, they also pick up two high-energy electrons, which store energy that can be coupled to do work in the cell. FAD (flavin adenine dinucleotide) is another, less common electron carrier. It carries energy when it is converted to FADH₂.

As you read the rest of this lesson, try not to lose your focus or get caught up in the details of the myriad reactions of respiration and photosynthesis. Instead, focus on *why* these reactions are taking place and what the products of each of these reactions are. If you understand the principles of reaction coupling and energy carriers, then respiration and photosynthesis will make much more sense.

RESPIRATION

We saw in the previous section that cells, in order to do work, need energy in some usable form and that ATP is the most common carrier of this usable energy. **Respiration** is the process by which cells break down the food they take in into usable energy. Respiration takes place in three main phases: glycolysis, the citric acid cycle, and oxidative phosphorylation.

Glycolysis

Respiration begins with a glucose molecule. Other carbohydrates must be converted into glucose before being metabolized. **Glycolysis** is the first step of respiration. In glycolysis, one glucose molecule is converted through a series of steps into two three-carbon **pyruvate** molecules. This process involves a large number of steps. Each step is catalyzed by a different enzyme, and each of these steps has a specific function. At each step, the glucose molecule is converted to an intermediate sugar. The steps in this process can be broken into three different phases, each of which is seen in Figure 6-19.

- During the first phase, the cell is required to invest energy. The glucose molecule is phosphorylated twice (that is, two phosphate groups are added to it), and it is slightly rearranged to form an intermediate six-carbon sugar. The phosphorylation of the glucose molecule requires the breakdown of two ATP molecules, which represent an investment of energy by the cell.
- In the second phase of glycolysis, the cell breaks down the phosphorylated intermediate sugar from a six-carbon molecule into two three-carbon

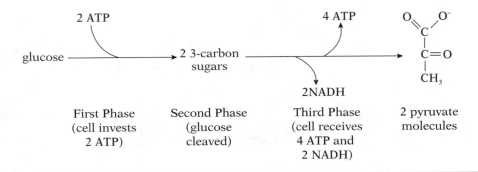

Figure 6-19 Glycolysis.

intermediate sugars. This process is known as cleavage. However, these three-carbon molecules are not yet the finished product.

- During the third phase of glycolysis, the cell slowly converts the two three-carbon intermediates into pyruvate. In the process, the cell is able to couple the breakdown of these intermediates to store energy in energy carriers. The third phase, thus, results in the conversion of two NAD^+ molecules into NADH, and converts four ADP molecules into ATP.

The last phase of glycolysis is the most crucial. The creation of ADP and NADH in these last steps represents energy that the cell can use to do work. Even though glycolysis required the investment of two ATP molecules, the ultimate output was four ATP molecules. This represents a net gain of two ATP molecules for the cell, plus the two NADH molecules.

The net reaction of glycolysis can thus be summed up as follows:

glucose + 2 NAD^+ + 2 ADP → 2 NADH + 2 ATP + 2 pyruvate.

Glycolysis is the only stage of respiration that prokaryotic cells can perform. Glycolysis occurs in the cytosol, and requires no specialized membranes or organelles. Thus, prokaryotic cells only receive two ATP molecules and two NADH molecules from each glucose molecule. This level of energy would not be sufficient, however, to provide a eukaryotic cell with the energy it requires. Eukaryotic cells thus have additional steps in respiration that allow them to gain more ATP from each molecule of glucose. These additional steps, however, require mitochondria. Prokaryotic cells, lacking mitochondria, cannot undergo these steps.

The Citric Acid Cycle

The **citric acid cycle,** also known as the Krebs cycle, for its discoverer, Hans Krebs, is a cycle of chemical reactions that further release the energy contained in pyruvate molecules, releasing carbon dioxide in the process.

Before they can enter the citric acid cycle, however, the pyruvate molecules must be modified, and a **coenzyme** must be added. This particular coenzyme is a small sulfur-containing molecule that renders the molecule it is attached to more reactive. These reactions are preformed by three enzymes known as the pyruvate dehydrogenase complex, which are located in the mitochondrion. In the process, each pyruvate is converted to a molecule known acetyl CoA. Acetyl CoA is a two-carbon sugar attached to a coenzyme. In the process of creating acetyl CoA from pyruvate, a carbon dioxide molecule is released, and one NAD^+ molecule is converted into an NADH. Recall, however, that because two pyruvate molecules are created in glycolysis for each glucose molecule, this process occurs twice for each glucose molecule that enters the cell.

The overall reaction for the reduction of pyruvate into acetyl CoA is as follows:

$$\text{pyruvate} + NAD^+ + \text{coenzyme A} \rightarrow NADH + CO_2 + \text{acetyl CoA}.$$

Acetyl CoA is the molecule that is able to enter the citric acid cycle. However, acetyl CoA is not just the products of the breakdown of glucose. If the body runs out of carbohydrates and needs energy from an alternative source, one such source comes from stored fat molecules, which contain a large amount of energy. However, as with glucose, these fat molecules need to be broken down. The breakdown of fat molecules converts two carbons in the fatty acid tails of a triacylglycerol into acetyl CoA molecules, which then enter the citric acid cycle.

The citric acid cycle is, as its name suggests, cyclic. As with glycolysis, it proceeds by breaking down its starting product bit by bit. However, this process occurs by adding the acetyl CoA (which has two carbons) to a four-carbon molecule, oxaloacetate, forming the six-carbon molecule citrate, from which the name of the cycle is derived. This citrate molecule is slowly broken down over ten steps, its energy carried off by various energy carriers, until at the very end, it reaches the same four-carbon molecule it began with. Another acetyl CoA can join with this molecule, and the cycle will begin again.

The citric cycle ends up exactly where it began—with an oxaloacetate molecule—but the benefits are great. For every acetyl CoA that enters the cycle, three molecules of NAD^+ are converted into NADH, one molecule of FAD is converted into $FADH_2$, and one molecule of GDP is converted into GTP. This represents a substantial gain of energy for the cell. The hydrogen atoms for the NADH and $FADH_2$ come from two water molecules that enter the cycle.

The oxygen from the water molecules, and the two carbon molecules from the acetyl CoA—the last carbons remaining of our original glucose molecule—are released as carbon dioxide (CO_2). This carbon dioxide is released in humans through the lungs. Every time we breathe, we exhale the carbon dioxide remnants of broken down glucose molecules. The coenzyme that was part of the acetyl molecule is also released, and can be reused to convert another pyruvate to acetyl CoA.

The net results of the citric acid cycle, shown in Figure 6-20, can be written as follows:

$$\text{acetyl Co A} + 2\,H_2O + 2\,NAD^+ + FAD + GDP \rightarrow 2\,CO_2 + 2\,NADH$$
$$+ FADH_2 + GTP + \text{coenzyme A}.$$

At the end of the citric acid cycle, the carbons from glucose will have all been released as carbon dioxide. The cell is left with a large number of electron carriers. For every glucose molecule, eight NADH molecules and two

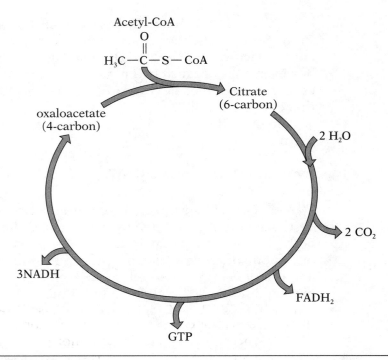

Figure 6-20 The citric acid cycle.

$FADH_2$ molecules are created. In the next section, we will see what becomes of these electron carriers.

There are a number of intermediate molecules in the citric acid cycle as it journeys from oxaloacetate to citrate and back again. And though its primary function is to serve as a generator of energy during respiration, the citric acid cycle also serves as the generator of a number of crucial molecules for the cell. Many of the intermediate molecules in the citric acid cycle are used to create amino acids, nucleotides, lipids, or other necessary molecules for the cell.

Oxidative Phosphorylation

Plants and animals require oxygen to live. In this section, we will learn why. **Oxidative phosphorylation** is the process through which the energy that has been stored in the electron carriers (NADH and $FADH_2$) is converted into usable energy in the form of ATP.

Recall from Lesson 6-2 that the inside of mitochondria contains a folded membrane with a large surface area. And recall from earlier in this Lesson that when there is a gradient across a membrane, that molecules will have a tendency to move with the gradient. Both of these concepts come into play in oxidative phosphorylation.

The electron carriers created by glycolysis and the citric acid cycle are on one side of the inner membranes of the mitochondrion. Using a series of proteins that are embedded into this inner membrane, known as the **electron-transport chain,** electrons from the NADH or the $FADH_2$ are transported across the inner membrane, leaving NAD^+ or FAD. Eventually, the electrons are received by an oxygen molecule, which is converted to water. In the process, a hydrogen proton (H^+) is transported across the membrane. As with the carbons, these Hs also came from the breakdown of glucose. This process is illustrated in Figure 6-21.

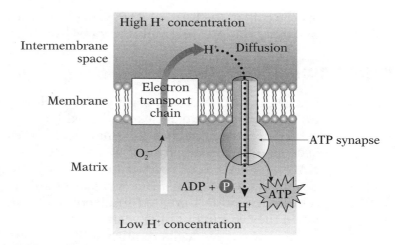

Figure 6-21 Oxidative phosphorylation.

As the electron transport chain continues, hydrogen ions start to accumulate on one side of the inner membrane. This creates a concentration gradient because there are many more hydrogen atoms on one side of the membrane than the other. As a result, hydrogen atoms will have a tendency to try to travel back across this membrane. They travel back through the membrane through a protein known as ATP synthase. Like a turbine using the downward flow of water, ATP synthase harnesses the energy of these protons as they cross the barrier, and uses it to convert ADP into ATP (see Figure 8-21).

Oxidative phosphorylation is very different from the other steps of respiration in that it does not produce ATP through a chemical reaction. Instead, it sets up a gradient, and uses that gradient to drive the synthesis of ATP. In the process, approximately 30 ATP molecules are created, many more than would be produced with simply glycolysis or the citric acid cycle. Oxidative phosphorylation is, thus, essential to deriving enough energy for the cell.

The most important feature of oxidative phosphorylation is its reliance on oxygen. Oxygen accepts the electrons from the electron transport chain. Without oxygen, the chain cannot proceed, no gradient will be created, and no ATP produced. As the cell runs out of electron carriers, the citric acid cycle will stop as well. It is for this reason that human beings and most organisms need oxygen—to ensure continued respiration. In the next section, we'll learn how cells respond to the absence of oxygen.

Overview

Respiration is a complicated process. But in the end, respiration has a very simple overall equation:

$$glucose \left(C_6H_{12}O_6 \right) + 6\,O_2 \rightarrow 6\,H_2O + 6\,CO_2 + energy.$$

As you can see, there are no atoms lost or created in this process. If you know the formula for glucose and the other molecules that are involved (oxygen, water, and carbon dioxide), this equation is easy to interpret. What's most important to remember about respiration, however, is that all the processes of respiration are aimed at converting glucose into usable energy for the cell, in the form of ATP. Glycolysis, the citric acid cycle, and oxidative phosphorylation are simply the steps by which the cell achieves that process.

FERMENTATION

Oxygen is not necessary for glycolysis. However, in eukaryotes, which also utilize the citric acid cycle and the oxidative phosphorylation, oxygen is necessary because it acts as the final electron acceptor. In eukaryotes, oxygen accepts the hydrogen from the electron carriers NADH and $FADH_2$, allowing NAD^+ and FAD to be regenerated. Water is then created as the "waste product" of these reactions. But what mechanisms do prokaryotic cells have to recycle the NADH created in glycolysis? And what do eukaryotic cells do when they've run out of oxygen?

Absent oxygen, cells require a different mechanism other than oxidative phosphorylation to regenerate NAD^+ from NADH. The process by which these electron carriers are regenerated is known as **fermentation.** Fermentation involves the derivation of energy from food sources in the absence of oxygen, conditions known as *anaerobic* conditions.

There are many different types of fermentation processes. What they all share is that instead of using oxygen to produce water as their waste product, they instead regenerate the energy carriers by forming other molecules as waste products, which accept the electrons. The two most common forms of fermentation are lactic acid fermentation and alcoholic fermentation, shown in Figure 6-22.

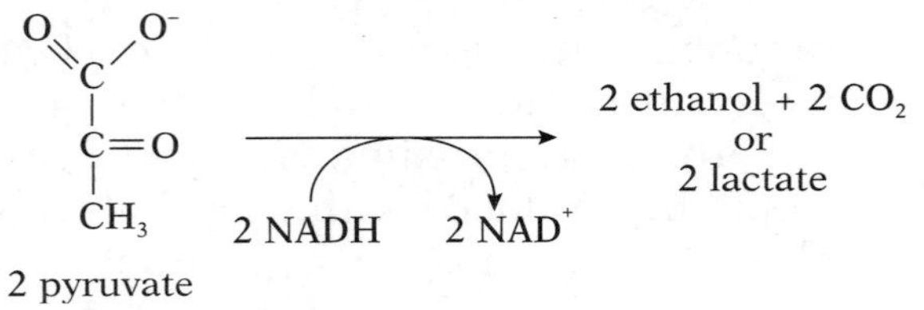

Figure 6-22 Fermentation.

Alcoholic fermentation is the process by which the pyruvate that results from glycolysis is converted into ethanol, a two-carbon alcohol. In the process, the cell is able to generate two additional ATP, and a carbon dioxide (CO_2) molecule is released. In addition, alcoholic fermentation regenerates two NAD^+ molecules from NADH, thus restoring them for glycolysis.

The production of alcohol by such organisms as yeast (which is a fungus) and a number of bacteria occurs through alcoholic fermentation. It is the release of carbon dioxide by this process that accounts for the holes in bread and the bubbles in champagne.

Lactic acid fermentation is the process by which the pyruvate molecule from glycolysis is converted into lactate, another waste molecule. Like alcoholic fermentation, it generates two additional ATP and regenerates two NAD^+ for use in glycolysis. Lactate must be properly broken down back into pyruvate, a process that requires energy.

If you've ever experienced a cramp from exercising, then you've experienced the effects of lactate buildup in the body. As oxygen in human muscle cells grows scarce, the cells turn to lactic acid fermentation. The lactate builds up, causing the muscle pain that we experience as cramps. Eventually, when the oxygen supply is more abundant, the lactate is carried to the liver for metabolism.

PHOTOSYNTHESIS

Photosynthesis is perhaps the most important biological process on Earth. Not only is photosynthesis responsible for the presence of most of the oxygen in the Earth's atmosphere, but it also generates most of the energy that is used by humans and other organisms. As we will see, photosynthesis uses many of the same principles of respiration—the use of energy carriers, for example—but in a process that produces and stores, instead of consumes, energy.

Overview

Photosynthesis, like respiration, is a complex process involving a number of steps, and specialized structures within the cell. Earlier in this lesson, we saw that respiration breaks down the energy stored in glucose into its usable form, ATP. In photosynthesis, we'll see the reverse process take place.

Photosynthesis is the process by which plants are able to capture the energy from sunlight. This energy from sunlight is harnessed and used to create a large sugar molecule, which, if necessary, can be broken down to release the energy contained within it. In the process, plants capture carbon dioxide from the atmosphere, harnessing it for use in organic molecules, and release oxygen. Photosynthesis as a whole can be described using the following reaction:

$$6\,H_2O + 6\,CO_2 + \text{light energy} \rightarrow \text{glucose}\,(C_6H_{12}O_6) + 6\,O_2.$$

The ability to harness sunlight and carbon dioxide and convert them into usable sugars is what makes photosynthesis unique among cellular process.

Because photosynthesis produces food in the form of glucose, organisms that undergo photosynthesis do not require energy from some outside source of food, as humans and other animals do. Such organisms that are capable of producing their own food are known as **autotrophs.** Organisms that rely upon organic molecules from some outside source for their food supply are known as **heterotrophs.**

Light Reactions

Photosynthesis can be broken up into two parts: the light reactions, and the dark reactions. As these names might suggest, these two reactions differ in their reliance on sunlight. The **light reactions** are the parts of photosynthesis that rely on sunlight. It is the light reaction that converts the light energy from the sun into some sort of usable chemical energy—that is, energy contained within some sort of molecule. These processes take place in the thylakoid membranes of the chloroplast.

The key molecule in the light reaction of photosynthesis is **chlorophyll.** Chlorophyll is a pigment within the chloroplast that gives leaves their green color. Pigments such as chlorophyll are important because they are capable of absorbing the energy carried by light. When light hits chlorophyll, one of the electrons of each chlorophyll molecule is "excited" by the reaction, giving it slightly more energy than its neighbors. There are also other pigments in the cell whose electrons can be excited by sunlight. When these other pigments are excited, they pass their excited electrons to chlorophyll. It is for this reason that these pigments are known as accessory pigments.

Photosynthesis works by harnessing the energy of these excited electrons, through a series of electron transport chains known as **photosystems.** These photosystems contain proteins and pigments, such as chlorophyll. As we have just seen, when light hits the photosystem, an excited electron in the chlorophyll molecule results, and the chlorophyll molecule is able to pass on this electron to another molecule, known as the primary electron acceptor, which is the first step in an electron transport chain. This process is similar to the transport of electrons across the membrane in the electron transport chain of oxidative phosphorylation.

These electron transport chains use a series of proteins known as the cytochrome complex to carry these electrons from molecule to molecule. Just as with oxidative phosphorylation, however, this electron transport chain is used to do work—in this case, it is used to actively transport protons (H^+) across the thylakoid membrane into the interior of the thylakoid, and to break up water molecules into hydrogen and oxygen (which is released). As in respiration, a concentration gradient is set up by the accumulation of these hydrogen ions. As the hydrogen ions build up on interior of the thylakoid, the net movement of these ions out of the thylakoid is harnessed using the transmembrane protein ATP synthase. The movement of these protons out of the thylakoid turns a proton pump, which converts ADP into ATP. As we know, ATP provides usable energy for the cell, stored in chemical form in the bond between its phosphate groups.

Eventually, with the additional input of energy from sunlight, another electron transport chain is used to capture the excited electron in the electron carrier $NADP^+$, which is simply an NAD^+ molecule with an extra phosphate group attached. At the end of these electron transport chains, the electrons that were excited by light are transferred to $NADP^+$, resulting in a molecule of NADPH.

The light processes of photosynthesis are rather complex, and it is easy to get mired in the details. Try hard, however, to focus on *why* the light reactions occur, and on the products, instead of its mechanisms. The light reactions take in sunlight, and produce ATP and NADPH. In the process, a water molecule is broken down, and oxygen is released.

What's most important to remember about the processes of the light reactions is that they enable the conversion of sunlight to chemical energy. No other biological process is able to harness sunlight in this manner. This chemical energy is necessary to drive all of the other processes of the cell; in fact, the light reactions are mechanism by which all of the energy that drives our cells was produced. And, as we will see in the next section, the dark reactions of photosynthesis store this chemical energy in the form of sugar molecules.

Dark Reactions: The Calvin Cycle

The purpose of the light reactions was to create usable chemical energy from sunlight. In the **dark reactions,** which take place in the stroma of the chloroplast, this usable chemical energy is harnessed to create sugar molecules such as glucose. The name "dark" is appropriate because these reactions rely only upon the chemical energy in NADPH and ATP and not on sunlight. Note, however, that these reactions can and *do* often occur during the day for many plants. This is why the "dark reactions" have also become known as the "light-independent" reactions.

As with the citric acid cycle of respiration, **the Calvin cycle,** which is the primary component of the dark reactions, is a series of chemical reactions that, in the end, reproduce their starting products. The citric acid cycle took in carbon molecules from pyruvate, released them as CO_2, and donated energy to a number of energy carriers in the process. The Calvin cycle works in the opposite direction. Instead of releasing CO_2, it *takes in* carbon from the atmosphere, converts it into an organic molecule, with the donation of energy from ATP and energy carriers, and then releases this usable sugar molecule so that the process can start over again, as shown in Figure 6-23.

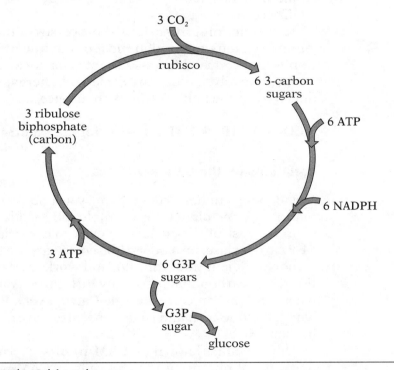

Figure 6-23 The Calvin cycle.

The most crucial aspect of the Calvin cycle is its first phase, the capture of carbon dioxide from the atmosphere for use in making carbohydrates. This process is extremely important because it allows gaseous molecules to be harnessed to create large organic molecules, of which all organisms are made. Photosynthetic organisms, then, can convert gaseous carbon into solid carbon. This process is performed using a protein known as **rubisco.** Rubisco incorporates the CO_2 molecule into a five-carbon ribulose biphosphate molecule, forming a six-carbon intermediate sugar that immediately splits into two three-carbon sugars. Because the Calvin cycle converts carbon dioxide into a three-carbon molecule (which is eventually used to make glucose), this process of carbon fixation must occur three times in order for a three-carbon sugar to be produced. The oxygen molecules from these carbons are combined with hydrogen to form water.

In the second phase of the Calvin cycle, the three-carbon sugars that are created are modified using a number of chemical processes. These processes are expensive: they involve the breakdown of 6 ATP molecules, and use the energy contained in 6 NADPH molecules, which are broken down into NADP+. Recall, however, that the cell has just produced these molecules using the energy of the light reactions. The end result is a number of glyceraldehyde-3-phosphate (G3P) molecules. Most of these G3P molecules are returned to the cycle, for use in re-creating the ribulose biphosphate molecule. However, some are removed from the cycle, and are used to create glucose and other organic compounds.

In the final phase of the Calvin cycle, the G3P sugars are converted into the starting product of the Calvin cycle: ribulose biphosphate. This process, too, requires a large input of energy, in the form of three ATP molecules. This energy, again, was derived from the light reactions of photosynthesis. As the ribulose biphosphate is re-created, the cycle of carbon fixation can start over again.

It is useful to summarize the processes of the dark reaction. But in such a summary, don't forget that most of the raw materials used in the dark reaction were produced from sunlight. This means that while the dark reaction seems to involve a large investment of energy, much of that energy was produced from the light reactions themselves.

$$3 \, CO_2 + 9 \, ATP + 6 \, NADPH \rightarrow \text{glyceraldehyde-3-phosphate} + 12 \, H_2O.$$

Variations on the Dark Reactions

Not all plants undergo the Calvin cycle and carbon fixation in the exact same manner. Some plants, for example, physically separate the carbon fixation from the rest of the citric acid cycle. These plants use an enzyme known as PEP carboxylase, instead of rubisco, to capture CO_2 from the air. This enzyme is more efficient than rubisco, and works more effectively in hot, dry conditions. The carbon that is fixed by PEP carboxylase is then transported to cells where the carbon can enter the Calvin cycle. Plants that use such a system, which include corn and sugarcane, also have a different arrangement of cells in their leaves.

Other plants, known as **CAM plants,** separate the times when the two reactions of photosynthesis take place. CAM plants are most often found in deserts, where water is scarce. CAM plants cannot afford to lose water, yet water is often lost when cells must open the pores in their leaves (known as stomata) to absorb carbon dioxide. CAM plants, then, have another solution: they only open these stomata at night. During the day, CAM plants are able to undergo the light reactions, and produce ATP and NADPH. At night, they open their stomata to let in carbon dioxide, and undergo the dark reactions of photosynthesis, at a time when the temperature is lower, and the plants will lose less water.

LESSON SUMMARY

- Enzymes carry out important cellular mechanisms by catalyzing reactions.
- Energy is required for a number of reactions in the cell. These reactions take place through reaction coupling.

- The cell uses energy carriers such as ATP, FAD^+, NAD^+, and $NADP^+$ to carry energy in its usable forms throughout the cell.
- Respiration is the breakdown of glucose into usable energy. It has three steps:

  - Glycolysis is the breakdown of glucose into pyruvate, resulting in the creation of ATP and NADH.
  - The citric acid cycle creates a number of electron carriers and releases the carbons from pyruvate as carbon dioxide.

- Oxygen is essential as the final electron acceptor in respiration.

  - Oxidative phosphorylation uses an electron transport chain to create a concentration gradient. This gradient is harnessed to produce a large number of ATP molecules.

- Fermentation is the process by which cells donate electrons to waste products such as alcohol or lactic acid in the absence of oxygen.
- Photosynthesis is the creation of organic molecules using energy from the sun and atmospheric carbon dioxide. It has two parts:

  - The light reactions use chlorophyll to harness light energy and use it to create ATP and NADPH.
  - The dark reactions use these energy carriers to convert atmospheric carbon dioxide into a sugar molecule.

REVIEW QUESTIONS

1. Which of the following statements about enzymes is NOT true?

   (A) They are usually proteins.
   (B) They speed up reactions within the body.
   (C) They create energy for reactions to take place.
   (D) They can couple favorable and unfavorable reactions.
   (E) They can break down molecules.

2. The role of energy carriers such as ATP is:

   (A) to break down molecules within the cell.
   (B) to transport molecules in the cell.
   (C) to fix carbon in the Calvin cycle.
   (D) to provide usable energy for chemical reactions.
   (E) to catalyze chemical reactions.

3. Which of the following processes involves gaseous oxygen?

   I.   Respiration
   II. Fermentation
   III. Photosynthesis

      (A) I only
      (B) II only
      (C) I and II only
      (D) I and III only
      (E) II and III only

4. Which of the following produces ATP?

   I.   Glycolysis
   II. Oxidative phosphorylation
   III. Lactic acid fermentation

     (A) I only
     (B) I and II only
     (C) I and III only
     (D) II and III only
     (E) I, II, and III

5. A biologist studies a plant, and finds that it does not consume carbon dioxide during the day. Which of the following is true about this plant?

     (A) It only performs the Calvin cycle during the day.
     (B) It only performs the Calvin cycle at the same time as the light reactions.
     (C) It only performs the Calvin cycle at night.
     (D) It only performs the Calvin cycle when it rains.
     (E) None of the above

6. Which of the following statements about oxidative phosphorylation is NOT true?

     (A) It requires oxygen.
     (B) It converts NAD^+ into NADH.
     (C) It harnesses a concentration gradient to produce ATP.
     (D) It takes place in the mitochondria.
     (E) It uses the energy carriers produced in the citric acid cycle.

Questions 7 and 8

Select which one of the following choices best matches the statement below. Some choices may be used once, more than once, or not at all.

     (A) carbon fixation
     (B) glycolysis
     (C) lactic acid fermentation
     (D) alcoholic fermentation
     (E) citric acid cycle

7. A scientist deprives an organism of oxygen. It cannot undergo this reaction.
8. Occurs in the chloroplast.

ANSWERS

1. **C** Although enzymes can *lower* the activation energy necessary for a reaction to take place and can harness the energy of one reaction to perform another, they cannot *create* energy for a reaction to take place.
2. **D** The role of energy carriers is providing energy in a usable form, which can be coupled to perform any number of functions.
3. **D** Respiration requires oxygen to take place, and photosynthesis releases oxygen. Only fermentation does not involve oxygen in some form.
4. **E** All of these processes produce ATP.

5. **C** This plant is a CAM plant. It does not use carbon dioxide during the day, which means that it does not undergo the Calvin cycle during the day. Instead, it undergoes the Calvin cycle at night.

6. **B** Oxidative phosphorylation requires oxygen as a final electron acceptor. It does indeed take place in the mitochondria, and it does harness a gradient in proton concentration to drive ATP synthesis. It sets up this gradient using an electron transport chain initiated by the energy carriers from the citric acid cycle. It does not, however, convert NAD^+ into NADH; in fact, the opposite reaction takes place in oxidative phosphorylation.

7. **E** Lacking oxygen, the energy carriers created in the citric acid cycle will not be recycled for use in oxidative phosphorylation. As a result, it will stall.

8. **A** Carbon fixation is part of the dark reactions of photosynthesis. These reactions take place in the chloroplast.

Lesson 6-4. DNA, RNA, Protein

VOCABULARY

- DNA polymerase
- DNA replication
- gene
- messenger RNA or mRNA
- transcription
- RNA polymerase
- promoter
- repressors
- inducer
- corepressor
- transcription factors
- introns
- exons
- translation
- codons
- transfer RNA or tRNA
- mutations

We saw in Lesson 6-1 that the conformation of a protein depends on its amino acid sequence. But there are thousands of different proteins in the cell, each necessitating its own amino acid sequence. In this lesson, we'll review the important processes that involve DNA, RNA, and proteins. The important processes through which cells convert the instructions contained in DNA into the proteins that carry out the work of the cell will be fully explained.

COPYING DNA

Each cell contains all of the necessary instructions to create any protein in the entire organism. This information is stored in the cell's DNA. But when cells need to divide—a process that we explore in Lesson 5—they must have some way of passing this necessary information to their daughter cells. To do so, cells must have a method with which they can copy their DNA. This process, **DNA replication,** is the focus of this section.

DNA Replication

As we saw in Lesson 6-1, the DNA in cells actually contains two versions of the same message, because the two strands of DNA are complementary. That is, the nucleotide sequence on one DNA strand is the opposite of the nucleotide sequence on the other. A cytosine is always opposite a guanine, and a thymine is always opposite an adenine. Because of this, the sequence of a strand can be easily deduced from looking at its opposite, complementary strand. For example, if you knew that a strand had a given sequence:

CTGTAATCGTAGCCTTG

Then you could deduce the nucleotide sequence of its complementary strand by simply filling in the opposite. For example, the first nucleotide will be guanine, which matches with cytosine. The second will be adenine, which matches with thymine. The third will be cytosine, which matches with guanine. Carrying on, you could deduce the entire sequence:

GACATTAGCATCGGAAC

The complementary nature of DNA allows DNA replication to take place. DNA replication uses each single DNA strand as a template for forming its complementary strand. This means that each half of the DNA is the basis for the cell to create the other half of the DNA double strand. At the end, from two halves of the original double-strand, two identical DNA double-strands will be formed. This is shown in Figure 6-24.

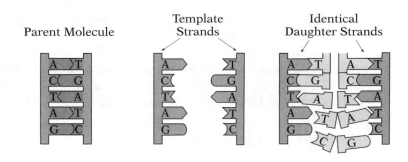

Parent Molecule   Template Strands   Identical Daughter Strands

Figure 6-24 Diagram of DNA replication.

Because the two identical strands of DNA will form the template strand for the new DNA molecules, the first step in replication must be the separation of the two identical strands of DNA. Because DNA molecules are so long, this process does not require the complete separation of the two strands of DNA from each other. Instead, the process starts at a site known as the replication origin. Somewhere in the middle of the DNA, a protein will separate a small section of DNA at the replication, allowing the other steps of replication to take place. As these steps continue, the DNA is further separated, creating replication forks, areas on either side of the origin of replication where the DNA is being separated and copied. Because there are multiple origins of replication on the DNA strand, then more than one part of the same DNA molecule can be copied at the same time. Eventually, the replication forks will meet each other, and the entire DNA molecule will be separated.

After the DNA strands have been at least partially separated, the cell may begin copying the template strands. This process occurs with the help of a protein known as **DNA polymerase.** Using the old DNA strand as the template, it matches the complementary nucleotides to the DNA strand. It then forms a bond between the newly added complementary nucleotide and the already-existing nucleotide strand, making the sugar-phosphate backbone of the new strand.

Recall that DNA nucleotides have two sides—a 5′ side and a 3′ side—and that the two strands of DNA connect in the opposite direction (see Lesson 6-1). DNA polymerase starts at the replication point, but on each strand it is only capable of moving in one direction, the 5′ to 3′ direction. This means that there are some areas of the DNA sequence that cannot be immediately copied as one long strand. These areas are replicated piecemeal, in the 5′ to 3′ direction, as the replication fork progresses. This creates DNA fragments, known as Okazaki fragments that must then be bound together with a protein known as DNA ligase.

This may be complicated, but try to think about DNA polymerase as a copy machine. Say you're trying to copy a book, for example, but that the copy machine only allowed you to turn the pages in one direction—from right to left, as the book progressed—so you could only copy pages in increasing number. Now, remember that DNA polymerase starts in the middle of the

DNA strand, at the origin of replication, and that only as the DNA strands continue to be split can replication progress. So now imagine you start at page 200 of your book, and you've copied to page 500—but now what? Well, you'd have to find another copy machine which would let you go back and copy pages 100–199, and then 50–99, and then 1–49. Then, you'd have to bind all these fragments together in a new book. This is somewhat how DNA polymerase progresses.

DNA replication ends when either the DNA polymerase runs out of template strand or when the two replicating forks run into each other. At the end, DNA ligase connects the gap in the new DNA strand, and, two, new, double-stranded DNA molecules are created where there was once one.

Correcting Mistakes

There are 2.9 billion—that's 2.9×10^9—nucleotide base pairs in the human genome. That's an astounding amount of information; if each base pair were a letter, it would be more letters than there are in 1,000 copies of this book. DNA polymerase must copy it all, and try to do so as accurately as possible. To do so, there are a number of double-checking mechanisms that it has to correct any mistakes that might be made.

DNA polymerase itself has an effective double-checking mechanism. As it adds nucleotides, it checks to see if the last nucleotide it just added is correct before moving on. DNA polymerase does this error-checking by looking at the shape of the DNA double-strand. If the newly added nucleotide formed the correct hydrogen bonds to the template strand, then the nucleotides of the two strands will form the correct double-stranded shape. Only the correctly matched nucleotide will form this shape, and the protein is able to detect an incorrectly placed nucleotide. If the nucleotide that was added is incorrect, it is removed, so that the correct nucleotide can be inserted in its place. Generally, DNA polymerase makes a mistake in only one out of every 10^7 molecules, making it an impressively accurate protein.

Still, there are other proteins that also check the DNA for mismatches or for damage, after the DNA polymerase finishes its job. These proteins, like the DNA polymerase, look for nucleotides that have been incorrectly matched, take them out, and then replace them with a matching nucleotide. These proteins, however, do not necessarily know which one was the template strand, so while they ensure that the two strands of DNA match, they cannot be sure that they have ensured the correct match.

These repair enzymes also help to fix "kinks" in the DNA strand caused by ultraviolet rays. UV rays can bring about misshapen DNA by causing two thymine molecules to link together in such a way that bends the sugar–phosphate backbone and distorts the shape of the DNA molecule. These repair enzymes can excise, or remove, these linked nucleotides, and replace them with new thymine nucleotides.

DNA TO mRNA

The information to create proteins is stored within the cell's DNA. Most of the DNA in our chromosomes do not contain useful instructions; instead, they consist of repeats of short nucleotide sequences. A part of a DNA strand that contains the instructions for a given protein is known as a **gene.** The human genome contains tens of thousands of genes. For the genes contained in DNA to be expressed as proteins, the DNA must be converted to a type of RNA known as **messenger RNA, or mRNA.** mRNA is a single strand of RNA that contains the necessary information to produce a polypeptide. mRNA is produced from DNA in a process known as **transcription.**

Transcription

Transcription of messenger RNA from DNA occurs in the nucleoid of prokaryotic cells and in the nucleus of eukaryotic cells. It is carried out by an enzyme known as **RNA polymerase.** RNA polymerase attaches to a strand of DNA at a specific site in the DNA known as **promoter.** The promoter is generally located a few nucleotides "upstream" from the gene that encodes for a protein. RNA polymerase recognizes the promoter sequences in the DNA, and binds to the DNA at these sites, causing the two complementary strands of DNA to come apart. One of these DNA strands serves as a template strand for the production of RNA. The RNA polymerase proceeds "downstream" along the template strand, attaching complementary mRNA nucleotides to the template strand, and forming a single strand of mRNA attached to the template strand of DNA.

The sequence of mRNA that is formed will be complementary to what is found in the template DNA strand. This means that it will contain complementary base pairs of each nucleotide found in the DNA strand, except that uracil (U) will complement with adenine (A) because mRNA is being created. For example, if a given template DNA strand has the sequence:

ATAGTCTTCCGC

then the mRNA strand that is created will have the sequence:

UAUCAGAAGGCG

because RNA polymerase creates a complementary strand to the template DNA.

As the RNA polymerase proceeds, the new single strand of mRNA detaches from the template DNA, and the original DNA molecule returns to its double-helical structure. The RNA polymerase continues downstream, creating mRNA, until it hits a termination point. At the termination point, which is generally slightly past the information necessary to create the protein, transcription ends. The RNA polymerase detaches from the DNA strand, and goes on to find another promoter, and produce another strand of mRNA.

Controlling Gene Expression

There are tens of thousands of genes that code for proteins in human DNA. But not all of the proteins that are coded for in DNA need to be expressed in every cell at all times. Organisms have developed a number of mechanisms to ensure only the proper proteins are expressed. One way in which cells are able to control protein production is by controlling which parts of the DNA are transcribed into mRNA. If a cell never produces the mRNA for a certain gene, then the protein coded for in that gene will never be produced.

One mechanism for controlling transcription is known as a repressor. **Repressors** are proteins that, when activated, bind to a section of the DNA known as an operator, which is between the promoter and the gene for the protein. When a repressor is active, it binds to the DNA, and prevents the DNA from being transcribed into mRNA. When the repressor is inactivated, however, it releases the DNA, and transcription proceeds normally.

Repressors are useful to cells because the activation of repressors to stop transcription allows the cell to respond to its changing needs. Certain repressors are always active, unless they are bound to a certain molecule known as an **inducer.** These repressors will always bind to the DNA, preventing transcription, unless the inducer molecule is present. Allolactose, which is an isomer of lactose found in cells with lactose, acts as such an inducer in the *lac* operon of the bacteria *E. coli* (an operon is a stretch of DNA in prokaryotes that codes for a series of proteins). The *lac* operon contains the genes for the proteins that digest lactose. Normally, *E. coli* cells have no need to digest lactose. Thus, in the absence of lactose, the repressor is activated, and the cell does not waste any energy producing unnecessary proteins. However, when lactose is present, the cell needs a way to digest it. The allolactose that accompanies lactose inactivates the repressor, allowing the cell to produce the lactose-digesting enzymes when they are necessitated.

Other repressors, however are activated only when they are bound to a certain molecule, known as a **corepressor.** One system that uses corepressors is the *trp* (or tryptophan) operon in *E. coli,* which contains the proteins that produce the essential amino acid tryptophan. The *trp* repressor requires tryptophan as a corepressor in order to be activated. When tryptophan is scarce, the cell needs tryptophan-producing proteins. Without tryptophan, the repressor is inactive, and the genes for tryptophan-producing proteins are expressed. If tryptophan is abundant, however, the cell needs a way to halt tryptophan production. The tryptophan binds to the repressor, and changes the shape of the repressor so that it binds the operon and halts the production of mRNA for tryptophan-producing proteins. In this way, the cell always ensures that it has an adequate supply of tryptophan.

In eukaryotic cells, transcription requires not only the presence of RNA polymerase, but also the presence of a number of proteins known as **transcription factors.** These transcription factors are what activate the RNA polymerase and allow it to transcribe the DNA. By limiting the activation of these transcription factors, eukaryotic cells are able to control which genes are transcribed.

RNA Processing

In eukaryotes, additional steps are necessary before the mRNA can be used to produce a protein. First, the mRNA is capped at either end. At the 5′ end of the mRNA, an enzyme adds a guanosine triphosphate molecule, forming what is known as a 5′ cap. At the 3′ end of the mRNA, another enzyme adds 50–250 adenosine nucleotides, known as the poly(A) tail. Because mRNA is not an especially stable macromolecule, it is subject to rapid degradation. The 5′ cap and the poly(A) tail are thought to add stability to the mRNA molecule and keep it from degradation. They also serve as markers that aid ribosomes in attaching to the mRNA.

The additions to the ends of mRNA are not the only way that mRNA is processed. The mRNA of eukaryotes contains a number of segments, known as **introns,** which are not necessary to produce the protein. If the mRNA were made into a protein with all of these segments, the protein would not function correctly. To remedy this, the cell cuts out, or excises, these introns, and then puts back together the coding regions, known as **exons,** into one mRNA strand, from which a protein can finally be made (see Figure 6-25). This process, known as RNA splicing, occurs at a large complex of proteins known as a spliceosome.

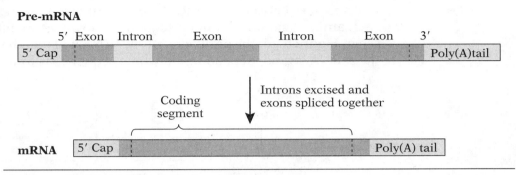

Figure 6-25 RNA processing: introns and exons.

Gene splicing might seem like a rather unnecessary step. But, in fact, gene splicing provides a way to allow one gene to code for more than one protein. Sometimes, genes can be spliced in two or more different ways, resulting in two or more different sets of exons being expressed, and two or more different proteins. These alternative splicings mean that the same stretch of DNA can be used to produce a large number of proteins. Although it is not known exactly how splicing is controlled, it is thought that alternative splicing might also serve as a way for cells to regulate gene expression.

mRNA TO POLYPEPTIDE

Making and processing mRNA is only the first step of creating a protein. In the second step, the mRNA must be read and converted into the desired polypeptide chain that will become a fully functional protein, in a process known as **translation.**

Translation

Translation is slightly harder to understand than transcription, because it is a slightly less intuitive process. Whereas transcription just involves copying one nucleic acid to another—DNA to mRNA—translation somehow starts with a nucleic acid and ends up with a protein.

Translation takes place inside the ribosome. For translation to occur, the two halves of the ribosome actually attach themselves to opposite sides of the mRNA. This occurs at the site where the ribosome recognizes the sequence **AUG** in the mRNA. This sequence signals the beginning of the useful portion of the mRNA molecule. Once this sequence is reached, mRNA is moved through the ribosome, three mRNA nucleotides at a time, and a polypeptide is produced.

In translation, mRNA is read three nucleotides at a time. In the sequence **AUGGGACUGCGA,** for example, the ribosome first reads **AUG,** the codon that gives the signal to start translation. It then proceeds to read **GGA,** and then

CUG, and then **CGA.** These three-nucleotide sequences are known as mRNA **codons.** There are 64 possible mRNA codons.

The key to translation is a small, folded stretch of RNA that is attached to an amino acid, called **transfer RNA,** or **tRNA.** There are 20 different types of tRNA molecules, each attached to a different type of amino acid. Because it is bonded to an amino acid, but can also match up to mRNA, tRNA acts as an intermediary between the mRNA and the finished polypeptide. The tRNA for each amino acid has a unique sequence known as an anticodon. As you can see in Figure 6-26, the anticodon of the tRNA will match up with the codon of the mRNA strand, depending on which sequence is found in the mRNA.

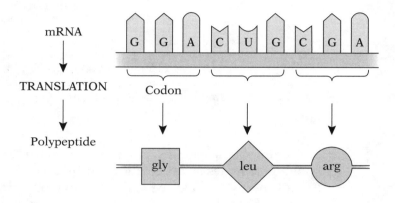

Figure 6-26 Transcription.

Above, for example, we considered the sequence **AUGGGACUGCGA.** After the start codon, the second codon, **GGA,** will match up with a tRNA for the amino acid glycine. The third codon, **CUG,** will match up with a tRNA for the amino acid leucine. And the fourth codon, **CGA,** will match up with a tRNA for the amino acid arginine.

Translation, thus, involves matching the mRNA codon to the complementary tRNA anticodon at the ribosome. When the correct tRNA molecule matches up to the mRNA codon, then it fits inside the ribosome. The amino acid that is attached is bonded via a peptide bond to the existing polypeptide chain (the start codon, **AUG,** results in a methionine amino acid, so there is always something to bind to).

As the process moves on, the tRNA is released. The tRNA, now devoid of its amino acid, then re-attaches to another amino acid, to be used again in translation. The mRNA then moves forward three nucleotides in the ribosome, and the process repeats itself—tRNA anticodon matching mRNA codon, the amino acids attaching via a peptide bond, and onto the next codon.

You may have noticed a slight discrepancy in the numbers involved here: there are 64 possible mRNA codons, but only 20 types of amino acids. This discrepancy is resolved because there is more than one mRNA codon for each amino acid. For example, the mRNA codons **CAU, CAC, CAA,** and **CAG** all code for the same amino acid—proline.

Translation ends when a **UAA, UAG,** or **UGA** mRNA codon is reached. These are known as "stop" codons. When one of these codons is reached, translation ends. The mRNA molecule is released from the ribosome, and the finished polypeptide is released.

Translation is a complicated process, involving a complex array of molecules. But remember that translation is not the end of the story—after translation, there are still a number of steps that need to take place in order for a protein to be made. These steps involve folding the protein into its proper shape. The forces that dictate how proteins fold are detailed in Lesson 6-1.

The Evolution of Transcription and Translation

The creation of mRNA might seem like a wasteful step and an added complication in creating proteins. In eukaryotes, the need for mRNA is clear, because there is a physical separation between DNA, which carries the instructions for proteins, and the endoplasmic reticulum, where proteins are made: they are separated by the nuclear envelope. Because DNA molecules are too large to travel through the nuclear envelope, there must be an intermediate molecule to transfer instructions outside of the nucleus. mRNA, a single-stranded molecule, is able to travel through the nuclear envelope to the ribosome.

In prokaryotic organisms, however, there is no nucleus or endoplasmic reticulum. In fact, *in prokaryotes, transcription and translation occur simultaneously.* One or more ribosomes can be at work, translating mRNA into polypeptides, while the downstream parts of the mRNA are still being transcribed from the DNA. Nevertheless, prokaryotic cells, which have no need for the transport of instructions outside a nucleus, still create mRNA. Why?

The explanation for the creation of mRNA as an intervening step is simply that the mechanisms to create proteins from RNA are thought to have evolved before DNA was used as the genetic code. It is thought that RNA was the original genetic material, and was used to encode all of the information necessary for creating enzymes. There is evidence to suggest that RNA might capable of replicating itself, without the use of DNA or even proteins, because certain RNA molecules known as ribozymes are capable of performing simple functions, and might once have been capable of replicating RNA.

You might wonder, then, why cells don't still use RNA as the genetic material. The reason is that RNA is not as stable a molecule as DNA. Ribose sugars, and uracil, are more easily mutated or broken down than DNA molecules and thymine, and therefore are a less reliable repository for genetic information.

MUTATIONS

No organism is perfect. DNA and RNA are no more than long molecules, and occasionally, mistakes can be made when DNA is copied, or environmental factors may cause damage to DNA. Such changes in the nucleotide sequence of DNA are known as **mutations.** Because the eventual function of a protein is dependent upon the proper DNA sequence, mutations can often have negative consequences, although they might also have positive consequences. Depending on the type of mutation, they will affect the protein differently.

Think of a mutation as a scratch on a DVD. Sometimes, a scratch is harmless, and doesn't affect the movie at all. Other times, it causes only a certain scene in the movie. But in the worst case scenario, a scratch can render a DVD completely unusable. Similarly, mutations sometimes have little or no effect; occasionally, however, they can cause life-threatening diseases.

There are different types of mutations in nucleic acids. A base-pair *substitution* is a mutation caused when one base-pair accidentally replaces another in the DNA. For example, if a cytosine nucleotide of a gene were to be replaced by an adenosine nucleotide, this would result in a substitution mutation. The effects of such base-pair mutations will vary, depending on how it affects the resulting polypeptide sequence:

- Sometimes, *the substitution may not change the polypeptide sequence at all.* This is possible because more than one mRNA codon will give the same amino acid, so that even with the mutation, the resulting protein is the same. This is most often true if the mutation involves the third base in an mRNA codon.
- Sometimes *the substitution may result in a different amino acid being inserted into a polypeptide.* This can happen if the point mutation causes the mRNA codon to give a different amino acid. If the amino acid is in an especially crucial part of a polypeptide sequence, this can have serious implications for protein function. This is true in sickle-cell anemia, a common disease resulting in misshapen red blood cells that are less able to carry oxygen in the bloodstream. Sickle-cell anemia is caused by a difference in only one polypeptide, resulting from a single point mutation.
- *The substitution may result in an incomplete polypeptide chain.* If the point mutation changes the mRNA codon to a stop codon, then translation will terminate prematurely, and the complete polypeptide will not be produced. This would likely result in a malfunctioning protein.

Mutations are not always caused by one nucleotide replacing another. Sometimes, they are caused when a nucleotide is incorrectly inserted or deleted. Such a mutation can have disastrous effects when it results in what is known as a frame-shift, as shown in Figure 6-27.

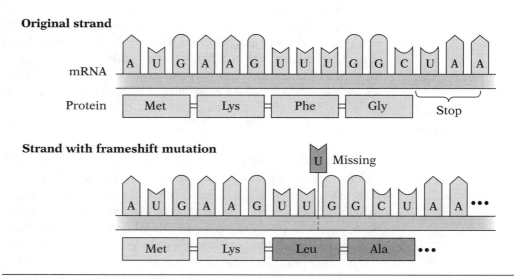

Figure 6-27 Frame-shift mutations.

As was discussed in the section on translation, mRNA is read three nucleotides at a time. As this figure shows, inserting or deleting one or two nucleotides will result in every remaining mRNA codon to be misread. This is because the three-codon "frame" that the ribosome translates into amino acids will be the wrong three nucleotide bases. This would likely result in the rest of the polypeptide being completely unusable.

Only if such an insertion or deletion involves three nucleotides—an entire codon—can such a dangerous frame-shift mutation be prevented. In this case, an amino acid would be either deleted or added from the polypeptide sequence. The effect of this added or deleted polypeptide would depend on how important the location of that amino acid is to the protein. In a crucial area of the protein, such a mutation could be disastrous; in a less important place, it might have little or no effect.

LESSON SUMMARY

- DNA is copied in a process known as DNA replication, carried out by a protein known as DNA polymerase.
- mRNA is produced from DNA in a process known as transcription. Transcription is carried out by a protein known as RNA polymerase. A number of mechanisms act to control the occurrence of transcription.
- In eukaryotes, mRNA is processed before exiting the nucleus.
- mRNA's messages are converted into polypeptides in a process known as translation. Translation occurs at the ribosome, using short RNA segments known as tRNA.
- RNA is thought to have been the original genetic material.
- Mutations in the DNA sequence can have significant effects on protein structure and function.

REVIEW QUESTIONS

Questions 1 and 2

A stretch of DNA in the middle of a gene is sequenced, and is found to have the following nucleotide sequence.

CCATGGAATGTT

1. Which of the following describes the nucleotide sequence that is complementary to this strand of DNA?

   (A) **CCATGGAATGTT**
   (B) **TTGTAAGGTACC**
   (C) **GGTACCTTAGAA**
   (D) **GGUACCUUAGAA**
   (E) **AAGAUUCCAUGG**

2. Which of the following describes the nucleotide sequence that would be produced if this part of the gene were to undergo transcription?

   (A) **CCATGGAATGTT**
   (B) **TTGTAAGGTACC**
   (C) **GGTACCTTAGAA**
   (D) **GGUACCUUAGAA**
   (E) **AAGAUUCCAUGG**

3. A scientist has eliminated, or "knocked out," the gene for one enzyme from a cell. He discovers that the cell that results is incapable of producing mRNA from its DNA. Which of the following statements about this cell is most likely?

    (A) This cell lacks a nucleus.
    (B) This cell lacks tRNA.
    (C) This cell lacks the enzyme DNA polymerase.
    (D) This cell lacks the enzyme RNA polymerase.
    (E) This cell lacks ribosomes.

4. An extra cytosine nucleotide was mistakenly entered into the middle of a gene. Which of the following is NOT true about this gene?

    (A) This gene has undergone a point mutation.
    (B) This gene will be transcribed.
    (C) The protein produced by this gene will most likely be misshapen.
    (D) This gene will likely not produce a functional protein.
    (E) The amino acid sequence of this gene will likely be affected.

Questions 5 and 6

Select which one of the following choices best matches the statements below. Some choices may be used once, more than once, or not at all.

    (A) Prokaryotic cells only
    (B) Eukaryotic cells only
    (C) Plant cells only
    (D) Animal cells only
    (E) All cells

5. Cells in which DNA is replicated
6. Cells in which mRNA is spliced before translation
7. Which of the following involve the matching of complementary base pairs?

    I.   Replication
    II. Transcription
    III. Translation

        (A) I only
        (B) I and II only
        (C) I and III only
        (D) II and III only
        (E) I, II, and III

8. Which of the following statements about transcription is NOT true?

    (A) Transcription is concurrent with translation in some cells.
    (B) Transcription occurs in the endoplasmic reticulum.
    (C) Transcription precedes translation.
    (D) Transcription involves the enzyme RNA Polymerase.
    (E) Transcription is carried out by bacteria.

ANSWERS

1. **C** A complementary stretch of DNA to this will have the complementary DNA base pairs at each position. This means that guanine will match with the first two cytosines, thymine will match with the adenine, and adenine will match with the thymine. (C) is the only answer to have even these first four nucleic acids in order.

2. **D** A complementary stretch of DNA will be identical to the complementary DNA strand, except that it will contain uracil instead of thymine. (D) is identical to (C), except that it has uracil instead of thymine.

3. **D** Whatever is missing from this protein is what allows mRNA to be created from DNA, the process known as transcription. There is no reason to believe this cell does not have a nucleus because even cells without a nucleus are capable of transcription. tRNA and ribosomes are only needed for translation, so they would not be necessary for transcription. DNA polymerase is used in DNA replication, not transcription. RNA polymerase is the only one of these options that is necessary for mRNA to be produced.

4. **A** This gene has, in fact, undergone a frame-shift mutation, which will cause the reading frame of translation to shift over. As a result, the amino acid sequence produced will be incorrect, and the protein produced will likely be misshapen and nonfunctional. This would have little to no effect on the transcription of the gene, however, because it occurs in the middle of the gene.

5. **E** DNA is replicated in all cells.

6. **B** Only eukaryotes undergo gene splicing.

7. **E** In replication, base-pair matching is what composes the new strands of DNA. In transcription, base-pair matching is how new strands of mRNA are created. And in translation, the matching of base pairs between mRNA and tRNA produces the correct polypeptide sequence.

8. **B** Transcription occurs in the nucleus of eukaryotic cells. Translation occurs at the ribosomes in the rough endoplasmic reticulum.

Lesson 6-5.　Mitosis and Meiosis

VOCABULARY

- interphase
- mitosis
- prophase
- metaphase
- anaphase
- telophase
- meiosis
- crossing over

Other terms: cytokinesis, centriole, centromere, cleavage, synapsis, tetrads, chromatin/chromatid/chromosome

In this chapter, we have discussed the chemical building blocks, the main physical features, and the significant processes that take place within a cell. In this last lesson, we'll explore a final important feature of cells: how they reproduce. These processes, known as mitosis and meiosis, are the crucial mechanisms through which cells can divide and thereby multiply.

THE CELL CYCLE

Cells have a natural cycle through which they progress before dividing. Newly formed cells enter a first "gap" phase, known as the G_1 phase, an S phase, and a second "gap" phase, known as the G_2 phase. Collectively, these phases are known as **interphase.** In all of these phases, cells grow and carry out their normal functions by producing the necessary proteins and organelles for life. What makes the S phase distinct from the other two parts of interphase is that it is during the S phase that the cell replicates its DNA, using the process described in Lesson 6-4.

After interphase, cells enter what is known as **mitosis.** It is during mitosis that cells perform the large number of tasks that are necessary to divide. During mitosis, cells divide to form two identical daughter cells. After mitosis, cells again enter the G_1 phase of interphase, in which they grow and produce the necessary molecules for life.

MITOSIS

Mitosis is the highly complex process by which cells divide into two daughter cells. Mitosis is responsible for almost all cell division that takes place in all eukaryotic organisms. Every cell in your body, except for sperm cells (in males) and oocytes (eggs, in females), was produced using mitosis. Though mitosis accounts for only about 10% of the time spent in the cell cycle, it is an extremely complex process that has been broken down into a number of shorter phases. Each of these phases is described at length below. It should be noted that this section concerns *animal* cell mitosis only (the process is slightly different in plant cells).

As you read through these phases, try not to get lost in the details of what happens in each phase. Instead, think about how each phase takes the cell one step closer to its ultimate goal: successfully dividing into two identical daughter cells. Also, follow along in Figure 6-28, which illustrates how the cell appears at each phase, to help you remember what occurs during each phase.

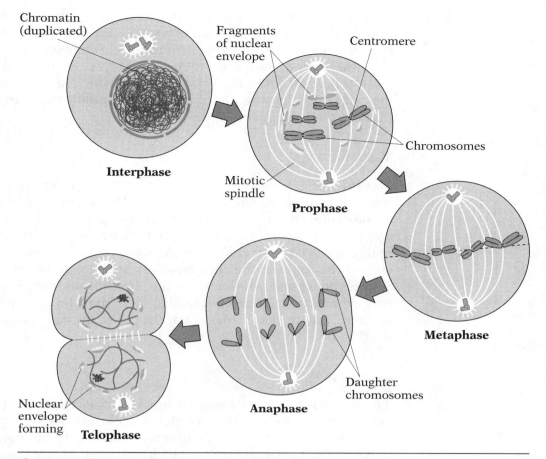

Figure 6-28 The stages of mitosis.

End of Interphase

To contrast with the activities that begin to take place during mitosis, Figure 6-28 shows how cells appear at the end of interphase. Note that in cells at the end of interphase, the DNA, or chromatin, within the cell has already been replicated. It has not yet, however, coalesced into chromosomes, meaning that the DNA is not yet visible using a light microscope. At this point, the nucleus and the nuclear envelope are still intact. In animal cells, two pairs of centrioles are present outside the nucleus. These centrioles are made of elements of the cytoskeleton, and are replicated from one centriole during interphase.

Prophase

During **prophase,** a number of changes occur both inside and outside the nucleus. First, inside the nucleus, the strands of DNA coalesce. They fold together to form tightly bound, dense structures known as chromosomes. Because the DNA has been replicated, there are now two copies of the DNA within the cell. There are, therefore, two copies of each chromosome as well. These two identical chromosomes are bound together with a microtubule known as the centromere.

Meanwhile, changes occur in the cytoplasm. The centriole pairs start to migrate to opposite ends of the cell. Between them, connecting the two centrioles, are microtubules which form the *mitotic spindle*. These microtubules will help to guide the chromosomes to opposite ends of the cell later in mitosis.

As the cell enters the end of prophase, the nuclear envelope breaks down, erasing the distinction between nucleus and cytoplasm. As this occurs, the microtubules start to migrate toward the chromosomes. These chromosomes are now even denser than they were before. At the end of prophase, the microtubules connect the two centrioles, which migrate to opposite poles of the cell. The microtubules of the mitotic spindle begin to attach to the centromere of each chromosome.

Metaphase

Metaphase is a very distinctive part of mitosis, during which the chromosomes line up in the middle of the cell. This occurs because the centromeres at the center of each set of chromosomes have attached to the mitotic spindle, and the chromosomes migrate to the center of the cell. The cell during metaphase looks rather symmetrical, with the two centriole pairs at opposite ends of the cell, and the chromosomes lined up in the middle between them.

Metaphase ensures that all of the chromosomes are in place to be equally divided among two daughter cells. Now that the chromosomes have been lined up, and the centrioles are at the poles, the cell is ready to begin pulling itself apart.

Anaphase

Anaphase is the part of mitosis in which the cell begins to pull itself apart. During this phase, each pair of identical chromosomes, which had been held together at the centromere, suddenly separate. The daughter chromosomes that were replicated during interphase are pulled toward opposite poles of the cell. As shown in Figure 6-28, the chromosomes appear as if they are tugged on at the center, with the loose sides trailing toward the center. In fact, the microtubules of the spindle are attached to the centromere and are pulling them toward opposite ends of the cell.

At the same time, the cell is elongating. The two poles of the cell are getting farther apart, as the cell prepares to divide into two new cells. By the time anaphase ends, the daughter chromosomes have completely migrated to opposite ends of the cell, each side having an identical and complete copy of the organism's DNA. The final acts of division are ready to begin.

Telophase

Telophase is the phase during which two daughter cells form. As the two poles of the cell move farther apart, a membrane begins to form between them, starting to separate the contents of the cytoplasm. The contents of the cell—the organelles—also migrate to different poles of the cell, a process known as *cytokinesis*. As the membrane between the two cells grows, a nuclear envelope begins to form around the chromosomes of each daughter cell. At the same time, the chromosomes start to become less dense, unfolding back into the chromatin. The cells begin to return to their normal, interphase state.

At the end of telophase, what results are two identical daughter cells—smaller, perhaps, but ready to grow in the G_1 phase of interphase. Each daughter cell inherits all of the organelles and the genetic material necessary to continue with its normal functions, and as they do so, they will prepare themselves to divide again. With telophase, the cell cycle is ready to begin again.

Plant cell division contains a few differences: there are no centrioles to organize the spindle fibers, and, because there is a rigid cell wall, cytokinesis occurs from *within* the cell. Vesicles secrete polysaccharides that become a cell plate, eventually creating a new cell wall between the cells.

Regulating the Cell Cycle

Cells are not constantly dividing. Though some cells—skin cells or red blood cells, for example—never stop dividing, other cells—brain cells, for example—do not divide frequently or at all. Growing and dividing, as we have seen, are complicated processes. Such processes involve the expenditure of large amounts of energy for the cell. Cells need some way to control how often they divide.

Cells use chemical signals to regulate how often they divide. There are certain points at which the cell can arrest, or stop, the cell cycle. One important checkpoint is right before the cell enters the S phase of interphase, in which the cell's DNA is replicated. This is known as the G_1 checkpoint. DNA replication is an expensive process; it makes sense that the cell would not want to undergo this process unless it were necessary. Thus, the cell requires a certain chemical signal in order to set off this process. If cells do not receive this chemical signal, they will continue to undergo their normal functions, but they will not grow or divide. Most of the cells in our bodies subsist at this state.

Occasionally, however, cells receive an erroneous signal. Sometimes, this results from a genetic mutation. When a cell receives an erroneous signal, it may pass through these checkpoints on its growth even though the body does not need more of this type of cell. Such cells often ignore signals that would indicate that mitotic division is not necessary. As they divide, their daughter cells, too, are not responsive to the checks on growth of normal cells. This condition of unchecked growth is what causes many forms of cancer in the body. When this occurs, a tumor, or a mass of extra, unneeded cells, can result. Often, such cells will impede normal functioning of tissues or organs.

MEIOSIS

Mitosis is responsible for almost all cell division in the body. Sometimes, however, organisms need to produce specialized cells for use in sexual reproduction. In sexual reproduction, genetic material from one organism is combined with the genetic material from another organism, to make a new organism with a different combination of genetic material. **Meiosis** is the process by which the specialized cells necessary for sexual reproduction are produced.

Diploid, Haploid, Zygotes

Normal cells in the body, known as somatic cells, carry two copies of each gene. One of these copies is inherited from each parent of this organism. For example, every human has one set of each of his genes from his mother, and one set from his father. Cells that carry two copies of each of their genes are known as *diploid* cells. During mitosis, one diploid cell is replicated into two identical daughter diploid cells. Because, as we know, genes are carried on chromosomes, it follows that diploid organisms will actually have two chromosomes, each with different versions of the gene for the same trait. For example, one chromosome may carry a gene for blue eyes, while the other carries a gene for brown eyes in the same place.

Organisms must have a way of forming a half-set of instructions to pass on to their descendants. Such a half-set of instructions, which could be combined with a similar half-set from another organism, describes a *haploid* cell. Haploid cells contain one set of all of the chromosomes necessary for an organism to survive. When two haploid cells combine, they form a cell that has the complete set of instructions—a new diploid cell.

The number of chromosomes necessary for each organism is different, and is often written using the letter n. Cells that are haploid, and contain one of each chromosome, are often written as n. Cells that are diploid, and thus contain two sets of each chromosome, are often written as $2n$ because they contain twice the number of chromosomes. In humans, $n = 23$. Each of our normal cells contains $2n$, or 46 chromosomes: two sets of 23.

Cells that are diploid are known as somatic cells, and cells that are haploid are known as *gametes*. In humans, egg and sperm cells serve as the gametes. In the rest of this section, we examine how these gametes are produced, using meiosis.

Meiosis I and II

Meiosis is a slightly more complex process than mitosis, because unlike mitosis, it is not trying to create *identical* daughter cells. Instead, meiosis is involved in halving the number of chromosomes in an organism. Thus, though the phases of meiosis are quite similar to the phases of mitosis, there are slight differences. Nevertheless, a good understand of mitosis will serve as a good guide to meiosis. One important difference is that meiosis is equivalent to *two* mitotic cycles, because cells undergoing meiosis divide twice. Because of this, meiosis is divided into meiosis I and meiosis II, as shown in Figure 6-29.

In the interphase before meiosis I, the cells that will eventually become gametes replicate their DNA, much as occurs in mitosis. The sister chromatids are attached at their centromeres, as in mitosis, but the prophase I of meiosis is a much more complicated process. At this point, the cell is $4n$, containing two copies of each of two different versions of the same chromosome. Each of these two different versions contains different genes for the same traits.

In prophase I, the different versions of the chromosomes trade lengths of their DNA segments, a process known as recombination, or **crossing over.** Think of the crossing over of DNA as mixing two decks of cards, each with a different design on the back, and trading all of clubs in one deck for the same cards in another. In the end, each of the decks will have a complete set of instructions, but the origins will be mixed up a bit, and the design might be slightly different. In the case of crossing over, each chromosome is complete, but the chromosomes have been "mixed up," so that segments coming from different chromosomes are now put together.

After prophase I, meiosis proceeds largely as mitosis does: the chromosomes line up (metaphase I), are pulled to opposite ends of the cell (anaphase I), and then two daughter cells are created (telophase I). The one important difference in meiosis is that instead of giving each daughter cell one complete set of directions, the cell now has two copies of the same half-set of directions.

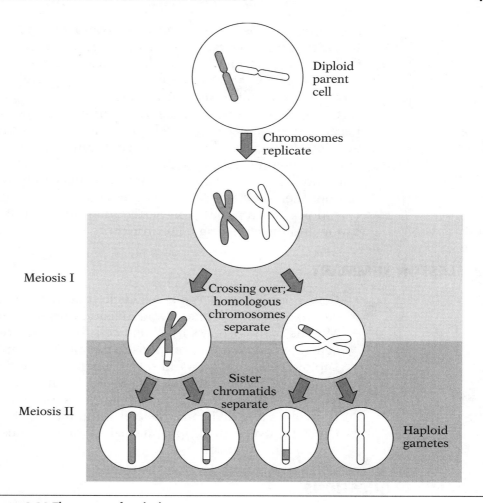

Figure 6-29 The stages of meiosis.

Whereas in mitosis, sister chromatids (i.e., copies of the same chromosome) are divided after metaphase, in meiosis I, they are not divided. Instead, the sister chromatids move *together*. The daughter cells that are created at the end of meiosis I are 2*n*, like cells at the end of mitosis, but instead of each cell containing two different versions of the same chromosome (one inherited from each of the organism's parents), the cells contain two almost identical versions of the same chromosome, different only for what has crossed over.

In meiosis II, the process of dividing repeats itself. Meiosis II also includes the steps of prophase, metaphase, anaphase, and telophase, except that there is no recombination in prophase II. The important part of meiosis II is that the cells do *not* replicate their DNA prior to meiosis II. Because of this, when the genetic material of each cell is divided in anaphase II, there is only one copy of each chromosome that goes to each daughter cell. Each daughter cell that is formed in telophase II is a haploid gamete, containing only one half-set of genetic instructions. Only by joining with another haploid gamete can a diploid organism with a full set of genetic instructions be created.

Why Meiosis?

You may wonder why cells would undergo such a complex process as meiosis, involving crossing over and not one, but two, divisions, simply to produce a gamete. The answer is that crossing over helps to produce genetic variation. If crossing over of chromosomes did not occur, then you would have inherited exactly one half of your father's genes and exactly one half of your mother's genes, and your child would inherit either the half from your mother or the half from your father.

Crossing over ensures genetic variation in the organisms of a population, because it ensures that your child will inherit genes from both your mother and your father. Instead of passing the same set of traits with each other over and over again (i.e., tall with black hair and brown eyes, or short with red hair and blue eyes), it ensures that the traits can be inherited in new combinations (i.e., short with black hair and blue eyes). As we will see later, genetic variation helps a population better adapt to the continued pressures of evolution and the changing environment.

LESSON SUMMARY

- Cells normally undergo a cell cycle that includes growth and DNA replication during interphase, and division during mitosis.
- Mitosis is the process by which cells divide to create identical daughter cells. It is divided into prophase, metaphase, anaphase, and telophase.
- Diploid cells contain a full set of genetic instructions, while haploid cells contain one half of the necessary genetic instructions.
- Meiosis is the process by which gametes, or haploid cells, are produced. It involves two divisions, meiosis I and meiosis II.
- Crossing over during prophase I of meiosis ensures genetic variation within a population.

REVIEW QUESTIONS

1. A haploid human cell has how many chromosomes?

   (A) 12
   (B) 23
   (C) 35
   (D) 46
   (E) 69

Questions 2–4

Select which one of the following choices best matches the statement below. Some choices may be used once, more than once, or not at all.

   (A) anaphase
   (B) telophase
   (C) prophase
   (D) interphase
   (E) metaphase

2. The phase of mitosis following metaphase
3. The phase of cell division in which DNA is replicated
4. The phase of mitosis in which chromosomes migrate to opposite sides of the cell

5. Which of the following statements about meiosis is NOT true?

   (A) Meiosis I involves "crossing over."
   (B) Meiosis produces identical daughter cells.
   (C) Meiosis ensures genetic variety.
   (D) Meiosis II results in gametes.
   (E) Meiosis produces haploid cells.

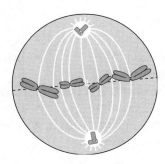

6. The cell above is in which stage of mitosis?

   (A) interphase
   (B) telophase
   (C) prophase
   (D) anaphase
   (E) metaphase

ANSWERS

1. **B** A normal human cell has 23 *pairs* of chromosomes, or 46 chromosomes. A haploid cell has half that number, or 23 chromosomes.
2. **A** Anaphase follows metaphase in mitosis.
3. **D** DNA is replicated in the S phase of interphase.
4. **A** During metaphase, the chromosomes line up at the metaphase plate. In anaphase, they are pulled towards opposite ends of the cell. By the time telophase starts, the chromosomes have been pulled to opposite sides of the cell.
5. **B** Meiosis does not produce four identical cells, because there is variation in the genetic content of each of the cells that it produces. This ensures genetic variation within the population. Meiosis does produce haploid gametes, which have been formed by crossing over.
6. **E** Metaphase is easily recognizable here by the chromosomes, which are lined up in the center of the cell.

CHAPTER 7

UNDERSTANDING GENETICS

Lesson 7-1. Mendelian Inheritance

VOCABULARY

- phenotype
- genotype
- alleles
- dominant allele
- recessive allele
- law of segregation
- homozygous

- homozygous dominant
- homozygous recessive
- heterozygous
- carriers
- Punnett square
- law of independent assortment

The saying goes, "like father, like son." Parents with brown eyes, for example, are more likely to have children with brown eyes. In this section, we'll examine the basic principles by which certain simple traits are inherited, by taking a look at the work of an Austrian monk named Gregor Mendel.

MENDEL: PATTERNS OF INHERITANCE

Gregor Mendel was a nineteenth-century Austrian monk who had received some training in botany and in conducting scientific research. Mendel took it upon himself to investigate the traits of pea plants that he harvested in the garden of the monastery where he lived. In doing so, Mendel discovered the patterns by which certain traits are inherited, patterns whose genetic basis would not be fully understood for one hundred years.

At the time Mendel was working, scientists had little real understanding of what inheritance meant. Although they may have seen that fathers resembled their sons, for example, they had no understanding of the mechanisms of how such similarities might occur.

It was Mendel who was the first to characterize properly what he called the "heritable factor," some discrete part of a parent that was passed on to its offspring and that, when combined with the heritable factor of the other parent, created certain traits in that offspring. Today, we know this "heritable factor" as a gene, and we know that genes exist on DNA and that DNA is passed from parent to offspring in gametes.

It is important to gain a thorough understanding of Mendel's research for a number of reasons. First, Mendel uncovered the important principles that determine how most traits are passed from one generation to another. Understanding these principles is essential to understanding the questions about inheritance that you will be asked on the SAT Biology exam.

Second, Mendel's research ties in to what we know about DNA and chromosomes; understanding Mendel makes it easier to understand how genes and chromosomes work. Finally, Mendel's experiments are a famous example of how the scientific method can be used to discover important facts about how life works. This means that understanding his experiments can help you better understand the scientific method, and it also makes his experiments ample fodder for questions on the exam.

Mendel's Experiment

If Mendel was going to explore how traits are passed from generation to generation, he needed to be able to control how the plants bred. Normally, pea plants will self-pollinate; that is, the pollen from a plant will generally fertilize an ovum (egg) of the same flower and of the same plant, producing offspring that are almost identical to their parents. Mendel's experiments, however, involved the controlled *cross-pollination* of pea plants; that is, Mendel wanted to be able to choose the parent organisms, to produce offspring with two different parents. To achieve this, he cut off the pollen-producing part of the flower, known as the stamen, before it produced pollen. This eliminated the ability of plants to self-pollinate. By taking pollen from one plant and transferring it to another, Mendel was able to cross two plants and be sure that the seeds that were produced had parents that he had chosen.

But if Mendel was going to carry out experiments on plant inheritance, he needed a control—some plant whose behavior was predictable, with which he could compare his results. Mendel, thus, started his research with true-bred plants, that is, plants which, when self-pollinated, always produced offspring with the same traits. For example, Mendel started with plants with yellow peas whose offspring only produced plants with yellow peas, or plants with green peas whose offspring only produced plants with green peas.

Mendel's experiment was simplified in that he chose to investigate traits of pea plants that are inherited in a discrete or "either-or" fashion. The peas of pea plants are either green or yellow. The flowers of pea plants are either purple or white. There are no intermediate shades of green-yellow peas, or lavender flowers. Had Mendel chosen to investigate traits exist on a continuum— something like the height of humans, for example, which varies across a range—it would have been much harder for him to interpret his results.

Mendel knew that his true-bred plants, when self-pollinated, would give predictable results. But what would happen when he mated them? To figure this out, Mendel took his true-bred plants, and performed controlled cross-pollinations of plants with different traits. He took true-bred plants with yellow peas, for example, and crossed them with true-bred plants with green peas.

Mendel's result was surprising: all of the plants in this first generation of offspring produced yellow peas. Whatever "heritable factor" that caused plants to have green peas seemed to disappear in this first generation. But Mendel took his experiment further: he then cross-pollinated these first-generation plants with the pollen from other first-generation plants. What he found was even more surprising that his first result: of the offspring in the second generation of plants, approximately one-quarter had green peas. 6,022 produced yellow peas, while 2,001 produced green peas, a ratio of approximately 3:1. A diagram of Mendel's results can be seen in Figure 7-1.

Mendel repeated this experiment with plants true-bred for other traits. When he crossed true-bred plants that had purple flowers with true-bred plants that had white flowers, the first generation always had purple flowers. The second generation had plants of both purple and white flowers, again in a ratio of 3:1. Time after time, one of the traits seemed to disappear in the first generation, only to re-appear in approximately one-quarter of the total population of the second generation. Mendel realized that something was at work: that something is genes.

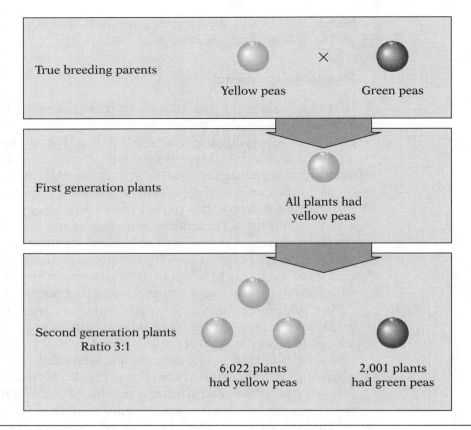

Figure 7-1 Mendel's results for his yellow-pea/green-pea experiments.

Law of Segregation

Mendel's discovery of the ability of certain traits to "skip" generations—that is, to completely disappear from one generation and then reappear in another— revealed an important principle of genetics: organisms with the same outward appearance could have different genes. Consider, for example, that Mendel's true-bred plants with yellow peas always produced offspring with yellow peas, whereas Mendel's first-generation plants were able to produce yellow-pea and green-pea offspring.

The word **phenotype** is used to describe the outward appearance created by a gene. Yellow seeds, purple flower petals, blue eyes—all of these are examples of phenotypes. Mendel's findings indicated that a distinction needs to be made between an organism's phenotype, or outward appearance, and its **genotype,** or the information contained in its genes, because two organisms with a similar phenotype could have a different genotype. Mendel observed two genotypes of yellow-seeded plants: one that always had yellow-seeded offspring, and one that occasionally had green-seeded offspring.

Mendel was able to draw a number of important conclusions from his results:

- *There are alternative versions of each gene, each of which corresponds to a different phenotype.* For example, there are versions of the gene for the color of the seed in pea plants: one yellow and one green. These different versions of the same gene are known as **alleles.**

- *Each organism has two alleles for each gene. One of these alleles came from each of the organism's parents.*
- *If the alleles are the same, then the organism will exhibit the phenotype for that allele.* If an organism has two copies of the allele for yellow seeds, it will have yellow peas. If it has two copies of the allele for green peas, it will have green peas.
- *If the alleles are different, then the phenotype for only one allele—the dominant allele—will be expressed.* The allele that is expressed is known as the **dominant allele.** The other allele, which is not expressed, is known as the **recessive allele.** For pea plants, the allele for yellow peas is the dominant allele, because plants with both yellow-pea and green-pea alleles have yellow peas.
- *An organism's alleles are segregated when it produces gametes.* This principle is known as the **law of segregation.** When an organism reproduces, it passes on only *one* of its alleles to its offspring. This segregation means that the offspring, too, will inherit two alleles, one from each parent, and so on. Each offspring has an equal chance of receiving one of the two alleles.

It should be noted that these ideas are only applicable to *sexually* reproducing organisms.

Mendel's conclusions provided an explanation for the results he obtained when he studied traits of the pea plant. Let's review his entire experiment using Mendel's theory of alleles.

- When Mendel began, his true-bred plants each had the same two alleles. The true-bred yellow-pea plant had two alleles for yellow peas, and passed these yellow-pea alleles on to its offspring, which were always yellow-pea plants. The true-bred green-pea plant had two alleles for green peas, and only passed these green-pea alleles on to its offspring, which were always green-pea plants.
- When Mendel crossed the two true-bred plants together, each one passed on one allele; all of the resulting plants had one yellow-pea allele, and one green-pea allele. Mendel observed that all of the plants in the first generation had the yellow-pea phenotype, indicating that the yellow-pea allele is the dominant allele, and that the green-pea allele is the recessive allele. This means that the green-pea allele, though present in all of the first generation plants, was not expressed physically.
- The law of segregation explains that when these first-generation plants were interbred, each one passed *either* a yellow-pea allele *or* a green-pea allele to its offspring. This process occurs randomly; on average, each allele will be passed on 50% of the time. This creates three possibilities for the offspring of the second gene.
  - Some of these offspring will inherit two yellow-pea alleles and will have yellow peas.
  - Some of these offspring will inherit one of each allele, but will have yellow peas because the yellow-pea alleles are dominant.
  - Some of these offspring will inherit two green-pea alleles and will have green peas.

Mendel, in fact, observed that while most of the offspring in the second generation had the yellow-pea appearance, the green-pea phenotype returned in the second generation.

Mendel's observation that one quarter of the second generation displayed the recessive trait (in this case, green peas) can be explained through the laws of probability. Mendel's law of segregation holds that each of the first-generation plants has a 50% chance of passing on the recessive (green-pea) allele. For a plant of the second generation to have green peas, however, it must inherit a green pea allele from *both* of their parents. To calculate the possibility that these two independent events will occur, we multiply the probability that each will happen. The chances are thus $0.50 \times 0.50 = 0.25$, or 25%, that a second-generation plant will have both of the recessive alleles, and will have green peas. And, indeed, Mendel observed that approximately 25% of his second-generation plants displayed the green-pea trait.

Today, we use specific terms to better describe the genotypes that Mendel observed. An organism is **homozygous** if it has the same two alleles for a trait. If the organism has both dominant alleles, it is known as **homozygous dominant;** if it has both recessive alleles, it is known as **homozygous recessive.** An organism that has two different alleles—carrying both the dominant and the recessive alleles—is known as **heterozygous.** (a.k.a. "hybrid").

Recall that heterozygous organisms will display the trait carried by the dominant allele, because the effect of the recessive allele will be masked. The recessive phenotype is displayed only in the homozygous-recessive phenotype. Because heterozygous organisms are able to pass on the recessive trait but do not themselves express the trait, they are often referred to as **carriers** of the recessive phenotype.

These terms are especially important in distinguishing between plants that are of the same phenotype but have two different genotypes. For example, Mendel's original true-bred plant that gave yellow peas was homozygous dominant. His first-generation plants, which were all yellow-pea plants, but had one of each allele, were heterozygous.

Modeling Mendel's Experiment: Punnett Squares

A **Punnett square** is a highly useful way to model the possible patterns of inheritance caused by the passing of alleles in Mendelian inheritance. Punnett squares allow biologists to look at all of the genotypic combinations that are possible from the mating of two organisms.

Punnett squares use letters to symbolize the different alleles that can be passed. A capital letter is generally used to describe the dominant allele, while a lower-case letter is used to describe the recessive allele. For yellow and green peas, for example, a "Y" indicates a dominant allele, while a "y" generally indicates a recessive allele. Homozygous dominant organisms are written as YY, heterozygous organisms are written as Yy, and homozygous recessive organisms are written as yy. This shorthand can be useful when trying to figure out the offspring that will result from a certain combination of parents.

Say, for example, we wish to model the potential offspring of the first-generation pea plants in Mendel's experiment. We would do so by writing all of the possible alleles that one parent could pass on the top of our Punnett square and the same for the other parent on the left of the Punnett square. In this example, there are two possibilities for each of these plants; they can pass on either a Y or a y. These would be indicated on the top and side of a diagram, as shown in Figure 7-2.

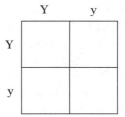

Figure 7-2 Punnett Square.

Then, to fill in the blanks of the Punnett square, we write in the allele that is indicated in each column and row. For example, in the top left square, there is a Y from one parent (on the top) and a Y from the other parent (to the left). This square should this be filled in YY. In the top right square, there is a y from one parent (on the top) and a Y from the other (to the left). Because, by convention, we write the capital first, the resulting organism will be Yy. Using this same pattern, the Punnett square can be filled in as shown in Figure 7-3.

	Y	y
Y	YY	Yy
y	Yy	yy

Figure 7-3 Punnett Square.

This filled-in Punnett square models all of the possible offspring that can result from the cross of two heterozygous organisms. It cannot tell us the exact number of each genotype that will be produced, but it can tell us the probability that each genotype will be produced. Each of these squares represents an equally likely offspring to be produced from these two parents. In this case, we can see that, on average 1/4 of the organisms will be heterozygous dominant, 1/2 will be heterozygous, and 1/4 will be homozygous recessive.

Figure 7-3 has also been shaded in to indicate which of these offspring will display the dominant phenotype, and which of these offspring will display the recessive phenotype. Here, the shaded organisms will have the dominant phenotype. Note that there is a 3:1 ratio of organisms with the dominant phenotype to organisms with the recessive phenotype. In other words, there is a 1/4 possibility—or 25% chance—that an organism of the second generation will display the recessive phenotype. Note that this corresponds closely to what Mendel observed in his second-generation offspring of pea plants. We'll learn more abut how to use Punnett squares to model patterns of inheritance in Lesson 7-4.

Law of Independent Assortment

Mendel's research was an important beginning, but he had more questions. Specifically, Mendel needed to establish whether or not there was a link in the inheritance of two different characteristics. For example: would the dominant "heritable factor" that caused a plant to have yellow peas the same one that caused them to have purple flowers? Or were the traits inherited by two different heritable factors?

Mendel set up a similar experiment to his first, starting with plants that were true-bred. This time, however, he looked at plants that were true-bred for two traits: certain plants always produced offspring with yellow and round peas, while other plants always produced offspring with green and wrinkled peas. In the first generation, all of the plants came out yellow and round, indicated that the alleles for yellow peas and round peas were dominant.

But it was the second-generation plants that were important for Mendel's conclusion. Mendel needed to know if it was possible for the two traits to be inherited independently of each other. The heterozygous plants of the first generation had received a set of dominant alleles from one parent, and one set of recessive alleles from the other parent. Was it possible for them to mix these up, passing on one dominant allele and one recessive allele? Or did they necessarily pass on the same set of all-dominant or all-recessive alleles? In terms of his plants, Mendel wanted to see if it was possible for the second-generation plants to have the dominant gene for one characteristic (pea color) while having a recessive gene for another characteristic (pea shape)?

Mendel's answer was that yes, the two genes are inherited independently of each other. In his second generation, there were many pea plants that had yellow and wrinkled peas, while there were others that had green and round peas, as shown in Figure 7-4. Although many of the plants did, indeed, display both of the dominant traits, or both of the recessive traits, there were some that did not. This indicates that just because an organism received dominant traits one parent and recessive traits from the other, it did not pass them along in the same way.

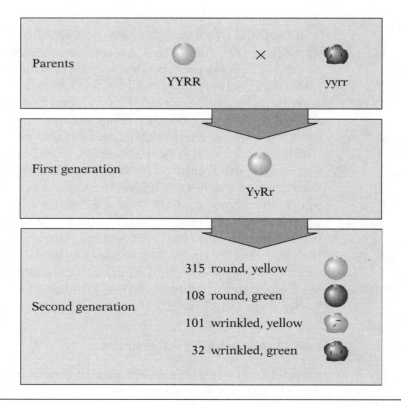

Figure 7-4 Results from Mendel's experiment leading to the Law of Independent Assortment.

Mendel, thus, developed his second law, the **law of independent assortment.** The law of independent assortment holds that the alleles for each trait are inherited separately from each other. This means that the inheritance of the alleles for pea color has nothing to do with the inheritance of the alleles for pea shape, or for flower color.

The law of independent assortment allows for a greater genetic variation in organisms, because it indicates that organisms are capable of passing on their alleles in different combinations from the ones that they inherited from their parents. This greatly increases the total number of genetic combinations that are possible, because it means that not all characteristics are inherited together. Think of our genes as a basket of characteristics that we pass onto our descendants. The law of independent assortment means that instead of coming in a small number of prepackaged combinations, our alleles are passed on in more of a mix-and-match fashion, which greatly increases the number of potential combinations.

Mendelian Inheritance in Humans

Although Mendelian inheritance is a relatively simple concept, it in fact dictates the way in which a number of human traits are inherited. Later, we'll look at a number of traits that are inherited in a more complex fashion, and we'll discuss the how the molecules we learned about in the last chapter—DNA, RNA, and proteins—relate to these concepts of inheritance. Before ending this lesson, however, we'll take a brief look at some of the many traits in human beings that are inherited through simple Mendelian inheritance—traits you might even look for in your own family.

- The ability to sense certain bitter tastes, which can be tested by giving individuals a test strip of paper with the chemical phenylthiocarbamide (PTC) on it, is a dominantly inherited trait. The 30% of the population that does not have this trait cannot taste PTC at all.
- Attached earlobes—earlobes that are attached to the side of the skull, as opposed to hanging freely at the bottom, are recessively inherited. Only individuals with both recessive alleles will have attached earlobes.
- The Rhesus, or Rh, factor, is the name for the "positive" or "negative" that is included in one's blood type (for example, A negative, or B positive). Like one's blood group (A, B, AB, or O) the Rhesus factor determines the compatibility of donated blood; Rh+ (Rh negative) individuals can receive both Rh+ and Rh– blood, while Rh– individuals can only receive Rh– blood. The allele that causes blood to be Rh+ is a dominant allele; only homozygous recessive individuals are Rh–.

Many human disorders are recessively inherited:

- Sickle-cell anemia is a disorder that causes the protein hemoglobin to have an abnormal shape. This results in deformed red blood cells, and can cause a number of serious problems including physical weakness and paralysis, brain damage, or heart failure. Individuals who are heterozygous for this gene, however, seem to have increased immunity to malaria, a mosquito-borne disease that is responsible for millions of deaths in the tropical regions of the globe.

- Cystic fibrosis is a disease that affects the ability of cells to transport chloride ions. As a result, affected individuals develop large amounts of mucus in their lungs and other organs, which leaves them prone to bacterial infections. It is especially common among Caucasians in the United States.
- Tay-Sachs disease is caused by the inability to break down certain lipids in the brain. The disease causes severe neural damage, leading to epilepsy, blindness, and death within the first few years of life. The gene that causes Tay-Sachs is especially common among Ashkenazi Jews, and many Ashkenazi Jews choose to have their genes examined to determine if they are heterozygous carriers of the disorder—a process known as *genetic screening*.

There are some disorders that are dominantly inherited:

- Polydactyly is a condition in which an individual has more than five fingers or toes. Occasionally, these extra fingers are fully developed and useful; other times they are not usable, and can be removed by surgery during childhood.
- Huntington's disease is a disease that causes deterioration of the nervous system. Most healthy individuals have both recessive alleles for this disease, but, because it is dominantly inherited, anyone with the heterozygous trait will develop the disease. Because the disease does not cause any known symptoms until the affected individual is 35 or 45, the affected heterozygous individual often has children who then have a 50% chance of developing the disorder themselves.

LESSON SUMMARY

- Gregor Mendel used experiments in pea plants to discover the basic principles of inheritance.
- Mendel discovered that each trait he studied was caused by two alleles, one from each of a plant's parents. Different traits (e.g., purple vs. white flowers) are caused by alternate versions of each allele.
- Genotype describes the alleles in an organism's genes. Phenotype describes the physical traits of that organism.
- Organisms may have two of the same allele (in which case they are known as homozygous) or may have two different alleles (in which case they are known as heterozygous). If an organism has two different alleles, the allele that is displayed in the phenotype is known as the dominant allele; the allele that is hidden is the recessive allele.
- Organisms pass one—not both—of these alleles on to their offspring; this is known as Mendel's law of segregation.
- Mendel's law of independent assortment holds that the alleles for different traits are inherited independently of each other. Organisms may pass on alleles in a different combination than how they inherited them.
- Many human traits and disorders are inherited through simply Mendelian inheritance, among which are sickle-cell anemia (which is recessively inherited) and Huntington's disease (which is dominantly inherited).

REVIEW QUESTIONS

1. Sickle-cell anemia is a recessively inherited disorder that affects the protein hemoglobin in red blood cells. The possible genotypes of individuals with sickle-cell anemia include the following:

    (A) *RR*
    (B) *Rr*
    (C) *rr*
    (D) *RR* or *Rr*
    (E) *Rr* or *rr*

2. Purple flowers are a dominant trait. Mendel used plants in his experiment that were true-bred for purple flowers, meaning that, when this plant was self-pollinated, its offspring always displayed purple flowers. Which of the following describes the possible genotype for this plant?

    (A) *PP*
    (B) *Pp*
    (C) *pp*
    (D) *PP* or *pp*
    (E) *Pp* or *pp*

3. Which of the following statements about dominantly inherited traits is NOT true?

    (A) Dominant traits may be passed on to offspring.
    (B) Some individuals in a population may not display dominant traits.
    (C) Individuals may be heterozygous and still display dominant traits.
    (D) To inherit these traits, they must occur in both parents.
    (E) Displaying this trait requires at least one dominant allele.

4. A mother is a carrier of the gene for a disorder but does not display the disorder. Which of the following statements is NOT true about this disorder?

    (A) It is not possible for her children to have this disorder.
    (B) The disorder is recessively inherited.
    (C) The mother is heterozygous for the disorder.
    (D) Her parents may not have been affected by this disorder.
    (E) One of her children may be a carrier for this disorder.

5. Polydactyly—having more than five fingers or toes—is a dominant trait. Which of the following is a possible genotype for someone with this trait?

    I.   homozygous dominant
    II. homozygous recessive
    III. heterozygous

    (A) I only
    (B) II only
    (C) I and II only
    (D) I and III only
    (E) I, II, and III

6. A researcher mates two mice who express a dominant trait. Yet three of the eight offspring display the recessive trait. Which of the following describes the genotypes of the parent mice?

   (A) Both are *GG*.
   (B) Both are *Gg*.
   (C) Both are *gg*.
   (D) One parent is *GG* while the other parent is *Gg*.
   (E) One parent is *GG* while the other parent is *gg*.

ANSWERS

1. **C** Sickle-cell anemia is recessively inherited. Individuals with this trait must, therefore, have both recessive alleles. The only possible phenotype, then, is *rr*.

2. **A** All of the offspring of this plant have the dominant trait. This means that it is passing on only dominant alleles to its children. It must be homozygous dominant—or *PP*—for this trait.

3. **D** Dominantly inherited traits, like all traits, may be passed on to offspring. Statement (B) may be eliminated because some individuals may be recessive for the trait. Because the trait is dominant, heterozygous individuals *will* display the trait, so statements (C) and (E) are true. Statement (D), however, is false; only one parent is required to display this trait in order for it to be inherited; the other parent may be recessive for the trait.

4. **A** Carriers of a disorder who do not display the disorder must be heterozygous for that trait. The disorder must be recessively inherited, because one cannot be a carrier of a dominant trait without expressing that trait. Her parents, as well, may have been carriers of this trait, as may one of her children, if they are also heterozygous. Her children, however, can inherit this trait if they inherit a recessive allele from their father as well.

5. **D** A dominant trait will be expressed by individuals who are either homozygous dominant or heterozygous for that trait.

6. **B** The parents express the dominant trait, so both must have at least one dominant allele, which rules out (C) and (E). (A) and (D) cannot possibly produce offspring with the recessive trait, because there is no way for the offspring to inherit two recessive alleles. (B) is the only way to produce the results that the scientist noted.

Lesson 7-2. The Genetic Bases of Inheritance

VOCABULARY

- gene
- mutant
- wild-type
- chromosomes
- autosomes
- sex chromosomes
- homologous
- genetic recombination
- linked genes
- nondisjunction
- monosomic

- trisomic
- Down syndrome
- translocation
- polymerase chain reaction
- DNA fingerprinting
- restriction enzymes
- gel electrophoresis
- recombinant DNA technology
- transgenic organism
- clone
- *Escherichia coli*, or *E. coli*

The diversity of life is truly remarkable, encompassing species from the microscopic to the enormous, occupying almost every habitat on Earth. What makes each of these species different are the instructions that are carried within each of their cells, in the form of DNA. In this section, we'll discover the molecular basis behind Mendelian inheritance. We'll tie in many of the cellular processes that we learned about in Chapter 6 and see how genetics is an essential part of how life propagates.

DNA: THE GENETIC MATERIAL

As we learned in the last chapter, DNA, or deoxyribonucleic acid, is a large molecule created by linking two strands of nucleotides, forming a shape known as a double helix. Nucleotides, as we learned, are the monomers of DNA. These nucleotides are named for the nitrogenous base which extends from the sugar–phosphate backbone of the nucleotide strand. There are four types of nucleotides found in DNA: adenine (A), cytosine (C), guanine (G), and thymine (T). Recall that nucleotides are only able to match up in specific combinations: adenine in one strand pairs only with thymine in the complementary strand, while cytosine pairs only with guanine. The double-helix shape of DNA, and the base-pairing that makes up the basic structure of DNA, was discovered in 1953 by James Watson and Francis Crick.

Today, we take for granted that DNA is the material that contains the instructions for cells. However, this fact was not widely accepted until the early 1950s. Before then, many scientists thought that the material that contained the instructions for the cell was not DNA, but proteins. Scientists thought that only proteins, with their wide variety of shapes and sizes, were versatile enough to make up the genetic material. DNA, with only four nucleotide bases (as opposed to the 20 different amino acids that are the monomers of proteins) did not seem to contain enough possible combinations to serve as a biological language for encoding information.

You may recall that RNA, or ribonucleic acid, serves as an intermediate product between DNA and the protein that it encodes for. RNA combines nucleotides into groups of three, known as codons. These codons serve as the basic unit that is in the ribosome read to make proteins. In this way, the "language" of RNA uses its four "letters" to form 64 different codons, which correspond to specific amino acids. As we learned in Chapter 6, Lesson 6-4, the first step in carrying out the instructions contained in DNA is converting the DNA into a single strand of RNA known as messenger RNA, or mRNA, in the process known as transcription. RNA, as we learned, is like DNA in that it is made up of nucleotides, although its nucleotides have a slightly different sugar present in the sugar–phosphate backbone. RNA does not have thymine nucleotides, either; instead, it uses uracil (U).

Messenger RNA serves as a template for the production of polypeptide chains in a process known as translation. In translation, mRNA is fed, three nucleotides (or one codon) at a time, into the ribosome, where it matches with a corresponding transfer RNA, or tRNA, molecule, carrying the appropriate amino acid. One by one, these amino acids are linked together by peptide bonds, forming the polypeptides that make up proteins. Proteins may be made up of one or many polypeptides, depending on the size of the protein.

Within our DNA, there are instructions for thousands of different proteins. Each section of DNA that codes for a discrete protein or polypeptide is known as a **gene.** The genes of our DNA are now known to be the heritable factor that Mendel described in his research. DNA is the raw information that codes for life. More than just an abstract molecule, DNA contains encoded instructions that determine much about us: How many limbs? How long? How many fingers? Opposable thumb? Nails? Our DNA contains a spectacular amount of information.

MENDEL AND MOLECULES

It is one thing to understand that DNA codes for proteins. But understanding the mechanisms of how that DNA is inherited, and how exactly Mendel's vision of dominant and recessive "heritable factors" relates to that DNA, requires more investigation. In this section, we'll investigate these genetic bases of inheritance.

Alleles and DNA

In the last chapter, you learned about sickle-cell anemia. This disease is actually caused by a single changed nucleotide; the gene that causes sickle-cell anemia has an adenine where it should have a thymine, resulting in the insertion of a valine into a polypeptide where there should be a glutamic acid. This different version of the gene is referred to as the **mutant** gene because it contains a mutation that causes abnormal function of the protein. The more commonly occurring version is known as the **wild-type** version of the gene.

Yet in the last lesson, you also learned that sickle-cell anemia is a recessively inherited trait, meaning that unless someone inherits two disease-causing alleles, they will not display symptoms of the disease. How can you reconcile this Mendelian view of sickle-cell anemia with the molecular view?

To understand this, it's important to understand the structure of DNA in the cell, as discussed in the last chapter. Our cell's DNA is generally tightly bound and folded into **chromosomes.** Each human cell contains not one, but sets of each chromosome; a normal human cell, then, has 23 *pairs* of chromosomes, for 46 total chromosomes. Twenty-two of these chromosomes are what is known as **autosomes;** the last pair constitutes the **sex chromosomes,** which, in humans, come in two varieties: X and Y (sex chromosomes will be discussed further in the next lesson). A cell that contains one pair of each chromosome is said to be diploid.

Each of these pairs of chromosomes (except, in males the sex chromosomes) constitutes what known as a **homologous** pair. This means that although the chromosomes may not be exactly the same in size or sequence, they are roughly the same size, and generally contain copies of the same genes. As you learned, through a process known as meiosis, organisms are able to create gametes, cells that are haploid (containing only one set of chromosomes). When a female gamete (egg, or ovum) is fertilized by a male gamete (sperm), the two haploid sets of DNA combine to form one diploid organism. This process then repeats in the next generation.

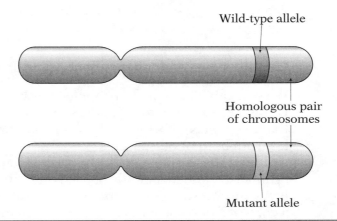

Figure 7-5 Two chromosomes, with the same gene on each chromosome, showing a different allele (wt vs. mutant).

Homologous pairs of chromosomes are the molecules behind Mendelian inheritance. Mendel observed that every organism contained two alleles for each characteristic, and we now know that organisms have homologous pairs of chromosomes, each chromosome containing one allele—a copy of a gene for a specific trait (see Figure 7-5). Mendel also observed that one of these alleles came from each of the organism's parents. We know now that organisms inherit one set of chromosomes from each of the haploid gametes that came from their parents. From each of these gametes, an organism inherits one allele for each trait.

How is it, then, that there can be different alleles for each trait? What is the molecular basis for these different alleles? And how can they be different? Here, the case of sickle-cell anemia is instructive. The gene for normal hemoglobin, the wild-type, has a different nucleotide sequence from the allele that causes the disease, the mutant version. Different alleles, then, are simply corresponding stretches of DNA with different sequences, producing different results. The wild-type, with the normal nucleotide sequence, corresponds to the dominant allele, and the mutant, with the slightly modified nucleotide sequence that leads to sickle-cell disease, corresponds to the recessive allele.

It is easy to see then, how an organism with two copies of each gene would display the phenotype caused by that gene. It makes sense that an organism with two normal copies of the hemoglobin gene would have normally functioning hemoglobin, and that an organism with two mutated copies of the hemoglobin gene might experience disease. But what about the heterozygous individual, who has one wild-type gene and one mutant gene? What makes the DNA of the wild-type dominant to the recessive DNA of the mutant?

The answer is that on a molecular level, there is nothing that makes one gene dominant while the other gene is recessive. What makes a gene dominant or recessive is its effect on the phenotype. If one copy of the wild-type gene is adequate to cover up for the existence of the mutant gene, for example, then the wild-type gene will be dominant. If not, then the mutant gene will be dominant. In the example of sickle-cell anemia, a heterozygous individual has both the wild-type and mutant genes, and produces both normal and the disease-causing hemoglobin. But heterozygous individuals have enough of the normal hemoglobin that, in most circumstances, they never experience any of the negative effects of sickle-cell disease. Thus, the wild-type gene is said to be dominant.

Chromosomes and Independent Assortment

We've established, then, the molecular basis for Mendel's law of segregation. But what accounts for Mendel's law of independent assortment? How is it that our alleles "mix themselves" so that our gametes inherit a mixture of alleles from both of our parents?

If two alleles are on different chromosomes, it's easy to see how they might be inherited independently of each other. It makes sense that, when an organism's chromosomes are separating during meiosis II, a gamete might inherit a copy of a chromosome that came from the organism's mother, while at the same time inheriting a copy of another chromosome that came from the father. Thus, the fact that our genes are on different chromosomes—discrete stretches of DNA that are copied and then segregated into our gametes—provides one mechanism for genes to "mix and match."

But what about genes that are located on the same chromosome? Are they inherited independently from each other, as Mendel's law of independent assortment dictates? Well, it's true that genes on the same chromosome are inherited together more often than genes on a different chromosome, which makes them to some extent an exception to Mendel's law. However, it is possible for genes that are located on the *same* chromosome to originate from different parents, making that chromosome somehow an amalgam of DNA from both your mother and your father.

This is a result of the process known as crossing-over. You learned in the last chapter that during meiosis I, a large amount of time is devoted to the exchange of DNA between homologous chromosomes. This crossing-over produces chromosomes that are made of DNA from both of our parents, allowing for the independent assortment even of genes that are on the same chromosomes (see Figure 7-6). This "mixing and matching" of DNA on the same chromosome, as a result of crossing over, is known as **genetic recombination.**

As discussed in the previous section, genetic recombination is an important process because it allows genes to be combined in new ways. This new combination of traits increases the genetic variation within a species. A greater amount of variation is important if species are to be able to adapt to changing environmental conditions.

Crossing over, however, is still a complicated and imperfect process, and it does not completely exchange all of the DNA on each pair of homologous chromosomes. Indeed, because crossing over only occurs a finite number of

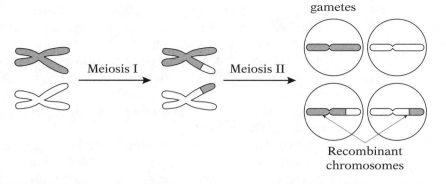

Figure 7-6 Chromosomes swap DNA during crossing over, creating genetic recombination.

times, genes that are located closer to each other on a chromosome are more likely to be inherited together. This provides an exception to Mendel's law of independent assortment, because it means that genes located close to each other on a chromosome are not always inherited independently.

Genes that are often inherited together, because of their proximity to each other on a chromosome, are known as **linked genes.** Linked genes are a useful tool for mapping the location of genes on a certain chromosome. Because genes that are closer to each other are linked more frequently than genes that are distant, scientists can tell which genes are located close to each other on the chromosome based on the frequency with which they are linked. This allows scientists to create what is known as a linkage map—a diagram of the relative distance between genes on the same chromosome.

These linked genes are another example of the limits of Mendel's laws when applied to the molecular level. The law of independent assortment, although it does apply for many genes, is nevertheless *not strictly adhered to* when one considers genes that are located on the same chromosome.

CHROMOSOMAL ABERRATIONS

One important topic of the last chapter was the possibility of a mistake in the replication of DNA. Such mutations can occur any time DNA is copied, and other environmental factors—the presence of certain chemicals, or of ultraviolet rays—can also contribute to the mutation of DNA. These mutations, as we learned, can occasionally have no effect at all, but can also occasionally cause potentially nonfunctional proteins.

Yet, it's also possible for mistakes to be made at the chromosome level. One of the most common mistakes occurs during meiosis I or II, when chromosomes are supposed to separate, creating haploid gametes. Occasionally, the two chromosomes in a homologous pair do not properly separate, and one or more gametes will end up short a chromosome, while others can end up with one chromosome too many. This failure of chromosomes to properly separate is a condition called **nondisjunction.** A cell that has only one copy of a given chromosome is said to be **monosomic,** while a cell that has three copies of a given chromosome is said to be **trisomic.**

Most embryos that are monosomic or trisomic are not able to survive to childbirth. Certain cases of nondisjunction, however, create viable embryos. **Down syndrome** is the most common form of human trisomy; it is caused by trisomy of chromosome 21. Down syndrome causes mental retardation, and a set of distinct physical and facial features; affected individuals generally have a shorter life span than normal, and are usually sterile.

Monosomy and trisomies of the sex chromosomes are especially well tolerated. Individuals with three X chromosomes (XXX) are generally healthy, as are males born with an extra Y chromosome (XYY). Males with an extra X chromosome (XXY), a condition known as Klinefelter syndrome, are generally sterile, as are females who only have one X chromosome, a condition known as Turner syndrome.

Occasionally, organisms are able to function with more than two copies of their entire set of chromosome—a condition known as polyploidy. Polyploidy is especially common in the plant kingdom (strawberries, for example).

Other chromosomal disorders are caused not by nondisjunction, but by breakage of a chromosome. Occasionally, a segment of a chromosome can be deleted, duplicated, or even inverted (turned around in order). Occasionally, the end of one chromosome will break off and switch places with the end of another, nonhomologous chromosome, a process known as **translocation.**

Such mistakes as these, which involve chromosome structure, and not number, are especially common in meiosis, during the process of crossing over. During crossing over, chromosomes are exchanging their DNA, It's not difficult to imagine that DNA may re-attach in the incorrect place, or may not be swapped correctly, leaving one chromosome with two copies of the same stretch of DNA, and the other with that stretch of DNA completely absent. Translocations, however, can and do occur at any time.

The absence of a significant number of genes, as occurs in deletion, is generally a lethal condition. However, even duplication, inversion, and translocation, although they provide the cell with a complete set of genes, can lead to disorders. This is because the structure of the cell's DNA is important for the control of gene expression. Translocation of certain chromosomes has been linked to a form of leukemia, a cancer that affects blood cells.

GENETIC TECHNOLOGY

Genetic research has led to a far greater understanding of the makeup and mechanisms of DNA and our genes, but as our understanding of genetics has improved, so, too, has our ability to use genetics as a tool for other ends. Our growing understanding of bacteria and viruses would be rather impossible without the genetic tools to understand the genomes of these organisms, as would our investigations into the workings of the human body. In this last section, we'll review some of the common mechanisms and methods that allow researchers to investigate the genome.

Copying and Sequencing DNA

One of the most important technologies are used today in dealing with DNA is the **polymerase chain reaction,** or PCR. PCR is a method of amplifying (that is, rapidly copying) DNA in the laboratory; it works by heating DNA so that the two complementary strands separate, and then allows DNA polymerase to duplicate each DNA strand. Essential to this process are short, artificially created DNA sequences known as primers, which attach to the DNA strands to be copied and provide an initiation point for the DNA polymerase. This cycle is repeated numerous times to produce multiple copies of DNA—which are necessary for a number of the technologies described below. Without PCR, few of the technologies we will discuss below would be available.

One common DNA technology that many people are familiar with is **DNA fingerprinting,** which is used to prove or disprove identity based on an individual's genetic sequence. DNA fingerprinting utilizes the activity of proteins known as **restriction enzymes,** which were found to cleave, or cut, DNA when they encountered a specific sequence in the DNA. Different sequences of DNA will be cleaved in different places, meaning that each individual's DNA sample will be broken up into fragments of different length, depending on their specific genetic makeup—allowing scientists who can measure the length of these fragments to differentiate between DNA from different individuals, or match a DNA sample to its owner.

The method that scientists use to determine the lengths of these fragments is known as **gel electrophoresis.** Gel electrophoresis uses an electric current to separate and arrange the different cleaved DNA fragments by length. DNA molecules have a negative charge and are thus attracted to the positive terminus of the gel. Shorter fragments will be pulled farther through the gelatin medium by the current, and so will separate from the larger, slower-moving fragments. DNA samples from the same individual will have fragments that travel equal distances; DNA from different individuals will have different lengths and will have traveled different distances.

Gel electropharesis is also an important tool that researchers use to identify the exact nucleotide sequence of a strand of DNA, a process known as DNA sequencing. The Human Genome Project, a worldwide DNA sequencing effort, was assembled in 1990 to give the exact DNA sequence of the human genome. Since then, the genomes of a number of other organisms has been sequenced; these organisms include viruses and bacteria, plants such as corn and rice, and such animals as mice. These sequences, it is hoped, will allow us to identify the location of genes for certain traits. It already allows us to identify individuals who carry the genes for certain genetic disorders, such as Huntington's disease or Tay-Sachs disease.

Recombination and Cloning

Perhaps the most significant DNA technology that has been developed is that known as **recombinant DNA technology.** Recombinant DNA (not to be confused with the natural process of genetic recombination that occurs during meiosis) is DNA that comes from more than one source. Recombinant DNA is often the result of researchers inserting a gene from one organism into the genome of another. This process requires first that scientists identify the specific gene that they want to insert in an organism, and that they have a vector—a method of inserting this specific gene into the cell so that it will be copied and expressed. Commonly used vectors include viruses (which are naturally able to inject their own genetic material into cells), bacteria, or special machines for injecting DNA into a cell known as "gene guns." This process of adding genes to organisms is known as genetic engineering.

Recombinant DNA technology has been used to create **transgenic organisms**—organisms whose genome contains DNA from another species. One famous example of a transgenic organism was a tobacco plant able to produce a protein that caused it to glow in the dark; recently, a transgenic rabbit able to glow under ultraviolet light was also created. Genetic engineering, however, has many practical applications: in plants, for example, genetic recombination has been used to produce specific chemicals that render crops immune to the effects of pests or disease. One breed of rice was genetically engineered to produce vitamin A, making this staple of much of the developing world also a cure for a common vitamin deficiency.

One of the more controversial uses of genetic engineering has been to **clone** organisms. Cloning is the process of taking the DNA from the cell of an organism and to create another, genetically identical organism. In mammals, cloning generally entails removing the DNA from a cell, and inserting this DNA in the place of the DNA of a fertilized egg, which then develops with this new set of genetic instructions. This process is often difficult, because, as we develop, many portions of our DNA are deactivated, so that cells can specialize for their specific function (nerve cells, for example, utilize genes that muscle cells do not need). Often, there are also complications resulting from the fact that our DNA can accumulate errors over time. However, several mammals have been cloned successfully, including sheep and cats.

Model Organisms

Studying genetics would be rather impossible without nonhuman model organisms in which to study the effects of genes. Understanding how the instructions of DNA are carried out requires the ability to alter DNA, and then see its effects in an organism. Doing such research on humans would be neither ethical nor especially effective because the time required to raise a human being is much longer than the time required to raise many other organisms.

Researchers use a number of model organisms to study the properties of genes. Such model organisms all have similar attributes: they all have rather short life cycles, so that many generations can be reproduced in a relatively short amount of time. They are all rather easily bred in controlled settings, which is necessary for researchers to be able to eliminate the influence of environmental factors on their research. And they all are able to reproduce in rather large numbers, which allows scientists a large number of organisms to test their hypotheses and develop results to a high degree of scientific certainty.

For studies into the genomes of bacteria (which, as prokaryotes, have a much more simple mode of inheritance than the complex mechanisms we've discussed here), the most common organism is a bacteria known as ***Escherichia coli,*** commonly abbreviated ***E. coli.*** Although most of the public knowledge of *E. coli* has centered on the potentially lethal effects of one strain of *E. coli* (strain O157:H7), *E. coli* is in fact a rather common bacteria that inhabits the lower intestinal tract of all human beings in enormous numbers—on the order of 10^{10} bacteria per person. Not only is *E. Coli* common, it's also quite useful to humans in that they synthesize much-needed vitamin K and B-complex vitamins in our intestines.

E. coli have been used to understand the basic mechanisms of gene control (operons) and have also proved ready organisms for genetic recombination. One of the first transgenic organisms was, in fact, a strain of *E. coli* with the gene for the human hormone insulin inserted into its genome. Insulin produced by *E. coli* provides the daily injection of insulin required by diabetics worldwide.

In the plant kingdom, the most common model organism is a member of the mustard family *Arabidopsis thaliana,* the common wall cress. *Arabidopsis* is especially useful because it has an extremely short life cycle—only 10 weeks are required for each generation—and because plants can be grown in a test tube. *Arabidopsis* also has a relatively small genome—which has already been sequenced—and rather easily takes up DNA that scientists try to insert. Other model organisms in the plant kingdom include the common crops corn and rice; the interest in these plants is largely driven by their agricultural importance.

There are, in addition, a number of model organisms that have been used to understand the animal kingdom. One of the most common in the early days of genetics was a species of fruit fly that is now often used to illustrate the principles of genetics in high school laboratory experiments: *Drosophila melanogaster*. *Drosophila*, which also have a rather small genome, were extremely useful in understanding the principles of genetics (sex-linked genes were first discovered in *Drosophila*) and continue to be important in understanding how organisms develop from a single cell to their mature form.

Another extremely important organism for understanding the development of organisms is *Caenorhabditis elegans*, a nematode worm, normally living in soil, that can be easily cultured in petri dishes. The development of *C. elegans* has been extensively studied (a feat made easier by the fact that *C. elegans* is completely transparent), so that we now understand the lineage of cells in *C. elegans* starting from its origins as a newly fertilized zygote, and can identify which cells will become the nervous system, or the intestine, or the skin.

Perhaps the most important animal model, especially for modeling many human diseases, is the common mouse, *Mus musculus*. Mice are especially useful for modeling diseases in mammals, and extensive genetic research has been done in mice by observing what are known as "knock-out" mice, mice in whom genes have been simply eliminated, or "knocked out" in an effort to determine their function. Using genetic recombination, we can, for example, replicate the human immune system in mice, which allows us to study many diseases of the immune system. Mice have the advantage of being relatively small—making them easy to keep in a laboratory—and have a much shorter life cycle than humans. Other rodents, such as the rat and hamster, also occasionally prove useful in genetic studies. Without the sacrifices of all of these model organisms, our understanding of genetics—and of ourselves—would not be nearly as advanced as it is today.

LESSON SUMMARY

- DNA is the genetic material. It encodes instructions for proteins in discrete units known as genes. These genes are responsible for all of our traits.
- Organisms have two alleles for the same gene result from copies of genes located on homologous chromosomes. Different alleles for a gene are caused by differing nucleotide sequences in a gene.
- Independent assortment of traits is a result of the independent assortment of chromosomes, and the crossing over of DNA during meiosis.
- Genes that are located close to each other on the same chromosome are often inherited together; these linked genes are an exception to Mendel's law of independent assortment.
- Nondisjunction—the improper separation of chromosomes during meiosis—can result in chromosomal aberrations, as can inversions, deletions, duplications, or translocations.
- Genetic technology can be used to sequence DNA and to rapidly copy it for other uses. Scientists can also use recombinant DNA technology to insert a gene from one organism into another.

- Many organisms such as *E. coli, C. elegans, Arabidopsis,* and the common mouse provide a useful model for performing genetic research in a controlled setting.

REVIEW QUESTIONS

1. Which is the name for the procedure that involves taking a gene from one species and inserting it into the genome of another?

   (A) gel electrophoresis
   (B) DNA sequencing
   (C) recombinant DNA technology
   (D) crossing over
   (E) DNA fingerprinting

Questions 2 and 3: Select which one of the following choices best matches the statements below. Some choices may be used once, more than once, or not at all.

   (A) 23
   (B) 24
   (C) 45
   (D) 46
   (E) 47

2. Down syndrome is caused by trisomy of chromosome 21. How many chromosomes will be present in the cells of an individual with Down syndrome?
3. How many chromosomes are present in a human gamete?
4. Which of the following statements about homologous chromosomes is NOT true?

   (A) They may carry different alleles for a given gene.
   (B) They may carry the same allele for a given gene.
   (C) They may exchange DNA during meiosis.
   (D) They are not present in haploid cells.
   (E) They come from the same parent.

5. Which of the following statements about genes is NOT true?

   (A) Genes may be transcribed into messenger RNA.
   (B) Genes are copied during translation.
   (C) Genes may contain the instructions for proteins.
   (D) Genes are located on chromosomes.
   (E) Genes consist of DNA.

6. An organism has two different alleles for the same gene. Which of the following statements about this organism is true?

   I.   It could be described as heterozygous.
   II. Its homologous chromosomes contain different DNA sequences.
   III. Its offspring cannot be homozygous for that gene.

   (A) I only
   (B) II only
   (C) III only
   (D) I and II only
   (E) II and III only

7. Which of the following terms describes the exchange of DNA between homologous chromosomes?

   (A) transgenic
   (B) crossing over
   (C) cloning
   (D) translation
   (E) nondisjunction

8. A teacher is trying to set up a lab experiment to illustrate Mendel's law of independent assortment to his students. He wants to show them how two traits in pea-plants are independently assorted, so he chooses traits whose genes are located close together on the same chromosome. Is this a good set-up for his experiment?

   (A) No, because homologous chromosomes separate during meiosis.
   (B) No, because only one allele for each gene will be passed on.
   (C) No, because genes on the same chromosome may be linked.
   (D) No, because one of the genes may be dominantly inherited.
   (E) No, because one of the genes may be recessively inherited.

ANSWERS

1. **C** Recombinant DNA technology involves taking DNA from one organism and inserting it into the genome of another.

2. **E** Trisomy involves having three copies of the same chromosome. Humans normally have 46 chromosomes (23 pairs), so an individual with an extra chromosome will have 46 + 1 = 47 chromosomes.

3. **A** Gametes are haploid cells, having one copy of each chromosome. Humans have 23 different chromosomes, so each gamete has 23 chromosomes.

4. **E** Homologous chromosomes carry alleles for a gene, but these alleles may be the same (as in homozygous organisms) *or* they may be different (as in heterozygous organisms), eliminating statements (A) and (B). Homologous chromosomes are able to exchange DNA during the process of crossing over, eliminating statement (C). Haploid cells, by definition, only have one set of chromosomes, and so they cannot have homologous chromosomes; statement (D) is thus true. Statement (E), however, is false; each of the chromosomes in a homologous pair comes from a different parent.

5. **B** Genes are made of DNA, and are arranged into long strands known as chromosomes, so statements (D) and (E) are true. DNA may be transcribed into messenger RNA—eliminating statement (A)—which is used to make proteins during the process known as translation; genes thus contain the instructions for proteins, eliminating statement (C). Copying genes occurs through replication, not translation; replication occurs during mitosis and meiosis.

6. **D** An organism that has different alleles for the same gene is, by definition, heterozygous, making statement I true. Because different alleles are caused by different DNA sequences, this organism's homologous chromosomes will have different DNA sequences, making statement II true. It will pass on only one of these alleles, however, so it is not certain if its offspring will be heterozygous or homozygous. Thus, statement III is false, and (D) is the correct answer.

7. **B** Crossing over is the exchange of DNA between homologous chromosomes. A transgenic organism contains DNA from more than one organism. Cloning is the process of creating a genetically identical organism to one already existing. Translation is the process of making a polypeptide from RNA. Nondisjunction is when homologous chromosomes do not separate properly during meiosis.

8. **C** The problem with this experiment is simply that genes on the same chromosome may not always assort independently. Such genes are known as linked genes. Thus, the teacher might not get the results he desires. For random assortment, he should pick genes that are located on *different* chromosomes.

Lesson 7-3. Beyond Simple Inheritance

VOCABULARY

- incomplete dominance
- codominance
- multiple alleles
- sex chromosomes
- sex-linked genes
- polygenic inheritance
- cytoplasmic genes

Recall that in Lesson 7-1 we discussed that Mendel chose traits that were inherited simply, in an either–or fashion. His pea plants, for example, have either white or purple flowers, without any intermediate shades. But not all traits are inherited so simply. In humans, for example, although many traits are indeed inherited in this simple, either–or fashion—among them, the ability to roll one's tongue into a u-shape—many traits are not. Consider, for example, that there are four different human blood groups: A, B, AB, and O. Because this trait is carried on only one gene, there must be some other mechanism than simple inheritance at work. In this section, you'll discover some of the many different mechanisms of inheritance.

Incomplete Dominance

When Mendel looked at the flower color of pea plants, he found that there were only two phenotypes expressed: white flowers and purple flowers. But what if you were to study, for example, snapdragons, which come in white, pink, and red?

Incomplete dominance is a term used to describe the pattern of inheritance that results when a heterozygous organism displays a phenotype that is in between the homozygous phenotypes. In snapdragons, the homozygous phenotypes are white or red. Snapdragons that are heterozygous for flower color produce flowers that are in between white and red: their flowers are pink. When these heterozygous pink flowers are bred, however, their offspring can have either red, white, or pink flowers, because they are able to pass on either the red or the white allele.

Patterns such as incomplete dominance are good examples of where the usefulness of Mendel's distinction between "dominant" and "recessive" traits starts to break down, and the picture of inheritance becomes more complicated. This third phenotype—pink flowers—results from the fact that the heterozygous organisms only have one gene that is able to produce red pigment. To have true red flowers, a plant must have two copies of the gene that produces the red pigment. Pink flowers simply do not produce enough of the pigment to be truly red.

Codominance is another alternate form of inheritance. It is similar to incomplete dominance in that the heterozygous phenotype is distinct from either of the homozygous phenotypes. However, whereas in incomplete dominance, the heterozygous phenotype is a phenotype that is "in between" the two homozygous phenotypes, in codominance, the heterozygous phenotype is an altogether different phenotype that is not an intermediate value of the two homozygous phenotypes An example of codominance is seen in the inheritance of fur on roan horses—individual red and white hairs.

The line between when a characteristic is inherited by incomplete dominance, codominance, or when it is inherited by simple dominant–recessive genetics is not often clear. Remember that this distinction between which allele is dominant and recessive, or whether they will display incomplete dominance or codominance, is not in the genes themselves. The different genes that make up dominant or recessive alleles simply code for alternate versions of proteins. It is the interaction of these proteins in the body that will determine whether or not one of these alleles is dominant, or whether a situation such as incomplete dominance or codominance arises.

Multiple Alleles

In each of the cases, we've discussed, there were two possible different versions of each gene—two alleles—at play. Sometime, however, there are **multiple alleles** for each characteristic, which gives way to more possibilities for the same characteristic. The most famous example of a characteristic that has multiple alleles is human blood groups.

The blood group of humans is determined by the existence of a marker on the surface of each of our red blood cells. This marker is a small carbohydrate, and comes in two different forms, known as A and B. The existence of these markers is important in giving blood transfusions, because the existence of these markers can provoke an immune response that can kill the recipient of an improper blood transfusion. Individuals will have such an immune response if their bodies encounter blood with markers that they do not possess. An individual with an A marker, then, will respond to blood with a B marker, and vice versa. Someone with neither marker will respond to both the A and B marker, while someone with both markers will not have an immune response to either.

As you may have guessed, these markers correspond to what are known as blood groups. Individuals with the A marker are said to be of the A blood group, while individuals with the B marker are said to be of the B blood group. Individuals with both markers are said to be AB, and individuals with neither are of the O blood group.

These markers for blood group are inherited on the same gene, even though there are three different alleles for this gene:

- The I^A allele, which confers the A marker
- The I^B allele, which confers the B marker
- The i allele, which confers neither marker

Each person has two of these alleles, one carried on each homologous chromosome. The blood group of an individual depends on the alleles that are inherited from the parents:

- Individuals with $I^A I^A$ or $I^A i$ are of the A blood group
- Individuals with $I^A I^A$ or $I^A i$ are of the B blood group
- Individuals with $I^A I^B$ are of the AB blood group
- Individuals with ii are of the O blood group

Because the presence of the marker in one allele masks its absence on the other, the I^A and the I^B allele are dominant to the i allele. These I^A and the I^B

alleles are codominant; however, an individual with both these alleles will have the AB blood group, which is not an "intermediate" phenotype to the A and B blood groups, but is its own blood group.

Our discussion of blood types is a good occasion to take note of an important characteristic of the inheritance of traits: *just because an allele is dominant does not mean that it is the most prevalent allele in a population.* In fact, the most common blood group in the United States is the O blood group, which requires both recessive alleles to be present. Although natural selection can affect the prevalence of certain alleles within a population (about which more in later chapters), the prevalence of alleles and phenotypes in a population generally remains stable.

SEX GENES AND SEX-LINKED GENES

Recall that in Lesson 7-2 you learned that the human genome consists of 23 pairs of chromosomes—22 pairs of autosomes, and 1 pair of **sex chromosomes.** These sex chromosomes are responsible for many of the attributes that differentiate humans between the male and female sexes.

Mendel discovered that organisms carry two copies of the gene for each characteristic (for example, pea color). He also discovered that there are different types of genes for each characteristic, called alleles. This finding was later understood to be a result of the fact that humans have one pair of every chromosome, each of which carries one copy of every gene carried on that chromosome. These are known as homologous chromosomes. In somatic chromosomes, each of the homologous chromosomes is of equal length, and these chromosomes cross over during meiosis.

Sex chromosomes, however, work slightly differently, in that there are two types of sex chromosomes in humans: the X chromosome, and the Y chromosome. The sex chromosomes are only partially homologous. There are genes that are present solely on the X or Y chromosome that have no homologue (additional copy) on the other. These sex chromosomes are not of equal length—the Y chromosome is much shorter than the X chromosome—and they do not often cross over.

The sex chromosomes, as one might gather from their name, form the basis for the inheritance of sex in humans. Female humans have two X chromosomes, while male humans have one X chromosome and one Y chromosome. When females produce ova (eggs), they are only able to pass on the X chromosome. When males produce sperm, the law of segregation dictates that 50% of the time they will pass on an X chromosome, producing a female, and the other 50% of the time they will pass on a Y chromosome, producing a male. The sex of an individual, as you can see, is determined by the chromosome that is inherited from the sperm.

Because the sex chromosomes are not homologous, the patterns of inheritance for genes that are carried on these chromosomes are quite different. Such genes that are carried on the sex chromosomes are known as **sex-linked genes.** Consider, for example, the gene that causes red–green colorblindness. The most common form of color blindness, red–greed colorblindness results from the inability to properly perceive the colors red and green. It is caused by a recessive allele that resides on the X chromosome. There is no homologous allele that resides on the Y chromosome.

In females, who have two X chromosomes, there are two homologous copies of this gene. This means that in order to manifest the disease, females must have *two* copies of the recessive allele. If a female has only one of the disease-causing alleles, she will not have the disease, but as a carrier of the gene, she can pass it to one of her sons or daughters.

In males, who only have only X chromosome, there is only one copy of this gene. This means that if a male inherits the recessive allele, there is no second copy that can be dominant to mask the recessive allele. As a result, males are much more likely to be afflicted with sex-linked disorders such as red–green color blindness, because they need only inherit *one* copy of the recessive allele in order to display the recessive phenotype.

This pattern of inheritance can be modeled using Punnett squares, as you can see in Figure 7-7. Note that because the genes in question are only carried on the X chromosome, they are listed as a superscript on the X chromosome.

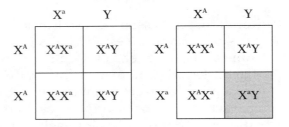

Figure 7-7 Two Punnett squares.

Inheritance in sex-linked genes has a number of differences from that in simple inheritance. Whereas simple inheritance is rather blind to sex, the outcomes in sex-linked inheritance are largely dependent on the gender of the offspring. In simple inheritance, males can pass on genes to their offspring regardless of gender, for sex-linked genes, males pass only a Y chromosome to their sons, and thus their genes have no bearing on the expression of sex-linked traits. As a result, if males inherit a sex-linked disorder, the gene must have come from their mother.

Other traits that are sex-linked include hemophilia, a disorder of the blood's clotting factors, which produces profuse bleeding from even minor scrapes and bruises, and Duchenne muscular dystrophy, a disorder that causes muscle tissue to waste away and generally results in death before the age of 30. Both of these disorders are recessive, and are found primarily in males.

Sex-linked inheritance does not only affect traits that are carried on the X-chromosome. There are certain genes that are expressed only on the Y chromosome as well. Because these genes have no corresponding copy on the X chromosome, this means that there is no crossing over, and that large sections of the Y chromosome are passed on, almost identically, from father to son, generation to generation. The patterns of inheritance that result are unique: fathers cannot pass any of these genes to their daughters, but pass all of them on to each of their sons. This allows scientists to perform a number of studies to establish male lineage across a number of generations—most famously, to establish a genetic link between someone in the family of President Thomas Jefferson and the descendants of one of his slaves, Sally Hemings.

It should be noted here that sex chromosomes do not work the same way in every species. In certain insects, such as bees and ants, there are no sex chromosomes; instead, males are haploid and are formed from unfertilized eggs, while females are diploid, formed from fertilized eggs. In some other organisms, such as birds and some fish, the chromosome that determines sex is not passed from the father (as in humans) but from the mother. And, as discussed later in this section, sex can occasionally be the result of environmental factors as well.

POLYGENIC INHERITANCE

The characteristics that you have studied so far have all had one thing in common: they have all determined by only one gene, copied onto two chromosomes. Sometimes, however, there is more than one gene that determines a trait. Many times, it is a combination of the effects of a large number of genes that determines the final phenotype of an organism.

Consider, for example, that there are three known genes that control for the height of certain plants. These genes are likely to be incompletely dominant; that is, a plant that is heterozygous for one of these genes will have a height that is between the heights of plants that display the recessive or dominant phenotype. A plant with the genes *ffgghh* will be much shorter than average, while a plant with the genes *FFGGHH* will be much taller than average, and a plant that is *FfGgHh* will have a height somewhere in the middle. This means that each of the six possible dominant alleles will add to the plant's height, leaving seven possible heights for this plant. Once environmental factors are taken into account, there will most likely be a continuum of heights from the very shortest to the very tallest, with most individuals fitting in somewhere in the middle of the range. Generally, this resembles a bell curve, as shown in Figure 7-8.

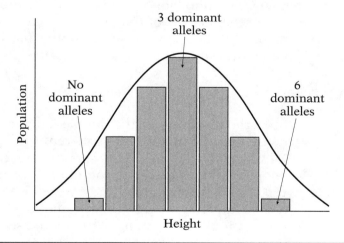

Figure 7-8 Description of the results of genes passed by polygenic inheritance.

Polygenic inheritance occurs in many human traits as well. Human height is known to be the result of a number of different genes, as is human weight, skin color, and a number of other characteristics that exist as a continuum of possibilities. The basic mechanism of inheritance for each of these traits is not very different from simple genes—one half of each individual's alleles still come from each parent—but it is the fact that so many alleles would contribute to create one trait that makes the expression of these traits different.

EXTRA-NUCLEAR GENES

Recall that in Chapter 6, Lesson 6-2 we discussed that mitochondria and chloroplasts are able to self-replicate, leading to speculation that they are the evolutionary descendants of fully functional cells that were swallowed up by another cell at some point. Mitochondria and chloroplasts, in fact, have their own DNA, which is quite separate from the DNA that resides in the nucleus. They reproduce themselves and their DNA in a process that is separate from the process by which nuclear DNA is replicated. How then, are mitochondria passed from generation to generation?

The answer is that mitochondria and chloroplasts, along with the other organelles of the cell, are passed to offspring in the cytoplasm of the ovum. Because they are passed in the cytoplasm of the ovum, such genes are known as **cytoplasmic genes.** The male gamete—sperm in humans, and pollen in plants—can donate mitochondria, but they are very quickly destroyed by the cell. This means that, in contrast to the nuclear DNA, half of which comes from each parent, the mitochondrial DNA in an organism is an almost exact copy of that which was present in its maternal parent. The pattern of inheritance is quite different: mothers will pass their cytoplasmic genes to *all* of their offspring, while fathers do not pass on any cytoplasmic genes.

There are a number of genes coded for in mitochondrial and chloroplast DNA. Certain plant disorders are known to be inherited in chloroplasts. Defects in ATP synthase and the electron transport chain—both important parts of the respiratory pathway that are found in mitochondria (see Chapter 6, Lesson 6-3)—are known to be caused by mitochondrial DNA and inherited from the mother.

The maternal inheritance of mitochondrial DNA means that it is passed relatively unchanged from mother to offspring over the generations. The only changes in mitochondrial DNA that occur are random mutations that occur during the lifetime of the mother. Because of this, mitochondrial DNA, like the DNA of the Y chromosome, is often used for genetic studies to prove common maternity in rather distant relatives.

BEYOND DNA

Since the discovery of the double helix, a much public attention has been focused on the possibilities inherent in the instructions that are carried in DNA. Science fiction writers spend much time imagining how genetic technology could be used to promote a program of eugenics. Meanwhile, the researchers who actually study genetics have made a great deal of progress in their understanding of how genetics works. But it will be a long while before our abilities reach the nightmare scenarios of the public imagination, for two important reasons, which are the topic of this section.

After Genetics: Proteomics

Our understanding of the genetic code continues to provide insight into the workings of biology. But as scientists progressed with such ambitious gene-focused projects as the Human Genome Project, it became clear that all of the answers we were looking for could not be found waiting in the genome. In fact, the number of genes that are currently thought to be in the human genome—between 20,000 and 25,000—is far fewer than most molecular biologists had guessed at the time the project started.

Consider Alzheimer's disease, which affects a large proportion of elderly persons. Although we do know that there are certain genes that predispose people to Alzheimer's disease, it is also thought that the accumulation in brain cells of β-amyloid, a form of a naturally occurring protein in brain cells, contributes to the disease. What is interesting about this β-amyloid is that it is made from the same gene as a normal, non-Alzheimer's protein. The difference between the two is the location where the amyloid protein is cleaved, or cut. This alternate cleavage causes the protein to take on a different, disease-causing shape, even though it was formed from the same DNA as the benign version of amyloid.

As you can see, there is another entire level of mechanisms that acts after the DNA has been transcribed. These mechanisms act at the level of polypeptides and proteins to regulate the ways in which proteins work and their abilities are applied. A new field—known as proteomics—has been developed to investigate the various ways in which the actions of proteins are regulated in the body. Although we are only beginning to understand how, for example, identical instructions in DNA can give way to vastly different phenotypes, it is nevertheless clear that the interactions of proteins in the body have as much to do with human inheritance as the instructions in the DNA themselves.

After Instructions: Environment

Over the last two centuries, the life of human beings has undergone remarkable changes. The average lifespan has more than doubled. Humans continue to set new speed records on foot. And the average height of humans has risen dramatically. How can these be explained? Is there some force that is systematically altering our genes to make people taller and live longer? It seems doubtful. A much more likely explanation is simply that people receive much better nutrition and health care than they did two hundred years ago. Given certain circumstances, our bodies are able to do more—go faster, grow taller, and live longer.

This illustrates an important fact about our genes: the instructions contained in our DNA and our proteins are constantly interacting with outside factors in our environment. Although our DNA can set a range of possibilities, it is the environment that does the final work in determining each individual. Any number of factors can determine exactly how we develop—from random chance to, as we saw above, nutrition.

Instead of exactly determining every facet of an organism, genes often create a *range* of phenotypes. The final traits that an organism displays will depend on the interaction of the organism's environment and the instructions contained in its DNA. Consider, for example, skin color in humans. Although we may have a "baseline" skin color determined by our genes, our actual skin color will depend to no small extent on how much time we spend in the sun. One might think that the characteristic pink color of flamingos is genetic; in fact, this coloring comes from a dye contained in the shrimp that flamingos eat. In alligators and crocodiles, for example, eggs incubated above a certain temperature (approximately 30 degrees Celsius) will develop to be males, while eggs incubated below that temperature will be female. And, although genetics may predispose humans to certain behavioral or personality traits, our childhood upbringing has much to do with our final personality.

One final example of the role of environment in creating organisms was discovered by scientists who recently developed the ability to clone cats genetically. You can now pay a company to create a genetically identical version of your beloved pet kitten. However, the company warns that the genetic clone it creates, although similar to your old pet, may not be identical. Not only is its personality not likely to be the same as its predecessor, but occasionally even the patterns in its fur—which can depend on environmental factors and chance—might also be different. These differences are a testament to the limits of genetics and genetic technologies.

LESSON SUMMARY

- Many genes are inherited in more complex ways than through simple Mendelian, dominant–recessive inheritance.
- Certain traits are inherited by incomplete dominance, in which a heterozygous individual has an intermediate phenotype between the dominant and recessive phenotype.
- For certain characteristics, there are more than two possible alleles for the trait, such as in blood group. This is known as multiple alleles.
- Certain traits are passed not on the somatic chromosomes, but on the sex chromosomes, which determine the sex of an individual (XX is female, XY is male). The patterns of inheritance for such sex-linked genes depend greatly on the sex of the individuals.
- Other traits, such as height and skin color, are influenced by the alleles on more than one gene; this is known as polygenic inheritance.
- Certain genes are carried on DNA found in mitochondria and chloroplasts. Such genes are called cytoplasmic genes because these organelles are carried in the cytoplasm of the mother to the offspring.
- Such factors as the interactions of proteins and an organism's environment will affect the way that genes are expressed.

REVIEW QUESTIONS

Questions 1 and 2

Select which one of the following choices best matches the statement below. Some choices may be used once, more than once, or not at all.

(A) polygenic inheritance
(B) incomplete dominance
(C) multiple alleles
(D) sex-linked genes
(E) codominance

1. The method of inheritance of traits that are passed on the X chromosome.
2. The method of inheritance in which genes from more than one chromosome may control a trait.
3. The gene for hair curliness in a species is inherited by incomplete dominance, with heterozygous organisms having wavy hair, and homozygous organisms having either straight or curly hair. How many different alleles are there for this trait?

(A) 0
(B) 1
(C) 2
(D) 3
(E) 4

4. Which of the following is the best example of the influence of environment on genetics?

   (A) A child has two copies of a gene that differ in their nucleotide sequence.
   (B) Two pea plants with purple flowers have some offspring with white flowers.
   (C) Trees that are planted close to each other tend to be shorter than those that are planted far apart.
   (D) Two mice are fed the same food, but have different colored fur.
   (E) Males are more likely to be affected by muscular dystrophy than in females.

5. Oscar and Ophelia are of blood group O. What is the probability that their newborn child will be of blood group O?

   (A) 0%
   (B) 25%
   (C) 50%
   (D) 75%
   (E) 100%

6. Kyle has a disorder that is carried on his mitochondrial DNA. His wife, Karen, does not have this disorder. What is the probability that one of their children will have this disorder?

   (A) 0%
   (B) 25%
   (C) 50%
   (D) 75%
   (E) 100%

7. Red–green color blindness is a recessively inherited sex-linked trait. Stephanie is red–green color blind. Her husband, Steve, is not. Which of the following statements accurately describes which of their children will have red–green color blindness?

   (A) None of sons or daughters will be red–green color blind.
   (B) None of the sons and some of the daughters will be red–green color blind.
   (C) Some of the sons and none of the daughters will be red–green color blind.
   (D) All of the sons and none of the daughters will be red–green color blind.
   (E) All of the sons and daughters will be red–green color blind.

8. A certain species of mouse has a coat that may be either tan, black, or dark brown. A scientist crosses a black mouse with a tan mouse and obtains four dark brown mice. He then crosses these dark brown mice with each other. Which of the following is a possible hair color that will be displayed in the offspring?

   I.   tan
   II. dark brown
   III. black

      (A) II only
      (B) I and II only
      (C) I and III only
      (D) II and III only
      (E) I, II, and III

ANSWERS

1. **D** Genes that are passed on the X chromosome are called sex-linked genes because the X chromosome is a sex chromosome. Sex-linked genes also exhibit a sex-dependent pattern of inheritance.

2. **A** The only way for genes on more than one chromosome to affect inheritance is if a trait is controlled by more than one gene, which describes polygenic inheritance.

3. **C** There are three phenotypes for this trait, each of which corresponds to a different genotype. However, there are only two different alleles for this trait: one allele that causes curliness, and another that does not.

4. **C** Environmental factors are factors that are not accounted for by genetic instructions. Different nucleotide sequences may occur because the child has two alleles for the same gene. Two pea plants with purple flowers may produce white-flowered offspring because white flowers are recessive, and the trait "skipped" a generation. The two mice can have the same upbringing, but different fur color, because of their genes. And the difference between the sexes in the occurrence of muscular dystrophy is because the gene is sex-linked. However, environment is the leading factor in choice (C), because it is not the genetic makeup of the tree, but their surroundings—their proximity to other trees—that helps to determine their height.

5. **E** Blood group O is a recessive phenotype. Two parents who have only these recessive alleles can pass on only recessive alleles to their children. All of Oscar and Ophelia's children, therefore, will have this recessive phenotype.

6. **A** Kyle will not pass on the disorder from his mitochondrial DNA to any of his children. Mitochondrial DNA is passed only from the maternal organelles, so this trait will not show up in any of the children.

7. **D** As someone displaying a recessive phenotype, Stephanie must have the recessive allele on both of her X chromosomes. This means that she can pass only recessive alleles on to her children. Because the sons will receive X chromosomes only from Stephanie, they will all be red–green color blind, eliminating all the answers except (D) and (E). Steve, with only one X chromosome, does not have the recessive allele; he will pass on a dominant allele to all of his daughters, meaning that none will be red–green color blind, eliminating answer choice (E).

8. **E** The offspring of two heterozygous individuals can be homozygous for either allele or heterozygous. This means that all of the fur colors can be displayed in the offspring.

Lesson 7-4. Using Punnett Squares

VOCABULARY

- probability
- test cross

Punnett squares are extremely useful tools for understanding the mechanisms of inheritance and for modeling the genetic characteristics of the off-spring of two individuals. Not only is it likely that you'll see a Punnett square somewhere on the test, it's also likely that the ability to create Punnett squares will be useful to solve questions about the possible offspring of two individuals. In this section, we'll take a detailed look at how to complete Punnett squares in all sorts of situations.

A QUICK REVIEW OF PROBABILITY

Punnett squares are an excellent example of how mathematics can be applied to a science such as biology. Very often you'll be required to express something in terms of a **probability** or a chance that something might happen. So before we launch into our discussion of Punnett squares, it might be helpful to review some simple facts about probability.

The probability, or chance, that an event will happen, is generally expressed as a number between zero and one. A probability of zero means that there is no chance of the event occurring; a probability of one means that an event will definitely occur. Probabilities can be written as decimals (0.5, 0.25, 0.133) or as fractions $\left(\dfrac{1}{2}, \dfrac{1}{4}, \dfrac{2}{15}\right)$. Probabilities can also be written as a percentage; doing so simply requires shifting the decimal place of a probability two places to the right:

$0.50 = 50\%$

$0.1875 = 18.75\%$

To calculate a probability, you need to know how often the event you're looking for will occur, compared to the total number of possible outcomes. For example, if you're picking one of four coins out of a bag, and two of these coins are pennies, then there are two chances of four possible outcomes that you will pick a penny. To get your probability, you simply divide two by four: a probability of $\dfrac{2}{4}$ is equivalent to $\dfrac{1}{2}$, or 0.5, or 50%.

The sum of the probabilities for all of the possible outcomes must add up to one. This fact is especially important when converting ratios to probability. Mendel, for example, observed a 3:1 ratio of dominant phenotypes to recessive phenotypes in his second generation. To convert this to a probability, we need to know the *total* number of possible outcomes. To do so, we simply add all of the numbers in the ratio: in this case, four (3 + 1 = 4). Thus, the probability that one will get a dominant phenotype is $\dfrac{3}{4}$, or 0.75. Be sure when you are working with ratios not simply to convert a 3:1 ratio to $\frac{1}{3}$, for example, or you will end up with mistaken results.

One final note about probability involves the combination of probabilities. If you are asked the probability of both of two independent events occurring, the proper way to calculate this is to multiply the two values—not add. For example, if there is a $\frac{1}{4}$ chance of a plant having yellow peas, and a $\frac{3}{4}$ chance of that plant having purple flowers (recalling that, because of the law of independent assortment, these are two independent events), then the chances that a plant will have both yellow peas and purple flowers is $\frac{1}{4} \times \frac{3}{4} = \frac{3}{16}$.

MAKING A PUNNETT SQUARE

Making a Punnett square is a rather simple process. Before you make your Punnett square, however, it's important to remember the proper way to write the genotype of individuals: dominant alleles are written as a capital letter, while recessive alleles are written as a lower-case letter. It doesn't matter what letter you choose to use for each trait; it might be useful, however, to choose letters whose upper-case and lower-case forms are not easily confused. And, if you're completing a Punnett square for more than one characteristic, it's important to choose different letters for each of those characteristics.

The first step in making a Punnett square is to identify the possible alleles that will be passed on by each parent. Let us say, for example, we wished to know the probability that the offspring of an individual with attached earlobes, who married someone heterozygous for that trait, will also have the attached earlobes. Because attached earlobes is a recessive trait, we know that the individual with attached earlobes has two recessive alleles for that trait. We'll indicate that with *ff*. We also know that the other parent is heterozygous, so we'll indicate that with an *Ff*.

Now, we need to know the possible alleles that could be passed on by each of these parents. In this case, the homozygous parent will always pass on one of her two recessive alleles. The heterozygous parent, however, can pass on either the recessive allele (*f*) or the dominant allele (*F*).

Once you have identified the possible alleles that will be passed on, then write the alleles for one parent on the top of your Punnett square, and the alleles for the other parent on the side. As you can see in Figure 7-9, we chose to write the alleles for the heterozygous parent along the top. It doesn't matter which side you choose, as long as you're consistent, and one parent is along each side of the square.

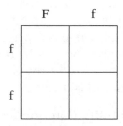

Figure 7-9

Now that you've identified the possible alleles, you need to fill in the blank spaces in your square. To do so, start with the alleles on the top. Write the allele that is found in the top in each space that appears in the column under that allele. Starting on the top left, then, you would write an *F* in the top left and bottom left squares, and an *f* in the top right and bottom right squares. Then, look to the left, and write the allele that appears to the left in the spaces that are to the right of the allele in each row. In this case, this means, that you would put an *f* in each of the spaces. When you're done, each space should reflect the alleles that appear at the top of its column and to the left of its row, as shown in Figure 7-10.

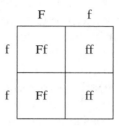

Figure 7-10

Remember, though, that simply completing your Punnett square is often not the end of your work. Now you have to interpret your results! One way to start is by listing each of the genotypes that you see. In this case, we found two genotypes:

- 2 *Ff*
- 2 *ff*

Then, list the corresponding phenotype for each of your genotypes:

- 2 *Ff*: free earlobes
- 2 *ff*: attached earlobes

In this case, there were only two genotypes, each of which had its own phenotype. Occasionally, however, you will have two genotypes that lead to the same phenotype. Be sure to watch out for occurrences where different phenotypes will lead to the same phenotype.

Finally, it's time to return to the question that was originally posed. *It's extremely important to be sure that you're answering the question that was asked in the problem.* The writers of the SAT tests are extremely adept at tricking test-takers by asking a question that does not seem the most obvious, and you're likely to get the question wrong, even though you could have found the correct answer had you been looking for it. So be sure that you're not writing the percentage of the offspring that are heterozygous, when you should be writing the percentage of offspring that are homozygous. It often helps to circle or underline the important part of the question.

In this case, our question asked the probability that the offspring will have attached earlobes. In this case, *attached* is our key word. Because we know that attached earlobes is a recessive trait, we need to look at our Punnett square to the see proportion of offspring that had attached earlobes. We found that 2 out of 4 offspring, corresponding to a probability of 0.50, or 50%, had the attached earlobes.

Test Crosses

Test crosses are matings of two individuals that are performed in order to figure out the genotype of one of the individuals. Most often, test-crosses are performed to figure out if an organism that is dominant for a trait is heterozygous or homozygous for that trait.

Test crosses are most easily performed on organisms capable of producing large numbers of offspring. This is because a larger number of offspring gives a greater chance for the alleles to combine in all of the ways that they might possibly combine. The greater the number of offspring, the more sure the results. Humans, for example, rarely have large enough numbers of offspring for such a test-cross to be reliable; plants on the other hand, produce many seeds, which grow quickly.

Say, for instance, that Mendel was investigating the color of pea pods, and wanted to know the genotype of one of his plants that had green pea pods. Pea pods come in two colors: yellow (which is dominant) and green (which is recessive). Because yellow pea pods is a dominant trait, Mendel has no way of knowing if his plant has one or two dominant alleles: is it *YY* or *Yy*?

A test cross generally involves the crossing of the plant whose phenotype is unknown with a plant whose phenotype is known—in other words, a plant that is homozygous recessive for that trait. In this case, we would cross our plant with yellow pea pods with a plant that has green pea pods, and a genotype of *yy*. Using two Punnett squares, we can model the possible outcomes of such a cross, and use them to interpret our results. If Mendel's plant is homozygous dominant, or *YY*, then the cross will go as shown in Figure 7-11.

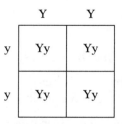

Figure 7-11

As you can see, all of the offspring in this cross are heterozygous—*Yy*—and so all will have green pea pods. If, however Mendel's plant with green pea pods is heterozygous, or *Yy*, then the cross will go as shown in Figure 7-12.

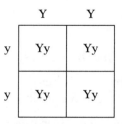

Figure 7-12

In this cross, half of the offspring are heterozygous—*Yy*—and half of the offspring are homozygous recessive—*yy*. This is quite a different outcome from the above, and that's why we do test-crosses: to determine an unknown genotype.

If Mendel were to run this experiment and find that all of the plants produced had yellow pea pods, he would be rather certain that his original plant was, indeed, homozygous dominant. If, however, he found that nearly half of the plants produced had green pea pods, then he would know that his original plant was heterozygous. And, as you can see, the ability to model test-crosses using Punnett squares makes the interpretation of the results much easier.

MODELING INHERITANCE

Punnett squares may not seem especially useful when only modeling one trait. But one instance when they're especially useful is when modeling two traits, or traits that are inherited in a more complicated fashion than simple inheritance.

Two or More Traits

Say we wanted to model the possible outcomes of Mendel's experiment involving two traits, which he used to investigate the law of independent assortment. In his first step, he crossed a plant that was true-bred for yellow, round seeds—we'll write this as *YYRR*—with a plant that was true-bred for green, wrinkled seeds—we'll write this as *yyrr*. All of his first generation plants inherited the *YR* alleles from the first parent, and the *yr* alleles from the second, making them *YyRr*. Such plants that are heterozygous for two traits are known as *dihybrids*.

Say we wanted to know the characteristics of the offspring of the cross of two dihybrid plants. This is a much more complicated process than the first-generation cross we just performed. Our first step is identifying the alleles that can be produced by such a plant. Remember that Mendel's law of independent assortment holds that each of these alleles is passed separately, so that the dominant alleles are not always passed on together, nor are the recessive alleles. This leaves us with four possible alleles that each of these dihybrid plants can pass on:

YR, Yr, yR, or *yr.*

Our Punnett square will have to be larger—this time, we'll need four rows and four columns. Because both of the parents are dihybrids, they'll have the same possibilities for alleles, so we write them on the top and side of our Punnett square, and fill the square in. When we're done, our Punnett square should resemble Figure 7-13.

Our last step is to interpret the results that we found. In this case, it's easiest to list all of the possible phenotypes, and then look at which (if any) of the genotypes that we found correspond to those phenotypes. In this care, there are four possible phenotypes:

- yellow, round: 1 *YYRR*, 2 *YYRr*, 2 *YyRR*, 4 *YyRr*
- yellow, wrinkled: 1 *YYrr*, 2 *Yyrr*

	YR	Yr	yR	yr
YR	YYRR	YYRr	YyRR	YyRr
Yr	YYRr	YYrr	YyRr	Yyrr
yR	YyRR	YyRr	yyRR	yyRr
yr	YyRr	Yyrr	yyRr	yyrr

Figure 7-13

- green, round: 1 *yyRR*, 2 *yyRr*
- green, wrinkled: 1 *yyrr*

As you can see, there are sixteen possibilities for the offspring of the second-generation. Nine of these possibilities give yellow, round peas, three give yellow, wrinkled peas, or green, round peas, and one gives green, wrinkled peas. This means that we would expect a 9:3:3:1 ratio of offspring in the second generation, something Mendel, indeed, observed in his pea plants.

The most difficult part of modeling Punnett squares for more than one gene is making sure that you've accounted for all of the possible alleles that can be produced, and then keeping track of the results. Be sure that, when dealing with more than one gene, you've properly accounted for the independent assortment of alleles, and have created all the combinations possible. As we saw, with only one gene, there are two possible alleles, but with two genes, there are four. If you were to model three genes, you'd get eight possibilities, and your Punnett square would need to have $8 \times 8 = 64$ squares! By going carefully, you can make sure you don't make mistakes.

Multiple Alleles

Punnett squares can also be used in cases that are more complex than simple inheritance, such as when there are multiple alleles for the same characteristic. Let's say we want to know the possible blood groups of children whose are of two different blood groups: group A and group B.

In this case, we don't know the genotype of the parents, so we're going to assume that they are heterozygous, so that we account for all of the possibilities. Although we would prefer to know the exact makeup of the parents so that we could give a probability of how many of their children will be of each genotype, in this case, we are only able to model the possible genotypes that can occur.

Let's start by determining the alleles. The parent of blood group A, if heterozygous, will have the genotype $I^A i$, meaning she can pass on either an I^A allele or an i allele. The parent of blood group B, if heterozygous, will have the genotype $I^B i$, meaning he can pass on either an I^B allele or an i allele. Now, let's put them into a Punnett square and see what the possibilities are for their children. Figure 7-14 shows the result.

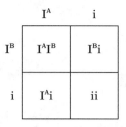

	I^A	i
I^B	$I^A I^B$	$I^B i$
i	$I^A i$	ii

Figure 7-14

In our Punnett square, we saw that there were four possible genotypes. Each of these genotypes corresponds to a different blood group:

- 1 *$I^A I^B$:* blood group AB
- 1 *$I^A i$:* blood group A
- 1 *$I^B i$:* blood group B
- 1 *ii:* blood group O

Now, we need to go back and look at our original question, which asked about which blood groups were possible if we didn't know the genotypes of the parents. As we saw from our Punnett square, it's possible for the offspring of these two parents to be of any blood group: A, B, AB, or O.

While we're discussing this Punnett square, it's important to note that this Punnett square also shows how one can do a Punnett square when one is dealing with a trait that displays co-dominance. To make it clear which alleles are dominant, we preserve the letters in upper case. To distinguish between the two dominant traits (A and B), however, we put a superscript above the letters.

Sex-Linked Genes

As a final example of the various ways to use Punnett squares, let's look at how they can be used to model sex-linked genes. Recall that with sex-linked genes, we are required to keep track of the gender of each of the children, because the expression of traits will depend upon how many X chromosomes the individual has. Because of this, it is convenient to write the alleles for sex-linked genes as superscripts of the chromosome on which they appear.

Say, then, we want to know the possibility of a mother who is a carrier of red–green color blindness passing on the trait to one of her sons, if the father is not red–green color blind. As with all of our other problems, the first step is determining which alleles the mother and the father will pass on. Recalling that red–green color blindness is a recessive trait carried on the X chromosome, the father would then have the genotype $X^N Y$, and can pass on either the X^N or the Y. The mother, who is a carrier, is heterozygous for the trait, so she has the genotype $X^N X^n$, and can pass on either X^N or X^n.

Using these alleles, we can now model the possible offspring in this cross, as shown in Figure 7-15.

	X^N	Y
X^N	$X^N X^N$	$X^N Y$
X^n	$X^N X^n$	$X^n Y$

Figure 7-15

Note that in this case, the question only asked about the sons (although neither of the daughters carry the disease). So, we'll look at the outcome for the sons:

- 1 $X^N Y$: normal vision
- 1 $X^n Y$: red–green color blind

As you can see, one of every two sons will have the disease. This means that there is a probability of 0.5 that one of the sons will develop red–green color blindness.

When you're doing crosses for sex-linked genes, be sure to keep track of the sex of each of the parents and of the offspring in the cross. Remember that no matter what genes they inherit, the individuals on the <u>right**</u> side of your Punnett square should both be male, and on the <u>left**</u> side should be female. (**This is only assuming you set up the square so that the female parent's genotype is listed on the side and the male's is across the top.)

LESSON SUMMARY

- Punnett squares are useful tools in modeling the possible outcomes of a specific cross.
- To complete a Punnett square, you must:
  - identify the alleles that will be passed on by the parents, and arrange them on the top and sides of your Punnett square;
  - figure out the genotypes of the alleles that will be produced, by filling in the square; and
  - match the genotypes that are produced to their respective phenotypes.
- Punnett squares may be used to model many different crosses, including the inheritance of more than one trait, inheritance of sex-linked genes, and the inheritance of traits with multiple alleles.
- When answering questions that require you to complete a Punnett square, be sure to look carefully at exactly what the question is asking you to figure out, so that you given the correct answer.

REVIEW QUESTIONS

1. Yellow pea pods are a dominant trait in pea plants. A scientist test-crossed a plant that has yellow pea pods with a plant that has green pea pods, and was able to determine that his yellow pea plant was homozygous dominant. Which of the following best resembles the scientist's results?

   (A) 789 plants with green pea pods
   (B) 630 plants with green pea pods, 185 plants with yellow pea pods
   (C) 409 plants with green pea pods, 397 plants with yellow pea pods
   (D) 594 plants with green pea pods, 242 plants with yellow pea pods
   (E) 812 plants with yellow pea pods

2. Two parents with the dominant phenotype for a characteristic already have a child who has the recessive phenotype. What is the probability that any of their future children will have the dominant phenotype?

   (A) 0%
   (B) 25%
   (C) 50%
   (D) 75%
   (E) 100%

3. Joyce is trying to make as many snapdragons with pink flowers as possible in one generation. The cross that would be most effective for Joyce is:

   (A) crossing two white-flowered plants
   (B) crossing a white-flowered plant and a pink-flowered plant
   (C) crossing a white-flowered plant and a red-flowered plant
   (D) crossing two pink-flowered plants
   (E) crossing a pink-flowered plant and a red-flowered plant

4. Nick has a cat that is homozygous dominant for one trait (*AA*) and homozygous recessive for another trait (*bb*). An offspring of Nick's cat could have which of the following genotypes?

   I. *AABb*
   II. *AaBB*
   III. *aabb*

   (A) I only
   (B) II only
   (C) I and II only
   (D) I and III only
   (E) I, II, and III

5. Morgan is crossing two pea plants that are heterozygous for pea color (*Yy*). One is heterozygous for pea shape (*Rr*), while the other is recessive for pea shape (*rr*). What proportion of the plants that offspring Morgan gets will have the dominant pea-color phenotype but the recessive pea-shape phenotype?

   (A) $\dfrac{1}{16}$

   (B) $\dfrac{1}{8}$

   (C) $\dfrac{3}{16}$

   (D) $\dfrac{1}{2}$

   (E) $\dfrac{9}{16}$

6. Both of Donna's parents are of blood group AB. Donna is of blood group A, and her husband, Don is of blood group B. Which of the following describes the possible blood groups of their son?

   (A) A only
   (B) A or B only
   (C) A or AB only
   (D) A, B, or AB only
   (E) A, B, or O only

7. Hemophilia is a recessively inherited sex-linked trait. Lauren's father was a hemophiliac, but neither Lauren nor her husband, Larry, is a hemophiliac. What is the probability that one of Lauren's daughters will have the same genotype as she does?

   (A) 0%
   (B) 12.5%
   (C) 25%
   (D) 50%
   (E) 100%

8. Blood type is determined by the blood group (A, B, AB, or O) and the Rhesus (Rh) factor, with Rh+ being dominant to Rh–. Luke has blood type B– and his mother has blood type O+. Which of the following is a possible blood type for Luke's father?

   I.   AB–
   II. B+
   III. O+

   (A) I only
   (B) I and II only
   (C) I and III only
   (D) II and III only
   (E) I, II, and III

ANSWERS

1. **E** A homozygous dominant plant crossed with a homozygous recessive plant will only produce plants that are heterozygous. All of the offspring, then, will display the dominant phenotype of green pea pods.

2. **D** The only way that two dominant parents with a dominant phenotype can have a child that has a recessive phenotype is if they each have a recessive allele to pass on. This would make them both heterozygous (*Hh*) for that trait. Using a Punnett square, we can calculate the possibility that their children will have the dominant phenotype.

	H	h
H	HH	Hh
h	Hh	hh

The offspring that are *HH* or *Hh* will display the dominant phenotype. These account for three of the four possibilities, giving a probability of $\frac{3}{4}$, or 75%.

If you answered (B) to this question, make sure you calculated the probability of the *dominant* phenotype and not the *recessive* phenotype.

3. **C** The pink phenotype is a heterozygous trait in snapdragons. The only way to achieve offspring that are all heterozygous is to cross a homozygous red-flowered plant with a homozygous red-flowered plant. All of the other crosses listed will give at most 50% pink snapdragons, including the cross of two pink snapdragons. This may be confirmed using Punnett squares, as shown below. The Punnett Square on the left shows the results of crossing a red plant with a white plant; the one on the right shows the results of crossing two pink plants.

The shaded squares are the ones that will give pink snapdragon plants.

	R	R			R	W
W	RW	RW		**R**	RR	RW
W	RW	RW		**W**	RW	WW

As you can see, crossing two pink plants gives only $\frac{2}{4}$, or 50% pink plants.

4. **A** Nick's cat has the phenotype *AAbb*. The alleles it passes on will, thus, be *Ab*. Its offspring must have both of these alleles. II does not have a *b*, and III does not have an *A*, making it impossible for either them to be the offspring of Nick's cat. I, however, does have an *A* and a *b*, and can, indeed, be an offspring of Nick's cat.

5. **C** Morgan's cross is of a plant that is *YyRr* with a plant that is *Yyrr*. The first plant is capable of passing on four types of alleles: *YR*, *Yr*, *yR*, and *Yr*. The second plant will have the alleles *Yr*, *Yr*, *yr*, and *yr*. We then create a Punnett square detailing these results.

	YR	Yr	yR	yr
Yr	YYRr	YYrr	YyRr	Yyrr
Yr	YYRr	YYrr	YyRr	Yyrr
yr	YyRr	Yyrr	yyRr	yyrr
yr	YyRr	Yyrr	yyRr	yyrr

The shaded squares are those that have the dominant pea-color phenotype and the recessive pea-shape phenotype. $\frac{6}{16}$, or $\frac{3}{8}$, of the offspring, will have this combination of phenotypes.

Another way to solve this problem would have been to produce a Punnett square for the inheritance of each of the traits, and calculating the probability of each of them being inherited ($\frac{3}{4}$ for pea-color, $\frac{1}{2}$ for pea-shape) and then multiplying these two values $\left(\frac{3}{4} \times \frac{1}{2} = \frac{3}{8}\right)$.

6. **C** Donna's parents are both of blood group AB. This means that Donna must have inherited two alleles for blood type A: her genotype is thus $I^A I^A$. Don may be either $I^B I^B$ or $I^B i$; we do not know, so we will assume it is the latter because this will account for all possibilities, and because we are not calculating a probability. Filling in our Punnett square, we get the following.

	I^A	I^A
I^B	$I^A I^B$	$I^A I^B$
i	$I^A i$	$I^A i$

Their son, then, may be of blood group A or of blood group AB.

7. **D** Lauren must have inherited a recessive allele from her father, but she does not display the trait. She is, thus, a heterozygous carrier of the trait. The question asks the probability that any of her daughters will have this same genotype as Lauren does. To calculate this, we can create a Punnett square, knowing that Lauren's husband is also not a hemophiliac:

	X^A	Y
X^A	$X^A X^A$	$X^A Y$
X^a	$X^A X^a$	$X^a Y$

The shaded square is the square that has the same heterozygous genotype as Lauren does. Because the question asks only about Lauren's daughters, then this represents one out of two $\left(\dfrac{1}{2}\right)$, or 50% of the possibilities for her daughters.

8. **B** This question is not hard if we break it down into its parts. Let's first address the issue of blood group. Luke is of blood group B, and his mother is of blood group O. This means he must have inherited an allele for blood group B from his father. This eliminates answer III.

Now, let's turn to Rh factor. Luke is Rh– and his mother is Rh+. Although Luke must have received an Rh– gene from his father, it's possible that his father is heterozygous for this trait, thus he could be either Rh+ or Rh–. Both I and II are, thus, viable answers.

Lesson 7-5. Using Pedigrees

Pedigrees are useful tools to trace the existence of a trait across generations. Although you will probably not have to create a pedigree of your own on this exam, you will most likely have to use the information contained in a pedigree to deduce certain facts about the genotype and phenotype of individuals. This section contains a basic explanation of pedigrees and includes a number of tips for interpreting them.

READING A PEDIGREE

Pedigrees can provide a large amount of information about the inheritance of a trait, and those you are likely to encounter will probably not be very complex. However, to interpret a pedigree, you must understand the symbols that you will encounter.

The basic symbols on a pedigree are a circle and a square, either empty, filled-in, or half-filled:

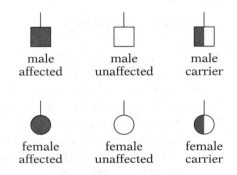

Figure 7-16

As you can see in Figure 7-16, a circle indicates a female, while a square indicates a male. A shape that is filled in indicates that an individual is affected by the trait in question, while an empty shape indicates that an individual is not affected by the trait. The half-filled shapes are not often used, but you may encounter them; they are used to indicate an individual who is a carrier for a trait but does not express the trait.

You may occasionally encounter a shape with a question mark inside. This generally indicates that it is unknown whether or not the individual displayed the trait or not. A small, typical pedigree might look something like what you see in Figure 7-17.

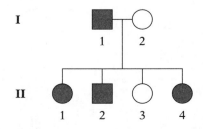

Figure 7-17

As you can see, this diagram contains six individuals: two affected males, two affected females, and two unaffected females. Generations of a pedigree are numbered with roman numerals (I, II, III, etc.); individuals within each generation are numbered left to right. Thus, each individual in the pedigree has a two-digit number that indicates his or her position on the diagram. The affected male in the second generation for example, could be referred to as II-2.

A horizontal line between two individuals, such as between I-1 and I-2 in the figure above, indicates a mating between those two individuals. The individuals on the branch that extends down from that mating are the children of that mating, placed in order of birth from left to right. Thus, II-1 is the eldest daughter of I-1 and I-2, while II-4 is their youngest daughter.

Generally, when you see a pedigree, you'll get a certain amount of information with which to decipher it. This information consists, at least, of the trait that the pedigree tracks. If you're not given the mode of inheritance for the trait (e.g., dominant or recessive), then you're generally be given some information about the genotype or phenotype of one or more individuals in the pedigree. The rest is for you to figure out; most commonly, there will be an unknown individual whose phenotype or genotype you will be required to deduce; occasionally, you will be asked to determine the mode of inheritance.

INTERPRETING FROM A PEDIGREE

A typical question from a pedigree might ask you to determine the genotype or phenotype of an individual. Such a question may resemble the following.

Polydactyly is a dominantly inherited trait that causes affected individuals to grow extra fingers or toes. Figure 7-18 is a pedigree that indicates the occurrence of polydactyly in a specific family.

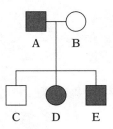

Figure 7-18

What is the genotype of the individual marked A?

The first step in answering such a question is to look at the diagram and indicate which of the organisms whose genotypes you *do* know. Because polydactyly is a dominantly inherited trait, we know that individuals who do *not* have the trait are homozygous recessive. This means that individuals B and C are homozygous recessive. It may help to write this down—perhaps using the letters *pp*—under the individual whose genotypes you know.

The next step, then, is figuring out the genotypes of the individuals that you don't know. To do so, a nice first step might be to list all of the possible genotypes for the individuals whose genotype you are trying to figure out.

Individuals A, D, and E all have polydactyly; they all may be either homozygous dominant or heterozygous for that trait.

Then, figuring out the genotypes of your unknowns is a matter of applying the information that you are given. In the case of individuals D and E, for example, we know that they inherited one recessive gene from their mother, so they must be heterozygous, or *Pp*. And in the case of individual A, we know that he had one son, individual C, who did not have polydactyly. The only way that individual C could not have the disorder is if he inherited one recessive allele from *each of his parents*. This means that he must have inherited a recessive allele from his father, individual A.

The hidden presence of a recessive allele is perhaps the most important factor to keep in mind when interpreting pedigrees for traits that are inherited simply. *Because recessive genes are only expressed as a phenotype when there are two copies, it's possible for these genes to remain unnoticed for generations before they finally appear as a recessive gene.*

It is, in reality, very uncommon that one can be entirely sure that an individual is not a carrier for a trait. This means that you should be careful that you do not assume that an individual who is dominant for a trait is homozygous dominant because these individuals may, in fact, be heterozygous for this trait. Only if you have a good reason to think that a trait is not present should you assume that an individual is not a carrier for the disease.

Another common question that you might see on a pedigree will ask you to determine the characteristics of the possible children of two individuals on the pedigree, as in the following.

Hemophilia is a disease that affects the ability of blood to clot properly. It is a recessively inherited disorder carried on the X chromosome. Figure 7-19 traces the occurrence of hemophilia in a family.

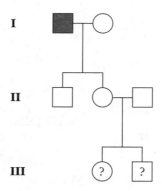

Figure 7-19

What is the likelihood that the individuals of the third generation marked with a question mark will have hemophilia? What is the likelihood that the female in the third generation will be a carrier for hemophilia?

Again, the first step in solving this problem is by listing the genotypes of each of the individuals in the pedigree that we know for certain. Because, in this pedigree, the individuals are not lettered, we'll use the traditional numbering system of I-1, I-2, etc.

We know, for example, that individual II-3, the father of the children about whom we have asked, does not have hemophilia. Because he is a male, and hemophilia is carried on the X chromosome, we know that his one X chromosome has a dominant allele. His genotype can, therefore, be written as $X^A Y$. We also know that individual I-1, who has the hemophilia, has a recessive allele on his X chromosome; his genotype can be written as $X^a Y$.

To figure out the likelihood of the third-generation children having hemophilia, we need to know the genotype of their mother, individual II-2 (we have already figured out the genotype of their father). We know that the mother does not have hemophilia. But is she a carrier? Well, we know that her father had hemophilia, and that her father passed on an X chromosome to her (otherwise she would not be female). Therefore, we know that she is indeed a carrier of hemophilia. We can thus write her genotype as $X^A X^a$.

Now, we must turn to our original question, which asks the probability that each of her children will have hemophilia, and the probability that the female child will be a carrier. To answer this question, we can complete a Punnett square—it's not hard to do because we already know the genotypes of the parents. We know that the father can pass on either an X^a allele or a Y allele; the mother can pass on either an X^A allele or an X^a allele:

	X^A	Y
X^A	$X^A X^A$	$X^A Y$
X^a	$X^A X^a$	$X^a Y$

Figure 7-20

Our Punnett square in Figure 7-20 provides many of our answers for us. What is the likelihood that the individual III-1 will have hemophilia? Well, of the two female squares in our Punnett square, we see that neither has both recessive alleles. There is, thus, no chance that III-1 will have hemophilia. For individual III-2, we see that $\frac{1}{2}$ of the male genotypes in our cross have hemophilia. Thus, there is a 50% chance that this individual will be affected by hemophilia.

Finally, the question asks what is the chance that the individual III-1 will be a carrier of hemophilia. Looking at our Punnett square, we see that 1/2 of the female genotypes in our cross have one recessive allele. This means that there is a 50% chance that individual III-1 will be a carrier of hemophilia.

As you can see, solving problems that involve pedigrees is not generally very difficult; it just requires patience and logic. The trick to solving such problems is to think through the pedigree, and start writing down what you know. Before long, you'll have your answer.

As with questions involving Punnett squares, however, it's important to be sure that you're answering the question that the test asks you to answer. There is no shortage of questions on the test that seem straightforward, but in fact ask a different question than you may think they are asking. Be especially sure that you pay attention to what the test is asking you to figure out.

One final type of question that you may encounter in pedigrees may ask you to determine the mode of inheritance for a specific trait: Is it a dominant trait or a recessive trait? Is the trait sex-linked or not? These questions may seem as if they are more difficult, but, in fact, they can be relatively easy to answer. It may often seem as if it would be impossible to tell the mode of inheritance simply by looking at a pedigree; remember, however, that you're taking a standardized test with thousands of other students—the writers of the test expect that there is a clear answer to the question, and they've left you a way to figure out this answer. All you have to do is know what to look for.

Consider, for example, pedigree in Figure 7-21, which traces the occurrence of a trait in a family.

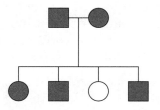

Figure 7-21

Is this trait a dominant or a recessive trait?

Well, let's hypothesize for a moment that this trait is inherited recessively. Why start here? Because it provides the least number of possibilities; if the trait is inherited recessively, then we know the exact genotypes of all the affected individuals. If that were true, then both of the individuals in the first generation would be recessive. We'll label them both *rr*. This being the case, all of their children would also have the genotype *rr* because these two parents would only be able to pass on the recessive alleles to their offspring. But this is, in fact, not the case; one of the children does not have the trait, and, therefore, is a different genotype than her parent. Thus, it's impossible for this trait to be inherited recessively. It must be inherited by a dominant allele.

To double-check our logic, let's consider the possibility of this trait being inherited by a dominant allele. Is it possible for two parents who have a dominant phenotype to have a daughter with the recessive phenotype? Indeed, this is possible: If both of the parents are heterozygous, then they can each pass on a recessive allele to their daughter, who will not display the trait. This trait, then, must be dominantly inherited.

This example illustrates an important rule you may have already observed from Punnett squares: the children of two parents with the recessive phenotype will always display the recessive phenotype. Therefore, if you ever see a pedigree like the one above, where two parents have the same phenotype, but one of their children has a different phenotype, then the two parents simply cannot be recessive.

Another pattern that you may notice is a pedigree in which a trait has simply skipped a generation.

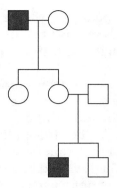

Figure 7-22

As you can see in Figure 7-22, the trait in question has simply "skipped over" the second generation, appearing only in the first and the third generations. Dominant traits, however, simply *cannot* skip generations; this is because in order for the allele to be passed down through generations, it must be present in an organism of each generation—even a heterozygous one. And while a recessive allele can be passed down and be hidden, a dominant allele—because it is dominant and will be reflected in the phenotype—cannot. If you should see a pedigree such as the above, in which a trait "skips" generations, it must be a recessive trait.

One final type of question you may be asked is to examine whether or not a trait is sex-linked. If you are asked such a question, one important way to identify a sex-linked gene is that it only affects males. Remember, that it's much more difficult for females to express sex-linked genes. If you see a pedigree in which a trait affects only males, it is likely—though not certain—to be sex-linked. Two other important characteristics of sex-linked traits that make distinguishing between the two types of inheritance much easier.

- Fathers *cannot* pass on traits carried on the X chromosome to their sons, because they do not pass an X chromosome to their sons.
- Daughters with recessively inherited sex-linked genes *must* inherit them from both their father *and* their mother, which means that the father *must* display the trait.

Consider, for example, the pedigree in Figure 7-23, which traces the occurrence of a trait in a family.

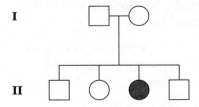

Figure 7-23

Is this trait recessive or dominant? And is it passed on a sex chromosome or on an autosome?

In this pedigree, we see that the trait has "skipped" the first generation of individuals and is present only in the second generation. This is an immediate clue that this trait is, indeed, a recessive trait. But is this trait sex-linked or not?

Let us assume for a moment that this trait is, indeed, sex-linked. For this trait to be sex-linked, the female who displays this trait must have inherited an allele from both her mother and her father; we'll indicate her genotype with an $X^n X^n$. For this individual to have this genotype, she must have inherited one of these alleles from each of her parents. This means that her father, individual I-1, would have the genotype $X^n Y$, and would display the trait; this, however, is not the case. In fact, her father does not have this trait, which indicates that this trait is *not* sex-linked, but is passed on autosomes.

LESSON SUMMARY

- Pedigrees are useful tools for examining the inheritance of traits across generations. They indicate the sex of an individual and whether or not the individual is affected by a trait.
- When interpreting a pedigree, start by marking the genotype of the individuals you know, and then try to logically figure out the genotype of the individuals you do not.
- Occasionally, a Punnett square may come in handy to figure out certain parts of a pedigree.
- When interpreting a pedigree, remember that a cross of two recessive individuals can never give a dominant result, and that a dominant trait can never "skip" generations.
- Sex-linked traits have unique, sex-dependent patterns of inheritance that can be used to identify them on a pedigree.

REVIEW QUESTIONS

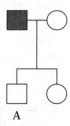

A

1. The above is a pedigree showing the occurrence of a dominantly inherited trait. Which of the following is a possible genotype of the individual marked A?

   I.   homozygous dominant
   II. heterozygous
   III. homozygous recessive

   (A) I only
   (B) II only
   (C) III only
   (D) I and II only
   (E) I, II, and III

Questions 2 and 3 refer to the following diagram:

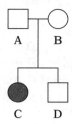

2. The above is a pedigree showing the occurrence of a recessively inherited trait. Which of the following is a possible genotype of the individual marked C?

   I. homozygous dominant
   II. heterozygous
   III. homozygous recessive

     (A) I only
     (B) III only
     (C) I and II only
     (D) I and III only
     (E) II and III only

3. Which of the following terms most accurately describes the individual marked A?

     (A) transgenic
     (B) homozygous
     (C) recessive
     (D) monosomic
     (E) carrier

Questions 4 and 5 refer to the following diagram.

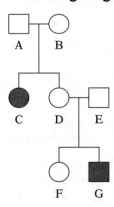

4. The above diagram tracks the inheritance of a certain trait through a family. Which of the following statements about this trait is NOT true?

     (A) This trait is dominantly inherited.
     (B) This trait could be inherited on the X chromosome.
     (C) This trait is capable of skipping generations.
     (D) This trait appears in both males and females.
     (E) This trait may not be sex-linked.

5. Which of the following statements about the trait that is tracked in this pedigree is CORRECT?

   (A) Individual B may be homozygous for this trait.
   (B) Individual D may be homozygous for this trait.
   (C) Individual F may be homozygous for this trait.
   (D) Individual C may be heterozygous for this trait.
   (E) None of the above

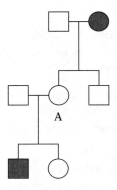

6. The above pedigree tracks the occurrence of a trait in a family. Which of the following statements accurately describe this trait?

   I.   This trait is recessively inherited.
   II. This trait is sex-linked.
   III. The individual marked A on this chart is heterozygous for this trait.

   (A) I only
   (B) I and II only
   (C) I and III only
   (D) II and III only
   (E) I, II, and III only

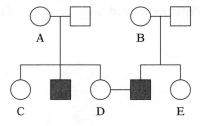

7. The above pedigree tracks the occurrence of a genetic disorder. Which of the following best describes the disorder?

   (A) dominant and autosomal
   (B) recessive and autosomal
   (C) recessive and Y-linked
   (D) dominant and X-linked
   (E) recessive and X-linked

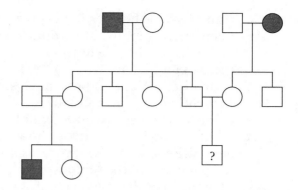

8. The above pedigree traces the occurrence of an autosomally inherited (that is, not sex-linked) trait in a family. What is the probability that the individual in the question mark will inherit this trait?

(A) zero

(B) $\dfrac{1}{8}$

(C) $\dfrac{1}{4}$

(D) $\dfrac{1}{2}$

(E) $\dfrac{3}{4}$

ANSWERS

1. **C** Individual A's box is unshaded, which indicates that he does not possess the trait and is, therefore, homozygous recessive. His *father* has the dominant trait, his box is shaded, and so he must be heterozygous in order to produce a son who is unaffected by the trait.

2. **B** Individual C has a recessive trait. She must have two recessive alleles and is, therefore, homozygous recessive.

3. **E** Individual A is heterozygous for this trait; otherwise, he could not have passed a recessive gene on to his daughter. He is, therefore, a carrier of this recessive trait, because he can pass it on without expressing it.

4. **A** Individuals D and E do not have this trait, yet they passed it on to their son (individual G) anyway. This is type of generation skipping is only possible with a recessive trait. This trait may or may not be sex-linked; there is not enough information to determine.

5. **C** Individuals B and D both passed on this trait. They must both be heterozygous. Individual C displays a recessive phenotype and, therefore, must be homozygous recessive. Individual F may be heterozygous or homozygous; there is no way to tell.

6. **C** This trait is recessive. We know this because the trait was able to "skip" generations, and dominant traits are not capable of skipping generations. Therefore, statement I is true. Statement II is false, however. If this were a sex-linked recessive trait, the male of the second generation (II-3) would have inherited the trait from his mother. He must have inherited two alleles (not one as he would have if this were a sex-linked

trait) because he does not express the recessive allele he inherited from his mother. Finally, individual A must be heterozygous to have passed on the recessive allele to her son (individual III-1). Therefore, statements I and III are true.

7. **E** Individuals A and B both have sons with this trait. These sons must have inherited the recessive allele from their mothers. Therefore, the disorder is recessive and sex-linked on the X chromosome.

8. **C** Our first job is to figure out how this trait is inherited. Because it skips generations, we know it is recessively inherited. We must then find out the genotype of the unknown individual's parents. Neither of them display the disorder, but each of them inherited one recessive allele from a homozygous recessive parent. Therefore, both are heterozygous (*Tt*) for this trait. We can now perform a Punnett square on the cross.

	T	t
T	TT	T*t*
t	T*t*	tt

The shaded squares are those that will display the trait. This represents $\frac{1}{4}$ of the possible offspring.

CHAPTER 8

UNDERSTANDING EVOLUTION AND DIVERSITY

Lesson 8-1. Evolution and Natural Selection

VOCABULARY

- evolution
- natural selection
- limiting factor
- homology
- convergent evolution

At largely the same time that Mendel was working with pea plants in his efforts to understand the principles of inheritance, a young British naturalist named Charles Darwin was exploring the diversity of life in Britain's globe-spanning empire. The principles of evolution and natural selection that he published would not only revolutionize the way biologists thought of the world, but would challenge long-held assumptions about the place of humans in the universe. In this lesson, we examine his basic theory of natural selection, which remains a fundamental underpinning of the modern understanding of biology.

DARWIN AND NATURAL SELECTION

As with Mendel, Darwin's theories have become so commonly accepted that it may be hard to understand why they were considered so revolutionary. It's important to remember that at the time of Darwin, there was little understanding of the nature of life. We take for granted much of our understanding of life: that it is made up of cells, that cells cannot spontaneously generate, and that traits are passed from generation to generation.

In Darwin's time, scientists were only beginning to understand that species might change over time. **Evolution,** strictly put, is this idea that the attributes of life change over time—that species have not always been the same throughout the history of the Earth. The opposing idea—that life had been created in the way it now exists—had been the prevailing thought in Western culture for approximately 2,000 years, since the days of the Greek philosophers Plato and Aristotle, and was confirmed by the teachings of the Old Testament.

Although Darwin is often credited with the theory of evolution, he was not the first to suggest it. The theory of evolution was first postulated in 1809 by Jean Baptiste Lamarck. Lamarck had examined fossils, and understood from his investigations into the new, growing field of paleontology that species did, indeed, change over time. Lamarck postulated that these changes occurred because of the acquired characteristics of an organism; a giraffe, the hypothesis goes, would develop a longer neck because of continual stretching to eat leaves on high branches. Over generations, Lamarck thought, these acquired characteristics could accumulate and change the form of species.

Darwin, however, postulated a different explanation for evolution's mechanism. While in his early twenties, Darwin sailed with the HMS *Beagle*, a British ship charged with making maps of the South American coast. During the voyage, Darwin observed the native plants and animals in the various locales that the ship visited and took a number of samples back for study. Most notably, Darwin observed the great variety of bird species—especially finches—that were present on a group of isolated islands in the Pacific Ocean far off the South American coast known as the Galapagos Islands. When Darwin returned home with his samples, he began to try to understand exactly how and why so many different species of finches existed on this small group of islands.

Darwin realized that the many different species of finches that he observed had features—most notably their beaks—that were well-suited to consuming a specific type of food. Certain finches had large beaks to crack seeds; others had smaller, more pointed beaks, better suited to eating insects than seeds. Darwin understood that these finches had probably all come from a common ancestor who had somehow ended up on the island.

Darwin, then, understood evolution as a process by which all life diverged from one common ancestor into many different species, some of which were able to survive, and some of which were not. Instead of looking at evolution as a line in which one species morphed into another, Darwin looked at evolution as a tree with hundreds of branches, some of which were successful and some of which were not.

This emphasis on success underscores the fundamental mechanism of Darwin's understanding of evolution: that of **natural selection.** Natural selection is often described as a simple story of "survival of the fittest" but there are a large number of underlying concepts that are involved in natural selection, each of which needed elucidating by Darwin. His theory can be understood by describing the following concepts.

- *Competition.* All organisms face some natural environmental limit— known as a **limiting factor**—on their ability to survive and reproduce. Otherwise, they would continue to reproduce infinitely. Often, this limiting factor is the availability of food or some other resource necessary for survival. Because of these limiting factors, organisms are forced to compete with one another for survival.
- *Variation.* There is a natural amount of variation within a population of organisms. This will leave certain organisms better able to survive in the current environmental conditions than others. These organisms are often referred to as "the fittest." Which organisms are best suited for an environment, will, of course, depend on the specific conditions of each environment because, as we know, environments can change, so too will the organisms that inhabit those environments.
- *Selection and Reproduction.* The organisms in a population that are the most fit will best be able to survive, meaning they will be most likely to reproduce. Their greater success at reproducing means that eventually, they and their offspring will make up most or all of the population, and those organisms that are less fit to the environment will die out. This is natural selection: the environment dictates which organisms will be able to procreate, and which will die out.

- *Adaptation.* The net result of this process is that the species best fit for an environment are the ones that are able to access the available resources in a given environment. This means that the tendency over time will be for organisms to adapt to their given environment.

Darwin's theory of natural selection isn't too difficult to understand. However, there are some points that bear elucidating. First, it's important to understand that Darwin understood evolution as process of trial and error. Whereas before, it had been assumed that evolution worked toward some finished product of species, Darwin's natural selection is a brutal process in which many, if not most, adaptations would not succeed. Darwin saw that species could come and go; his theory necessitated that there had been species on Earth that were no longer here, and raised the possibility—indeed, the great likelihood—that the species on Earth today might not be here tomorrow. And he makes it clear that the history of life on Earth is a history of how species on the planet have variously changed and adapted over time, into the forms we recognize today.

Second, it's important to understand that Darwin placed a large focus on the *interaction of the environment with natural variation in a species.* This does not mean that there are "good" or "bad" variations in a species—only that certain features of organisms are more or less fit for a given environment. This focus was different from previous theorists in that Darwin placed the driving force for evolution squarely within the natural world—in the surroundings of an organism. This meant that understanding how species changed over time was a matter of understanding how environmental conditions had promoted the survival of one feature over another.

Finally, the importance of *reproduction* in Darwin's theory of evolution cannot be understated. Reproduction is the heart of Darwin's theory, because it states that those species that are best able to reproduce will survive. Darwin understood that the only important features were the ones that allowed organisms of a species to produce more of themselves, thereby allowing them to pass on their traits to their offspring.

For the species of finches on the Galapagos Islands, developing beaks that allowed them to access various sources of food was what made certain species survive, and thus live to reproduce. This means that often, a favorable adaptation is one that allows an organism to survive better to adulthood, when they can reproduce. Sometimes, however, the mechanism directly affects the *ability* to reproduce; an insect that is not able to perform the correct mating dance, for example, would be less able to reproduce, while a male bird with colorful flowers that is more able to attract females might reproduce more than his less-colorful counterparts.

There is a tendency to think that natural selection acted to produce all of the attributes of a given species. But this is not always the case. If organisms have attributes that do not affect their ability to reproduce—or, indirectly, their survival to the age of reproduction—then there is little chance for natural selection to affect the prevalence of that trait. Consider, for example, Huntington's disease and Alzheimer's disease, both of which generally affect humans *after* their child-bearing years. Because these diseases have no effect on an individual's ability to reproduce—only the person's survival after he or she has already reproduced—they are neither favorable nor unfavorable from an evolutionary standpoint.

EVIDENCE FOR EVOLUTION

To this day, Darwin's ideas about evolution stir controversy. However, the scientific evidence overwhelmingly supports the theory. Evolution provides powerful explanations for much of what we observe in biology. In this section, we briefly discuss the evidence for evolution.

Humans can directly witness evolution by observing the natural selection of certain traits over others in species. Consider, for example, the continued existence of insects such as cockroaches despite the best efforts of humans to eradicate them. When humans first developed insecticides to fight infestations of such pests, they were highly effective. However, the small proportion of the cockroach population that was somehow naturally resistant to such insecticides survived these onslaughts, and continued to reproduce while their susceptible brethren died out. Eventually, these resistant ones made up more and more of the cockroach population, until almost all of the population was resistant to such insecticides.

A similar resistance regularly develops in bacteria, in response to antibiotics. Penicillin, the first antibiotic discovered, works by attacking a bacterial protein that produces the cell wall, causing the bacterial cells to lyse (break open). Soon, however, penicillin-resistant bacteria developed that were able to fabricate their cell walls despite treatments of penicillin. Today, resistance to penicillin and a number of other antibiotics has become very common, forcing researchers to continuously develop new antibiotics to fight against bacteria, so that we are not left without any drugs to fight bacterial infections.

Yet, aside from the occurrence of natural selection in everyday life, there are a number of indications that the organisms on Earth all share a common ancestor from which they diverged. At the molecular level, the simplest example is the fact that all organisms share the same basic mechanisms: they all utilize DNA, RNA, and proteins. The genetic code and its ability to code for proteins is a common feature of all life forms, inherited from the earliest organisms on Earth. Within our DNA and proteins, too, there is evidence of common ancestry. The amino acid sequence of the protein hemoglobin, for example, is rather similar between humans and many other primates. Our DNA, then, indicates that we have relatives among other species.

Indeed, **homology**—similarity in the characteristics of species, resulting from their common ancestry—is one of the best pieces of evidence for evolution. The molecular homologies discussed above, however, are just one type of homology. There are also a number of anatomical homologies between creatures. Consider, for example, that the wing of a bat more resembles a cat's paw in its skeletal structure than it does the wing of a bird, and that a whale's fin is much more like a human hand than it is any analogous structure found in fish, even though these structures perform vastly different functions. The explanation for this is that both whales and bats are mammals—they share a much more recent common ancestor with humans and other mammals than they do with fish or birds. As a result, their structure is more similar to other mammals than these fish or birds.

The homologies between creatures allow scientists to determine how closely related they are. Consider, for example, that humans and chimpanzees are much more closely related than are humans and mice. This is indicated not only in their anatomy—human anatomy much more closely resembles that of chimpanzees and other primates—but also at the molecular level. The amino acid sequence of human hemoglobin, for example, is much closer to that of chimpanzees than of mice. By investigating these differences, scientists have been able to come up with a "tree of life," developing a picture of how closely related the organisms on earth really are.

Scientists must be careful when relying upon homologies when determining the degree of relatedness of two different species. Very often, similar structures may evolve to perform the same function in vastly different species, a process known as **convergent evolution.** Both porcupines and cacti, for example, have needles to protect themselves; one, however, is an animal, while the other is a plant. Both species evolved a similar solution—sharp, pointy needles—to solve the problem of protection. Very often, these analogous structures often have very different anatomies—as is the case in the quills of porcupines and the needles of cacti.

The fossil record is a great aid in this attempt to put together such a tree of life. A number of fossils, for example, have been discovered for creatures that are not quite modern humans, but are not quite apes; these transitional fossils provide scientists with a way to observe how, from a common ancestor, humans evolved to a species that is quite distinct from chimpanzees. At their very least, the numerous fossils that have been uncovered—from dinosaurs, which are thought to be the ancestors of birds, to the predecessors of modern horses, felines, and humans—prove that Earth's current complement of species is not the one it has always had.

Indeed, it is certain that creatures have evolved over time. But explaining the mechanisms of natural selection—and providing a physical basis for it— were beyond the abilities of biologists at the time of Darwin, and these questions still occupy evolutionary biologists to this day. It is these topics that will occupy us in the next lesson.

LESSON SUMMARY

- Evolution is the change in the species present on Earth over time. Evolution was first proposed by Jean Baptiste Lamarck, best remembered for his theory of acquired characteristics as an explanation for evolution.
- Charles Darwin, a British naturalist, developed the theory of natural selection to explain the evolution of species. Natural selection holds that:

  — There is competition between organisms in a population for survival.
  — Natural variations in a population will render certain organisms better able to reproduce in the given environmental circumstances.
  — These most fit organisms in a population will eventually represent the greatest part of the population.
  — The overall trend of evolution will thus be for populations to adapt to the changing conditions of the environment.

- There is extensive evidence for the evolution of species over time. Molecular similarities in all life, and anatomical similarities between closely related species, indicate that all organisms share a common ancestor from which they evolved—a fact backed up by the extensive fossil record.

REVIEW QUESTIONS

1. Which of the following would NOT be useful to prove that two species were closely related?

   (A) the DNA sequence of a gene from each
   (B) anatomic homology between the two species
   (C) a map indicating that their habitats overlap
   (D) transitional fossils
   (E) a diagram of the skeletal structure of each

2. Evolution is

   (A) a change in the habitat of a species over time
   (B) a change in the species present over time
   (C) a change in the environment over time
   (D) a change in the availability of water over time
   (E) a change in the attributes of an individual over time

3. Which of the following is an example of anatomic homology?

   (A) two species live in the same area
   (B) the DNA sequence of a protein in two species is very close
   (C) two species consume the same food
   (D) two species both have green coloring
   (E) the skulls of two species resemble one another

4. Males of a certain species of bird are easily identified by their bright colors. Why might this be an advantageous adaptation?

   (A) it may allow this bird to access food that other species cannot
   (B) it may allow this bird to reproduce in greater numbers
   (C) it may allow this bird to live in harsh climates
   (D) it may allow this bird to produce greater genetic variation
   (E) this is not an advantageous adaptation

5. Which of the following is an example of convergent evolution?

   (A) both birds and insects have wings
   (B) chimpanzees and humans have a similar amino acid sequence in the protein hemoglobin
   (C) both lemon trees and orange trees have chlorophyll
   (D) bacterial cells do not have organelles
   (E) fish have gills, while mammals have lungs

6. Which of the following statements about natural selection is NOT true?

   (A) it promotes traits that allow organisms to survive longer
   (B) it promotes traits that allow organisms to reproduce in larger numbers
   (C) it uses the natural variation within a species
   (D) it occurs if there is no competition for survival
   (E) can cause species to change over time

ANSWERS

1. **C** DNA sequencing and anatomic homology (choices (B) and (E) involve anatomic homology) are useful to prove that two species are related, as would a fossil that shows a species that is intermediate in its characteristics. Simply because two organisms live in the same area, however, does not mean that they are related.

2. **B** Evolution is the change of the species that are present over time, or a change in the attributes of those species. A change in the habitat of a species is not evolution (it is migration). A change in environment or in the availability of water may bring about evolution, but are not themselves evolution. And evolution does not work to change the attributes of an individual over time, as Lamarck thought; it works to change species over time.

3. **E** Anatomic homology is a similarity in the anatomic structure of organisms. Choice (B) is a form of homology; but it is a genetic homology, not an anatomic one. Choice (D) is a tempting choice, but should be ruled out, because very different organisms could exhibit similar coloring (e.g, a frog and a plant).

4. **B** This is an example of an adaptation that increases the ability of an organism to reproduce, because it allows the males and females of the population to easily identify one another.

5. **A** Convergent evolution is the creation of similar structures in organisms that are distantly related. Both birds and insects have developed wings, even though their wings are very different in structure. The similarities mentioned in choices (B), (C), and (D) are similarities that result from a common ancestry, not similarities that result in spite of it.

6. **D** Natural selection cannot occur if there is no competition for survival. It assumes that there is some natural limit to the amount of resources that are available to support a population.

Lesson 8-2. Mechanisms of Evolution

VOCABULARY

- population
- gene pool
- Hardy–Weinberg equation
- genetic drift
- bottleneck effect
- founder effect
- mutations
- relative fitness
- directional selection

- diversifying selection
- stabilizing selection
- vestigial structures
- speciation
- species
- allopatric speciation
- gradualism
- punctuated equilibrium

It's one thing to understand how organisms change over time, but quite another to understand the specific mechanisms that make evolution possible. What is the genetic basis of the variations that Darwin talked about? How do these genetic mechanisms apply in a population? And how is it that evolution can create the many different species we see on Earth today? In this lesson, we explore the mechanisms of evolution and natural selection, starting at the genetic level, and working our way up to the creation of species.

EVOLUTION IN A POPULATION

It is tempting to think of individual organisms as the units of evolution. Indeed, our discussion has focused on the way that one organism is more fit than another. But one individual being more fit than another is not evolution. Evolution is the change in the characteristics displayed in a population of organisms—sometimes an entire species—over time.

Populations and Gene Pools

A **population** is a group of organisms from the same species in the same localized area. A population consists of a group of organisms among which there is regular breeding. The total sum of all of the different genes that are available within a population is known as the **gene pool.**

The gene pools of different populations may differ in the availability of alleles of a certain gene (recall from the last lesson that alleles are different versions of the same gene). In certain populations, for example, all members might express one trait (say, blue eyes), meaning they are homozygous for that trait. In another population, however, there may be more than one trait present in the gene pool (for example, blue and brown eyes), accounted for by the presence of different alleles in that population. A gene pool, then, describes the specific alleles that are present in a population.

Each population, then, can be described by the frequency of a given allele within it. A population in which 10% of the individuals are homozygous recessive (*rr*) for a certain trait, for example, is different from a population that is 90% homozygous recessive, or one in which no one is homozygous recessive.

The Hardy–Weinberg Equation: Nonevolving Populations

It is theoretically possible that the frequency of alleles within a population will not shift. For this to happen, a number of conditions must be met:

- a very large population
- no migration of organisms into or out of the population
- mating in the population is random and does not depend on the presence of one allele
- there are no mutations that regularly alter one allele into the other
- natural selection is not acting to affect the survival of organisms with one or the other allele

We elucidate these conditions here because the characteristics of such a population in which the frequency of alleles will not change has been described using a famous equation, known as the **Hardy–Weinberg equation.** The above, then, are preconditions for the Hardy–Weinberg equation.

The Hardy–Weinberg equation describes the frequency of the three genotypes in a population given the frequency of each of the alleles in that population (or, gives the frequency of the alleles in that population given the frequency of any one of the genotypes). Generally, the letter p is used to describe the proportion of the dominant allele in a population (that is, the percentage of all alleles in that population that are dominant), while the letter q is used to describe the frequency of the recessive allele. For a population with only two alleles for each trait (the only type of population we discuss), $p + q = 1$. So, if 85% of the alleles in a population are dominant (R), then 15% will be recessive (r), because $0.85 + 0.15 = 1$.

The Hardy–Weinberg equation says that in a nonevolving population, the frequency of the three resulting genotypes can be described using the following equation:

$$p^2 + 2pq + q^2 = 1,$$

where p^2 is the frequency of the homozygous dominant (RR) genotype, $2pq$ is the frequency of the heterozygous genotype (Rr), and q^2 is the frequency of the homozygous recessive phenotype (rr).

The Hardy–Weinberg equation is useful for describing the genetic features of a population. For example, take the above population where $p = 0.85$. In this population:

- the homozygous dominant genotype would occur in $p^2 = 0.85^2 = 72.25\%$ of the population
- the heterozygous genotype would occur in $2pq = 2 \times 0.85 \times 0.15 = 25.5\%$ of the population
- the homozygous recessive genotype would occur in $q^2 = 0.15^2 = 2.25\%$ of the population

Note that the total of these three numbers is 100%, or 1.00.

It's also possible, using the Hardy–Weinberg equation, to figure out the prevalence of a gene knowing only the frequency of one of the homozygous genotypes. We very often only know the proportion of a population that is homozygous recessive, but can use this to estimate how much of that population will be homozygous dominant and heterozygous.

For example, if we know that for a certain population, 36% of the population is homozygous recessive, then we know that:

- $q^2 = 0.36$, so $q = 0.6$ (the square root of 0.36), meaning 60% of the alleles are recessive
- $p = 0.4$ because $p + q = 1$, meaning 40% of the alleles are dominant
- $p^2 = 0.16$, meaning 16% of the population is homozygous recessive
- $2pq = 0.48$, meaning 48% of the population is heterozygous
- in total, $p^2 + 2pq = 0.16 + 0.48 = 0.64$, meaning 64% of the population will have the dominant phenotype

The Hardy–Weinberg equation, then, is a useful tool for modeling phenotypes within a given gene pool. But a population in which the Hardy–Weinberg equation applies is, by definition, a population in which there is no change in the frequency of the alleles, and is, therefore, a nonevolving population. In an evolving population, the proportion of the alleles within a population is, indeed, shifting.

Evolution by Chance

If a nonevolving population is one in which the frequency of alleles is stable, then an evolving population is one in which the frequency of alleles is changing. This definition of evolution is important because it allows us to understand evolution in genetic terms: evolution occurs when one allele becomes more or less common.

This change in the frequency of the alleles can be brought about by anything that causes one of the necessary requirements for the Hardy–Weinberg equation to be violated. Perhaps the most important of the preconditions for the Hardy–Weinberg equation is that of a very large population size. As Mendel understood when working with his pea plants, a larger population of organisms means that results are more likely to be close to what would be expected by the laws of probability. When a population is small, there is a good possibility that, as a result of simple chance, the inheritance of alleles from one generation to another will not follow what would be expected in the Hardy–Weinberg equation.

This change in the frequency of alleles within a population attributable to chance is known as **genetic drift.** Genetic drift is important because it describes a mechanism of evolution in the absence of natural selection—there is nothing in the environment that is causing one of the alleles to be favored over the other; simple chance is dictating that one is being selected over the other.

A good example of genetic drift is what is known as the **bottleneck effect.** The bottleneck effect is genetic drift that occurs when the size of a population is drastically reduced by some event. Say, for example, that you had 50 pennies and 50 nickels in your pocket, and you lost all but four of them through a hole in the bottom of your pocket. It's technically possible that you'll end up with two pennies and two nickels, but it's also quite possible, for example, that you might end up with all nickels. If this were the case, then your reduced population does not at all resemble the population that existed before the bottlenecking event. The bottleneck effect, then, results from the fact that the gene pool of a drastically reduced population may not resemble the gene pool of the original population.

Another example of genetic drift is a result of what is known as the **founder effect.** The founder effect is genetic drift that occurs when a small number of individuals populate a new area. Because the gene pool of this small group of individuals may not have the same genetic diversity as the original population, this new population often has very different attributes from the original population.

If there is movement between populations, however, it is likely to make the gene pools of the two populations more similar, as they share their alleles. This movement between two populations is known as gene flow. Gene flow can be caused when, for example, two mouse populations previously separated by a body of water are suddenly able to migrate across over a human-built bridge or tunnel, or when pollen is transported to one population from another by the wind.

Mutations, random changes in an organism's DNA that create new alleles for a gene, are also able to cause a population to evolve. However, mutations alone rarely cause evolutionary changes. First of all, the mutation, in order to be passed on, must take place in one of the cells that eventually develops into a sperm or an egg. Otherwise, although an organism may have a mutation in some of its cells, it will not be passed on to its offspring. Second, because mutations are random and occur in individuals, it's unlikely that a mutation alone will drastically affect the frequency of alleles in a population. Only if, for example, a person with a mutation survives a bottlenecking event, or if natural selection is at work on the population, will a mutation cause evolution in a population.

Evolution by Natural Selection

You may recall that the absence of natural selection was one of the preconditions for a nonevolving population. As you might imagine, natural selection can act to affect the frequency of alleles within a population drastically. Say, for example, that a previously isolated population of mice was suddenly faced with the encroachment of mouse-eating birds into its territory. If this were to happen, any mice that had a trait that made them less likely to be bird food would have a greater chance of survival. This situation, for example, might favor mice with a darker hair color, which were less able than their white or light-colored counterparts to be spotted by their predator.

When environmental conditions cause organisms with one allele to be somehow more fit than another, natural selection is at work, and the frequency of alleles within that population can change. Often, these alleles that are favored by natural selection are alleles that confer some survival advantage, as darker fur color did for mice in the case above.

Sometimes, however, natural selection may select alleles that do not cause a difference in survival, but confer the ability to reproduce in greater numbers. The males of certain species of geckos, for example, develop a bright red sac under their throat that allows them to attract females. Any male who somehow did not have the allele for this trait would face a severe disadvantage in finding a mate.

The term that is used to describe the differences between organisms that are more or less able to survive or reproduce in an environment is **relative fitness.** Organisms whose attributes make them better able to survive or reproduce are said be more relatively fit than their counterparts.

Natural selection is an especially significant force behind evolution because it is the most likely to favor adaptations that make an organism more fit for its environment. Genetic drift, gene flow, and mutations all occur rather randomly and will not necessarily cause an organism to accrue favorable mutations. Natural selection, however, continually acts to make organisms more fit for their environments.

There are a number of ways in which natural selection can act upon a population. Often, natural selection acts to shift the overall genetic makeup of a population toward one end; as, for example, happened in the case of the introduction of birds into the mouse environment, when darker mice were favored. In that case, the allelic makeup of the population was likely to tend toward darker alleles. Such a selection is known as **directional selection.**

Occasionally, however, natural selection might work to cause the phenotypes of a population to tend to the extremes of a range. This might happen if, for some reason, the predator birds were more able to see mice of the middle-range fur colors than those who were either very dark or very light. This is known as **diversifying selection.** Other times, natural selection can cause the culling of extreme phenotypes from a population. This might happen in the case of our mice if, for example, predator birds were able to see only the light and dark mice, but not mice of the intermediate phenotype. This is known as **stabilizing selection.**

Limits of Natural Selection

Before we turn from our discussion on natural selection, it's important to remember that there are limits to what natural selection can accomplish. First and foremost, it's important to remember that natural selection is not a process that was "designed" simply to lead to humans. Although humans are one product of evolution, natural selection only acts to cull those organisms that are unfit for the environment.

Second, natural selection cannot create anything new. Natural selection can only work with the given genetic variation within a species to favor certain attributes in that species. Only mutations can create a new genetic variant—and though this does often happen, the accretion of such mutations does not take place over one generation, but over thousands or millions of years.

Finally, natural selection does not create perfect organisms. As we learned in the last section with the example of traits that do not greatly affect the ability of humans to reproduce (Alzheimer's disease and Huntington's disease), sometimes different alleles simply have no effect on the relative fitness of an organism. This means that natural selection cannot act on that trait.

Influences other than natural selection, such as genetic drift, mutations, or gene flow, are also at work on organisms. These influences may act randomly, and not necessarily in a way that makes an organism more fit for its environment. It's also important to remember that there is no one definition of what a perfect organism is. What is imperfect for one environment, for example, might once have been very suitable for a past environment. And often, an adaptation that allows an organism to be "perfect" for one environment makes it less suitable for another environment, so trade-offs must be made. Take the human appendix for example. This is an organ in our bodies that serves no useful function. In fact, it only causes trouble. In our distant past, the appendix served an important purpose in the digestive process, however, now it is no longer needed. Such structures (other examples include our wisdom teeth and coccyx, or tailbone) are called vestigial. The presence of **vestigial structures** lends further support to evolution because organisms apparently were not designed perfectly.

Although natural selection is not a perfect process, and is, as we've learned, not even the only process by which evolution can occur, it has, indeed, allowed organisms to inhabit almost every environment on Earth. We've seen clearly how populations can evolve; now, we'll see how these evolutions can give rise to new species.

CREATING DIVERSITY: SPECIATION

The discussion above of evolution has said much about how the properties of a population can evolve over time. But we've yet to arrive at an understanding of what causes two populations to diverge into two different species of organisms. This process, known as **speciation,** is what accounts for the great diversity of species on Earth today. Evolution must be able to account for the process of speciation, showing how different species of closely related species are able to emerge (for example, different species of squirrels or finches), but also showing how the great diversity of life—from bacteria to birds—was created.

Before we discuss speciation, however, we must define the term "species." For the purposes of understanding evolution, a **species** can be defined as the populations of organisms that are capable of breeding to produce viable off-spring. For example, all humans, despite their ethnic differences and the long distances that separate them, are capable of interbreeding, making them members of the same species. Alligators and crocodiles, however, appear similar and live in approximately the same locations, but are not capable of interbreeding; they, then, are members of different species.

Barriers between Species

An important concept to understand is that there are a number of differences between two populations of closely related organisms that might make them members of different species. Given our definition of the term species as the ability to interbreed, it makes sense that most of these differences are generally barriers that prohibit interbreeding in the two populations. If one of these barriers develops between two populations, then they will be unable to interbreed and can be defined as two different species.

One type of barrier is a barrier to the mating of organisms. The two populations may live in different habitats in the same area—for example, living in the water versus on land, or, in the case of parasites, living on a different host organism. The two populations may simply not want to mate with each other; they may not recognize members of the other species as male or female, or may have different mating rituals that prevent them from mating. Sometimes, the two populations may mate or flower at different times of the day, resulting in the temporal isolation of two populations. In any of these cases, there will be a barrier to breeding between these populations.

Even if two organisms are capable of mating, they may be incapable of producing a fertilized egg. Sometimes, for example, different anatomy prevents organisms from successfully copulating or transferring pollen. And even if the two populations are capable of mating, their gametes may somehow be incompatible, and unable to produce a viable, fertilized egg.

But even the production of a fertilized egg does not mean that two organisms are members of the same species. The hybrid organism created by the mixture of the two organisms may not develop to birth or to sexual maturity. And, even if sexually mature, it may be infertile. This is the case with donkeys and horses; they are capable of successfully mating, creating a mule. Mules, however, are sterile, which ensures that horses and donkeys remain separate species. Finally, even if a hybrid is viable, its offspring may not be very robust and be incapable of retaining their fertility. Any one of these possibilities creates a barrier between two closely related populations that would make them members of a different species.

The Origin of Species

One population of organisms is not likely simply to diverge into two different species without some other factor at work. This is because in a population, organisms are constantly interbreeding, and so there is little chance for one of these barriers to emerge naturally within an existing population. How is it, then, that one of these barriers can develop, and lead to additional species?

One of the most common ways this occurs is through the geographic segregation of a population, which splits the gene pool of the population into two populations, which may then each evolve differently. This would happen if, say, a lake were to partially dry up and split into two different lakes, which are no longer connected. The fish in the two lakes were once one population, but, if they are unable to share genes because of this geographic separation, then they will not evolve together.

It's possible, as a result of any number of factors, for the two populations to evolve apart from each other, because the forces of genetic drift, mutation, and natural selection will affect these populations differently. When these two populations are reunited, they may no longer be able to interbreed because their separate evolution has caused them to develop some difference that prohibits mating—this may include any of the barriers that we discussed above. Perhaps they no longer recognize each other as a member of the same species, or perhaps one population has developed some genetic change that no longer allows it to successfully produce a fertilized egg with a member of the other population. When this happens, the two populations have become two different species. If, however, they are reunited and still able to breed, then speciation has not occurred.

Allopatric speciation is the term for the creation of species when a population is somehow separated by a geographic barrier. Allopatric speciation has been observed in a number of scenarios. This is very common in groups of islands, such as the Hawaiian or Galapagos Islands, because each island provides a segregated environment in which different species may evolve. As organisms are swept from one island to another—birds may be blown from one island to another by a storm, for example, carrying with them seeds for plants—there are plenty of opportunities for the two populations on each island to evolve separately. This is especially likely if the number of organisms that started the new population is small—an example of the founder effect. The many unique organisms that inhabit the continent of Australia, such as the kangaroo and koala, despite a common ancestry with those organisms from Asia and the Americas, are a good example of how geographic separation can lead to the creation of different species.

It is, however, technically possible for one population to produce another species without some form of geographic separation. This is known as sympatric speciation. Although it is more rare than allopatric speciation, sympatric speciation is possible if, for some reason, a barrier to mating somehow spontaneously emerges within a population. This might happen if, for example, an insect were to develop a mutation that caused it to live in a different habitat than its predecessors. A genetic barrier to breeding can emerge in plants, where occasionally tetraploid organisms (that is, organisms with four copies of each chromosome) can emerge because of nondisjunction. Such organisms might be incapable of breeding with their diploid ancestors, and so may form a new population in the same spot as the old.

The Pace of Evolution

There is much debate among evolutionary biologists about the pace at which speciation takes place. There is no doubt that two populations of organisms can diverge to form two different species. But how quickly does this change occur? Darwin originally postulated that the most likely scenario is that of **gradualism**—that two species emerge as only slightly different at first, and then, over time, eventually accumulate small differences that make them into vastly different species. Gradualism holds that evolution is a slow, steady process, taking millions of years to create new species and that species are likely to constantly change their form.

Another theory, known as **punctuated equilibrium,** has become very popular with evolutionary biologists. Punctuated equilibrium holds that the great majority of the differences between two species emerge shortly after their divergence—say, over the first 30,000 years—and that for the rest of the life of the species (which may be millions of years) they will most likely change very little.

Which of these theories is more accurate? Probably neither. Both theories describe one way in which organisms have evolved over time. Geologic evidence and the fossil record, however, do indicate that there have been "explosions" of speciation after certain mass extinctions in history, which does tend to support punctuated equilibrium. What's important to remember, however, is that *both* theories describe change that takes place over millions of years. In the next lesson, we explore this vast history of evolutionary change, a process known to have started approximately four billion years ago.

LESSON SUMMARY

- A population is a group of organisms of the same species that regularly interbreeds. The gene pool of a population can have specific characteristics, depending on the frequency of alleles within that population.
- A nonevolving population is one in which the frequency of alleles does not change. Such a population is described by the Hardy–Weinberg equation ($p^2 + 2pq + q^2 = 1$).
- Evolving populations are ones in which the preconditions of the Hardy–Weinberg equation are not met. In such a population, the frequency of alleles is changing.
- Genetic drift is evolution caused by chance. The bottleneck effect is genetic drift caused by the reduction of a population after an event. The founder

effect is genetic drift attributable to a small number of individuals starting a new population.

- Gene flow and mutation may also cause a population to evolve.
- Natural selection causes evolution in a population that adapts that population to its environment. Alleles that cause an organism to be relatively more fit than its counterpart will eventually become more frequent in the population.
- Natural selection cannot act on all traits simultaneously, nor can it create any "new" traits in an organism.
- A species is all of the populations of an organism capable of interbreeding. Speciation describes the creation of two different species.
- Species may be separated by barriers to mating, barriers to fertilization of the egg, or barriers to producing fertile and viable offspring.
- Allopatric speciation is the divergence of two populations separated by a geographic barrier into two (or more) species.
- Gradualism holds that speciation occurs slowly, with differences in species accreting slowly over time. Punctuated equilibrium holds that species diverge greatly in a short period of time, followed by long periods of stability.

REVIEW QUESTIONS

1. In a given nonevolving population, 20% of the alleles for a given gene are recessive (s). What percentage of individuals in this population have the dominant phenotype?

   (A) 4%
   (B) 32%
   (C) 64%
   (D) 80%
   (E) 96%

2. In a given nonevolving population, 51% of the individuals display the dominant phenotype. What proportion of the alleles in this population are dominant?

   (A) 0.09
   (B) 0.3
   (C) 0.49
   (D) 0.51
   (E) 0.7

3. It is discovered that 128 out of 200 individuals in a population display the dominant phenotype. Assuming the Hardy–Weinberg equation holds for this population, what proportion of individuals in this population display the heterozygous phenotype?

   (A) 0.18
   (B) 0.28
   (C) 0.38
   (D) 0.48
   (E) 0.58

4. Which of the following is an example of natural selection?

(A) Pollen from a flower is carried across a river by the wind, and polli-
nates another flower.
(B) Three mice are carried on a boat to an island and start a new mouse
population.
(C) An eagle is able to spot more mice than his counterparts, and lives
longer.
(D) A large proportion of a deer population dies in a forest fire, and the
remaining population is darker than before.
(E) Bees are attracted to both the pink and red varieties of a flower.

5. A flood leaves only 5% of a mouse population intact. This is an example of

(A) gene flow
(B) natural selection
(C) mutation
(D) bottleneck effect
(E) founder effect

6. A large canyon separates two populations of squirrels, which subsequently
diverge into different species. This is an example of

(A) genetic variation
(B) allopatric speciation
(C) bottleneck effect
(D) gene flow
(E) mutation

7. Which of the following statements about natural selection is NOT true?

(A) It can change the traits of an individual.
(B) It can cause speciation.
(C) It can change the frequency of alleles in a population.
(D) It can cause the extinction of species.
(E) It cannot create new traits.

8. Punctuated equilibrium describes

(A) a barrier between two species that prevent them from mating
(B) the accretion of mutations in individuals over time
(C) the frequency of alleles in a nonevolving population
(D) evolution that occurs in short periods of rapid change
(E) mechanisms for promoting genetic variation in a species

9. Which of the following involves a change in the frequency of the alleles in
a population?

I. genetic drift
II. evolution
III. natural selection

(A) I only
(B) III only
(C) I and II only
(D) II and III only
(E) I, II, and III

ANSWERS

1. **E** This question requires we use the Hardy–Weinberg equation. We are given that $q = 0.20$. Multiplying, we get that $q^2 = 0.04$, which means that 4% of the population is homozygous recessive. The rest of the population—96%—will display the dominant phenotype.

2. **B** Here again, we use the Hardy–Weinberg equation. We are given that 51% of the individuals have the dominant phenotype. This means that 49% of the individuals have the recessive phenotype and that $q^2 = 0.49$. Taking the square root of both sides, we get that $q = 0.7$. Because $p + q = 1$, solving for $p = 0.3$.

3. **D** Here, we must first figure out the number of dominant individuals as a proportion. Dividing the top and bottom of $\frac{128}{200}$ by two, we get that $\frac{64}{100}$, or 64%, of the individuals are dominant. This means that 36% of them are recessive and that $q^2 = 0.36$. Taking the square root of both sides, we get that $q = 0.6$. Because $p + q = 1$, $p = 0.4$. The number of heterozygous individuals is given by $2pq = 0.48$.

4. **C** Choice (A) is an example of gene flow from one population to another. Choice (B) is an example of the founder effect, and choice (D) is an example of the bottleneck effect. Choice (E) is an example of a variation within a species that does not make a difference. Choice (C), however, is a difference between organisms in which one trait (seeing better) gives an organism an advantage, and, thus, is an example of natural selection.

5. **D** Such a catastrophic event, which leaves only a small amount of the population intact, is an example of the bottleneck effect.

6. **B** Here, the organisms are separated by a geographic barrier. Although the founder effect may, in fact, be at work in this example, it is not an option. This divergence of two populations because of a geographic feature is known as allopatric speciation. In fact, different species of squirrels do reside on opposite sides of the Grand Canyon.

7. **A** Natural selection cannot change the traits of an individual organism. Although natural selection can cause change in the traits that are expressed in a population, it cannot specifically change one organism; populations, not individuals, are the units of evolution.

8. **D** Punctuated equilibrium holds that evolution occurs in short periods of rapid change, followed by a period of relative stability. The opposing theory to punctuated equilibrium is gradualism.

9. **E** Evolution is defined as a change in the frequency of alleles over time. Genetic drift and natural selection are two possible causes of such a shift. Thus, all of the three choices involve such a change in the frequency of the alleles in a population.

Lesson 8-3. Origins of Diversity

VOCABULARY

- abiotic
- Miller–Urey experiment
- ribozymes
- protobionts
- panspermia
- fossil record
- sedimentary rock
- relative dating
- radiometric dating
- half-life
- Cambrian explosion
- Carboniferous period

- Cretaceous extinction
- taxonomy
- genus (pl., genera)
- family
- order
- class
- phylum (pl., phyla)
- kingdom
- domain
- scientific name
- binomial nomenclature

The history of Earth has been one of stunning change. Today we see creatures from simple, unicellular bacteria to complex, multicellular plants and animals with specialized tissues. But what is perhaps more stunning than the diversity of life is the fact that it even exists at all: from an ooze of primordial chemicals evolved functional cells, complete with their own molecular method of information storage, and capable of reproducing themselves. The question of how life developed and came to resemble the creatures we see today is the subject of this lesson.

CREATING CELLS

Cells are by no means simple things. Even prokaryotic cells have specialized molecules that perform a variety of functions. Cells have DNA to store information, proteins to interpret and replicate that DNA and phospholipids to surround these parts and segregate the inner environment of a cell from its surroundings. Moreover, all of these cells are capable of producing other cells just like them.

All of the cells we see today were made from other cells. As we've learned, one of the important findings of science through cell theory is that the cells we see today did not spontaneously generate; instead, they came from other cells. But where, then, did the first cell come from? There must be some way for cells to have emerged in the absence of other cells. Such a synthesis is known as **abiotic** synthesis.

Scientists have been trying since the early 1900s to replicate the processes by which abiotic synthesis may have taken place. Replicating these processes is not a guarantee that, indeed, abiotic synthesis did occur; it does, however, tell us that abiotic synthesis could occur. One of the first important discoveries was that the conditions of early Earth were very different from conditions today, especially in one crucial manner: there was very little oxygen present in the early Earth atmosphere. This lack of oxygen is important because oxygen is not conducive to the spontaneous formation of large organic molecules. For the macromolecules of life to have formed naturally, an environment in which oxygen is largely lacking is necessary.

Perhaps the most significant experiment into abiotic synthesis was performed by Stanley Miller and Harold Urey, researchers at the University of

Chicago, who were investigating the conditions of early Earth. In 1953 (incidentally, the same year that Watson and Crick discovered the double helix), they tried to recreate the conditions of primordial Earth. They put water into a chamber of chemicals thought to have composed the primordial Earth atmosphere: methane (CH_4), ammonia (NH_3), hydrogen gas (H_2), and water. To mimic lightning, which is thought to have been a major source of energy for early chemical reactions, they discharged electric sparks into the mixture, and they put the water under constant heat.

What Miller and Urey found 1 week later was surprising: they discovered that the system had somehow synthesized amino acids, the constituents of proteins. While the amino acids in organisms today are synthesized by living things, these amino acids had spontaneously formed without any cellular synthesis. The **Miller–Urey experiment,** then, was important because it discovered that amino acids could be created abiotically, and it raised the very real possibility that the complexity of life as we know it could, indeed, have arisen from the early Earth conditions.

Subsequent to the Miller–Urey experiment, many scientists have taken up the search for an explanation of how life could have evolved abiotically. One important question that faced scientists was dealing with the chicken-and-egg conundrum of DNA and proteins: DNA needs proteins to replicate, but proteins are coded for in DNA. Which, then, came first; DNA or proteins?

Today, as we discussed in Chapter 6, it is thought that RNA, not DNA, was the first genetic material. We know now that RNA is capable of spontaneously forming short single strands, and that, through the spontaneous formation of complementary strands, RNA even replicates itself abiotically. We also know that RNA is capable of forming complex shapes through folding, and that these structures, known as **ribozymes,** are capable of performing functions such as splicing introns in eukaryotes. RNA, then, may have been not only the first genetic material, but also the first enzyme. Over time, RNA somehow ceded these functions to the more stable macromolecules of DNA and proteins.

Scientists have also been able to abiotically produce cell-like compartments known as liposomes, small droplets of certain lipids that can naturally form a lipid-bilayer membrane (much like normal cells). These liposomes are capable of having environments that are separate from their exterior environments, and can also spontaneously replicate by forming smaller liposomes if they grow too large. Such abiotically produced structures with some of the simple features of cells are known as **protobionts.**

The debate on the exact origins of life continues unabated. Some scientists assert that it is most likely that the complex organic molecules of life were not created on Earth, but may have been brought to Earth on a comet or a meteorite. This theory is known as **panspermia.** Other scientists have focused on deep-sea vents as the locus of the origin of life. These vents, which are caused by volcanic activity on the ocean floor, are extremely hot, providing a good environment for molecular synthesis, and also contain inorganic sulfur compounds that many organisms can use for energy.

Scientists look to other planets for clues on how life may develop. It is now known through the work of the rovers *Spirit* and *Opportunity* that Mars once had liquid water on its surface that could have supported life; Europa, a moon of Jupiter, is thought to have liquid water below its icy surface that could also support life. The European spacecraft *Huygens* landed on Titan, a moon of Saturn, and discovered that its surface contains a sea of liquid methane, and that its atmosphere may share many features with that of primordial Earth.

▨▨▨ **AFTER CELLS**

While some scientists continue to investigate how life may have evolved abiotically, others focus on what happened after the first prokaryotic cell is known to have emerged. These paleontologists focus on fossils, looking for evidence of cells within rocks to indicate that life was present when these rocks were formed.

Studying Fossils

The part of human existence during which we were capable of creating written records is thought to have begun about 3,500 BCE. This period represents less than 1/100,000th of the time in which life has been around. For the rest of this period, we must deduce events based on the **fossil record,** the term used to describe the evidence of past life on Earth.

There are a number of types of fossils. Rarely, but occasionally, we can find actual remains of an organism, such as bones or specimens preserved in ice or amber. **Sedimentary rock**—rock formed by the accumulation of sediment that settles out of water—is an important source of such fossils because it is able to cover up quickly fossils and preserves them until they are found. More commonly, however, we will find a hint that an organism once existed. Very often we can find a cast of an organism. Casts occur when the organic material of an organism decays, and the space taken up by that organic material is filled with a different mineral than the surrounding rock, thus forming an impression in stone of the organism that once existed. And occasionally, we will find trace fossils, the remnants of an organism such as its footprints or burrow, that have been left behind.

The existence of a fossil, however, cannot explain the history of life unless we know how old it is. Thus, one of the most important techniques that paleontologists have developed is the ability to date fossils. There are a number of ways of doing so. One way of dating a fossil is simply by understanding that it is older or younger than other fossils. This is known as **relative dating** because it focuses on the relative age of fossils, not their absolute age. Because sedimentary rock is laid down in layers over time, we are able to tell by examining these layers which organisms existed first. The deeper the layer the fossil came from, the older the fossil.

To give an absolute date of a fossil's age, however, we use **radiometric dating.** As we learned in Chapter 6, many of the elements have isotopes—atoms with a different number of neutrons—that give off radiation, and thus decay, and are converted to a more stable isotope, at a known rate. This rate is measured by the **half-life,** the time it takes for one-half of the material to decay. For more recent fossils, the decay of the isotope carbon-14, which has a half-life of approximately 5,700 years, is often used. For older fossils, other elements—such as uranium-238, which is laid down in volcanic rock, and has a half-life of more than four billion years—can be used to determine the age of much older fossils.

A Brief History of Life

In this section, we review a number of the important events in the history of life on Earth. This review is necessarily short, first because there's no need for you to remember all of the times that are mentioned in this history, but also because a few of these events are more important than others. What's more important than remembering the specific date of these events, however, is remembering in which order these events occurred. Remembering that prokaryotes came before eukaryotes, or that dinosaurs came before humans, for example, is more important than remembering exactly when eukaryotes emerged and dinosaurs died. If you get lost in this narrative, refer to the following chart.

Time	Event
2.5–1.6 million years ago	Humans emerge
7–5 million years ago	Human ancestors appear
65 million years ago	Cretaceous extinction allows mammals and flowering plants to emerge
250 million years ago	Permian mass extinction allows dinosaurs to dominate land, sea, and air
500 million years ago	Land is colonized; vascular plants dominate in the Carboniferous period
543–525 million years ago	Cambrian explosion results in emergence of animals
1.2 billion years ago	Multicellular eukaryotes emerge
2.1 billion years ago	Eukaryotes emerge
2.7 billion years ago	Oxygen becomes prevalent
4.0–3.5 billion years ago	Prokaryotic life emerges
4.5 billion years ago	Earth is formed

4.5 Billion Years Ago: Earth Created

Earth is thought to have been created approximately 4.5 billion years ago, although it was not completely solid until approximately 3.9 billion years ago. At this point, the matter in the solar system was still coalescing into planets and moons.

4.0–3.5 Billion Years Ago: Prokaryotic Life Emerges

The oldest rocks on Earth are 3.8 billion years old, and they contain evidence that life may have been present at that time; we have no direct fossils of life, however, from that time. We do, however, have direct evidence that life was present on Earth approximately 3.5 billion years ago, in the form of a fossil (found in Western Australia) that resembles primitive bacteria. However it may have emerged (see the previous section), it's clear that life emerged relatively soon after Earth developed.

2.7 Billion Years Ago: Oxygen Becomes Prevalent

Although the early Earth atmosphere may have contained oxygen, it was certainly not present in the amount that it is today. Oxygen was introduced into the atmosphere in large quantities by the emergence of cyanobacteria capable of carrying out photosynthesis that produces oxygen as its byproduct. This introduction of oxygen, at first into the oceans and later into the atmosphere, was a traumatic event for much life on Earth. Oxygen gas is a highly volatile molecule, and a number of organisms whose metabolisms required the absence of oxygen most certainly died out because of the increased presence of O_2 in the atmosphere. But in the process, many bacterial organisms adapted, and new chemical processes such as respiration, which use oxygen in the production of energy, emerged. We'll discuss the different metabolic abilities of bacteria in the next lesson.

2.1 Billion Years Ago: Eukaryotes Emerge

Eukaryotic cells are not only much larger than prokaryotic cells, but they are tremendously more complex, representing a significant amount of evolution from their prokaryotic predecessors. Fossilized cells that share some of the features of eukaryotic cells have been found that are approximately 2.2 billion years old; the first cells thought to be definitely eukaryotic are approximately 2.1 billion years old. As we discussed in Chapter 6, eukaryotic cells are thought to have emerged with the help of a process known as endosymbiosis, in which one cell swallows up another, incorporating the metabolism of the swallowed cell into its own. This explains how eukaryotic cells developed within themselves such highly specialized structures as mitochondria and chloroplasts.

1.2 Billion Years Ago: Multicellular Eukaryotes Emerge

Multicellular organisms represent yet another significant evolutionary step, in that suddenly one cell is no longer required to perform all of the functions of the organism. This specialization, however, adds a layer of complexity to the processes of development. The oldest multicellular fossil is an extremely small algae that has been dated to approximately 1.2 billion years ago, but it's possible that multicellular organisms existed as far back as 1.5 billion years ago. The majority of multicellular organisms, however, were relatively simple until the end of a severe ice age, approximately 570 million years ago, when a number of larger multicellular organisms, such as jellyfish, emerged. The origins and advantages of multicellularity are investigated in Lesson 8-5.

543–525 Million Years Ago: Cambrian Explosion

The **Cambrian explosion** is a phrase used to describe the emergence of a great variety of animals during the beginning of the Cambrian era. Although certain animals, such as sponges and jellyfish, had emerged prior to this period, this relatively short period of time saw an immense diversification of the animal kingdom, in such a short period of time that it's difficult to determine the exact manner in which these different groups emerged. What is known is that by the end of this period, all of the known animal forms, from worms to vertebrates (animals with a backbone and spinal cord), had emerged.

500 Million Years Ago: Land Is Colonized

Although bacteria had covered the land before this point, it was approximately 500 million years ago that plants, animals, and fungi began moving onto the land. This event required a number of changes to prevent water loss and allow reproduction without the aid of water. Plants, especially, would diversify during this period, providing animals that moved onto land with a food source. Seedless plants would their reach their apex during the **Carboniferous period,** from 290–360 million years ago, producing so much organic material that we are still using it today, in the form of coal, oil, and natural gas. (These are commonly known as "fossil fuels.")

250 Million Years Ago: Permian Mass Extinction

Over a five-million-year period starting approximately 250 million years ago, 90% of marine animal species, and much of the terrestrial animal life, died out, in an event known as the Permian mass extinction. The causes of this extinction are not clear; it may have resulted from changing geography, as the continents merged to form one supercontinent, known as Pangaea. An extreme amount of volcanic activity in what is now Siberia (northeastern Russia) is also thought to have caused an oxygen deficit. When conditions became conducive again for life, starting the Mesozoic era, reptiles greatly diversified, as the dinosaurs took over much of the land, sea, and air. In plants, gymnosperms (plants with cones) would become especially prevalent.

65 Million Years Ago: Cretaceous Extinction

Approximately 65 million years ago, the Mesozoic era ended abruptly, ending the age of the dinosaurs, killing a number of marine animals, and ushering in the Cenozoic era. Although it's possible that volcanic activity, as well, may have contributed to this extinction, the most likely explanation is that the **Cretaceous extinction** was caused by the impact of a large asteroid—on the order of 10 km in diameter—near the Yucatan peninsula, in Mexico. Such an impact could cause a fire that eliminated most of the life in North America, and could darken the Earth's skies for months, if not years. Absent sunlight, many plants, and the animals that depend on them, would die out. Whatever its cause, the Cretaceous extinction created a new opportunity for new organisms to colonize land. Mammals, especially, took hold and greatly diversified, as did birds. Angiosperms (flowering plants)—and, with them, pollinating insects—emerged not long afterward.

5–7 Million Years Ago: Human Ancestors Appear

The first primates emerged more than 45 million years ago. For most of that period, humans and other apes shared a common ancestry; it was only about 5–7 million years ago that humans and apes are thought to have diverged. The oldest fossil that appears to be human-like is approximately four million years old, and belongs to the genus *Australopithecus*, although new fossils are being discovered all the time (mainly in southeastern Africa), and the exact relationship between all of these species is far from clear, as many of these early species seem to have co-existed with each other. The most significant feature of these early prehumans was that they developed into bipedal creatures, walking on land using two feet instead of living in trees.

1.6–2.5 Million Years Ago: Humans Emerge

The first distinctly human species are thought to have emerged approximately 2.5–1.6 million years ago. These species are defined as human by a number of features: they have a larger brain size, their jaws take on a different, more human-like shape, and there is evidence from as far as two million years ago of individuals using tools. There have been many hominid (human-like) species, among which the better known are the early *Homo habilis,* known for using tools, and *Homo erectus,* named because it has a more upright skeleton. Modern humans, *Homo sapiens,* are thought to have emerged from Homo erectus—whom we eventually replaced—approximately 100,000 years ago.

There are at least three mass extinctions noted in this short history (one when oxygen emerged, the Permian mass extinction, and the Cretaceous extinction). Each of these extinctions provided the opportunity for a different group of organisms to develop and colonize different areas of Earth. Even the Cambrian explosion was preceded by an ice age, which would have greatly limited the ability of life to flourish. These extinctions, followed by periods of rapid diversification, tend to support the view that, at least on the level of macroevolution, speciation occurs in relatively short bursts, followed by periods of rather slow change.

Do not forget, however, that the time periods that we have discussed above are massive. Even counting the oldest prehuman ancestors, humanity has been around for little more than 1/1000th of the time-span of life. The evolutionary time-scale encompasses four billion years of change; animals have been present for probably no more than 1/8 of that time. So, although we may talk of a "short burst" of diversification, this period may be anywhere from tens of thousands to millions of years. Evolution has wrought great change, but these changes have come over great periods of time.

CLASSIFYING LIFE

One of the earliest activities of biology, going back to Aristotle, has been to make sense of the great diversity of life. Today, armed with an understanding of evolution, we seek to classify species in a way that acknowledges the evolutionary relationships between them. To that end, an entire field, known as **taxonomy,** has been developed to name and classify different species of life.

Modern Taxonomy

The first modern taxonomist was a Swedish physician named Carolus Linnaeus. Linnaeus worked in the mid-18th century to classify organisms. He recognized the need for a systematic way to classify organisms, although he classified organisms based on their similarities in features. To do so, Linnaeus first identified individual species; he then grouped these different species into increasingly large groups, based on common characteristics between those groups. Species that share similar characteristics, for example, are grouped into the same **genus (plural, genera);** similar genera are grouped into a **family,** similar families are grouped into an **order,** orders into a **class,** classes into a **phylum (plural, phyla),** phyla into a **kingdom,** and kingdoms into a **domain.**

This classification is known as a hierarchical classification; each group, as one travels up, is more comprehensive, encompassing more organisms. A phylum, for example, can contain more than one class; a class can contain more than one order.

Many of the classifications that Linnaeus developed are still in use today, although a number of modifications to the system have been made to reflect better understandings of the evolutionary relationship between organisms. The motivation behind taxonomy is to make apparent the evolutionary relationships between organisms. The idea is that two members of the same genus should be more closely related than organisms of the same class, or family.

Linnaeus understood that there was a need for a **scientific name** for organisms—a name that would accurately describe a species, even though the name that was commonly used for the species might differ from region to region. Thus, Linnaeus developed what is known as **binomial nomenclature.** Binomial nomenclature allows for a two-word identification of all species. In binomial nomenclature, species are named by their genus (with the first letter capitalized) and then the specific epithet (which appears in all lower-case). These names are written in italics. The common house cat, for example, is *Felis domesticus;* human beings are *Homo sapiens,* and horses are *Equus caballus.* All of these organisms are members of the domain Eukarya (for eukaryotes) kingdom Animalia (which includes animals), phylum Chordata (which includes vertebrates), and the class Mammalia (mammals).

Occasionally, scientists will split populations of the same species into a subspecies. For example, the Florida panther (*Felis concolor coryi*) and the cougar (*Felis concolor cougar*) are both members of the same species, but have an additional taxon, the subspecies, to distinguish between them. They are called subspecies because the two populations rarely meet and have different characteristics, but they are capable of interbreeding successfully. Often, the line between what makes two different populations a species, versus what makes them a subspecies, is unclear. For example, some scientists would place Neanderthals, early humans that inhabited Europe until approximately 30,000 years ago, as a subspecies of *Homo sapiens* (*Homo sapiens neanderthalensis*), while others label them as their own species, *Homo neanderthalensis.*

This underscores an important point about classification: classifications are not natural features of organisms that can be observed. They are a human invention, used to make the task of understanding organisms much easier. As a result, systems of classification can often change as our understanding of the relationships between organisms change.

LESSON SUMMARY

- The first cells must have somehow emerged spontaneously, without the aid of existing life—a process known as abiotic synthesis. This process was aided by the lack of oxygen in the early Earth environment.
- The Miller–Urey experiment showed that amino acids could form from the early Earth environment.
- RNA is thought to have been the first genetic material.
- The fossil record allows us to determine the history of life on Earth. Fossils can be dated using relative dating, or by using radiometric dating to give a more exact age.
- Life first emerged approximately four billion years ago, with eukaryotes emerging approximately 2.1 billion years ago. Multicellular life emerged approximately 1.2 billion years ago.

- The Cambrian explosion, approximately 525 million years ago, saw a sudden increase in animal diversity.
- Extinctions are common events. Mass extinctions allow other evolutionary branches to diversify:
  - Approximately 2.7 billion years ago, the advent of oxygen-producing photosynthesis in cyanobacteria caused the death of many prokaryotes; respiration emerged as a result.
  - The Permian mass extinction, about 250 million years ago, paved the way for reptiles (most notably, dinosaurs) and gymnosperms (cone-bearing plants) to diversify.
  - The Cretaceous extinction, about 65 million years ago (possibly because of an asteroid impact) allowed flowering plants and mammals to diversify.
- Human-like creatures emerged in Africa 4–6 million years ago, with the first hominids emerging approximately 1.6–2.5 million years ago. Modern *Homo sapiens* are thought to be no more than 100,000 years old.
- Taxonomy is the classification of species to reflect their similarities. Currently, species are divided into a series of groups, with each being larger than the former: genus, family, order, class, phylum, kingdom, and domain.

REVIEW QUESTIONS

1. Which of the following is an example of abiotic synthesis?

   (A) the emergence of eukaryotic cells
   (B) the Miller–Urey experiment
   (C) the Hardy–Weinberg equation
   (D) the Permian mass extinction
   (E) the emergence of oxygen into the atmosphere

2. Which of the following is thought to have emerged first?

   (A) bacteria
   (B) plants
   (C) fungi
   (D) animals
   (E) protists

3. The emergence of oxygen in the atmosphere is a result of:

   (A) mammals
   (B) fungi
   (C) amino acids
   (D) photosynthesis
   (E) the Cretaceous extinction

4. The choice that lists the items correctly from more inclusive to least inclusive is:

   (A) domain, family, class, species
   (B) kingdom, domain, phylum, order
   (C) kingdom, order, genus, phylum
   (D) kingdom, phylum, class, genus
   (E) species, class, phylum, domain

5. Which of the following statements about mass extinctions is NOT thought to be true?

(A) A mass extinction allowed mammals to diversify.
(B) A mass extinction resulted in the emergence of prokaryotic cells.
(C) A mass extinction followed the impact of an asteroid with Earth.
(D) A mass extinction followed the emergence of oxygen.
(E) A mass extinction resulted in the end of the dinosaurs.

6. Two organisms are members of the same family. They might not be a member of the same

(A) order
(B) class
(C) kingdom
(D) phylum
(E) genus

ANSWERS

1. **B** Abiotic synthesis is the spontaneous synthesis of the organic compounds needed for life. The events in choices (A), (B), and (E) all occurred as a result of life forms reproducing. The Hardy–Weinberg equation involves nonevolving populations. The Miller–Urey experiment, which produced amino acids (the elements of primordial Earth), is an example of such a synthesis.

2. **A** Prokaryotic cells emerged before any of the eukaryotic cells. Bacteria, which are prokaryotic cells, emerged long before any of the other choices.

3. **D** Photosynthesis in cyanobacteria is responsible for the creation of the oxygen in Earth's atmosphere. The Cretaceous extinction and the emergence of fungi and mammals all occurred very much after the emergence of oxygen in the atmosphere. Amino acids alone were present for almost two billion years before the presence of oxygen.

4. **D** The question requires that the answers be listed with the largest groupings first, followed by subsequently smaller groups. Because a class is larger than a family, choice (A) is incorrect. Choice (B) is incorrect because domains are larger than kingdoms; choice (C) is incorrect because a phylum is much larger than a genus. Finally, choice (E) lists the groups from least inclusive (smallest) to most inclusive (largest).

5. **B** Mass extinctions are known to have caused the extinction of the dinosaurs and the divergence of mammals. The Cretaceous extinction is thought to have followed an asteroid impact, and the introduction of oxygen also precipitated a mass extinction. Mass extinctions, however, did not account for the emergence of prokaryotic cells; they emerged before there was any life to go extinct.

6. **E** The two organisms are a member of the same family. They are necessarily members of the same domain, kingdom, phylum, class, and order. They are not, however, necessarily members of the same genus.

Lesson 8-4. The Three Domains and the Five Kingdoms

VOCABULARY

- domain Bacteria
- domain Archaea
- domain Eukarya

Domains and Kingdoms

Today, we recognize that there are three domains: **domain Bacteria, domain Archaea,** and **domain Eukarya.** The domain Bacteria includes prokaryotes that are found everywhere in nature. The domain Archaea includes prokaryotes that live in Earth's harshest environments, such as thermal vents deep in the oceans. The domain Eukarya includes all eukaryotic organisms, whether they are unicellular or multicellular, autotrophic or heterotrophic.

Before the three-domain system, scientists used a system in which the highest classification was a kingdom, and there were no domains. In this system, all life was divided into five kingdoms:

- Kingdom Monera, containing the Eubacteria and Archaebacteria
- Kingdom Protista, containing the protists. Protists are the simplest of eukaryotes, and are extremely diverse, ranging from unicellular to multicellular.
- Kingdom Fungi, containing fungi
- Kingdom Plantae, or plants
- Kingdom Animalia, or animals

However, there were a number of problems with this system. For example, there was too much diversity in the kingdom Protista to be contained in one kingdom, especially because the grouping of these organisms did not reflect the actual evolution of organisms. Many of the protists, for example, are in fact more closely related to plants, animals, and fungi than to other protists. Nonetheless, the five-kingdom classification is still used and reflects the similarities that the members in each kingdom share.

KINGDOM MONERA

Members of this kingdom are prokaryotes. We may feel very removed from the microscopic life of prokaryotes that inhabit so much of this world. Nevertheless, these microbes have an important role in the environment. Microorganisms are responsible for the presence of oxygen in Earth's atmosphere, and for recycling the necessary elements of life.

Prokaryotic cells are much simpler than eukaryotic cells. Not only are they much smaller than eukaryotic cells, they also have none of the membrane-bound organelles that carry out specialized functions in eukaryotic cells. Unlike eukaryotic cells, which have a nucleus and DNA in chromosomes, prokaryotic cells simply have a region in which the DNA resides. Their DNA is not arranged into tightly packed, linear chromosomes the way eukaryotic DNA is; instead, prokaryotic DNA is circular, with the genome generally consisting of one circular strand of DNA. This does not, mean, however, that prokaryotic cells do not have many specialized functions of their own.

Prokaryotes do have certain unique specialized structures. For example, certain bacteria are capable of forming a structure known as an *endospore* when faced with conditions that are unfavorable for growth, such as a lack of nutrients or water. The endospore is protected from harsh conditions, capable of withstanding even boiling water for extended periods of time, and only reactivating when it finds conditions that are favorable for growth.

The reason that prokaryotes are capable of living in such diverse environments is that they are capable of using a wide variety of substances as an energy source. Prokaryotes can be divided by their ability to use certain sources of food for energy. Recall that heterotrophs are organisms that require carbon in the form of organic molecules in order to function. Heterotrophic bacteria that simply consumed available organic materials in their surroundings were most likely the first bacteria to have evolved. Some autotrophic bacteria carry out photosynthesis. Other autotrophic bacteria convert inorganic substances, such as ammonia or hydrogen sulfide, into organic compounds.

The diversity of extreme environments in which prokaryotes live is quite stunning. Certain bacteria, for example, are capable of living in extremely salty environments, such as the salt flats of the Great Salt Lake or San Francisco Bay. Other prokaryotes are capable of living in areas of extreme heat (60–80°C), such as geysers or deep-sea vents.

KINGDOM PROTISTA

Protists are an extremely diverse group of organisms. All protists are eukaryotes. Most protists are unicellular. Some, however, are multicellular and can grow quite large. For example, a protist known as kelp can grow more than 60 m in a single season. This represents the fastest growth rate in height of any living thing.

Like prokaryotes, protists can be either heterotrophic or autotrophic. Perhaps the most familiar heterotrophic protist is the paramecium. This organism belongs to a group of protists called *ciliates* because they move with the help of cilia that cover their bodies. A paramecium feeds mainly on bacteria, using its cilia to sweep these prokaryotes into its body where they are digested with the help of *food vacuoles*. Another common heterotrophic protist is amoeba. This organism moves with the help of cytoplasmic extensions called *pseudopods*. Slime molds are also heterotrophic protists that resemble overgrown amoebae.

Autotrophic protists include algae, which are divided into three different types based on the pigment they contain: red, brown, and green. Red algae are the most abundant large algae in warm tropical seas. Brown algae include many of the species commonly called seaweed. Green algae live mostly in fresh water. Others like *Ulva*, commonly called sea lettuce, thrive in salt water.

Some protists can be autotrophic at times and heterotrophic at other times. Euglena is an example of such a protist. This protist contains a chloroplast and can, therefore, carry out photosynthesis. However, when sunlight is unavailable, Euglena converts to its heterotrophic mode of nutrition by consuming organic materials.

Protists also live in a wide variety of environments. They are found almost anywhere there is water and in most terrestrial habitats. Reproduction among protists also varies considerably. Some protists reproduce by simply dividing their unicellular bodies into two new individuals. Other protists carry out meiosis before they reproduce.

KINGDOM FUNGI

Fungi are heterotrophic eukaryotes that feed by absorbing organic materials. Most are multicellular, such as the mushroom. However, some fungi are unicellular such as yeast. What distinguishes fungi from other heterotrophs is the way in which they obtain their nutrients. Heterotrophs that belong to the kingdoms Monera, Protista, and Animalia ingest, or eat, their food. In contrast, heterotrophic fungi digest their food while it is still in the environment. Fungi secrete powerful digestive enzymes that break down complex organic molecules into simpler substances. The fungi then slowly absorb these digested nutrients. In this way, fungi can digest a fallen log.

This method of nutrition has resulted in fungi having a powerful impact on all organisms, including humans. Fungi are responsible for breaking down the organic compounds in dead and decaying matter. As of result of this decomposition, fungi return vital nutrients to the environment. You will learn more how these materials are recycled in nature in Chapter 10.

KINGDOM PLANTAE

Deciding in which kingdom to place an organism is sometimes difficult. For example, green algae are usually classified in the kingdom Protista. However, some scientists suggest that green algae should be classified as members of the kingdom Plantae. The main reason is that plants descended from green algae that colonized the land. Even today, green algae and plants have much in common.

Plants are multicellular autotrophs that obtain the energy they need through photosynthesis. Plants are divided into two main groups: *nonvascular* and *vascular*. Vascular plants have true roots, stems, and leaves to transport materials such as water and carbohydrates. In contrast, nonvascular plants lack these structures and must live in water where diffusion and osmosis sustain their existence. Nonvascular plants include mosses, liverworts, and hornworts.

Vascular plants are subdivided into seed plants and seedless plants. Seedless plants include the ferns, which produce spores instead of seeds to reproduce. Seed plants are still further divided into *gymnosperms* and *angiosperms*. Gymnosperms are nonflowering plants and include evergreen trees such as pines, firs, and cedars. Angiosperms are the flowering plants and represent the most highly evolved of all the plants. Angiosperms account for about 90% of all plant species. The flower of an angiosperm is a highly specialized reproductive organ.

KINGDOM ANIMALIA

All members of this kingdom are eukaryotic, heterotrophic, and multicellular. Animals are divided into two major groups: *invertebrates* and *vertebrates*. Invertebrates are animals that do not have a backbone. Invertebrates account for almost 95% of all animal species. They also account for all but one of the roughly 35 phyla that make up the animal kingdom. Common invertebrates include sponges, hydra, jellyfish, sea anemones, flatworms, roundworms, segmented worms, arthropods, starfish, sea urchins, clams, squids, and snails. Arthropods are the most varied phylum. This phylum includes insects, which are represented by more than one million different species.

Vertebrates belong to the phylum Chordata. Vertebrates include fishes, amphibians, reptiles, birds, and mammals. Vertebrates have a backbone, or spinal column, made of bone. While the insects are represented by over one million species, the vertebrates account for only slightly more than 50,000 species. However, what vertebrates may lack in diversity has been more than overshadowed by their complexity and success. As proof, consider just one species of vertebrates—*Homo sapiens*.

LESSON SUMMARY

- Organisms belonging to the kingdom Monera are all prokaryotes. Some monerans are autotrophic, while other monerans are heterotrophic.
- Organisms belonging to the kingdom Protista are eukaryotic. They can be either unicellular or multicellular. Some protists are autotrophic, while other protists are heterotrophic.
- Organisms belonging to the kingdom Fungi are eukaryotic and heterotrophic. They digest their food while it is still part of their environment. Almost all fungi are multicellular.
- Organisms belonging to the kingdom Plantae are eukaryotic, autotrophic, and multicellular. All members of this kingdom carry out photosynthesis.
- Organisms belonging to the kingdom Animalia are eukaryotic, heterotrophic, and multicellular. Invertebrates make up most of this kingdom. Vertebrates are classified as part of the phylum Chordata, which includes humans.

REVIEW QUESTIONS

Each set of lettered choices below refers to the numbered statements immediately following it. Select the one-lettered choice that best fits each statement. A choice may be used more than once or not at all.

- (A) Kingdom Monera
- (B) Kingdom Protista
- (C) Kingdom Fungi
- (D) Kingdom Plantae
- (E) Kingdom Animalia

1. All of its members consist of cells that contain chloroplasts.
2. This kingdom contains unicellular eukaryotes that are autotrophic.
3. None of its members have cells that contain a nucleus.
4. You would find a green alga among its members.
5. You would find a green moss among its members.
6. You would find a green mold among its members.

ANSWERS

1. **D** All plants, but not all protists, contain chloroplasts to carry out photosynthesis.
2. **B** Some protists, such as Euglena, are unicellular organisms that contain a chloroplast and, therefore, can manufacture organic compounds through photosynthesis. Plants are multicellular.
3. **A** All monerans are prokaryotes.
4. **B** Green algae are autotrophic protists.
5. **D** Green mosses are nonvascular plants.
6. **C** Green molds, such as *penicillium*, are fungi.

CHAPTER 9

UNDERSTANDING ORGANISMAL BIOLOGY

Lesson 9-1. Support and Movement

VOCABULARY

- homeostasis
- exoskeleton
- endoskeleton
- ligaments
- cartilage
- hydrostatic skeleton
- cardiac muscle

- smooth muscle
- skeletal muscle
- tendons
- flexor
- extensor
- actin
- myosin

With the evolution of multicellular organisms, specialization of structure and function became possible. The structure and function of a group of cells, organized into tissues and organs, could be focused on one task. For example, they could be specialized for locomotion or reproduction. As a result, these processes would function more efficiently. However, specialization of structure and function also posed a challenge. Somehow, the workings of all the various tissues and organs had to be coordinated so that all the functions carried out by a multicellular organism proceeded in a controlled and coordinated manner.

An understanding of homeostasis involves an understanding of the various organ systems that make up a multicellular organism. These include systems for support, movement, transport, digestion, protection, defense, reproduction, development, and communication. The coordination of all these systems in animals is the responsibility of still another two systems—the endocrine and nervous systems.

Animals have mechanisms to regulate their biological processes within very narrow limits. This regulation results in a stable internal environment. The maintenance of a stable internal environment is known as **homeostasis.** Homeostasis is essential if an animal is to survive in the face of a constantly changing environment.

SUPPORT

The bodies of some animals are protected by a hard covering. For example, a lobster is completely covered by a shell made of protein and chitin. This external covering is called an **exoskeleton.** An exoskeleton provides both support and protection for the animal. Muscles attached to the exoskeleton enable the animal to move. Animals that belong to the phylum Arthropoda have exoskeletons. In addition to lobsters, these animals include horseshoe crabs, insects, spiders, and crustaceans.

Although an exoskeleton protects and supports these animals, it does pose one limitation. An animal with an exoskeleton cannot grow very large, especially if it flies. Large animals then must have some other means of support. This support is provided by an **endoskeleton,** which is found inside an organism's body. All vertebrates (fish, amphibians, reptiles, birds, and mammals) have an endoskeleton. An endoskeleton provides not only support but also protection. Bones that make up the endoskeleton protect delicate internal organs such as the heart and lungs.

THE HUMAN SKELETAL SYSTEM

More than 200 bones make up the human skeleton. Some bones are fused together, such as those that make up an adult's skull. Most of the bones, however, are connected at joints. Bones are connected to one another by **ligaments.** Ligaments allow these bones to move freely. As they move, **cartilage** prevents bones from rubbing against one another. Cartilage is a tissue that is firm but much softer than bone.

Cartilage is firm enough to form the endoskeleton of some animals, such as sharks and rays. In fact, the long bones of the human skeleton, such as those found in the arms and legs, are first made of cartilage. This cartilage is slowly replaced by bone as the organism develops. However, this process does not occur in the center of each long bone. Instead, this area becomes a hollow cavity filled with bone marrow, where new blood cells are formed.

The cartilage in some structures is never replaced by bone, no matter how old a person gets. These structures include the tip of the nose and the external ear. Cartilage makes these structures flexible and less likely to break when struck.

In addition to support, protection, and production of blood cells, the skeletal system has another function. It is involved in homeostasis by helping to regulate the mineral level in the blood. Consider what happens when the calcium level in the blood begins to drop. Calcium that is stored in bones is released into the blood. The calcium level in the blood must be maintained so that the muscles can function.

MOVEMENT

Animals use their muscles to move their bodies and also move substances within their bodies. Even animals that lack a skeleton can move with just the help of their muscles. These animals include flatworms and annelids. The contraction of their muscles puts pressure on the fluids inside their bodies. The fluids cannot be compressed. As a result, the fluids flow along the length of the body and cause it to lengthen. When the muscles relax, the fluids retreat and the animal's body shortens. This type of motion is brought about by muscles and fluids which form a **hydrostatic skeleton.**

THE HUMAN MUSCULAR SYSTEM

The muscular system works with the skeletal system to support, protect, and move the body. There are three types of muscular tissue in the human body. One type is called **cardiac muscle.** This type of muscle is found only in the heart. Cardiac muscle is responsible for heart contractions that pump blood to all parts of the body. Cardiac muscle is involuntary. This means that a person does not have conscious control over the muscle's contraction.

The second type of muscular tissue in humans is called **smooth muscle.** This type of muscle lines the walls of internal organs and structures, such as the intestines, stomach, blood vessels, bladder, and uterus. Like cardiac muscle, smooth muscle is involuntary.

The third type of muscle is called **skeletal muscle.** As its name suggest, this type of muscle makes up the muscles that are attached to bones. Skeletal muscle is voluntary, meaning that a person can consciously control its contractions. Skeletal muscles are attached to bones by **tendons.**

Two opposing skeletal muscles work together to move a bone. One is known as a **flexor.** The contraction of a flexor brings two bones together. For example, contraction of the biceps muscles brings the forearm and upper arm together. The opposing muscle is called an **extensor.** The contraction of an extensor straightens the two bones. In this case, contraction of the triceps muscle straightens the arm. When an extensor contracts, a flexor relaxes, and vice versa.

When viewed under a microscope, skeletal muscle is seen to have alternating dark and light bands. These bands form a pattern or striations. As a result, skeletal muscle is also called striated muscle. These bands are formed by two muscle proteins—**actin** and **myosin.** Muscle contraction involves the sliding of these two proteins past one another. To get an idea of how this works, take the fingers on one hand and slide them between the fingers on your other hand. This action simulates what happens when a muscle contracts. Now move your fingers apart. This action simulates what happens when a muscle relaxes.

LESSON SUMMARY

- Homeostasis is the maintenance of a stable internal environment despite changes in the external environment.
- An external skeleton is known as an exoskeleton; an internal skeleton is called an endoskeleton.
- Both an exoskeleton and an endoskeleton provide protection, support, and help in movement.
- Bones of the human endoskeleton also produce blood and regulate the mineral level in the blood.
- A hydrostatic skeleton enables some animals to move through the interaction of muscles and fluids.
- Three types of muscles are found in humans: cardiac, smooth, and skeletal.
- Cardiac and smooth muscle are involuntary, while skeletal muscle is voluntary.
- Skeletal muscle contracts and relaxes when actin and myosin protein molecules slide past one another.

REVIEW QUESTIONS

1. Muscles are attached to bones by

    (A) ligaments
    (B) tendons
    (C) actin
    (D) myosin
    (E) flexors and extensors

2. Which of the following organisms has an exoskeleton?

   (A) shark
   (B) frog
   (C) snake
   (D) crayfish
   (E) protist

3. The human skeletal system

   (A) protects internal organs
   (B) is involved in body movement
   (C) produces blood cells
   (D) regulates the blood calcium level
   (E) all of the above

4. Which human muscle types are classified as involuntary?

   I.   skeletal
   II. smooth
   III. cardiac

   (A) I and III only
   (B) I and II only
   (C) II and III only
   (D) II only
   (E) I, II, and III

5. Examine the following illustration of human muscle tissue.

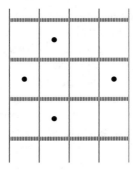

Figure 9-1

Where in the body would you expect to find this type of muscle tissue?

   (A) face
   (B) stomach
   (C) intestines
   (D) heart
   (E) bladder

ANSWERS

1. **B** Tendons attach a muscle to a bone, while ligaments attach one bone to another bone.
2. **D** Like all arthropods, a crayfish has an exoskeleton.
3. **E** The human skeletal system provides support and protection, helps move the body, produces blood cells, and regulates blood calcium levels.
4. **C** Smooth and cardiac muscles cannot be consciously controlled.
5. **A** The illustration shows skeletal (striated) muscles which is found in the muscles of the head where they control facial expressions, chewing, and eye movements.

Lesson 9-2. Transport

VOCABULARY

- open circulatory system
- closed circulatory system
- atrium
- ventricle
- septum
- vein
- artery
- pulmonary circulation
- systemic circulation
- capillaries
- plasma
- erythrocytes
- leukocytes
- platelets
- pharynx
- larynx
- trachea
- bronchus
- alveolus
- diaphragm

Transport of materials in some organisms simply involves the processes of diffusion and osmosis. For example, unicellular organisms such as protozoa depend on diffusion of nutrients from their environment and the diffusion of waste products out of their cells. Water moves in and out of these organisms by osmosis. Even some multicellular organisms depend only on diffusion and osmosis for the transport of substances. Hydra, for example, consist of two cell layers. Both layers are in direct contact with the environment, allowing for nutrients and wastes to enter and leave the cells by diffusion and osmosis. In contrast to protozoa and hydra, most animals need a specialized transport system. Only then can cells not in direct contact with their environment get the nutrients they need and eliminate the wastes they produce.

OPEN AND CLOSED SYSTEMS

Transport of nutrients and wastes is mainly the responsibility of the circulatory system. Some organisms have an **open circulatory system.** In such a system, blood flows within vessels only some of the time. At other times, blood seeps through open spaces called sinuses. Both mollusks and arthropods have an open circulatory system.

Other multicellular organisms have a **closed circulatory system.** In such a system, blood continuously flows within vessels. For example, annelids have a closed circulatory system where blood flows toward the head in a dorsal vessel. The blood then flows to five vessels called aortic arches, which pump the blood to a ventral vessel that transports it toward the posterior. By pumping the blood, the aortic arches act like hearts that are found in vertebrates.

Fish, for example, have a two chambered heart, consisting of one **atrium** and one **ventricle.** The atrium is the chamber that collects the blood returning from various parts of the body. The atrium pumps the blood to the ventricle, which is the chamber that then pumps the blood to all parts of the body. Amphibians have a three-chambered heart. Birds and mammals have a four-chambered heart, consisting of two atria and two ventricles.

THE HUMAN CIRCULATORY SYSTEM

Figure 9-2 illustrates how blood flows through the human heart.

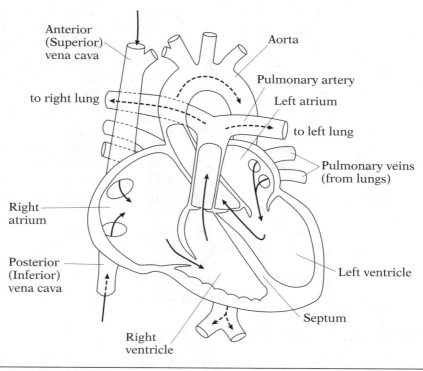

Figure 9-2

Be sure to refer to the above illustration when reading about the human circulatory system. Notice that the illustration shows how the heart appears in a person looking at you. Locate the **septum,** which is a muscular wall that separates the left side of the heart from the right side. Now locate the structures labeled anterior (superior) vena cava and posterior (inferior) vena cava. These are the blood vessels that return blood from all parts of the body except the lungs. A blood vessel that returns blood from a part of the body to the heart is called a **vein.** Notice that a pulmonary vein returns blood from the lungs to the left atrium.

Blood is then pumped from the atria into the ventricles. Valves in the heart prevent the blood from flowing backward. Locate the right ventricle. Notice that it pumps blood to the lungs through the pulmonary artery. A blood vessel that transports blood from the heart to all parts of the body is called an **artery.** Arteries are thicker and more muscular than veins. What is the name of the artery that transports blood from the right ventricle to the lungs? From the left ventricle to the body?

Blood flow between the heart and lungs is known as **pulmonary circulation.** Blood flow between the heart and the rest of the body is called the **systemic circulation.** Use the illustration shown above to trace with your finger how these two systems are related. Do this by tracing how blood flows from the leg through the posterior vena cava and eventually flows back to the leg.

Blood returning from the body to the right atrium is low in oxygen and high in carbon dioxide. This blood has a purplish color is known as deoxygenated blood. Deoxygenated blood is pumped to the right ventricle and then out the pulmonary artery. The pulmonary artery splits, sending a branch to each lung. At the lung, the blood gives up its carbon dioxide and picks up oxygen. This exchange takes place in blood vessels called **capillaries.** A capillary is the blood vessel where materials are exchanged between the blood and cells. Substances, such as oxygen and carbon dioxide, are exchanged by diffusion. The wall of a capillary is only one-cell thick so that these processes can occur easily.

Blood that leaves the lungs is called oxygenated blood, which has a red color. Oxygenated blood flows from each lung through a pulmonary vein. These two veins join to form the large pulmonary vein that enters the left atrium. The septum prevents oxygenated blood from mixing with deoxygenated blood in the heart.

Blood, whether oxygenated or deoxygenated, consists of a liquid called **plasma.** Plasma is mostly water containing dissolved substances such as nutrients, hormones, and gases. Plasma makes up about 50% of the blood volume. The rest is made up of solids that are suspended in the plasma. These solids include **erythrocytes,** or red blood cells. These cells make up about 45% of the blood volume. Red blood cells contain a protein called hemoglobin that transports oxygen. In contrast, carbon dioxide is transported in the plasma. The remaining 5% of the blood volume is made up of **leukocytes** and **platelets.** Leukocytes are white blood cells, which play a major role in protecting the body against disease. Platelets are needed for blood clotting.

THE HUMAN RESPIRATORY SYSTEM

The various systems in the human body work closely together. This is especially true of the circulatory and respiratory systems. You read that the pulmonary circulation is responsible for supplying oxygen to the blood and removing carbon dioxide. The respiratory system must get oxygen to the lungs and take away the carbon dioxide that is brought there by the circulatory system.

Air containing oxygen enters the nose and then passes to the **pharynx,** which is an area located at the back of the throat. Next, air travels to the **larynx,** or voice box. From here, air passes into the **trachea** or windpipe. Then air flows to a **bronchus,** which divides into two bronchi with one going into each lung.

The air passage in each lung continues to branch and branch. Eventually, each tiny branch ends in an **alveolus,** or tiny air sac. The lungs contain millions of alveoli. These alveoli are the sites where gases are exchanged between the circulatory system and the respiratory system. The following illustration shows how these gases are exchanged.

Like a capillary, an alveolus is surrounded by a wall that is only one cell thick. Oxygen, which is in higher concentration in the alveolus, can easily diffuse into the blood in the capillary. Carbon dioxide can easily diffuse in the opposite direction. Notice in Figure 9-3 that water vapor also diffuses from the capillary into the alveolus. This is why you breathe out water vapor that can condense on a mirror when you exhale.

Breathing is controlled by a muscle called the **diaphragm.** The diaphragm forms the bottom wall of the chest cavity. When you inhale, the diaphragm contracts and moves downward. This increases the volume of the chest cavity and reduces the air pressure inside. As a result, air rushes into the nose and begins its journey to the lungs. When you exhale, the diaphragm relaxes and

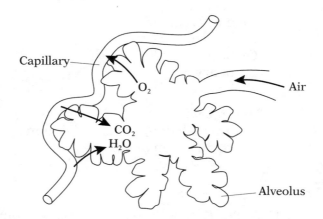

Figure 9-3

moves upward. This decreases the volume of the chest cavity and increases the air pressure inside. As a result, air is forced out the lungs and begins it journey to the nose.

LESSON SUMMARY

- Most multicellular organisms require a transport system to deliver nutrients and remove wastes from cells not in direct contact with the environment.
- Transport systems include the circulatory and respiratory systems.
- Some organisms possess an open circulatory system where blood at times seeps through open spaces.
- Most organisms possess a closed circulatory system where blood is always confined to a vessel or heart.
- The human circulatory system consists of a four-chambered heart, arteries, veins, and capillaries that transport blood throughout the body.
- The human circulatory system consists of pulmonary and systemic circulations.
- Blood consists of plasma, erythrocytes, leukocytes, and platelets.
- The human respiratory system consists of the pharynx, larynx, trachea, bronchus, and alveoli.
- Oxygen and carbon dioxide gases are exchanged between capillaries of the circulatory system and alveoli of the respiratory system.

REVIEW QUESTIONS

Each set of lettered choices below refers to the numbered statement immediately following it. Select the lettered choice that best answers each statement.

(A) left ventricle
(B) right atrium
(C) pulmonary vein
(D) pulmonary artery
(E) aorta

1. Receives blood returning from the arm
2. Blood vessel that contains oxygenated blood
3. Blood vessel that contains deoxygenated blood

> (A) diaphragm
> (B) alveolus
> (C) bronchus
> (D) pharynx
> (E) larynx

4. The voice box
5. Controls inhalation and exhalation
6. Site of diffusion of gases

ANSWERS

1. **B** The right atrium receives blood from the arm through the anterior vena cava.
2. **C** The pulmonary vein carries oxygenated blood from the lungs to the left atrium.
3. **D** The pulmonary artery carries deoxygenated blood that is on its way to the lungs.
4. **E** The larynx is the voice box.
5. **A** The diaphragm contracts during inhalation and relaxes during exhalation.
6. **B** Gases are exchanged between the alveolus and a capillary.

Lesson 9-3. Nutrition

VOCABULARY

- intracellular digestion
- extracellular digestion
- alimentary canal
- mechanism digestion
- salivary glands
- amylases
- chemical digestion
- epiglottis
- esophagus
- peristalsis
- proteases
- bile

- lipase
- villi
- nephron
- glomerulus
- Bowman's capsule
- proximal convoluted tubule
- loop of Henle
- distal convoluted tubule
- collecting tube
- ureter
- bladder
- urethra

Every cell of an organism needs nutrients. Organisms whose cells are in direct contact with the environment obtain nutrients by diffusion. Some unicellular organisms, such as paramecium, ingest tiny food particles. A food vacuole forms around these particles. Enzymes are secreted into the vacuole to break down the food. Digestion that takes place within a cell is known as **intracellular digestion.**

Some organisms, such as hydra, use their tentacles to sweep food into their body's cavity. Enzymes are released into the cavity where they break down the food. Digestion that takes place outside a cell is called **extracellular digestion.** As a result of extracellular digestion, the food particles are small enough to diffuse into the cells. The food particles are then further digested through intracellular digestion. Undigested materials are then expelled through the same opening through which the food particles entered.

More complex multicellular animals have more specialized mechanisms for nutrition. For example, annelids, such as the earthworm, have what is sometimes called a "tube-within-a-tube" digestive system. This consists of a digestive tract (one tube) that extends the length of its body (second tube). The digestive tract is also known as an **alimentary canal.** Food enters through a mouth, and wastes pass out through an anus. Specialized structures aid in the digestive process as the food passes through the alimentary canal.

THE HUMAN DIGESTIVE SYSTEM

Figure 9-4 illustrates the various parts that make up the human digestive system.

As you read about the human digestive system, follow the process in the above illustration. Food enters through the mouth. Here the food is chewed. Teeth break down the food into smaller pieces in a process known as **mechanical digestion.** Mechanical digestion is the process by which nutrients are physically changed into smaller pieces. However, these pieces have not been changed chemically.

The human digestive system also consists of accessory organs that contribute to the digestive process taking place in the alimentary canal. The **salivary glands** in the mouth are examples of the accessory organs. The salivary

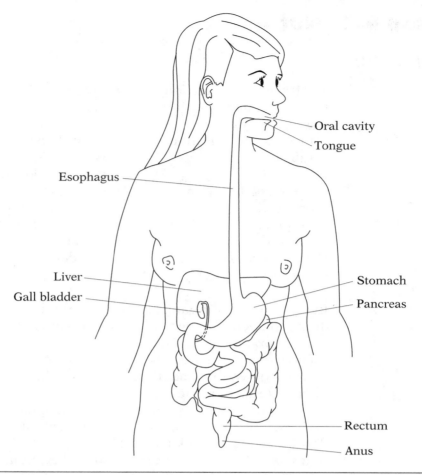

Oral cavity

Tongue

Esophagus

Liver

Gall bladder

Stomach

Pancreas

Rectum

Anus

Figure 9-4

glands secrete enzymes known as **amylases** that travel through ducts to enter the mouth. Amylases begin the process of **chemical digestion.** Chemical digestion is the process by which nutrients are chemically changed into new substances. For example, if you chewed a piece of bread long enough, amylases in your mouth would break down the polysaccharides into simple sugars. The digested bread would taste sweet.

The partially digested food then passes to the pharynx. Swallowing causes a tiny flap called the **epiglottis** to close off the trachea. As a result, the food passes into the **esophagus** and not the trachea where it would cause choking. The esophagus is a narrow tube that connects the pharynx to the stomach. Smooth muscles in the esophagus move the food along through waves of contractions called **peristalsis.** No digestion occurs in the esophagus.

Food next enters the stomach. Smooth muscles churn the stomach walls, continuing the process of mechanical digestion. Specialized cells in the stomach release digestive enzymes called **proteases.** With the help of hydrochloric acid, proteases begin the chemical digestion of proteins.

Food next enters the small intestine. **Bile** produced by the liver and stored in the gall bladder enters the small intestine through a duct. Bile is not an enzyme. Rather, the bile helps to break down the lipids so that they mix with water. Chemical digestion can only proceed in the presence of water. Lipids do not mix well with water. Bile sees to it that they do.

The pancreas secretes digestive enzymes that also enter the small intestine. Specialized cells in the small intestine also secrete digestive enzymes. These enzymes include amylases, proteases, and lipases. A **lipase** is an enzyme that speeds the chemical digestion of lipids. The digestive process is completed in the small intestine. Carbohydrates have been digested to simple sugars, proteins into amino acids, and lipids into fatty acids and glycerol. These products of digestion are now small enough to be absorbed by the small intestine. Tiny structures called **villi** greatly increase the surface area so that as many nutrients as possible are absorbed.

Undigested materials pass from the small intestine to the large intestine. If you examine the illustration of the human digestive system closely, you will see a tiny structure that is attached to the alimentary canal where the small and large intestine meet. This is the appendix. The large intestine stores the undigested wastes until they are eliminated through the rectum and anus. In addition to serving as a storage area, the large intestine also removes any excess water from the solid wastes before they are eliminated.

EXCRETION

Elimination is the term used for the removal of undigested materials by the digestive system. Excretion is the term used for the removal of metabolic wastes produced by an organism. You read that the respiratory system excretes carbon dioxide, a waste product of aerobic respiration. In addition to carbon dioxide, organisms also produce nitrogenous wastes from the metabolism of proteins and nucleic acids. Again, organisms, such as protozoa and hydra, can excrete these wastes directly into the environment because their cells are in direct contact with the environment. These organisms excrete nitrogenous wastes in the form of ammonia.

Most organisms, however, need specialized structures and even entire systems to deal with their nitrogenous wastes. Arthropods excrete nitrogenous wastes in the form of solid uric acid crystals through specialized structures called *Malphigian tubules.* Annelids secrete nitrogenous wastes in the form of urea through *nephridia.* Urea is also excreted by the human excretory system.

THE HUMAN EXCRETORY SYSTEM

Urea is made by the liver and transported by the blood to the kidneys. The functional unit of the kidney is the **nephron.** Each kidney contains about one million nephrons. The illustration on the following page shows the structure of a nephron.

Use Figure 9-5 to trace how urine is formed. Blood carrying wastes is delivered to the afferent arteriole, which is a small artery. This arteriole forms a tuft of capillaries known as a **glomerulus.** Surrounding the glomerulus is **Bowman's capsule,** which is part of the nephron. Notice how Bowman's capsule leads to the **proximal convoluted tubule,** then to the **loop of Henle,** next to the **distal convoluted tubule,** and finally to the **collecting duct.** Both urea and nutrients pass by diffusion from the glomerulus into Bowman's capsule. This process is known as filtration.

As the nutrients and wastes pass through the nephron, the nutrients are removed and returned by active transport to a second capillary network that surrounds the nephron. This process is known as reabsorption. If needed by the body, some water is also removed by osmosis before the fluid passes to

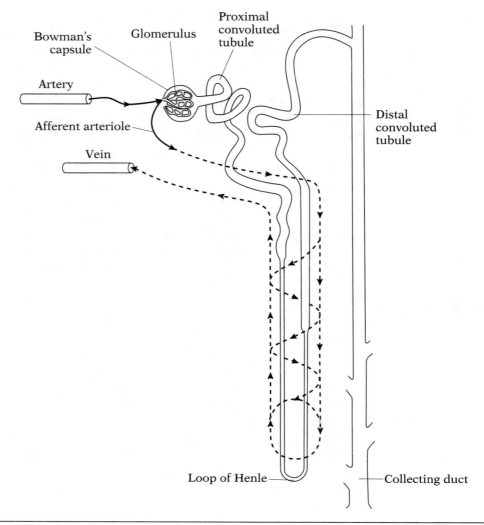

Figure 9-5

the collecting tubule. Additional water can also be removed as the fluid passes through the **collecting tube.**

The collecting tubes from all the nephrons in a kidney merge and lead to a **ureter.** Each ureter leads to the **bladder** where the urine is stored until it is excreted through the **urethra.**

LESSON SUMMARY

- Digestion within a cell is called intracellular digestion, while digestion occurring outside a cell is known as extracellular digestion.
- Mechanical digestion breaks down food physically, while chemical digestion changes it into new substances.
- Carbohydrate digestion begins in the mouth and is completed in the small intestine. Amylases change carbohydrates into simple sugars. The pancreas contributes by secreting amylases into the small intestine.
- Protein digestion begins in the stomach and is completed in the small intestine. Proteases change proteins into amino acids. The pancreas contributes by secreting proteases into the small intestine.

- Lipid digestion begins and is completed in the small intestine. Lipases change lipids into fatty acids and glycerol. The liver contributes by producing bile that mechanically breaks down lipids. The pancreas contributes by secreting lipases into the small intestine.
- Nutrients are absorbed by villi lining the small intestine.
- Undigested wastes are stored in the large intestine.
- Nitrogenous wastes are excreted by the kidneys as urea.
- The functional unit of a kidney is a nephron.

▨ REVIEW QUESTIONS

1. Which structure plays a role in mechanical digestion?

   (A) pancreas
   (B) large intestine
   (C) salivary gland
   (D) stomach
   (E) appendix

2. Which structure contributes three types of enzymes that aid in the digestion of carbohydrates, lipids, and proteins?

   (A) pancreas
   (B) esophagus
   (C) salivary gland
   (D) stomach
   (E) liver

3. Bile

   (A) breaks down lipids into fatty acids and glycerol
   (B) contributes to digestion by allowing lipids and water to mix
   (C) is produced in the gall bladder
   (D) is an enzyme involved in lipid digestion
   (E) passes from the gall bladder into the large intestine

Base your answers to questions 4 and 5 on Figure 9-6.

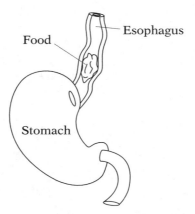

Figure 9-6

4. Notice where the food is found. What nutrient can be found in the food at this point?

   (A) amino acids
   (B) fatty acids
   (C) glycerol
   (D) partially digested proteins
   (E) partially digested carbohydrates

5. What process is being shown in this illustration?

   (A) absorption
   (B) diffusion
   (C) peristalsis
   (D) elimination
   (E) ingestion

6. Which structure is part of a nephron?

   (A) bladder
   (B) villi
   (C) ureter
   (D) urethra
   (E) loop of Henle

ANSWERS

1. **D** As the stomach muscles contract and relax, they aid in mechanical digestion.
2. **A** The pancreas secretes amylases, proteases, and lipases.
3. **B** Bile "emulsifies" lipids by breaking them down mechanically so that they can mix with water.
4. **E** Amylases secreted by the salivary glands would have partially digested the carbohydrates in the mouth.
5. **C** Food passes through the esophagus by peristalsis.
6. **E** The loop of Henle is part of the nephron where nutrients are reabsorbed.

Lesson 9-4. Protection

VOCABULARY

- ectothermic
- homeothermic
- thermoregulation
- epidermis
- dermis
- hypodermis
- phagocyte

- phagocytosis
- lymphocytes
- B-cell
- pathogens
- T-cell
- lymph nodes
- lymphatic system

Some organisms are unable to regulate their body temperature. Instead, their body temperature changes as the external temperature changes. These animals are **ectothermic,** or cold-blooded animals. Among the vertebrates, these animals include fishes, amphibians, and reptiles. In contrast, **homeothermic,** or warm-blooded, animals can maintain a fairly stable internal temperature despite fluctuations in their external environment. Among vertebrates, these animals include birds and mammals. In humans, one organ that plays a role in **thermoregulation** is the skin.

THE SKIN

The skin consists of three layers. The outermost layer is the **epidermis.** The epidermis helps protect the body from disease by preventing microbes from entering the body. The epidermis also contains specialized cells called *melanocytes.* These cells produce a pigment called *melanin* that protects the body from the damage caused by ultraviolet light from the sun.

Beneath the epidermis is the **dermis.** This layer of the skin contains sweat glands and oil glands. Sweat glands secrete a mixture of water, salts, and a small amount of urea. Tiny ducts carry these materials to the epidermis where they are excreted. The evaporation of water from the epidermis also helps in thermoregulation. In colder weather, capillaries in the dermis constrict. As a result, blood flow to the surface is restricted. This restriction retains heat and helps in thermoregulation. The opposite happens in warm weather when the capillaries dilate to allow more heat to escape from the body.

The deepest layer of the skin is called the **hypodermis.** Here fat cells help insulate the body against the cold. The thickness of the hypodermis layer can vary greatly between individuals.

THE IMMUNE SYSTEM

You learned that white blood cells play a role in protecting the body against disease. White blood cells are part of the immune system, a major player in keeping the body healthy.

There is only one type of red blood cell, but there are many types of white blood cells. One type of white blood cell is called a **phagocyte.** As its name suggests, this type of white blood cell carries out **phagocytosis.** This is a process by which a cell engulfs a tiny object, such as a bacterium, takes it inside the cell, and then digests or destroys it. There are several types of phagocytes, each specialized for a different role in protection. Some of these phagocytes present their digested components to other white blood cells in the immune system. These cells, in turn, carry out certain protective functions. These cells include **lymphocytes.**

Two main types of lymphocytes are involved. One is known as a **B-cell.** B-cells produce antibodies that destroy invading microbes, including viruses, bacteria, and parasites. Organisms that can cause disease are known as **pathogens.** Each pathogen brings about the response of a particular B-cell. Because there are millions of different pathogens, there are millions of different B-cells circulating in the blood that protect the body.

Another type of lymphocyte is called a **T-cell.** There are two different types of T-cells. One type of T-cell helps B-cells and other T-cells multiply and coordinate their actions. These are known as helper T-cells. Another type of T-cell is called a killer T-cell. These killer T-cells directly destroy a pathogen.

Lymphocytes travel in the blood stream. They also make up structures called **lymph nodes.** Lymph nodes are part of the **lymphatic system,** which is closely associated with the circulatory system. Unlike the circulatory system, the lymphatic system transports materials in only one direction—from body tissues back to the blood through lymphatic vessels. Lymph nodes are scattered along the way where lymphocytes can destroy pathogens that pass by. When confronted by a large number of pathogens, the lymphocytes will multiply. As a result, the lymph node gets larger. Swollen lymph nodes are a sign of infection.

LESSON SUMMARY

- The skin acts as a barrier to protect the body against pathogens and helps in homeostasis through thermoregulation.
- The immune system includes several types of white blood cells that protect the body against pathogens.
- Phagocytes engulf and destroy pathogens.
- B-cell lymphocytes produce antibodies to destroy pathogens.
- Helper T-cells coordinate the immune response, while killer T-cells directly destroy pathogens.
- Lymph nodes contain lymphocytes that destroy pathogens.

REVIEW QUESTIONS

1. The skin helps to maintain body temperature

    (A) by synthesizing melanin
    (B) by acting as a barrier against pathogens
    (C) through the action of its sweat glands
    (D) when capillaries in the dermis constrict in warm weather
    (E) when oil glands release their secretion onto the surface

2. Which type of white blood cell protects the body by making antibodies?

    (A) B-cells
    (B) helper T-cells
    (C) killer T-cells
    (D) phagocytes
    (E) all type of lymphocytes

3. The HIV virus that causes AIDS destroys helper T-cells. As a result, the body

    (A) is more prone to infections
    (B) has a compromised immune system
    (C) has a weakened defense system against pathogens
    (D) cannot produce enough B-cells to mount a proper immune response
    (E) all of the above

4. Millions of different kinds of B-cells are found in the blood because they

    (A) are needed for phagocytosis of pathogens
    (B) transport oxygen in addition to fighting disease
    (C) each form in response to a particular pathogen
    (D) are needed to attack the bodies various types of tissues
    (E) will no longer form after a certain age

ANSWERS

1. **C** Sweat glands in the dermis release water to the surface that evaporates in warm weather to keep the body cool.
2. **A** Antibodies are made by B-cells.
3. **E** Without helper T-cells, the body's immune system is compromised. All types of white blood cells are affected.
4. **C** Each pathogen triggers a particular type of B-cell. With millions of different pathogens, millions of different B-cells exist.

Lesson 9-5. Coordination

VOCABULARY

- neuron
- dendrite
- cell body
- axon
- resting potential
- action potential
- myelin sheath
- nodes of Ranvier
- synapse
- neurotransmitters
- central nervous system
- peripheral nervous system
- cerebrum
- cerebellum
- medulla oblongata
- hypothalamus
- somatic nervous system

- autonomic nervous system
- sympathetic division
- parasympathetic division
- reflex action
- endocrine gland
- hormone
- peptide hormones
- steroid hormones
- pituitary
- pineal
- thyroid
- parathyroid
- insulin
- glucagon
- adrenal gland
- testis
- ovary

For all the various systems to work well and maintain homeostasis, they must function in a coordinated manner. Coordination of the various systems is controlled by two specialized systems. These are the nervous system and the endocrine system.

The nervous system allows an organism to receive, process, and respond to stimuli. These stimuli arise in both the external and internal environments. For example, consider what happens when a hydra is touched on its body. The entire body contracts to protect the organism from danger. Nerve cells are scattered throughout the hydra's body to form what is called a nerve net. Obviously, humans have a much more complex nervous system.

THE HUMAN NERVOUS SYSTEM

The basic unit of the nervous system is a **neuron,** or nerve cell. Billions of neurons make up the human nervous system. Their structure depends on their function. However, all neurons have three basic parts. One part is a **dendrite.** A dendrite is an extension of the cell that receives signals either from the environment or other neurons. The signal next travels to the **cell body,** where the nucleus and organelles are located. Then the signal continues its journey on to an **axon,** which is an extension that transmits the signal to a muscle, gland, or other neurons.

A neuron that is not conducting a signal exhibits a **resting potential.** This is a small electrical potential that is established by an unequal concentrations of ions on either side of the cell membrane. At rest, more positive ions than negative ions are located on the outside of the cell membrane of a neuron. These include sodium ions. In contrast, more negative ions than positive ions are located inside the cell. Potassium ions are included among those positive ions inside a neuron.

When a neuron is stimulated, a signal, or impulse, travels along its length, moving in only one direction: dendrite → cell body → axon. The conduction of an impulse is known as an **action potential.** At the point of an action potential, the permeability of the membrane changes so that the outside of the cell has a net negative charge, while the inside has a net positive charge. The action potential travels across the neuron. After the action potential has passed a particular point, the ion concentrations are returned to the resting potential state. The neuron is then ready to conduct another impulse.

Some neurons are specialized to conduct impulses much faster than others. The axons of these neurons are wrapped with special cells that form a **myelin sheath.** The myelin sheath does not cover the entire axon. Rather, gaps exist along the axon. These gaps are called **nodes of Ranvier.** As the action potential moves along these neurons, the action potential jumps across the nodes of Ranvier. As a result, the impulse travels at a faster rate across the axon. Figure 9-7 shows how a neuron transmits an impulse.

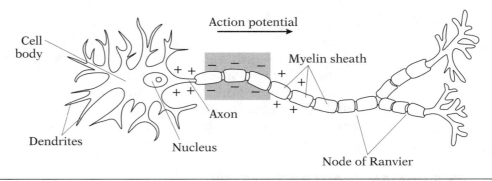

Figure 9-7

Neurons do not come in direct contact with one another. Rather, a small gap, known as a **synapse,** is present between the axon of one neuron and the dendrite of another neuron or a muscle or gland cell. Chemical messengers, called **neurotransmitters,** carry the impulse across the synapse. Once the neurotransmitters have crossed the synapse, they are destroyed. If they were not destroyed, the neuron would continue to "fire" or transmit impulses. Not all neurotransmitters stimulate a neuron. In fact, some neurotransmitters inhibit a neuron by raising the action potential that is necessary for the neuron to transmit an impulse. A dendrite, muscle, cell, or gland cell actually can receive several different neurotransmitters. Some stimulate, while others inhibit. Whatever is present in a greater concentration determines what happens.

Neurons are found everywhere in the body. They make up the two basic divisions of the nervous system. One is called the **central nervous system.** This division consists of the brain and spinal cord. The other division is called the **peripheral nervous system.**

The brain can be divided into four major parts. The **cerebrum** is the largest portion of the brain. The cerebrum is the part of the brain that consciously directs the body's responses to stimuli, such as answering the door when someone knocks or putting on a coat when the weather is cold. The cerebrum also is the center of learning, memory, and all higher cognitive skills associated with human behavior.

The **cerebellum** coordinates balance and muscle movements. The **medulla oblongata** controls vital functions like breathing and heart rate. The **hypothalamus** controls functions such as response to hunger, thirst, pain, and temperature changes.

The peripheral nervous system is further subdivided into the **somatic nervous system** and the **autonomic nervous system.** The somatic nervous system is under voluntary control and directs the actions of skeletal muscles. The autonomic nervous system involves involuntary actions. The autonomic system is divided into the **sympathetic division** that directs so-called "fight-or-flight" responses. For example, the sympathetic division acts when a person is suddenly startled, such as when confronted by a mean-looking dog. The sympathetic activation brings about such changes in your body as an increase in heart rate, respiration and blood pressure. Another division of the autonomic nervous system is the **parasympathetic division.** This division directs the so-called "rest-and-digest" responses by slowing down the activities of muscles and glands. For example, the parasympathetic system division acts after a person has eaten by dilating the blood vessels in the villi of the small intestine that transport nutrients.

Another function carried out by the nervous system is a **reflex action.** An example of a reflex action would be the response a person has after touching a hot stove. The person responds without thinking by quickly removing his or her hand from the stove. In this case, an impulse travels from neurons in the finger that response to heat, to the spinal cord, and then back out to muscles in the finger and hand. At the same time, the impulse travels up the spinal cord to the brain where the cerebrum interprets the signals as pain. Traveling to the brain takes a little longer. This is why the person feels the pain after the hand has been withdrawn from the hot stove.

THE HUMAN ENDOCRINE SYSTEM

You learned that the autonomic nervous system controls involuntary actions. Among these actions are the functions of the endocrine glands. An **endocrine gland** is a structure that produces and secretes a **hormone** directly into the bloodstream. A hormone is a chemical substance that is produced by a gland that travels in the blood to work on another structure in the body. The structure affected by a hormone is called the target organ.

Hormones are classified into two groups. One group includes the **peptide hormones.** Peptide hormones are large protein compounds that are too large to diffuse across a cell membrane. As a result, peptide hormones attach to receptors on the cell membrane where they initiate their action. A second group of hormones includes the **steroid hormones.** These hormones are lipid molecules. Lipids are also present in the cell membrane. As a result, steroid hormones can diffuse across the cell membrane. Steroid hormones enter the nucleus where they bind to regions in the genes to control transcription. Compared to peptide hormones, steroid hormones may take longer to produce a response. However, their effects may last longer.

You read that the hypothalamus is a part of the brain. The hypothalamus is also an endocrine gland. It is not unusual for an organ to be involved in more than one system. The hypothalamus secretes hormones known as releasing factors. These releasing factors stimulate another endocrine gland called the **pituitary.** The pituitary was once known as the "master gland" because it controls the functions of many of the other endocrine glands. However, this term is rarely used for the pituitary after scientists discovered that it is under the control of the hypothalamus.

The pituitary produces many different hormones. One of its hormones is *prolactin,* which stimulates milk production and secretion in a female. In fact, several of the pituitary hormones are involved in reproduction and development, which is discussed in the next lesson.

Located at the base of the brain is an endocrine gland called the **pineal.** The pineal gland produces a hormone called *melatonin,* which regulates our day–night cycles.

Another endocrine gland is the **thyroid.** The thyroid secretes a hormone called *thyroxin,* which stimulates metabolism. Attached to the thyroid is another endocrine gland called the **parathyroid.** The parathyroid secretes a hormone that regulates the calcium and phosphate levels in the bone and blood.

The pancreas is not only involved in digestion but also in hormone production. The pancreas secretes two hormones that regulate the sugar level in the blood. One hormone is **insulin,** which lowers blood sugar by stimulating glucose uptake by cells. The other hormone is **glucagon,** which raises blood sugar by changing glycogen into glucose.

Located on each kidney is an **adrenal gland.** The most familiar hormone that this endocrine gland produces is *epinephrine,* more commonly known as *adrenalin.* Adrenalin is the hormone that is most closely associated with the "fight-or-flight" responses that are controlled by the sympathetic division.

The **testis** of a male is another endocrine gland. The testes produce steroid hormones known as *androgens. Testosterone* is the most familiar androgen. The **ovary** of a female is still another endocrine gland. The ovary produces steroid hormones called estrogens. Figure 9-8 shows the location of the major endocrine glands in the body. Looking just at this illustration, can you identify what each endocrine gland does?

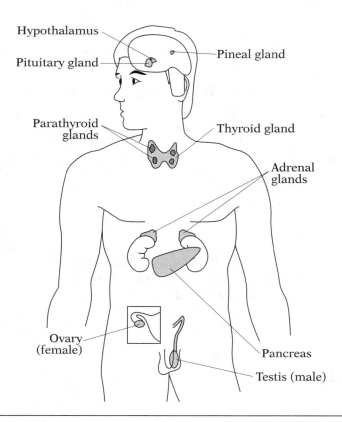

Figure 9-8

LESSON SUMMARY

- The functional unit of the nervous system is the neuron, which consists of an axon, cell body, and dendrite.
- A nerve impulse is an action potential that proceeds in only one direction along a neuron.
- Neurotransmitters are responsible for impulses crossing synapses.
- The nervous system is divided into the central nervous systems, which consists of the brain and spinal cord, and the peripheral nervous system.
- Major portions of the brain include the cerebrum, cerebellum, medulla oblongata, and hypothalamus.
- The peripheral nervous system is divided into the somatic nervous system and the autonomic nervous system. In turn, the autonomic system is divided into the sympathetic and parasympathetic divisions.
- The major glands of the endocrine system include the hypothalamus, pituitary, pineal, thyroid, parathyroid, adrenal, pancreas, testis, and ovary.
- The nervous system and endocrine system play a major role in homeostasis by coordinating the actions of the other body systems.

REVIEW QUESTIONS

Each set of lettered choices below refers to the numbered statement immediately following it. Select the lettered choice that best answers each statement.

(A) central nervous system
(B) somatic nervous system
(C) autonomic nervous system
(D) sympathetic division
(E) parasympathetic division

1. controls "fight-or-flight" responses
2. controls skeletal muscles
3. stores information
4. spinal cord

(A) parathyroid
(B) pineal
(C) pancreas
(D) ovary
(E) adrenal

5. involved in "flight-or-fight" responses
6. controls daily rhythm cycles
7. regulates blood calcium level
8. located on the kidney

▓▓▓ ANSWERS

1. **D** The sympathetic division of the autonomic nervous system helps prepare the body for stressful situations.
2. **B** Nerves of the somatic nervous system stimulate skeletal muscle to contract.
3. **A** The brain, which is part of the central nervous system, stores information.
4. **A** The spinal cord is also part of the central nervous system.
5. **E** The adrenal gland secretes epinephrine, a hormone involved in the "fight-or-flight" reactions.
6. **B** Night–day rhythms are controlled by the pineal gland.
7. **A** A hormone produced by the parathyroid regulates the calcium level in the blood stream.
8. **E** The adrenal gland is located on the kidney. The word *renal* refers to kidney.

Lesson 9-6. Reproduction and Development

VOCABULARY

- asexual reproduction
- sexual reproduction
- seminiferous tubules
- vas deferens
- Fallopian tube
- uterus
- cervix
- vagina
- menstrual cycle
- fertilization
- menstruation
- follicular phase
- ovulation
- corpus luteum
- luteal phase
- negative feedback
- zygote
- inner cell mass
- blastocyst
- embryo
- placenta
- gastrula
- ectoderm
- mesoderm
- endoderm

Reproduction is the key to survival of a species. There are two types of reproduction. **Asexual reproduction** involves the division of either a single cell or an entire organism to form a new individual. Asexual reproduction involves only one parent. For example, bacteria and protozoa undergo binary fission in which the single cell divides to form two new cells. Starfish can also undergo asexual reproduction. New starfish can regenerate from one of their arms cut off along with a small portion of their central body.

In contrast **sexual reproduction** involves two parents, one male and the other female. Because two parents are involved, sexual reproduction results in greater genetic diversity among the offspring. Keep in mind that some organisms can carry out both asexual and sexual reproduction, depending on conditions. For example, two bacteria can exchange genetic material in a process called *conjugation*. However, most organisms carry out only sexual reproduction. Such is the case with humans.

THE HUMAN REPRODUCTIVE SYSTEM

The hormone testosterone is responsible for the maturation of sperm cells. Mature sperm are produced within tiny coiled tubes within the testes. These tubes are called **seminiferous tubules.** The sperm then exit the testes through the **vas deferens,** which leads to the urethra. In males, both sperm and urine exit through the urethra and out the penis.

In females, hormones mature an egg cell in the ovary. After maturation, the egg cell is swept by cilia into the **Fallopian tube.** The Fallopian tube is also called an oviduct. The Fallopian tubes leading from each ovary meet at the **uterus.** The neck of the uterus is called the **cervix,** which leads to the **vagina.**

Hormones control the events that take place in the female reproductive cycle. These events form the **menstrual cycle.** The menstrual cycle is the period of time, usually lasting about 28 days, in which the female reproductive tract is prepared should **fertilization** take place. Fertilization is the fusion of an egg with a sperm, a process that usually occurs in the upper portion of the Fallopian tube.

The menstrual cycle involves four stages. Although these four stages form a cycle, it is convenient to begin at some point in the cycle. The first stage is known as **menstruation,** which starts at day 1. During menstruation, the uterine lining is shed. The lining includes blood vessels. As a result, menstruation results in bleeding as these blood vessels are broken down and discarded along with the uterine lining. Menstruation lasts for about 5 days.

The second stage, called the **follicular phase,** begins about day 6. The follicular stage is also known as the *proliferative phase.* During this stage, hormones from the pituitary gland stimulate the maturation of an egg in the ovary. In response to these hormones, the ovary in turn produces a hormone called estrogen. Estrogen from the ovary stimulates the division of cells in the uterus. As a result, the uterine lining thickens. Estrogen also promotes the formation of new blood vessels in the uterus. The follicular stage lasts until about day 13 of the menstrual cycle.

The third stage, **ovulation,** usually occurs about day 14. Ovulation involves the release of a mature egg from the ovary. This egg cell is swept into the Fallopian tube where it can be fertilized should sperm be present. Ovulation is stimulated by another hormone produced by the pituitary gland. Following ovulation, the structure that housed the egg while it was being matured in the ovary becomes a **corpus luteum.** The corpus luteum secretes *progesterone,* a hormone that brings on the fourth and final stage of the menstrual cycle.

The fourth stage, known as the **luteal** phase, begins on about day 15. The luteal phase is also known as the *secretory phase.* During this stage, the uterus continues to enlarge and become enriched with more blood vessels. These changes are attributable to progesterone. The uterus is now prepared to receive a fertilized egg descending from the Fallopian tube. However, if no fertilized egg becomes implanted in the uterus, the uterine lining is shed and the menstrual cycle starts again.

Estrogen and progesterone are just two of the hormones involved in the menstrual cycle. The interaction between all the hormones is quite complex. The level of each hormone must be controlled. These levels must also be adjusted, depending on whether or not a fertilized egg implants itself in the uterus. These hormones are controlled by a mechanism known as **negative feedback.**

Consider how the estrogen level is controlled by negative feedback. Recall that the pituitary gland secretes a hormone that stimulates the ovary to produce estrogen. As a result, the estrogen level continues to rise during the follicular phase.

Also recall that the pituitary is under the control of the hypothalamus. When the estrogen level rises to a certain level, estrogen in the bloodstream inhibits the hypothalamus from stimulating the pituitary. As a result, the pituitary stops secreting the hormone that stimulates the ovary to make estrogen. Therefore, the estrogen level starts to drop. In effect, there is feedback from the ovary to the hypothalamus. Because the estrogen level drops as a result of this feedback, the result is a negative impact on this hormone's level in the bloodstream.

DEVELOPMENT

If fertilization has taken place, then a **zygote,** or fertilized egg, will implant itself in the uterine lining. The zygote will start to undergo mitosis, usually within 24–36 hours of fertilization. The zygote continues to divide to form a small, solid ball of cells. Mitotic divisions continue. More cells are produced. In addition, a cavity forms inside the ball. The result is an outer ring of cells. Attached to this outer ring on one side is the **inner cell mass.** Together, the outer ring of cells and the inner cell mass form a structure called a **blastocyst.**

The inner cell mass will continue to develop and form the **embryo.** The embryo is the term given to the early stages of the development of an individual. The outer ring of cells will form the embryo's contribution to the **placenta.** Uterine tissue will also contribute to the placenta. The placenta is the structure that serves as the site of exchange of materials between the two. For example, nutrients will pass from mother to embryo across the placenta. The nutrients will then pass into the embryo via an umbilical cord that attaches the growing embryo to the placenta.

Mitotic divisions continue in the blastocyst, which now begins to get larger. The next stage of development is called a **gastrula.** For the first time, groups of cells become distinct and form three different layers. One layer, called the **ectoderm,** will develop into external structures such as the skin and also form the nervous system. A second layer, called the **mesoderm,** will form structures such as bones, muscles, blood vessels, and kidneys. The third layer, the **endoderm,** will develop into the inner linings of the digestive and respiratory systems. Keep in mind that almost all structures develop from more than one of these layers. For example, the epidermis of the skin comes from ectoderm, while the blood vessels in the dermis derive from mesoderm.

LESSON SUMMARY

- Asexual reproduction involves only one parent, whereas sexual reproduction involves two parents of opposite sex.
- In a human male, sperm are matured in the seminiferous tubules in the testes where they next pass into the vas deferens and exit the body through the urethra.
- In a human female, an egg is matured in the ovary and then released into a Fallopian tube. The egg then moves down to the uterus, and if it is not fertilized, will pass out the vagina.
- The menstrual cycle last about 28 days, during which hormones prepare the uterus should an egg be fertilized and implanted.
- The menstrual cycle consists of the menstruation, follicular phase, ovulation, and the luteal phase.
- A fertilized egg is known as a zygote, which develops into a blastocyst that consists of an outer wall of cells and an inner cell mass.
- At the gastrula stage, cells specialize to form ectoderm, mesoderm, and endoderm.

REVIEW QUESTIONS

Each set of lettered choices in Figures 9-9 and 9-10 refers to the numbered statement immediately following it. Select the lettered choice that best relates to each statement.

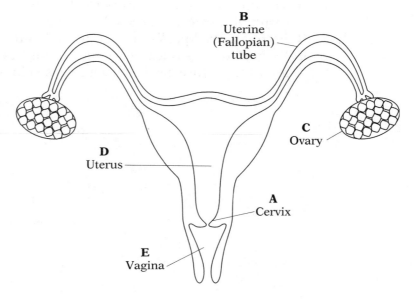

Figure 9-9

1. the usual site of fertilization
2. site of placenta formation
3. site that produces the hormone estrogen

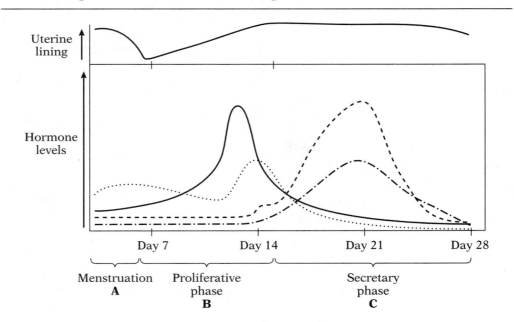

Figure 9-10

4. part of cycle where uterine lining builds up
5. part of cycle where estrogen level peaks
6. hormone secreted by the corpus luteum after ovulation has occurred

ANSWERS

1. **B** A sperm travels up the oviduct to fertilize an egg cell.
2. **D** The placenta forms in the uterus.
3. **C** Estrogen is produced by the ovary.
4. **B** The uterine lining becomes thicker during the proliferative phase as a result of estrogen secreted by the ovary.
5. **B** Estrogen level peaks toward the end of the proliferative phase.
6. **E** Progesterone is released by the corpus luteum that forms in the ovary after the mature egg has been released in ovulation.

CHAPTER 10

UNDERSTANDING ECOLOGY

Lesson 10-1. Population Growth

VOCABULARY

- ecology
- population
- population growth
- exponential growth
- limited growth
- carrying capacity

Darwin recognized that organisms are continuously interacting with their environment. As the environment changes, those organisms with the necessary adaptations are likely to survive. In contrast, organisms that lack these adaptations have less chance, if any, of surviving. Since Darwin's time, scientists began to appreciate the importance of the interactions between organisms and their environment. This awareness led to the field of biology known as **ecology,** which is the study of the interactions between organisms and their environment.

POPULATIONS

Perhaps there is a sign posted on the main road leading to your city or town that lists its population. This number indicates how many people are believed to be living in your city or town. In ecology, the term population has a specific meaning. A **population** is defined as a group consisting of all the members of a species who live in a defined area. In the case of your city or town, the population number refers to all the members of *Homo sapiens* who live there.

A population can be huge or tiny, depending upon the defined area. For example, the human population of a city may be several million. In contrast, the human population of a rural village may be fewer than one hundred. No matter what their size, all populations share certain characteristics. One such characteristic is growth. **Population growth** refers to the change in the number of its members over a period of time. The size of a population may grow, stay the same, or shrink.

EXPONENTIAL GROWTH

Darwin recognized that under ideal conditions, population growth can increase dramatically. As an example, Darwin calculated that one pair of elephants could produce 19 million offspring in just 700 years. Such a rapid increase in the size of a population is known as **exponential growth.** If Darwin's data were plotted, Figure 10-1 shows how the graph would look. Notice that the number of individuals in the population increases exponentially over time. Notice also that an exponential growth of a population produces a line on the graph that has the shape of the letter J. As a result, exponential growth results in a J-curve.

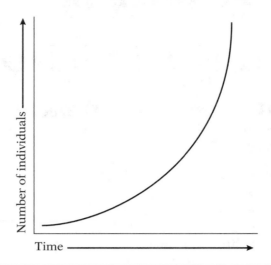

Figure 10-1

To experience exponential growth, a population must live under certain ideal conditions. Food must be abundant. The population members must be able to reproduce at maximum capacity. In turn, their offspring must survive at least to reach reproductive age. Darwin realized that such conditions rarely existed. When they did, these conditions could exist for only a relatively short time. As a result, Darwin realized that the exponential growth of a population for any significant period of time, such as 700 years, was not likely to happen. Rather, population growth was kept in control. Darwin recognized that nature was the controlling force.

Nature eventually sets a limit on the maximum size a population can reach. For example, the hunting of elephants in Kruger National Park in South Africa was banned. From the early 1900s until the mid-1960s, this elephant population underwent an exponential growth. With so many elephants, their food supply became limited. Their growth came to a stop and leveled off.

LIMITED GROWTH

The elephant population in Kruger National Park followed a growth pattern typical of what happens in nature. This type of growth is known as **limited growth.** The following illustration shows a population that experiences limited growth.

Notice in Figure 10-2 that the population experiences a period of exponential growth. At some point, the population reaches its maximum size. The maximum population size that a particular environment can support is known as the **carrying capacity.** Notice that the carrying capacity corresponds to the point on the graph where it levels off. At this point, the birth rate in the population equals the death rate. When this point is reached, the population is said to display zero growth. Take another look at Figure 10-2. Notice that the curve follows the shape of the letter S. Therefore, limited growth is characterized by an S-curve.

Keep in mind that populations do not grow as smoothly as either a J-curve or an S-curve suggests. Rather, the size of most populations often exceeds the carrying capacity before settling down. This is what happened to the elephant population in Kruger National Park. For a period of time, the size of this population exceeded the carrying capacity until starvation caused the death rate

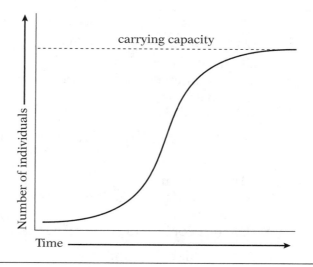

Figure 10-2

to increase. Only then did the population size decline to stabilize at the carrying capacity.

Also keep in mind that the carrying capacity can change if the environment changes. In the case of the elephants in Kruger National Park, the carrying capacity could have been increased by bringing in vegetation for the elephants to eat. This increased food supply would have raised the carrying capacity. At some point, however, the population growth would eventually level off.

Rather than raise the carrying capacity above the level set by nature, park managers took other steps to prevent starvation from occurring again. They instituted measures to limit the elephant population by using birth control and shipping elephants to other countries. In effect, what they did was to try to get the elephant population to reach its carrying capacity as smoothly as possible. Like Darwin, they realized that nature ultimately controls population growth.

LESSON SUMMARY

- A population consists of members of the same species that inhabit a particular environment.
- A population can experience exponential growth, characterized by a rapid increase over a short period of time.
- Exponential growth is characterized by a J-shaped curve on a graph.
- Over time, populations undergo limited growth in nature, characterized by an increase in size followed by a stabilization at its maximum size.
- Limited growth is characterized by an S-shaped curve on a graph.
- The maximum population size that a particular environment can support is called the carrying capacity.

REVIEW QUESTIONS

1. A population reaches the carrying capacity of its environment when the

    (A) food supply is insufficient to support the population
    (B) birth rate exceeds the death rate
    (C) environmental conditions are ideal
    (D) birth rate and death rate are equal
    (E) number of individuals in the population starts to decrease

2. To experience exponential growth, a population must have

   (A) a high birth rate and a low death rate
   (B) limited resources
   (C) few individuals that have reached sexual maturity
   (D) a large size
   (E) a small size

3. Which of the following is considered to be a population?

   (A) all the fish in a pond
   (B) all the animals in a zoo
   (C) all the tigers in a nature preserve
   (D) all the birds in a tree
   (E) the people living in Los Angeles and the people living in New York City

4. A population that undergoes limited growth

   (A) follows a J-curve growth pattern
   (B) also undergoes exponential growth for a limited time period
   (C) rarely reaches its carrying capacity
   (D) must inhabit a very limited geographic area
   (E) has access to an unlimited food supply

5. How can the carrying capacity for a population be decreased?

   (A) increase the food supply
   (B) increase the birth rate
   (C) introduce another population that consumes the same food supply
   (D) export members of the population to another environment
   (E) move the population to a less favorable environment

ANSWERS

1. **D** The carrying capacity is attained when the growth rate is zero. Therefore, at this point, the birth rate equals the death rate.
2. **A** A high birth rate and a low death rate can result in a dramatic increase in population size over a short period.
3. **C** Tigers constitute the only example of a single species inhabiting a particular environment.
4. **B** An S-curve includes a period of time where there is a rapid increase in population size.
5. **C** Introduction of another species would cause the original population to decrease in size as its members confront a dwindling food supply.

Lesson 10-2. Food Chains and Food Webs

VOCABULARY

- biotic factor
- abiotic factor
- community
- ecosystem
- trophic structure
- producer
- consumers
- herbivore

- carnivore
- food chain
- omnivore
- food web
- decomposers
- pyramid of energy
- pyramid of biomass

A population interacts with both the living and nonliving factors found in its environment. A living factor is known as a **biotic factor.** For example, some of the abiotic factors that mice in a small field interact with include the grasses, owls, and snakes. A nonliving factor is known as an **abiotic factor.** Some of the abiotic factors that these mice interact with include water and temperature. Taken together, the biotic and abiotic factors make up higher levels of biological organization beyond a population.

COMMUNITIES AND ECOSYSTEMS

Rarely does a single population inhabit a particular environment. Rather, the environment is more likely to serve as home to several populations, each consisting of a different species. Just consider a place you may have visited. For example, a stroll through a park would reveal a variety of plants, including grasses, ferns, mosses, colorful flowering plants, bushes, and trees. In addition, you could come across a variety of animals, including birds, squirrels, chipmunks, and insects.

The park represents a **community.** A community consists of all the populations of various species that live and interact in a particular environment. A community includes only the biotic factors present in a given area. If the abiotic factors are included, then you have an **ecosystem.** An ecosystem is defined as all the populations and abiotic factors that are interacting in a given area. In other words, an ecosystem consists of a community and its physical environment.

FOOD CHAINS

The interactions that take place in a community depend in large measure on the feeding relationships between the various populations. These feeding relationships make up the **trophic structure** of a community. Each population makes up a trophic level within the community.

The lowest trophic level within a community is made up of organisms that use energy from the sun or from inorganic molecules to make the organic compounds needed to survive. These organic compounds include carbohydrates, proteins, and lipids. The most familiar organisms found at this trophic level are green plants. Recall that green plants carry out photosynthesis, using light energy from the sun to convert water and carbon dioxide into oxygen and organic compounds. In effect, they are producing chemical energy that is stored in these organic compounds. As a result, these organisms are known as **producers.** Producers form the foundation of a trophic structure.

The next higher trophic level is made up of animals that eat, or consume, producers. These organisms are known as **consumers.** For example, a mouse that eats grass seeds is an example of a consumer. In this case, the mouse is classified as a primary consumer because it eats a producer. The mouse is also known as a **herbivore,** which is an animal that eats plants.

A snake that eats the mouse would represent the next higher trophic level. In this case, the snake is classified as a secondary consumer because it consumes the mouse. The snake is also known as a **carnivore,** which is an animal that eats other animals.

A hawk that eats the snake would be a tertiary consumer in this trophic structure. Keep in mind that positions within a trophic level can change. For example, when the hawk consumes a mouse rather than a snake, the hawk represents a secondary consumer.

The relationship between seeds, mouse, snake, and hawk is referred to as a **food chain** and can be diagrammed as follows.

seeds ──────▶ mouse ──────▶ snake ──────▶ hawk

Figure 10-3

Notice in Figure 10-3 that the arrow points to the next higher trophic level. In other words, the arrow points to show that the mouse serves as a primary consumer by eating grass seeds. Notice also that the mice eat both grasses and insects. An animal that eats both plants and other animals is known as an **omnivore.**

FOOD WEBS

The trophic structure that exists within a community is rarely as simple as a food chain depicts. Instead, a population often depends on more than one source of food. Recall that a hawk may eat a snake or a mouse, depending on which is available. In nature, feeding relationships are even much more complex than this. In the 1920s, an English scientist named Charles Elton recognized that a food chain does not exist as an isolated unit. Rather, several food chains are linked together to form a **food web.**

Food webs can be very complicated, especially in an environment where a wide variety of animal and plant species exist. But even food webs found within a rather harsh environment that limits biological diversity are still quite complex. Consider the following food web that exists among the marine life found in the Antarctic.

Notice in Figure 10-4 that the elephant seals depend upon two food sources: fishes and squids. In turn, the elephant seals serve as a food source for smaller toothed whales and humans. Notice that a food web enables you to predict the impact of what happens when just one population is affected. For example, assume that humans overhunt the elephant seals in a community. Forced to search elsewhere for food, the smaller tooth whales will eat more crab-eater seals, birds, leopard seals, and squids. As a result, these populations may decline in size. Their decline will affect other populations. For example, the food web illustrated above shows that a decline in the crab-eater seal

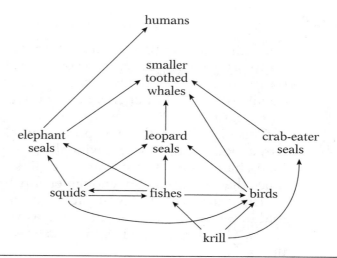

Figure 10-4

population can result in an increase in the krill population. As you can see, a food web is like a spider's web. Touch just one area and the effects are felt everywhere.

ENERGY FLOW

A food chain and a food web may give the impression that the flow always proceeds in one direction, ending with the organisms at the top of the trophic structure. This picture changes when an organism dies. As the dead organism decays, other organisms known as **decomposers** break down the organic matter into simpler inorganic substances such as carbon dioxide, nitrogen, and phosphorus. The main decomposers include bacteria and fungi. These decomposers also break down the organic matter found in fallen leaves and trees and in the solid wastes deposited by animals.

The inorganic substances produced by decomposers are released into the soil, water and air. From here, the inorganic substances can be used by producers for the synthesis of new organic compounds. These compounds then become part of the lowest trophic level and are ready to be used by those in successively higher levels. As a result, the flow of nutrients in a food chain or a food web does not proceed solely in one direction but rather in a cycle.

What flows through food chains and food webs is energy. This flow begins with light energy from the sun. Producers convert this light energy into chemical energy that is then transferred from one trophic level to the next. However, this transfer of energy involves only a fraction of the energy that is present in a trophic level.

Energy transfers are not 100% efficient. With each transfer, energy is usually given off and therefore considered "lost" as heat. In addition, the organisms within each trophic level use much of the energy stored in their organic compounds to survive. Scientists calculate that between 5 and 20% of the energy stored in one trophic level gets stored at the next trophic level. The percentage that gets transferred depends on the type of community. For most purposes, an average value of 10% is used when calculating how much energy is transferred.

PYRAMIDS

The unit that scientists use for energy is the joule (J). Consider that it takes 1 J to bring a cheeseburger to your mouth. Assuming you bring the cheeseburger to your mouth ten times means that you require a total of 10 J. To obtain 10 J, 100 J of energy are required at the next lower trophic level (a cow). In turn, 1,000 J of energy are required at the next lower level (grass).

This loss of energy as you proceed up through trophic levels is one reason why a food chain, either individually or as part of a food web, is limited. Most food chains consist of five or fewer links. After flowing through this many links, there is simply not enough energy left to support any additional links.

The transfer of energy in a food chain is sometimes illustrated as a pyramid because the numbers decrease as you proceed up through the trophic levels. This illustration is known as a **pyramid of energy,** as shown in Figure 10-5.

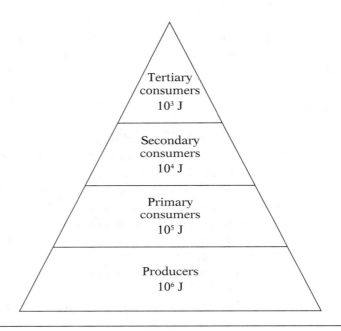

Tertiary
consumers
10^3 J

Secondary
consumers
10^4 J

Primary
consumers
10^5 J

Producers
10^6 J

Figure 10-5

A **pyramid of biomass** is another way to show how the numbers decrease as you proceed up through the trophic levels. Biomass refers to the dry weight of the organic matter present in a population. Again assume that each trophic level requires an amount ten times greater at each successively lower level. Therefore, a 50-kilogram (kg) person must be supported by 500 kg of biomass at the next lower trophic level (cows). In turn, 5,000 kg of biomass are required at the next lower trophic level (grass).

Not all trophic structures, however, can be diagrammed as a pyramid. In fact, some trophic structures are represented by an inverted pyramid. In this case, the number of individuals increases as you proceed up through the trophic levels. Such an inverted pyramid of numbers can be seen in a tropical rain forest where one producer, a tree, supports a large number of primary consumers such as birds or insects.

LESSON SUMMARY

- A community consists of all the populations of various species that live and interact in a particular environment.
- An ecosystem consists of a community and its physical environment.
- The feeding relationships between different populations in a community can be represented by a food chain.
- A food chain includes producers and consumers.
- In nature, several food chains are linked to form a food web.
- A food chain can be represented by a pyramid to illustrate that the quantity of energy and the amount of biomass decrease as you move up through the chain.

REVIEW QUESTIONS

1. Which of the following cannot be part of a community?

   (A) a species
   (B) a population
   (C) sunlight
   (D) organisms
   (E) *Homo sapiens*

2. The least amount of biomass in a forest community would consist of the

   (A) grasshoppers
   (B) mice
   (C) grass
   (D) snakes
   (E) hawks

3. In an ecosystem, the greatest amount of stored energy is usually found in the

   (A) primary consumers
   (B) secondary consumers
   (C) producers
   (D) small animals
   (E) large animals

4. A food chain consists of the following populations: grass → insects → owls → lynx. Which population represents the tertiary, or third-level, consumers?

   (A) grass
   (B) insects
   (C) owls
   (D) lynx
   (E) both insects and owls

5. Examine the following food web.

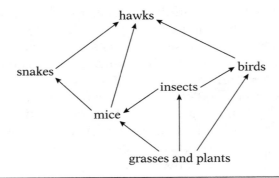

Figure 10-6

Which population would be most likely be the first to increase in size if the snake population were reduced?

(A) hawks
(B) mice
(C) birds
(D) insects
(E) grass and plants

ANSWERS

1. **C** Sunlight is an abiotic factor and, therefore, is not part of any community, which includes only biotic factors.
2. **E** As the final trophic level, hawks would have the smallest biomass.
3. **C** Producers contain the greatest quantity of stored energy as a result of photosynthesis.
4. **D** A tertiary consumer (lynx) eats a secondary consumer (owl), which in turn, feeds upon a primary consumer (insect).
5. **B** With fewer snakes to eat them, the mouse population would likely increase.

Lesson 10-3. Ecological Relationships

VOCABULARY

- habitat
- niche
- symbiosis
- mutualism
- nitrogen fixation
- commensalism
- parasitism

- parasite
- host
- interspecific competition
- predators
- prey
- intraspecific competition

You read that all organisms interact with their environment, including both biotic and abiotic factors. Within its environment, each organism has a **habitat.** A habitat is the physical environment in which the organism lives. Your habitat is your home. Within its environment, each organism also occupies a **niche.** A niche is the way the organism lives in its habitat. For example, an organism's niche includes what it eats, when it sleeps, how it moves, and when it reproduces. You can think of an organism's habitat as the place where it lives and its niche as the role its plays. Part of its role usually involves maintaining an ecological relationship with other organisms, including members of other species.

SYMBIOTIC RELATIONSHIPS

An ecological relationship between members of different species that are in direct contact is known as **symbiosis.** Symbiotic relationships are classified in three ways. One way is called **mutualism.** As its name suggests, mutualism is a relationship in which both organisms benefit. This type of relation is sometimes symbolized as +/+. Mutualism exists everywhere in nature, from the coral reefs in tropical seas to the farm fields in agricultural areas.

An example of mutualism can be seen in the giant clams that live in coral reefs. When fully grown, this clam can reach a length of 1.2 meters (4 feet) and weigh as much as 225 kilograms (500 pounds). Living inside these giant clams are algae that carry out photosynthesis. The food the algae make is used to feed themselves and the giant clams. In turn, the algae benefit by being protected from harm inside the giant clam's shell.

Another example of mutualism is found on the roots of legumes such as peas, beans, peanuts, soybeans, and clover. Bacteria living on the roots of these plants carry out a process called **nitrogen fixation.** This process converts the nitrogen in the soil into a form that can be used by plants. In return, the plants provide nutrients for the bacteria.

Mutualism also plays an important role in humans. Scientists estimate that between 500 and 1,000 species of bacteria live in the human intestines. Many of them synthesize substances such as vitamins that humans need to stay healthy. In return, the bacteria benefit by receiving shelter and nutrients they require.

A second type of symbiotic relationship is known as **commensalism.** In this relationship, one organism is benefited, while the other organism is not affected in any way. Commensalism is symbolized as +/0. An example of commensalism can be seen in whales, whose bodies can be covered with barnacles. Getting a "free" ride, the barnacles have more opportunities to get the nutrients they need. The whale is unaffected.

The third type of symbiotic relationship is called **parasitism.** This relationship involves one organism that benefits at the expense of another organism. Parasitism is symbolized as +/−. The organism that benefits is known as the **parasite.** The other organism is called the **host.** Most parasites are small. However, some parasites can be quite large. Consider the pearl fish that lives in coral reefs. Its body can grow as long as 65 centimeters (25 inches). During the night, pearl fish hunt for food. During the day, they live inside the body of another organism known as a sea cucumber. There, the pearl fish feeds on the sea cucumber. Like all parasites, the pearl fish rarely kills its host. If it did, the pearl fish would no longer have a host to keep it alive.

COMPETITION

Organisms belonging to different species can occupy the same habitat without any problem. They may depend on different food sources, seek shelter in different ways, or reproduce at different times of the year. However, organisms belonging to different species cannot occupy the same niche without a problem. If they do, competition is sure to follow.

Competition between different species is known as **interspecific competition.** The degree of competition depends on how much their niches overlap. The more overlap, the greater the competition. The competition can be so fierce that both species may be harmed. This outcome is symbolized by −/−. This can happen in the northern forests of Canada and Alaska where foxes and lynx compete for snowshoe hares. The fox and lynx are known as **predators,** which are animals that eat other animals. The snowshoe hare is the **prey,** or the animal that is eaten. If the predators compete and eat too many prey, then both the foxes and the lynx may suffer from a dwindling food supply.

When two different species occupy the same niche, one of two outcomes is likely to result. One species may be successful in driving the other species to seek another niche. Or the two species may evolve in different directions so that over time, they will eventually occupy two different niches. For example, either the foxes or lynx may resort to depending more on sources of food other than snowshoe hares.

Competition between members of the same species is known as **intraspecific competition.** The members of a species are always competing for food, shelter, or the ability to reproduce. Darwin recognized that those organisms with the necessary adaptations were more likely to survive. In other words, natural selection would again settle the issue.

LESSON SUMMARY

- A habitat is the place where an organism lives, while its niche is the role it plays in that habitat.
- Symbiosis includes mutualism, commensalism, and parasitism.
- Mutualism is symbolized as +/+ to show that both organisms benefit.

- Commensalism is symbolized as +/0 to show that one organism benefits while the other organism is unaffected.
- Parasitism is symbolized as +/− to show that one organism benefits at the expense of another organism.
- Competition can occur between different species (interspecific competition) and between members of the same species (intraspecific competition).

REVIEW QUESTIONS

1. Which of the following best describes an organism's niche?

    (A) its color
    (B) its activities
    (C) its age
    (D) its community
    (E) its sex

2. Protozoa are protected by living inside the digestive tract of termites that eat wood. The protozoa possess an enzyme that can digest the cellulose in wood into a form that can be used by both organisms. This symbiotic relation is an example of

    (A) parasitism
    (B) commensalism
    (C) mutualism
    (D) predation
    (E) interspecific competition

3. Two bird species inhabit the same tree on an island where they eat the same fruit. How might both these species survive without engaging in competition?

    (A) One species lives near the top of the tree, while the other species inhabits the lower portion.
    (B) One species can fly faster.
    (C) One species is larger.
    (D) One species eats during the day, while the other species eats at night.
    (E) Both species continue to occupy the same niche.

4. The occupation of the same niche by two different species can bring about

    (A) mutualism
    (B) intraspecific competition
    (C) similar mating behaviors
    (D) natural selection
    (E) parasitism

5. Figure 10-7 illustrates how two species grow alone and when they are mixed with each other.

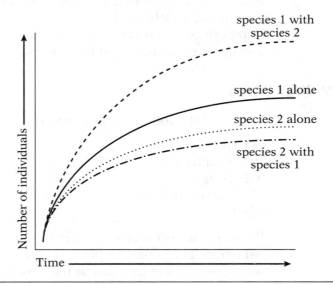

Figure 10-7

Which of the following ecological relationships between Species 1 and Species 2 is illustrated in the graph shown above?

(A) mutualism
(B) parasitism
(C) competition
(D) predation
(E) commensalism

ANSWERS

1. **B** A niche describes all of the elements of an organism's role within a community.
2. **C** This relationship is an example of mutualism because both organisms benefit.
3. **A** Only by living in different parts of the tree can the two species not compete for the same food supply.
4. **D** The interspecific competition that results can bring about either one species being excluded from the niche or natural selection that causes the two species to evolve in different directions.
5. **E** Notice that Species 1 has an increased growth rate when it is present with Species 2 than it does by itself. In turn, Species 2 has about the same growth rate whether it is alone or in the presence of Species 2.

Lesson 10-4. Biomes

VOCABULARY

- biome
- biosphere
- ecological succession
- pioneer organisms
- climax community

Let's review the levels of biological organization that you have studied so far: cell → tissue → organ → organism → population → community → ecosystem. You are now ready to look at the final and the two highest levels of biological organization.

TERRESTRIAL BIOMES

Ecosystems are organized into the next higher level of biological organization known as a **biome.** A biome is considered a large geographic area that is characterized by a predominant type of vegetation. The type of vegetation that predominates in each biome depends on the abiotic factors found in that geographic area. Most biomes are terrestrial—found on land. Some biomes are aquatic—found in water. Taken together, the terrestrial and aquatic biomes make up the **biosphere.** The biosphere is the entire portion of Earth inhabited by life.

Let's start our look at the terrestrial biomes by beginning at the equator and working our way toward the poles. A terrestrial biome found along the equator is a tropical rain forest. The abiotic factors that have a significant impact on a tropical rain forest are rain, temperature, and sunlight. A tropical rain forest receives more rainfall than any other biome on Earth. Temperatures are warm year around with little seasonal variation. With ample water and warm temperatures, life thrives in a tropical rain forest. Animal life includes monkeys, exotic birds, lizards, snakes, and tapirs. Plant life includes orchids, vines, and broadleaf trees. With so much water and mild temperatures, the trees grow very tall. Some trees grow as high as 60 meters (200 feet), or as high as a 20-story building. The tall trees form a canopy that covers much of what lies beneath. As a result, very little sunlight filters down to the ground.

Another biome found along the equator is a savanna, which is sometimes called a grassland. Rainfall is seasonal. A dry spell can last for 8 to 9 months. Temperatures are mild year around. A dry season is not favorable for the growth of many trees. Those trees that do grow are scattered, thorny, and have small leaves. Grasses are the primary vegetation. Animal life includes zebras, lions, hyenas, elephants, and giraffes.

As we move away from the equator, we come across a desert biome. This biome receives the smallest amount of annual rainfall, receiving only a fraction of what a tropical rain forest gets. Temperatures fluctuate widely in a desert, both daily and seasonally. In fact, in some areas, this biome is referred to as a cold desert. With so little water, cacti are the primary plants. Animals include snakes, lizards, and scorpions. Many of these animals are nocturnal, venturing out to feed only when it is cool enough.

The next biome we come across is a chaparral. This biome has rainy winters and dry summers. While summer is warm, the other seasons are cool. The chaparral is dominated by small trees and shrubs. Deer, goats, and a variety of amphibians, reptiles, and birds live in the chaparral.

Next, we find a temperate forest. This biome can receive almost as much rain each year as a tropical rain forest. However, the cool autumns and cold winters prevent a diversity of life from flourishing in a temperate forest. This biome contains broadleaf trees, including oaks, maples, chestnuts, and hickories. Deer, squirrels, black bears, beavers, and raccoons are some of this biome's animal life.

A biome known as a coniferous forest is next. This biome is also called a taiga. A coniferous forest receives about the same amount of rainfall as a temperate forest. In fact, the coniferous forests in the Pacific Northwest of the United States receive as much rainfall as a tropical rain forest. The cold winters, however, limit plant life to mainly cone-bearing trees such as pines, firs, and hemlocks. Animals that live in this biome include brown bears, wolves, and moose.

The biome that covers most of the Arctic is the tundra. Temperatures are cold year around so that the topsoil is permanently frozen. Plants that can survive here are short and have a very short growing season. Many of the animals in this biome, such as caribou, migrate south in winter.

There are two points you should keep in mind about terrestrial biomes. One, the Antarctic is the only place on Earth that does not have a biome. Two, the distinction between biomes is not a clear-cut line. In other words, as you walk along the land, you do not abruptly move from one biome to another type of biome. Rather, the change is gradual with areas that contain the features of both biomes.

AQUATIC BIOMES

Aquatic biomes are divided into two categories—freshwater and saltwater (marine). Freshwater biomes include ponds, lakes, streams, and rivers. Organisms living in freshwater biomes face a challenge. The concentration of water is higher outside the organism than it is in its cells. As a result, water moves into the cells by osmosis. To survive, freshwater organisms must have a mechanism to eliminate this excess water. Some unicellular organisms such as protozoa have contractile vacuoles that excrete water. Some multicellular organisms such as fish excrete a dilute urine which contains a high concentration of water.

Oceans form the largest saltwater biomes. These biomes are the most stable ecosystems on Earth. With so much water, abiotic factors such as salinity and temperature do not fluctuate to any significant degree, except near the surface and shorelines. With little change in abiotic factors, organisms do not face the challenges of a changing environment. One challenge, however, that marine organisms do face is the loss of water. With a higher water concentration inside their cells, water moves out by osmosis. Fish in marine biomes drink seawater and excrete the salts through their gills. They also produce a concentrated urine that contains little water.

Figure 10-8 shows how a marine biome is divided into various zones, depending on depth and distance from shore.

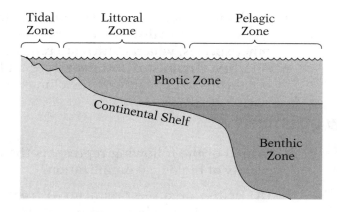

Figure 10-8

ECOLOGICAL SUCCESSION

All biomes experience occasional disturbances, some of which may cause serious destruction. For example, a fire may rage across a temperate forest or a tsunami may flood a tropical forest. All that may be left after the fire is extinguished and the waters dry up is a barren land. What naturally follows is a process known as **ecological succession.** This process involves the introduction of organisms into the disturbed environment and their gradual replacement by other species, which in turn are replaced by still other species.

Consider what may happen after a forest fire. The first organisms to inhabit the barren landscape are known as **pioneer organisms.** Lichens are often pioneer organisms, which can live on rocky surfaces. Acids produced by the lichen slowly erode the rock. As a result, the environment is no longer suitable for lichens. However, as the rocks eroded, the soil was built up. This change makes it possible for mosses to establish themselves. Mosses continue to build up the soil. Now, grasses and small bushes can start to grow. As the soil continues to build up and contains more nutrients, small trees appear. These may include birch and poplar trees that grow well in full sun. As more of these trees grow, they compete for sunlight and other resources. Slowly, they are replaced by white pines. As more white pines take hold, less sunlight penetrates to lower levels. Trees that grow best in the shade now start to appear. These include beeches and maples. The final organisms that appear establish a **climax community.** The climax community is stable, unless another disaster strikes.

LESSON SUMMARY

- The levels of biological organization from smallest to largest are: cell → tissue → organ → organism → population → community → ecosystem → biome → biosphere.
- A biome is a large geographic area that is characterized by a predominant type of vegetation. The biosphere is the entire portion of Earth inhabited by life.
- Terrestrial biomes include tropical rain forest, savanna, desert, chaparral, temperate forest, coniferous forest, and tundra.
- Aquatic biomes include freshwater biomes and saltwater biomes, which include the oceans.

- Ecological succession is the process that involves the introduction of organisms into a disturbed environment and their gradual replacement by other species, which in turn are replaced by still other species.
- The first organisms to appear are called pioneer organisms. The last organisms to appear form the climax community.

REVIEW QUESTIONS

1. Which of the following represents the correct order of increasing complexity of biological organization?

    (A) cell → organ → organism → tissue → population → community → ecosystem → biome → biosphere
    (B) tissue → cell → organ → organism → population → community → ecosystem → biome → biosphere
    (C) cell → tissue → organ → organism → ecosystem → community → population → biome → biosphere
    (D) cell → tissue → organ → organism → population → community → ecosystem → biome → biosphere
    (E) cell → tissue → organ → community → population → organism → ecosystem → biome → biosphere

2. Which biome has the greatest biological diversity?

    (A) tundra
    (B) temperate forest
    (C) tropical rain forest
    (D) desert
    (E) ocean

3. Another name for a coniferous forest biome is a

    (A) taiga
    (B) savanna
    (C) temperate deciduous forest
    (D) tundra
    (E) chaparral

4. The climax community

    (A) consists of pioneer organisms
    (B) is a temporary ecosystem that will be eventually displaced
    (C) is the same in all cases of ecological succession
    (D) consists of only one species
    (E) is stable as long as the environment remains relatively unchanged

5. Which biome is correctly paired with its description?

    (A) marine biome: unstable
    (B) tundra: limited diversity of life
    (C) chaparral: tall trees
    (D) desert: little temperature fluctuation
    (E) taiga: mild winters

ANSWERS

1. **D** This is the only choice that proceeds in the correct sequence from the smallest level of organization (cell) to the largest level (biosphere).
2. **C** With plentiful rain and mild temperatures year around, a tropical forest is home to the greatest diversity of life.
3. **A** Taiga is the same as a coniferous forest.
4. **E** The climax community represents the last stage of ecological succession and is, therefore, stable.
5. **B** With such harsh environmental conditions, the tundra can support only a limited variety of life.

Lesson 10-5. Nutrient Cycles

VOCABULARY

- water cycle
- carbon cycle
- nitrogen cycle
- nitrogen-fixing bacteria
- nitrifying bacteria
- denitrifying bacteria

You read that decomposers break down decaying organic matter into simpler substances. These substances can then be recycled through a food chain. If substances were not recycled, then the flow of energy through a food chain would stop. In other words, life would cease to exist. The recycling of substances, then, is essential if organisms are to survive. Substances that are recycled in nature include water, carbon, and nitrogen.

WATER CYCLE

Without water, organisms would die. Some organisms can obtain the oxygen they need from photosynthesis. However, almost all organisms must obtain water from an external source. Most of the water on Earth is found in the oceans. The **water cycle** is responsible for getting the water from the oceans to the land and back, as you can see in Figure 10-9.

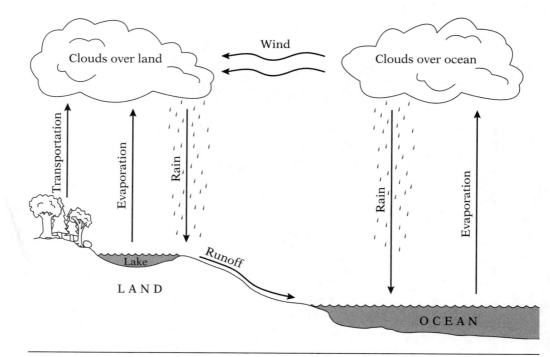

Figure 10-9

CARBON CYCLE

Carbon is the basic building block of all organic compounds. Carbon is also part of carbon dioxide, which is a common inorganic compound. Organisms produce carbon dioxide during aerobic respiration. In turn, carbon dioxide is used in photosynthesis. Therefore, respiration and photosynthesis are the two processes that form the **carbon cycle,** as shown in Figure 10-10.

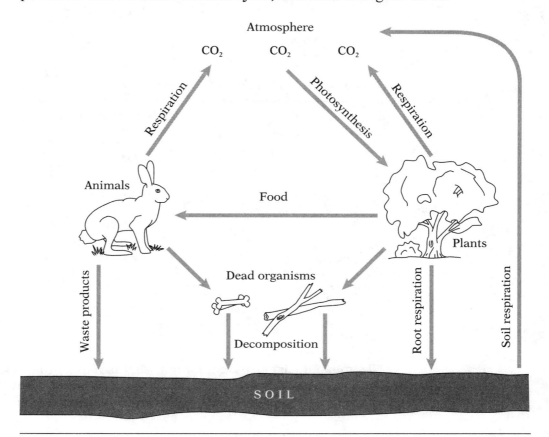

Figure 10-10

Following the Industrial Revolution, another process was added to the carbon cycle. This is combustion. Combustion of fuels such as gasoline and propane release carbon dioxide into the atmosphere. The amount of carbon dioxide that is being released cannot be used by plants. As a result, this excess carbon dioxide accumulates in the upper atmosphere where it can contribute to global warming.

NITROGEN CYCLE

Nitrogen is an element that is used by plants to make proteins. Most of the nitrogen on Earth is found as N_2, which is a gas in the atmosphere. This form of nitrogen cannot be used by plants. Rather, they use nitrate, NO_3^-, to make proteins. The **nitrogen cycle** is responsible for cycling nitrogen and nitrate so that plants can continue to make proteins. As you can see from the following illustration, the nitrogen cycle is more complex than those you have examined so far.

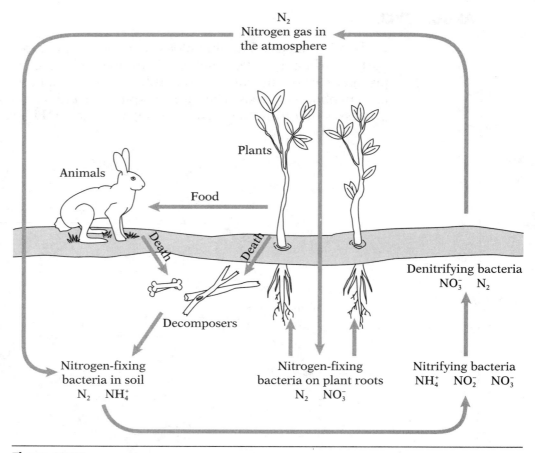

Figure 10-11

To make it easier to understand what is happening, refer to Figure 10-11 as you read through the following steps. Remember that the aim is to cycle nitrogen gas, N_2, in the atmosphere and nitrate, NO_3^-, in the soil.

1. **Nitrogen-fixing bacteria** in the soil convert N_2 to NH_4^+. **Nitrifying bacteria** then convert NH_4^+ to NO_2^- and then to NO_3^-.
2. Nitrogen-fixing bacteria on the roots of legumes directly convert N_2 to NO_3^-.
3. **Denitrifying bacteria** convert some of the NO_3^- produced by nitrifying bacteria into N_2, which is released into the atmosphere.

Also notice in the illustration shown above that decomposers break down proteins in decaying organic matter to form NH_4^+, which can then enter the nitrogen cycle.

▬ LESSON SUMMARY

- In the water cycle, transpiration and evaporation release water into the atmosphere, while precipitation returns water to the ground.
- In the carbon cycle, photosynthesis uses carbon dioxide, while respiration releases carbon dioxide. Combustion also contributes to the release of carbon dioxide.
- In the nitrogen cycle, nitrogen-fixing bacteria and nitrifying bacteria convert nitrogen in the atmosphere into nitrates in the soil, while denitrifying bacteria convert nitrates into nitrogen.

REVIEW QUESTIONS

1. Transpiration

   (A) returns water to the atmosphere
   (B) is involved in the carbon cycle
   (C) is the process by which nitrogen is converted to nitrates
   (D) returns carbon dioxide to the atmosphere
   (E) is one of the processes plants use during the carbon cycle

2. Identify the process that is NOT involved in the carbon cycle.

   (A) photosynthesis
   (B) respiration
   (C) decomposition
   (D) combustion
   (E) evaporation

3. Denitrifying bacteria convert

   (A) nitrogen to nitrates
   (B) nitrates to nitrogen
   (C) nitrates to proteins
   (D) decaying organic matter to nitrates
   (E) NH_4^+ to NO_2^-

4. During the nitrogen cycle, bacteria

   I.   release nitrogen from the soil
   II.   take in nitrogen from the atmosphere
   III. convert nitrates into proteins

   (A) I only
   (B) II only
   (C) I and II
   (D) III
   (E) I, II, and III

ANSWERS

1. **A** Transpiration is the process used by plants to release water into the atmosphere.
2. **E** Evaporation is involved in the water cycle.
3. **B** Denitrifying bacteria convert nitrates into nitrogen, which is then released into the atmosphere.
4. **C** Bacteria are responsible for cycling nitrogen between the atmosphere and the soil.

PART III
FOUR PRACTICE TESTS

PRACTICE TEST 1
BIOLOGY-E

The following Practice Test is designed to be just like the real SAT Biology-E test. It matches the actual test in content coverage and level of difficulty. The test is in two parts. Part A (Questions 1–60) is for everyone taking Biology-E or Biology-M. Part B (Questions 61–80) is ONLY for students taking Biology-E.

When you are finished with the test, determine your score and carefully read the answer explanations for the questions you answered incorrectly. Identify any weak areas by determining the areas in which you made the most errors. Review these chapters of the book first. Then, as time permits, go back and review your stronger areas.

Allow 1 hour to take the test. Time yourself and work uninterrupted. If you run out of time, take note of where you ended when time ran out. Remember that you lose $\frac{1}{4}$ of a point for each incorrect answer. Because of this penalty, do not guess on a question unless you can eliminate one or more of the answers. Your score is calculated using the following formula:

Number of correct answers $-\frac{1}{4}$(Number of incorrect answers)

This Practice Test will be an accurate reflection of how you'll do on test day if you treat it as the real examination. Here are some hints on how to take the test under conditions similar to those of the actual exam.

- Complete the test in one sitting.
- Time yourself.
- Tear out your Answer Sheet and fill in the ovals just as you would on the actual test day.
- Become familiar with the directions to the test and the reference information provided. You'll save time on the actual test day by already being familiar with this information.

PRACTICE TEST 1

BIOLOGY-E

ANSWER SHEET

Part A

1.	(A) (B) (C) (D) (E)	21.	(A) (B) (C) (D) (E)	41.	(A) (B) (C) (D) (E)
2.	(A) (B) (C) (D) (E)	22.	(A) (B) (C) (D) (E)	42.	(A) (B) (C) (D) (E)
3.	(A) (B) (C) (D) (E)	23.	(A) (B) (C) (D) (E)	43.	(A) (B) (C) (D) (E)
4.	(A) (B) (C) (D) (E)	24.	(A) (B) (C) (D) (E)	44.	(A) (B) (C) (D) (E)
5.	(A) (B) (C) (D) (E)	25.	(A) (B) (C) (D) (E)	45.	(A) (B) (C) (D) (E)
6.	(A) (B) (C) (D) (E)	26.	(A) (B) (C) (D) (E)	46.	(A) (B) (C) (D) (E)
7.	(A) (B) (C) (D) (E)	27.	(A) (B) (C) (D) (E)	47.	(A) (B) (C) (D) (E)
8.	(A) (B) (C) (D) (E)	28.	(A) (B) (C) (D) (E)	48.	(A) (B) (C) (D) (E)
9.	(A) (B) (C) (D) (E)	29.	(A) (B) (C) (D) (E)	49.	(A) (B) (C) (D) (E)
10.	(A) (B) (C) (D) (E)	30.	(A) (B) (C) (D) (E)	50.	(A) (B) (C) (D) (E)
11.	(A) (B) (C) (D) (E)	31.	(A) (B) (C) (D) (E)	51.	(A) (B) (C) (D) (E)
12.	(A) (B) (C) (D) (E)	32.	(A) (B) (C) (D) (E)	52.	(A) (B) (C) (D) (E)
13.	(A) (B) (C) (D) (E)	33.	(A) (B) (C) (D) (E)	53.	(A) (B) (C) (D) (E)
14.	(A) (B) (C) (D) (E)	34.	(A) (B) (C) (D) (E)	54.	(A) (B) (C) (D) (E)
15.	(A) (B) (C) (D) (E)	35.	(A) (B) (C) (D) (E)	55.	(A) (B) (C) (D) (E)
16.	(A) (B) (C) (D) (E)	36.	(A) (B) (C) (D) (E)	56.	(A) (B) (C) (D) (E)
17.	(A) (B) (C) (D) (E)	37.	(A) (B) (C) (D) (E)	57.	(A) (B) (C) (D) (E)
18.	(A) (B) (C) (D) (E)	38.	(A) (B) (C) (D) (E)	58.	(A) (B) (C) (D) (E)
19.	(A) (B) (C) (D) (E)	39.	(A) (B) (C) (D) (E)	59.	(A) (B) (C) (D) (E)
20.	(A) (B) (C) (D) (E)	40.	(A) (B) (C) (D) (E)	60.	(A) (B) (C) (D) (E)

Part B

61.	(A) (B) (C) (D) (E)
62.	(A) (B) (C) (D) (E)
63.	(A) (B) (C) (D) (E)
64.	(A) (B) (C) (D) (E)
65.	(A) (B) (C) (D) (E)
66.	(A) (B) (C) (D) (E)
67.	(A) (B) (C) (D) (E)
68.	(A) (B) (C) (D) (E)
69.	(A) (B) (C) (D) (E)
70.	(A) (B) (C) (D) (E)
71.	(A) (B) (C) (D) (E)
72.	(A) (B) (C) (D) (E)
73.	(A) (B) (C) (D) (E)
74.	(A) (B) (C) (D) (E)
75.	(A) (B) (C) (D) (E)
76.	(A) (B) (C) (D) (E)
77.	(A) (B) (C) (D) (E)
78.	(A) (B) (C) (D) (E)
79.	(A) (B) (C) (D) (E)
80.	(A) (B) (C) (D) (E)

Part C

81.	(A) (B) (C) (D) (E)
82.	(A) (B) (C) (D) (E)
83.	(A) (B) (C) (D) (E)
84.	(A) (B) (C) (D) (E)
85.	(A) (B) (C) (D) (E)
86.	(A) (B) (C) (D) (E)
87.	(A) (B) (C) (D) (E)
88.	(A) (B) (C) (D) (E)
89.	(A) (B) (C) (D) (E)
90.	(A) (B) (C) (D) (E)
91.	(A) (B) (C) (D) (E)
92.	(A) (B) (C) (D) (E)
93.	(A) (B) (C) (D) (E)
94.	(A) (B) (C) (D) (E)
95.	(A) (B) (C) (D) (E)
96.	(A) (B) (C) (D) (E)
97.	(A) (B) (C) (D) (E)
98.	(A) (B) (C) (D) (E)
99.	(A) (B) (C) (D) (E)
100.	(A) (B) (C) (D) (E)

PRACTICE TEST 1
Time: 60 Minutes

▓▓ PART A (Core Questions 1–60–for Both Biology-E and Biology-M)

> **Directions:** Determine the BEST answer for each question. Then fill in the corresponding oval on the answer sheet.

Questions 1–4

    (A) ribosome
    (B) mitochondria
    (C) chloroplast
    (D) endoplasmic reticulum
    (E) Golgi apparatus

1. Site where photosynthesis takes place

2. Extensive series of membranes throughout the cell

3. Powerhouse of the cell

4. Packaging and distribution system of a cell

Questions 5–7

    (A) lipids
    (B) proteins
    (C) carbohydrates
    (D) nucleic acids

5. long chains of amino acids

6. composed of only carbon, hydrogen, and oxygen

7. also known as fats

Questions 8–11

    (A) commensalism
    (B) mutualism
    (C) parasitism
    (D) symbiosis

8. Two or more organisms in a close, long-term association

9. One organism benefits, while the other suffers from the relationship.

10. Both organisms benefit from the relationship.

11. One organism benefits and the other does not benefit nor is it harmed from the relationship.

Questions 12–15

    (A) organ
    (B) cell
    (C) tissue
    (D) organ system

12. Group of cells with a similar function

13. Smallest unit of organization in living things

14. Many different groups of cells working together

15. The highest level of organization that carries out important body functions

16. Protists are classified by their

    (A) method of feeding
    (B) method of moving
    (C) method of reproducing
    (D) size
    (E) habitat

17. The part of the human brain that controls balance, posture, and coordination is the

    (A) cerebrum
    (B) cerebellum
    (C) medulla oblongata
    (D) thalamus
    (E) hypothalamus

18. The characteristics that gymnosperms and angiosperms share are

    (A) leaves, rhizomes, and spore
    (B) leaves, stems, roots, and seeds
    (C) flat leaves, trunks, and naked seeds
    (D) lack of vascular tissue and small leaflets
    (E) needle-like leaves, stems, roots, and fleshy fruits

GO ON TO THE NEXT PAGE ▶

PRACTICE TEST—*Continued*

19. All of the following are characteristics of living things EXCEPT for the ability to

    (A) perform cellular respiration
    (B) regulate their internal environment
    (C) reproduce
    (D) change their external environment
    (E) pass traits to offspring

20. What happens to an enzyme during a biochemical reaction?

    (A) It becomes part of the product.
    (B) It is unchanged.
    (C) It is broken down into amino acids.
    (D) It reacts with fatty acids.
    (E) It becomes a polypeptide.

21.

    I.   monera
    II. plants
    III. protists

    Which kingdom(s) contain(s) chemotrophs as members?

    (A) I only
    (B) II only
    (C) III only
    (D) I and III only
    (E) I, II, and III

22. Which bird has feet that are modified for grasping prey?

    (A)

    (B)

    (C)

    (D)

    (E)

23. In RNA molecules, uracil is complementary to

    (A) thymine
    (B) guanine
    (C) cytosine
    (D) adenine
    (E) uracil

24. Most mutations result from

    (A) certain chemicals
    (B) ionizing radiation
    (C) infrared radiation
    (D) ultraviolet radiation
    (E) random events

25. The first vertebrates to evolve a three-chambered heart that ensured all cells in the body received the proper amount of oxygen are the

    (A) fishes
    (B) reptiles
    (C) amphibians
    (D) birds
    (E) mammals

26. Which is the correct order of stages for an insect that undergoes complete metamorphosis?

    (A) egg→larva→adult
    (B) egg→nymph→adult
    (C) egg→nymph→larva→adult
    (D) egg→larva→pupa→adult
    (E) egg→nymph→pupa→adult

27. Which process brings carbon into the living portion of its cycle?

    (A) photosynthesis
    (B) cellular respiration
    (C) combustion
    (D) decomposition
    (E) fixation

28. Microspores of gymnosperms eventually develop into

    (A) seeds
    (B) cotyledons
    (C) female gametophytes
    (D) pollen grains
    (E) archegonia

GO ON TO THE NEXT PAGE

PRACTICE TEST—*Continued*

29. Bacteria are an important part of most food chains because they serve as

    (A) primary consumers
    (B) secondary consumers
    (C) scavengers
    (D) decomposers
    (E) producers

30. Ground tissue provides all of the following functions in plants EXCEPT

    (A) protection of other tissues
    (B) supporting the plant
    (C) storage of water and carbohydrates
    (D) transport of materials
    (E) photosynthesis

31. Which of the following scientific names is written in the correct form to identify a species?

    (A) *meleagris gallopavo*
    (B) *Meleagris Gallopavo*
    (C) Meleagris Gallopavo
    (D) Meleagris gallopavo
    (E) *Meleagris gallopavo*

32. Which best describes the source of genes in an offspring resulting from sexual reproduction?

    (A) The offspring gets a full set of genes from the mother and from the father.
    (B) The offspring gets half the genes from the mother and half the genes from the father.
    (C) The offspring gets all of its genes from the father.
    (D) The offspring gets a random mixture of genes from the mother and father.
    (E) The offspring gets all of its genes from the mother.

33. Which best describes how the following ecosystem will change over time?

    ```
    ┌──────────────┐
    │ Secondary    │
    │ Consumers    │
    └──────────────┘

    ┌─────────────────────────────────────┐
    │            Herbivores                │
    └─────────────────────────────────────┘

    ┌──────────────────────────────┐
    │          Producers           │
    └──────────────────────────────┘
    ```

    (A) The herbivores will decline because there is not enough food to support them.
    (B) The herbivores will increase and the secondary consumers increase.
    (C) The populations of producers, herbivores, and carnivores will remain the same.
    (D) The secondary consumers will decline and the producers will increase.
    (E) The producers will increase to support the herbivores.

34. If an organism has a haploid number of 28, how many chromosomes does it have?

    (A) 7
    (B) 14
    (C) 28
    (D) 42
    (E) 56

35. A pea plant with a genotype of YY produces yellow seeds. A pea plant with a genotype of yy produces green seeds. If the pea plants are crossed, which describes the possible genotypes of the offspring?

    (A) all are YY
    (B) all are Yy
    (C) all are yy
    (D) half YY and half yy
    (E) half YY and half Yy

GO ON TO THE NEXT PAGE

PRACTICE TEST—*Continued*

36. Which set of offspring would result from a cross that was controlled by the law of independent assortment?

    (A) Half the offspring are tall with white flowers and half are short with white flowers.
    (B) All the offspring are tall or short and have white or purple flowers.
    (C) All the offspring are short and have purple flowers.
    (D) All the offspring are tall and have white flowers.
    (E) All the offspring are tall and have purple flowers.

37. Which of the following statements about evolution is accurate?

    (A) Populations evolve while individuals do not evolve.
    (B) Populations do not evolve while individuals evolve.
    (C) Populations evolve only when individuals evolve.
    (D) Populations evolve only when isolated individuals evolve.
    (E) Populations evolve only through mutations.

38. On the human skeletal system, which type of joint allows rotational movement?

    (A) slightly moveable joint
    (B) ball-and-socket joint
    (C) pivot joint
    (D) plane joint
    (E) saddle joint

39. Which of the following best describes what will happen if cells are placed in a very salty solution?

    (A) The cells remain unchanged.
    (B) Water moves from inside of the cell to the outside.
    (C) Water moves from outside of the cell to the inside.
    (D) The cells burst.
    (E) The cells dissolve.

40. The color red and the color white are codominant in horses. What would you expect if you crossed a homozygous red horse with a homozygous white horse?

    (A) The offspring is white.
    (B) The offspring is red.
    (C) The offspring has both red and white hairs.
    (D) The offspring is brown.
    (E) The offspring is black.

41. The DNA of two closely related species would likely be

    (A) completely different
    (B) somewhat different
    (C) very different
    (D) very similar
    (E) identical

42. All of the following are mechanisms of reproductive isolation EXCEPT

    (A) geographical isolation
    (B) ecological isolation
    (C) temporal isolation
    (D) reproductive failure
    (E) niche overlap

43. The process of photosynthesis produces many products. Which of these products are used for starting cellular respiration?

    (A) oxygen and ATP
    (B) water and carbon dioxide
    (C) NADP and hydrogen
    (D) glucose and oxygen
    (E) carbohydrates and NADP

Questions 44 and 45

This diagram is a cross section through the primary stem of a woody plant.

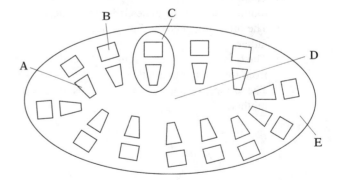

44. Which part of this stem is the vascular tissue?

    (A) A
    (B) B
    (C) C
    (D) D
    (E) E

GO ON TO THE NEXT PAGE

PRACTICE TEST—*Continued*

45. Which part of this stem will develop into the bark of the woody plant?

    (A) A
    (B) B
    (C) C
    (D) D
    (E) E

46. Sequences of DNA that are easily and naturally copied from one location in the genome and inserted elsewhere are called

    (A) duplication genes
    (B) jumping genes
    (C) crossing over genes
    (D) recessive genes
    (E) deletion genes

47. A bat wing and a human's arm are examples of

    (A) homologous structures
    (B) analogous characters
    (C) vestigial structures
    (D) adaptive structures
    (E) derived traits

48. A type of mutation that occurs when part of a chromatid breaks off and attaches to its sister chromatid resulting in the duplication of a gene on a chromosome is called

    (A) deleting
    (B) inserting
    (C) separating
    (D) substituting
    (E) inverting

49. Cellular respiration in the absence of oxygen is called fermentation. What is the product of fermentation in animal cells?

    (A) Acetyl-CoA
    (B) alcohol
    (C) carbon dioxide
    (D) pyruvic acid
    (E) lactic acid

50. Natural selection is an evolutionary force that can affect an entire population. One species can evolve into two species when only the extreme forms of a trait are favored and intermediate forms are selected against. This is known as

    (A) artificial selection
    (B) directional selection
    (C) targeted selection
    (D) disruptive selection
    (E) stabilizing selection

51. An example of a density-dependent factor is

    (A) weather
    (B) climate
    (C) air
    (D) food
    (E) drought

52. Which best describes the advantage of crossing over during meiosis?

    (A) makes for healthy offspring
    (B) provides a source of genetic variation
    (C) creates a random mix of chromosomes
    (D) allows gametes to have half the number of chromosomes
    (E) increases the number of gametes

53. A segment of a DNA molecule that carries instructions for a specific trait is called a

    (A) gene
    (B) chromosome
    (C) nucleotide
    (D) codon
    (E) chromatid

54. Small, round bacteria that grow in a chain are called

    (A) streptococci
    (B) staphylobacilli
    (C) spirillium
    (D) diplococci
    (E) bacillus

55. According to Darwin, organisms best suited to their environment

    (A) are most likely to evolve
    (B) are more likely to survive and reproduce
    (C) are most likely to live the longest
    (D) are the fastest organisms
    (E) have the same chance of survival as other organisms

56. When lions and hyenas fight over a dead zebra, their interaction is called

    (A) mutualism
    (B) competition
    (C) commensalism
    (D) parasitism
    (E) predation

GO ON TO THE NEXT PAGE

PRACTICE TEST—*Continued*

57. Which is the best method for preserving the bio-diversity of an ecosystem?

    (A) creating a preserve in an urban area
    (B) building botanical gardens based on the ecosystem
    (C) preserving a few very large areas on an ecosystem
    (D) preserving many small areas of an ecosystem
    (E) creating greenbelts along creeks and roadways in urban areas

58. Gregor Mendel found that the inheritance of one trait had no affect on the inheritance of different trait. He described this observation as the

    (A) law of dominance
    (B) law of universal inheritance
    (C) law of segregation
    (D) law of independent assortment
    (E) law of separate chromosomes

59. Meiosis is the process of making sex cells or gametes. In humans, how many mature egg cells result from meiosis?

    (A) 1
    (B) 2
    (C) 3
    (D) 4
    (E) 6

60. Which of the following are considered prokaryotes?

    (A) animals
    (B) plants
    (C) fungi
    (D) protists
    (E) bacteria

GO ON TO THE NEXT PAGE ➔

PRACTICE TEST—*Continued*

PART B (Biology-E Questions 61–80)

61. Which represents the correct order from simplest to most complex?

    (A) organ system, organ, tissue, cell
    (B) cell, tissue, organ, organ system
    (C) tissue, cell, organ, organ system
    (D) cell, organ, tissue, organ system
    (E) cell, organ, organ system, tissue

62. Which property of a population may be described as even, clumped, or random?

    (A) habitat
    (B) dispersion
    (C) size
    (D) density
    (E) growth rate

63. The process of evolution where an ancestral species evolves into an array of species that occupy different niches is called

    (A) gradualism
    (B) convergent evolution
    (C) adaptive radiation
    (D) punctuated equilibrium
    (E) divergent evolution

64. Natural selection is often described as survival of the fittest. Which of the following species would likely be best able to survive in rapidly changing environmental conditions?

    (A) a tree that takes 20 years to reach maturity and produces thousands of seeds
    (B) a weed that only lives one year and produces hundreds of seeds
    (C) a mouse that reproduces six to eight times a year with a litter of six mice
    (D) a bird that reproduces once a year but lays four to six eggs
    (E) a tree that lives for more than 500 years and produces many slow growing seeds

65. Bryophytes are nonvascular plants. In which of the following habitats would you most likely find bryophytes growing?

    (A) in a desert
    (B) on the top of a high tree
    (C) in a cave
    (D) under the soil
    (E) at the mouth of a spring

66.
    I.   temperature
    II. humidity
    III. vegetation

    Which of the above are abiotic factors?
    (A) I only
    (B) II only
    (C) III only
    (D) I and II only
    (E) I, II, and III

67. When energy is transferred from one trophic level to the next, about 90% of the energy is lost. If plants produce 1,000 kcal of energy, how much of the energy is passed to the next trophic level?

    (A) 10,000 kcal
    (B) 1,000 kcal
    (C) 100 kcal
    (D) 10 kcal
    (E) 1 kcal

68. Which main factor(s) determine(s) which biome exists in a certain area?

    (A) temperature
    (B) elevation
    (C) precipitation
    (D) temperature and moisture
    (E) temperature and elevation

GO ON TO THE NEXT PAGE

PRACTICE TEST—*Continued*

Questions 69–74

Some Land (Terrestrial) Biomes:

Biome	Water	Temperature	Soil	Plants	Animals
Desert	Almost none	Hot or cold	Poor	Sparse—succulents (like cactus), sage brush	Sparse—insects, arachnids, reptiles and birds (often nocturnal)
Chaparral (scrub)	Dry summer, rainy winter	Hot summer, cool winter	Poor	Shrubs, some woodland (like scrub oak)	Drought and fire-adapted animals
Tundra	Dry	Cold	Permafrost (frozen soil)	Lichens and mosses	Migrating animals
Taiga (coniferous forest)	Adequate	Cool year around	Poor, rocky soil	Conifers	Many mammals, birds, insects, arachnids, etc.
Temperate deciduous forest	Adequate	Cool season and warm season	Fertile soil	Deciduous trees	Many mammals, birds, reptiles, insects, arachnids, etc.
Grassland	Wet season, dry season	Warm to hot (often with a cold season)	Fertile soil	Grasses (few or no trees)	Many mammals, birds, insects, arachnids, etc.
Tropical rain forest	Very wet	Always warm	Poor, thin soil	Many plants	Many animals
Swamp	Very wet	Warm	Nutrient-rich soil	Many plants	Many animals
Cave (terrestrial)	Variable	Cool (and dark)	Rocks	Almost no plants	Few animals
Biome	**Water**	**Temperature**	**Soil**	**Plants**	**Animals**

69. A biome that is characterized by warm temperatures throughout the year and seasonal heavy rainfall is found in the

   (A) temperate deciduous forest
   (B) taiga
   (C) tundra
   (D) tropical rain forest
   (E) savannah

GO ON TO THE NEXT PAGE ▶

PRACTICE TEST—*Continued*

70. Which pair of biomes would most likely be found adjacent to each other?

    (A) temperate deciduous forest–taiga
    (B) taiga–tundra
    (C) tundra–swamp
    (D) tropical rain forest–deciduous forest
    (E) chaparral–tundra

71. Which describes the change you most likely see when moving from the equator toward the North Pole?

    (A) tropical rain forests→deserts→taiga
    (B) tundra→deserts→grasslands
    (C) grasslands→ tundra→rainforests
    (D) temperate deciduous forests→taiga→rain forests
    (E) tropical rainforest→taiga→grasslands→tundra

72. Which biome produces much of our wheat crop?

    (A) taiga
    (B) grassland
    (C) chaparral
    (D) tropical rain forest
    (E) temperate deciduous forest

73. Which two biomes are most similar in annual rainfall?

    (A) taiga and tundra
    (B) taiga and grassland
    (C) grassland and tropical rain forest
    (D) taiga and temperate deciduous forest
    (E) tundra and grassland

74. The biome that has the highest biodiversity is the

    (A) temperate deciduous forest
    (B) taiga
    (C) tundra
    (D) savannah
    (E) tropical rain forest

Questions 75–77

This chart shows the number of genera of brachiopods, a type of mollusk, throughout geologic time. Brachiopods were once numerous but today they are rare. They resemble clams but they are very different in form and structure. Most of the brachiopods living today are found in very cold waters or in the deep ocean. Brachiopods are very important to paleontologists because they give information about both time sequence and past environmental conditions.

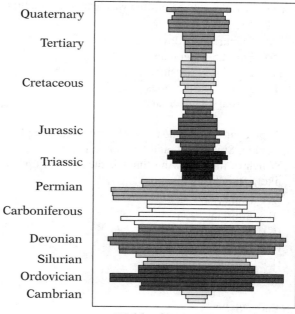

Width of Bars Is Proportional to the Number of Genera Known from Each Geologic Time Period

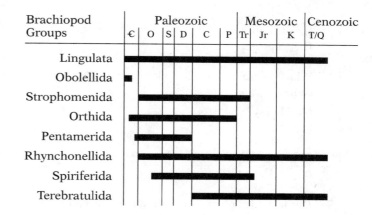

75. During which of the following times did a mass extinction occur?

    (A) Cambrian–Ordovician
    (B) Silurian–Devonian
    (C) Permian–Triassic
    (D) Jurassic–Cretaceous
    (E) Tertiary–Quaternary

GO ON TO THE NEXT PAGE

PRACTICE TEST—*Continued*

76. During which period of time was there a population explosion of species?

    (A) Cambrian–Ordovician
    (B) Silurian–Devonian
    (C) Permian–Triassic
    (D) Jurassic–Cretaceous
    (E) Tertiary–Quaternary

77. A paleontologist finds a rock unit with Strophomenida, Spiriferida, and Pentamerida brachiopods. Which of the following times is the rock unit most likely from?

    (A) Cambrian
    (B) Silurian
    (C) Triassic
    (D) Cretaceous
    (E) Tertiary

Questions 78–80

The diagram represents the events of the cell cycle:

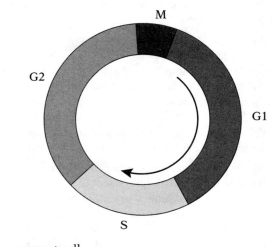

78.
    I.   mitosis
    II. G1 phase
    III. S phase

    Which phase of the cell cycle involves DNA replication?

    (A) I only
    (B) II only
    (C) III only
    (D) I and III only
    (E) I, II, and III

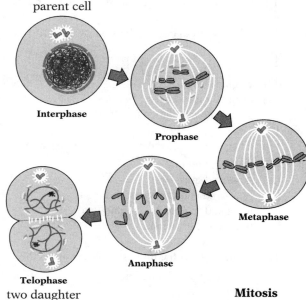

79. During which phase of mitosis do the chromosomes uncoil at opposite ends of the cell followed by the formation of the nuclear membrane?

    (A) interphase
    (B) prophase
    (C) metaphase
    (D) anaphase
    (E) telophase

80. During which phase of mitosis do the chromosomes begin condensing and become visible?

    (A) interphase
    (B) prophase
    (C) metaphase
    (D) anaphase
    (E) telophase

S T O P

IF YOU FINISH BEFORE TIME RUNS OUT, GO BACK AND CHECK YOUR WORK.

PRACTICE TEST 1
BIOLOGY-E

ANSWER KEY

Part A

1. C	11. A	21. A	31. E	41. D	51. D
2. D	12. C	22. A	32. B	42. E	52. B
3. B	13. B	23. D	33. A	43. D	53. A
4. E	14. A	24. E	34. E	44. C	54. A
5. B	15. D	25. C	35. B	45. B	55. B
6. C	16. B	26. D	36. B	46. B	56. B
7. A	17. B	27. A	37. A	47. A	57. C
8. D	18. B	28. D	38. B	48. B	58. D
9. C	19. D	29. D	39. B	49. E	59. A
10. B	20. B	30. A	40. C	50. D	60. E

Part B

61. B	71. A
62. B	72. B
63. C	73. D
64. B	74. E
65. E	75. C
66. D	76. A
67. C	77. B
68. D	78. C
69. D	79. E
70. B	80. B

SCORE SHEET

Number of questions correct: _____

Less: 0.25 × number of questions wrong: _____

(Remember that omitted questions are not counted as wrong.)

Raw score: _____

Raw Score	Scaled Score	Raw Score	Scaled Score	Raw Score	Scaled Score	Raw Score	Scaled Score	Raw Score	Scaled Score
80	800	57	690	34	520	11	380	−12	250
79	800	56	680	33	520	10	370	−13	240
78	800	55	670	32	510	9	370	−14	240
77	800	54	670	31	510	8	360	−15	230
76	800	53	660	30	500	7	350	−16	230
75	800	52	650	29	500	6	350	−17	230
74	800	51	650	28	490	5	340	−18	220
73	790	50	640	27	490	4	330	−19	220
72	790	49	630	26	480	3	330	−20	220
71	780	48	620	25	480	2	320		
70	780	47	620	24	470	1	320		
69	770	46	610	23	470	0	310		
68	760	45	600	22	460	−1	310		
67	760	44	600	21	450	−2	300		
66	750	43	590	20	440	−3	300		
65	740	42	580	19	440	−4	290		
64	740	41	580	18	430	−5	290		
63	730	40	570	17	420	−6	280		
62	720	39	560	16	420	−7	270		
61	710	38	560	15	410	−8	270		
60	710	37	550	14	400	−9	260		
59	700	36	540	13	400	−10	260		
58	700	35	530	12	390	−11	250		

Note: This is only a sample scoring scale. Scoring scales differ from exam to exam.

ANSWERS AND EXPLANATIONS

Part A

1. **C** Chloroplasts are the organelles that contain chlorophyll and other photopigments used during photosynthesis.

2. **D** The endoplasmic reticulum is an extensive network of membranes that are in the cytoplasm. The endoplasmic reticulum is a transportation network to move molecules around the cell.

3. **B** The mitochondria are the site where ATP is produced, providing energy for cellular functions.

4. **E** The Golgi apparatus consists of flattened sacs that collect and distribute molecules produced by cellular functions.

5. **B** Proteins are long chains of amino acids linked together. Proteins serve many different functions in cells.

6. **C** Carbohydrates are used by the body for energy. Carbohydrates range from such simple sugars as glucose to complex polysaccharides such as starch.

7. **A** Lipids are a diverse class of organic compounds that include olive oil, vegetable oil, and even beeswax. Lipids do not dissolve in water.

8. **D** Symbiosis is two or more organisms that live together in a long-term association. Symbiosis has different forms depending on whether organisms benefit from the relationship or not.

9. **C** Parasitism is a type of symbiotic relationship where one organism benefits at the expense of the other organism. Tapeworms are an example. Tapeworms get food from the digestive system of their host.

10. **B** Mutualism is a type of symbiotic relationship where both organisms benefit from the relationship. Some ants and aphids are an example. The ants care for and protect the aphids. In return, the aphids provide the ants with a sweet liquid.

11. **A** Commensalism is a type of symbiotic relationship where one organism benefits, while the other neither benefits nor is harmed. Barnacles growing on a whale is an example of commensalism. The barnacles are carried across the oceans while the whale is not affected.

12. **C** A tissue is a group of cells that are serve a similar function.

13. **B** A cell is the smallest unit of life capable of carrying out all functions.

14. **A** Organs are composed of a group of tissues. The tissues collectively work to perform different functions within the organ.

15. **D** Organ systems are groups of organs that work together to make up a system.

16. **B** Protists are classified by the way they move or method of locomotion. The methods are pseudopods, cilia, flagella, or nonmotile.

17. **B** The cerebellum is a small region at the back of the brain. The cerebellum controls smooth, coordinated movements, helps maintain muscle tone, posture, and balance.

18. **B** Gymnosperms and angiosperms are advanced plants. They have many similarities including their leaves, stems, roots, and reproduction with seeds.

19. **D** Most organisms do not have the ability to change their external environments.

20. **B** An enzyme acts as a catalyst for the biochemical reaction. Catalysts lower the activation energy required for a reaction but they are not changed in any way during the reaction.

21. **A** Chemotrophs are able to breakdown inorganic chemical molecules to obtain energy. This has only been found in the Kingdom Monera. Some members of this kingdom are able to break down hydrogen sulfide to obtain energy. Chemotrophs do not depend on sunlight for energy.

22. **A** Birds such as hawks and falcons have strong feet with long talons for grasping prey.

23. **D** In RNA, uracil replaces thymine and is complimentary to adenine.

24. **E** There are many causes of mutations in cells. The most common are the random processes that take place in cells.

25. **C** Amphibians were the first to have a three-chambered heart. This advancement allowed the circulatory system to include lungs.

26. **D** Complete metamorphosis occurs when an organism has a different body shape at different stages of its life cycle. For example, in butterflies, the larva state, called a caterpillar, is very different from the adult butterfly.

27. **A** Photosynthesis is the fixing of atmospheric carbon into molecules that can be used by organisms.

28. **D** Microspores result from meiosis that takes place in the pollen cone of a gymnosperm. The microspores develop into pollen grains, or more correctly, microgametophytes.

29. **D** Bacteria break down or decompose organic matter. Because of their actions, they are considered decomposers in an ecosystem.

30. **A** Ground tissues in plants serve many different functions. Ground tissues do not protect other tissues.

31. **E** The proper way of writing a species name is with the genus capitalized and the specific epithet lower case. The entire name is written in italics or, in older texts, underlined.

32. **B** When gametes are formed in parents; each gamete has half the genetic material of the parent. When the gametes unite, the resulting offspring will receive half the genetic material of each parent.

33. **A** An ecosystem only has so much energy available to pass up to each level of the trophic pyramid. Only about 10% of the energy is actually passed up to the next higher level. When one level of the pyramid is larger than the level below it, there must be a shift to reduce the energy demands.

34. **E** The haploid number of chromosomes is the number of pairs found in an organism. In this case a haploid number of 28 translates to 28 pairs or 56 chromosomes.

35. **B** In this type of cross, the offspring get one allele from each parent. The result is that all offspring will be Yy.

36. **B** The law of independent assortment only applies to traits that are on different chromosomes. The common traits in pea plants all happen to be on different chromosomes so this law applies.

37. **A** Evolution affects populations, not individuals. Individuals can have traits that give them an advantage, and they may pass the traits on, but they do not evolve.

38. **B** The ball-and-socket joint is the type of joint found in the shoulder. The joint allows rotational movement.

39. **B** When a cell is placed in a very salty solution, water moves from the area of higher concentration, inside the cell, to the area of lower concentration, outside the cell.

40. **C** Both codominant traits are always expressed. In horses, the offspring has both red and white hairs.

41. **D** Species that are very closely related have very similar DNA with only minor differences. They are related through a common ancestor.

42. **E** Niche overlap is a form of competition instead of reproductive isolation.

43. **D** Glucose and oxygen are products of photosynthesis. They enter the cellular respiration pathway where they are used to release energy.

44. **C** The vascular tissue in plants moves water up the plant from the roots and moves sugars from the leave, throughout the plant, and down to the roots.

45. **B** The phloem becomes the bark in woody plants.

46. **B** Jumping genes are genes that easily jump or move from one location on a chromosome to another. Jumping genes are what cause some corn to have multicolored kernels.

47. **A** Homologous structures are structures that are similar in two different species. In this case, the bones in the human arm are similar to those in a bat. The finger bones in a human are similar to the thin bones in the bat wing.

48. **B** Inserting is a type of mutation. As the name implies, a repeat of a sequence is inserted into a different chromosome.

49. **E** In animal cells, when fermentation takes place, lactic acid is formed.

50. **D** Disruptive selection takes place when some environmental pressure works to make the extremes in variation the most successful organisms. These organisms are those that reproduce and pass their traits to their offspring.

51. **D** Density-dependent factors are ones that affect a population differently depending on its size and density.

52. **B** Crossing over is a process where genetic material is exchanged by two different chromosomes during meiosis. This is similar to shuffling a deck of cards and increasing variation in the genes.

53. **A** Genes are segments on DNA that on a chromosome that have a specific function.

54. **A** Streptococci means long chain of small round bacteria. *Strepto* refers to a chain and *cocci* refers to round.

55. **B** The concept of the survival of the fittest states that those best able to survive are the ones most likely to reproduce and pass on their genes.

Part B

61. **B** The cell is the smallest unit of life. When a group of similar cells works together, it is called a tissue. Groups of tissues are linked together to form organs. Organs that work together are called organ systems.

62. **B** The dispersion of a population is a way of describing how members of a population are spread out in their habitat.

63. **C** Adaptive radiation describes how a species moves into new, unfilled niches and becomes more specialized to fill each niche.

64. **B** Natural selection works best in a rapidly changing environment when an organism is capable of producing many offspring in a short amount of time.

65. **E** Bryophytes do best in an environment that is constantly wet. Of the ones listed, the mouth of a spring is the best habitat.

66. **D** Abiotic factors are things that are not living. Vegetation is living; therefore it is a biotic factor.

67. **C** Each trophic level only passes about 10% of its energy to the next higher level.

68. **D** Temperature and moisture are the two main controlling factors that determine biome type. Plants and animals have specific requirements on needs and these are the most basic.

69. **D** Tropical rain forests are found in warm regions near the equator.

56. **B** The ecological concept of competition is when two species try for a limited resource. The species best suited to exploit the resource gets the larger share of the resource.

57. **C** Preserves usually work better as larger areas. The same amount that is fragmented does not have the same healthy exchange of genetic material as one large area.

58. **D** Mendel explained that different traits are inherited independently if they are found on different chromosomes.

59. **A** During meiosis, three of the resulting cells are called polar bodies and are discarded. Only one of the cells becomes an egg.

60. **E** Bacteria are prokaryotes because they lack a true nucleus and membrane bound organelles.

70. **B** The taiga and tundra are both found in cold climates. The permafrost is much shallower in tundra so it cannot support large plants.

71. **A** Tropical rain forests are found at the equators. Deserts are found in the midlatitudes. Taiga is found at high latitudes.

72. **B** Grain crops are grasses so they grow best in a grassland biome.

73. **D** The taiga and temperate deciduous forest have similar rainfall amounts. The main difference is the temperature.

74. **E** The tropical rain forest has a warm temperature year round, which gives it a high biodiversity.

75. **C** The chart clearly shows a large drop in number of genera at the end of the Permian.

76. **A** At the end of the Silurian, there was a big increase in the number of genera of brachiopods.

77. **B** Of the times listed, the Silurian is the only one where all three brachiopod groups are present.

78. **C** DNA is replicated during the S, or synthesis phase of the cell cycle.

79. **E** Telophase takes place close to the end of mitosis. The cell is getting ready to split into two daughter cells.

80. **B** Prophase occurs at the beginning of mitosis. The chromosomes condensing is the first step in preparation for mitosis.

PRACTICE TEST 2
BIOLOGY-E

The following Practice Test is designed to be just like the real SAT Biology-E test. It matches the actual test in content coverage and level of difficulty. The test is in two parts. Part A (Questions 1–60) is for everyone taking Biology-E or Biology-M. Part B (Questions 61–80) is ONLY for students taking Biology-E.

When you are finished with the test, determine your score and carefully read the answer explanations for the questions you answered incorrectly. Identify any weak areas by determining the areas in which you made the most errors. Review these chapters of the book first. Then, as time permits, go back and review your stronger areas.

Allow 1 hour to take the test. Time yourself and work uninterrupted. If you run out of time, take note of where you ended when time ran out. Remember that you lose $\frac{1}{4}$ of a point for each incorrect answer. Because of this penalty, do not guess on a question unless you can eliminate one or more of the answers. Your score is calculated using the following formula:

Number of correct answers $- \frac{1}{4}$(Number of incorrect answers)

This Practice Test will be an accurate reflection of how you'll do on test day if you treat it as the real examination. Here are some hints on how to take the test under conditions similar to those of the actual exam.

- Complete the test in one sitting.
- Time yourself.
- Tear out your Answer Sheet and fill in the ovals just as you would on the actual test day.
- Become familiar with the directions to the test and the reference information provided. You'll save time on the actual test day by already being familiar with this information.

PRACTICE TEST 2

BIOLOGY-E

ANSWER SHEET

Part A

1. Ⓐ Ⓑ Ⓒ Ⓓ Ⓔ	21. Ⓐ Ⓑ Ⓒ Ⓓ Ⓔ	41. Ⓐ Ⓑ Ⓒ Ⓓ Ⓔ
2. Ⓐ Ⓑ Ⓒ Ⓓ Ⓔ	22. Ⓐ Ⓑ Ⓒ Ⓓ Ⓔ	42. Ⓐ Ⓑ Ⓒ Ⓓ Ⓔ
3. Ⓐ Ⓑ Ⓒ Ⓓ Ⓔ	23. Ⓐ Ⓑ Ⓒ Ⓓ Ⓔ	43. Ⓐ Ⓑ Ⓒ Ⓓ Ⓔ
4. Ⓐ Ⓑ Ⓒ Ⓓ Ⓔ	24. Ⓐ Ⓑ Ⓒ Ⓓ Ⓔ	44. Ⓐ Ⓑ Ⓒ Ⓓ Ⓔ
5. Ⓐ Ⓑ Ⓒ Ⓓ Ⓔ	25. Ⓐ Ⓑ Ⓒ Ⓓ Ⓔ	45. Ⓐ Ⓑ Ⓒ Ⓓ Ⓔ
6. Ⓐ Ⓑ Ⓒ Ⓓ Ⓔ	26. Ⓐ Ⓑ Ⓒ Ⓓ Ⓔ	46. Ⓐ Ⓑ Ⓒ Ⓓ Ⓔ
7. Ⓐ Ⓑ Ⓒ Ⓓ Ⓔ	27. Ⓐ Ⓑ Ⓒ Ⓓ Ⓔ	47. Ⓐ Ⓑ Ⓒ Ⓓ Ⓔ
8. Ⓐ Ⓑ Ⓒ Ⓓ Ⓔ	28. Ⓐ Ⓑ Ⓒ Ⓓ Ⓔ	48. Ⓐ Ⓑ Ⓒ Ⓓ Ⓔ
9. Ⓐ Ⓑ Ⓒ Ⓓ Ⓔ	29. Ⓐ Ⓑ Ⓒ Ⓓ Ⓔ	49. Ⓐ Ⓑ Ⓒ Ⓓ Ⓔ
10. Ⓐ Ⓑ Ⓒ Ⓓ Ⓔ	30. Ⓐ Ⓑ Ⓒ Ⓓ Ⓔ	50. Ⓐ Ⓑ Ⓒ Ⓓ Ⓔ
11. Ⓐ Ⓑ Ⓒ Ⓓ Ⓔ	31. Ⓐ Ⓑ Ⓒ Ⓓ Ⓔ	51. Ⓐ Ⓑ Ⓒ Ⓓ Ⓔ
12. Ⓐ Ⓑ Ⓒ Ⓓ Ⓔ	32. Ⓐ Ⓑ Ⓒ Ⓓ Ⓔ	52. Ⓐ Ⓑ Ⓒ Ⓓ Ⓔ
13. Ⓐ Ⓑ Ⓒ Ⓓ Ⓔ	33. Ⓐ Ⓑ Ⓒ Ⓓ Ⓔ	53. Ⓐ Ⓑ Ⓒ Ⓓ Ⓔ
14. Ⓐ Ⓑ Ⓒ Ⓓ Ⓔ	34. Ⓐ Ⓑ Ⓒ Ⓓ Ⓔ	54. Ⓐ Ⓑ Ⓒ Ⓓ Ⓔ
15. Ⓐ Ⓑ Ⓒ Ⓓ Ⓔ	35. Ⓐ Ⓑ Ⓒ Ⓓ Ⓔ	55. Ⓐ Ⓑ Ⓒ Ⓓ Ⓔ
16. Ⓐ Ⓑ Ⓒ Ⓓ Ⓔ	36. Ⓐ Ⓑ Ⓒ Ⓓ Ⓔ	56. Ⓐ Ⓑ Ⓒ Ⓓ Ⓔ
17. Ⓐ Ⓑ Ⓒ Ⓓ Ⓔ	37. Ⓐ Ⓑ Ⓒ Ⓓ Ⓔ	57. Ⓐ Ⓑ Ⓒ Ⓓ Ⓔ
18. Ⓐ Ⓑ Ⓒ Ⓓ Ⓔ	38. Ⓐ Ⓑ Ⓒ Ⓓ Ⓔ	58. Ⓐ Ⓑ Ⓒ Ⓓ Ⓔ
19. Ⓐ Ⓑ Ⓒ Ⓓ Ⓔ	39. Ⓐ Ⓑ Ⓒ Ⓓ Ⓔ	59. Ⓐ Ⓑ Ⓒ Ⓓ Ⓔ
20. Ⓐ Ⓑ Ⓒ Ⓓ Ⓔ	40. Ⓐ Ⓑ Ⓒ Ⓓ Ⓔ	60. Ⓐ Ⓑ Ⓒ Ⓓ Ⓔ

Part B

61. Ⓐ Ⓑ Ⓒ Ⓓ Ⓔ
62. Ⓐ Ⓑ Ⓒ Ⓓ Ⓔ
63. Ⓐ Ⓑ Ⓒ Ⓓ Ⓔ
64. Ⓐ Ⓑ Ⓒ Ⓓ Ⓔ
65. Ⓐ Ⓑ Ⓒ Ⓓ Ⓔ
66. Ⓐ Ⓑ Ⓒ Ⓓ Ⓔ
67. Ⓐ Ⓑ Ⓒ Ⓓ Ⓔ
68. Ⓐ Ⓑ Ⓒ Ⓓ Ⓔ
69. Ⓐ Ⓑ Ⓒ Ⓓ Ⓔ
70. Ⓐ Ⓑ Ⓒ Ⓓ Ⓔ
71. Ⓐ Ⓑ Ⓒ Ⓓ Ⓔ
72. Ⓐ Ⓑ Ⓒ Ⓓ Ⓔ
73. Ⓐ Ⓑ Ⓒ Ⓓ Ⓔ
74. Ⓐ Ⓑ Ⓒ Ⓓ Ⓔ
75. Ⓐ Ⓑ Ⓒ Ⓓ Ⓔ
76. Ⓐ Ⓑ Ⓒ Ⓓ Ⓔ
77. Ⓐ Ⓑ Ⓒ Ⓓ Ⓔ
78. Ⓐ Ⓑ Ⓒ Ⓓ Ⓔ
79. Ⓐ Ⓑ Ⓒ Ⓓ Ⓔ
80. Ⓐ Ⓑ Ⓒ Ⓓ Ⓔ

Part C

81. Ⓐ Ⓑ Ⓒ Ⓓ Ⓔ
82. Ⓐ Ⓑ Ⓒ Ⓓ Ⓔ
83. Ⓐ Ⓑ Ⓒ Ⓓ Ⓔ
84. Ⓐ Ⓑ Ⓒ Ⓓ Ⓔ
85. Ⓐ Ⓑ Ⓒ Ⓓ Ⓔ
86. Ⓐ Ⓑ Ⓒ Ⓓ Ⓔ
87. Ⓐ Ⓑ Ⓒ Ⓓ Ⓔ
88. Ⓐ Ⓑ Ⓒ Ⓓ Ⓔ
89. Ⓐ Ⓑ Ⓒ Ⓓ Ⓔ
90. Ⓐ Ⓑ Ⓒ Ⓓ Ⓔ
91. Ⓐ Ⓑ Ⓒ Ⓓ Ⓔ
92. Ⓐ Ⓑ Ⓒ Ⓓ Ⓔ
93. Ⓐ Ⓑ Ⓒ Ⓓ Ⓔ
94. Ⓐ Ⓑ Ⓒ Ⓓ Ⓔ
95. Ⓐ Ⓑ Ⓒ Ⓓ Ⓔ
96. Ⓐ Ⓑ Ⓒ Ⓓ Ⓔ
97. Ⓐ Ⓑ Ⓒ Ⓓ Ⓔ
98. Ⓐ Ⓑ Ⓒ Ⓓ Ⓔ
99. Ⓐ Ⓑ Ⓒ Ⓓ Ⓔ
100. Ⓐ Ⓑ Ⓒ Ⓓ Ⓔ

PRACTICE TEST 2
Time: 60 Minutes

PART A (Core Questions 1–60–for Both Biology-E and Biology-M)

Directions: Determine the BEST answer for each question. Then fill in the corresponding oval on the Answer Sheet.

Questions 1–3

    (A) Krebs cycle
    (B) electron transport chain
    (C) fermentation
    (D) glycolysis
    (E) Calvin cycle

1. Cellular respiration in the absence of oxygen

2. A biochemical pathway that utilizes pyruvate to produce ATP, NADH, and $FADH_2$

3. A biochemical pathway that breaks down glucose into pyruvate

Questions 4–7

    (A) primary consumers
    (B) secondary consumers
    (C) scavengers
    (D) decomposers
    (E) producers

4. Earthworms eat organic matter and return nutrients to the soil.

5. Cows eat grass.

6. Lions are hunters on the African plains.

7. Buzzards soar in the sky looking for dead animals.

Questions 8–12

    (A) geographical isolation
    (B) mechanical isolation
    (C) temporal isolation
    (D) hybrid sterility
    (E) behavioral isolation

8. Groups are not attracted to each other for mating.

9. Structural differences prevent mating between individuals of different groups.

10. Groups are physically separated.

11. Groups reproduce at different times of the year.

12. Matings between groups do not produce fertile offspring.

Questions 13–15

    (A) dominance
    (B) reflex
    (C) instinct
    (D) imprinting
    (E) habituation

13. Learned behavior that occurs only at a certain, critical time in an animal's life

14. Automatic, unconscious reaction

15. Simple form of learned behavior

16. You are trying to identify a plant. If you look closely at the leaves, you see the veins are all parallel. What does this tell you about the plant?

    (A) The plant is a dicot.
    (B) The plant is a monocot.
    (C) The plant is a gymnosperm.
    (D) The plant is an angiosperm.
    (E) The plant is a bryophyte.

17. Populations tend to grow because

    (A) the large number of individuals reduces the number of predators
    (B) the more individuals there are, the more likely they will survive
    (C) random events or natural disturbances are rare
    (D) there are always plentiful resources in every environment
    (E) individuals tend to have multiple offspring over their lifetime

GO ON TO THE NEXT PAGE

PRACTICE TEST—*Continued*

18.
　I.　jellyfish
　II.　mollusk
　III.　earthworm

Which of the above organisms lacks a complete digestive tract?

(A)　I, II, and III
(B)　I only
(C)　II only
(D)　III only
(E)　I and III only

19. The internal need that causes an animal to act and is necessary for learning is called

(A)　trail-and-error
(B)　motivation
(C)　habituation
(D)　conditioning
(E)　imprinting

20. The rigid shape of plant cells is due to the

(A)　cell membrane
(B)　cell wall
(C)　cytoskeleton
(D)　chloroplasts
(E)　centrioles

21. An invertebrate that displays two distinct body forms, medusa and polyp, at different stages in its lifecycle belong to the phylum

(A)　Porifera
(B)　Cnidaria
(C)　Nemotoda
(D)　Mollusca
(E)　Echinodermata

22. The failure of homologous chromosomes to separate during meiosis is called

(A)　nondisjunction
(B)　translocation
(C)　mutation
(D)　crossing over
(E)　disjunction

23. Which characteristic of fungi is used to classify them into different phyla?

(A)　the type of food they grow on
(B)　the type of hyphae they have
(C)　the type of mushroom they produce
(D)　the way they produce spores
(E)　the material that makes up their cell wall

24. A rancher moved his herd of cattle to a different pasture. Which example below indicates that the carrying capacity of that pasture was exceeded?

(A)　The herd increased in size.
(B)　The pasture became overgrazed and barren.
(C)　The pasture had more grasses.
(D)　The cows gained weight.
(E)　The cows had more calves.

25. Some mutations are a source of genetic variation. Which type of cell is mostly likely to cause a genetic variation that could lead to evolution?

(A)　skin cells
(B)　body cells
(C)　brain cells
(D)　sex cells
(E)　embryo cells

26. What is the expected phenotypic ratio of a dihybrid cross between two heterozygous individuals?

(A)　3:1
(B)　1:2:1
(C)　3:3:1
(D)　9:3:3:1
(E)　6:4:4:2

27. Which of the following nucleotide bases is found in RNA but not in DNA?

(A)　uracil
(B)　adenine
(C)　cytosine
(D)　thymine
(E)　guanine

28. Some bacteria are able to reproduce with a simple form of sexual reproduction called

(A)　binary fission
(B)　fragmentation
(C)　meiosis
(D)　replication
(E)　conjugation

GO ON TO THE NEXT PAGE

PRACTICE TEST—*Continued*

29. Mendel's law of segregation states that

    (A) genes are separated on different chromosomes
    (B) pairs of alleles separate during mitosis
    (C) pairs of alleles separate during meiosis
    (D) pairs of alleles exchange material during crossing over
    (E) genes are passed from parents to offspring

Questions 30 and 31

This is a segment of DNA.

   CGATGGCTA

30. Which represents the complimentary strand of DNA for the segment?

    (A) CGATGGCTA
    (B) GCTACCGAT
    (C) UAGCCAUCG
    (D) CGTAGGCAT
    (E) ATCGGTAGC

31. What is the messenger RNA strand for the DNA segment?

    (A) GCUACCGAU
    (B) UCTACCGUA
    (C) GUTAUUGAT
    (D) CGATGGCTA
    (E) ATCGGTAGC

32. The classification system set forth by Linneaus grouped organisms based on their

    (A) similar coloring
    (B) similar structures
    (C) similar habitats
    (D) genetic similarities
    (E) evolutionary relationships

33. Which of the following best describes an ecosystem?

    (A) a group of individuals of the same species that live together in the same area at the same time
    (B) all populations of different species that live and interact in the same area
    (C) all populations of different species that live and interact in the same area and the abiotic environment
    (D) all the organisms that depend on the resources in a specific region
    (E) the part of Earth where life exists

34. The diploid number of a human cell is 23. How many actual chromosomes are in a normal body cell?

    (A) 22
    (B) 23
    (C) 44
    (D) 46
    (E) n

35. Which tissue transports carbohydrates and water through plants?

    (A) epidermal tissue
    (B) vascular tissue
    (C) ground tissue
    (D) epithelial tissue
    (E) endodermal tissue

36. According to the cell theory, which of the following statements is correct?

    (A) All organisms are made up of one or more cells.
    (B) All organisms must be able to reproduce.
    (C) Cells have organelles to carry on their functions.
    (D) Cells evolved from a primordial soup on early Earth.
    (E) Cells are able to regulate their external environment.

37. Which bird uses its beak to probe flowers for nectar?

    (A)

    (B)

    (C)

    (D)

    (E)

GO ON TO THE NEXT PAGE

PRACTICE TEST—*Continued*

38. Which of the following best describes what will happen if cells are placed in distilled water?

   (A) The cells remain unchanged.
   (B) Water moves from inside of the cell to the outside.
   (C) Water moves from outside of the cell to the inside.
   (D) The cells shrink.
   (E) The cells dissolve.

Questions 39 and 40

In an experiment in a laboratory, a population of bacteria in a petri dish is exposed to an antibiotic. The antibiotic kills most of the population. However, a few bacteria survive and soon repopulate the Petri dish with antibiotic-resistant bacteria.

39. According to modern evolutionary theory, which of the following explanations is correct for this experiment?

   (A) Some of the bacteria tried and successfully adapted to the new conditions in the petri dish.
   (B) Some members of the bacteria population developed a resistance to the antibiotic immediately after exposure.
   (C) Some members of the bacteria population already had a resistance to the antibiotic so they were not killed.
   (D) Some of the bacteria quickly evolve into a new species that resists the antibiotic.
   (E) Some of the bacteria protected themselves from the antibiotic long enough to develop a resistance.

40. Which best describes what happened in the petri dish?

   (A) macroevolution
   (B) microevolution
   (C) adaptive radiation
   (D) divergent evolution
   (E) speciation

41. All of the following are cycled though biogeochemical cycles EXCEPT

   (A) water
   (B) carbon
   (C) energy
   (D) phosphorus
   (E) nitrogen

42. You cross a red flowered plant with a white flowered plant, and all of the offspring have pink flowers. What is the most probable explanation?

   (A) Red is dominant.
   (B) White is dominant.
   (C) Pink is dominant.
   (D) Red and white exhibit incomplete dominance.
   (E) Red and white exhibit codominance.

43. If an organism has a haploid number of 24, how many chromosomes does it have?

   (A) 6
   (B) 12
   (C) 24
   (D) 36
   (E) 48

44. Bats and insects both have wings. The wings of bats and insects are examples of

   (A) homologous structures
   (B) analogous characters
   (C) vestigial structures
   (D) adaptive structures
   (E) derived traits

45.
   I.   vitamin synthesis
   II. absorb water
   III. absorb nutrients

   In humans, what function does the small intestine serve?

   (A) I and II only
   (B) II and III only
   (C) II only
   (D) I only
   (E) III only

46. A codon is

   (A) a group of three nucleotide sequences
   (B) the nucleotide units between the start and stop codes
   (C) the nucleotide sequence that serves as the instructions for a protein
   (D) a single nucleotide in an mRNA sequence
   (E) the sequence of nucleotides that signals the start or stop of protein synthesis

GO ON TO THE NEXT PAGE

PRACTICE TEST—*Continued*

47. Which of the following conditions is necessary for a virus to attack a host cell?

    (A) The virus must have the DNA or RNA key sequence to enter the host cell.
    (B) The virus must have the enzymes to cause the host cell to burst so that the host cell may be used as raw materials.
    (C) The virus must have the proper enzyme to puncture the membrane of the host cell.
    (D) The virus must have a particular shape that will match up with the proteins on the surface of the host cell.
    (E) The viral DNA or RNA must have a sequence that is recognized by the ribosomes of the host cell.

48. Cytochrome–c is a protein that scientists often use to compare the evolutionary relationships among species. There is one difference in the cytochrome–c sequence between humans and rhesus monkeys. There are ten differences between humans and kangaroos. What can you infer about the relationship between these species?

    (A) Humans and kangaroos have the same proteins coded in their genes.
    (B) Humans and kangaroos share a more recent ancestor than humans and rhesus monkeys.
    (C) Humans are not closely related to either kangaroos or rhesus monkeys.
    (D) Humans and rhesus monkeys share a more recent ancestor than humans and kangaroos.
    (E) Rhesus monkeys and kangaroos share a more recent ancestor than humans and rhesus monkeys.

49. A man with type A blood marries a woman with type B blood. Their child is blood type O. What are the genotypes of the parents?

    (A) AO and BO
    (B) OO and AB
    (C) Aa and BO
    (D) AO and Bb
    (E) Aa and Bb

Questions 50 and 51

Each corn kernel in an ear of corn is ready to grow into a new plant.

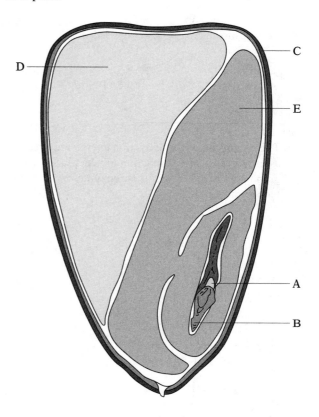

50. Which part of this seed makes up the plant embryo?

    (A) A, B
    (B) A, D
    (C) B, C
    (D) A, B, E
    (E) B, C, D

51. Which part of the seed stores the energy for the plant embryo?

    (A) A
    (B) B
    (C) C
    (D) D
    (E) E

GO ON TO THE NEXT PAGE ▶

PRACTICE TEST—*Continued*

52.

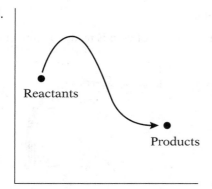

This graph shows the activation energy required for a certain biochemical reaction to take place. Which graph shows the effect of an enzyme on the same biochemical reaction?

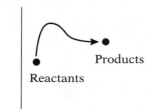

(A)

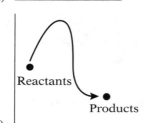

(B)

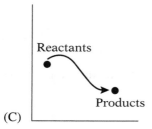

(C)

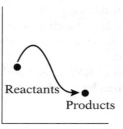

(D)

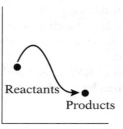

(E)

53. Which is the correct order of stages for an insect that undergoes incomplete metamorphosis?

(A) egg→larva→adult
(B) egg→nymph→adult
(C) egg→nymph→larva→adult
(D) egg→larva→pupa→adult
(E) egg→nymph→pupa→adult

54. The number of trophic levels that are maintained in an ecosystem is limited by

(A) the number of species
(B) the population size
(C) the loss of potential energy
(D) the number of individuals
(E) the hours of sunshine

55. The law of independent assortment applies to

(A) two genes on different chromosomes
(B) two genes on the same chromosome
(C) two alleles on different chromosomes
(D) two alleles on the same chromosome
(E) two chromosome strands

GO ON TO THE NEXT PAGE

PRACTICE TEST—*Continued*

56. Which is the correct order for the cell cycle beginning with the phase that most cells spend the majority of their time?

   I. G_2 Phase—growth and preparation for mitosis
   II. Mitosis
   III. G_1 Phase—cell growth
   IV. S Phase—DNA copied
   V.   Cytokinesis

   (A) III, IV, I, II, V
   (B) III, I, IV, V, II
   (C) II, III, I, IV, V
   (D) IV, III, I, II, V
   (E) V, III, IV, I, II

57. For natural selection to occur, which of the following must be true?

   (A) Individuals must evolve.
   (B) The environment must be constant.
   (C) Variation among organisms must exist.
   (D) Traits must be acquired.
   (E) Many species must be present.

58. What is the phenotypic ratio for a cross between a pea plant with purple flowers (PP) and a pea plant with white flowers (pp)?

   (A) all white
   (B) all purple
   (C) half purple, half white
   (D) 1PP, 2Pp, 1pp
   (E) all Pp

59. Natural selection is a part of evolution of a species. Which of the following best describes the driving force that leads to evolution within a species?

   (A) Individuals within a population change their behavior to accommodate changes in the environment and pass these to offspring.
   (B) Individuals within a population develop new adaptations as selective pressures force change.
   (C) Individuals within a population find new ways to adapt to environmental pressures.
   (D) Individuals within a population use different parts of their body as conditions change and pass those changes to offspring.
   (E) Individuals within a population have variations that give those individuals a better chance of survival.

60. Which of the following organisms is INCORRECTLY paired with its trophic level?

   (A) tree–producer
   (B) hawk–primary consumer
   (C) fungi–detritivore
   (D) fox–secondary consumer
   (E) grasshopper–primary consumer

GO ON TO THE NEXT PAGE

PRACTICE TEST—*Continued*

PART B (Biology-E Questions 61–80)

61. All of the following could cause a large number of density-dependent deaths in a population EXCEPT

    (A) winter storms
    (B) disease-carrying insects
    (C) predators
    (D) limited resources
    (E) small forest fire

62. Which of the following seeds depends on wind for dispersal?

    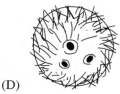
    (A)

    (B)

    (C)

    (D)

    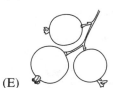
    (E)

63. Which group of animals was the first to have internal fertilization?

    (A) fishes
    (B) amphibians
    (C) reptiles
    (D) birds
    (E) mammals

64. Where would you most likely find nitrogen-fixing bacteria?

    (A) on the stems of some plants
    (B) in the leaves of trees
    (C) on the roots of some plants
    (D) on atmospheric dust particles
    (E) in blue-green algae

65. Earthworms are hermaphroditic, meaning that they

    (A) reproduce asexually
    (B) only come up to the surface at night
    (C) reproduce both sexually and asexually
    (D) have specialized segments for specialized tasks
    (E) have both male and female sex organs

66. According to the Hardy–Weinberg principle, allele frequencies change when evolutionary forces act on a population. All of these are possible evolutionary forces EXCEPT

    (A) mutations
    (B) gene flow
    (C) genetic drift
    (D) random mating
    (E) natural selection

Questions 67–69

This is a typical food web in a pond.

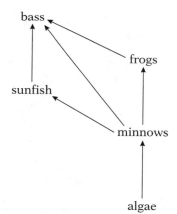

GO ON TO THE NEXT PAGE

PRACTICE TEST—*Continued*

67. Which two organisms in this food web are in direct competition?

    (A) bass and minnows
    (B) minnows and sunfish
    (C) frogs and sunfish
    (D) bass and algae
    (E) frogs and algae

68. Which shows one possible direct pathway for energy flow to the bass?

    (A) algae→minnows→frogs→bass
    (B) algae→bass
    (C) algae→frogs→sunfish→bass
    (D) minnows→frogs→bass
    (E) bass→frogs→minnows→algae

69. Based on this food web, what would happen if the bass disappeared due to over fishing?

    (A) The algae population would increase.
    (B) The frogs and sunfish would disappear.
    (C) The minnow population would increase and the sunfish population would decrease.
    (D) The frog and sunfish populations would increase.
    (E) The minnow population and algae would increase.

70. Which of the following time periods shows a mass extinction of animals?

    (A) end of the Ordovician
    (B) end of the Silurian
    (C) end of the Devonian
    (D) end of the Permian
    (E) end of the Triassic

71. Which of the following time periods showed a boom in all echinoderm groups?

    (A) Ordovician
    (B) Silurian
    (C) Mississippian
    (D) Permian
    (E) Jurassic

72. All of the following statements are correct EXCEPT

    (A) The Blastoids are extinct.
    (B) The Echinodermata will become extinct in the near future.
    (C) The Echinoids are a successful group.
    (D) The Blastoids were not able to adapt to the same changes as the Crinoids.
    (E) The Crinoids have been living in a stable environment since the Triassic.

Questions 70–72

This chart shows the relative abundance of different groups of echinoderms throughout geologic time. The width of the band indicates the number of species for each group.

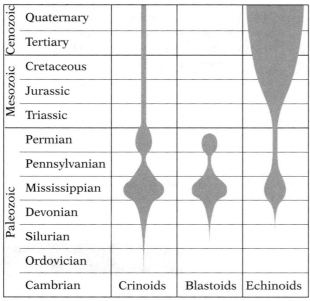

Phylum Echinodermata

GO ON TO THE NEXT PAGE

PRACTICE TEST—*Continued*

Questions 73–77

Vegetation follows established patterns of regrowth and change after disturbances by farming, timber harvesting, hurricanes, or fire. This process of patterned regrowth and change is called plant succession. The rate of succession and the species present at various stages depend on the type and degrees of disturbance, the environment of the particular sites, and the species available to occupy the site. In the Piedmont of North Carolina, land subjected to disturbances will grow back in a century or two to become mixed hardwood forest.

1st year	2nd year	3rd to 18th year	19th to 30th year	30th to 70th year	70th to 100th year	100th year plus
Horseweed dominant; crabgrass, pigweed	Asters dominant; crabgrass	Grass scrub community; broomsedge grass, pines coming in during this stage	Young pine forest	Mature pine forest; Understory of young hardwoods	Pine to hardwood transition	Climax oak-hickory forest

73. Based on this diagram, after 80 years, which will make up the majority of trees?

    (A) young pines
    (B) mature pines
    (C) oak trees
    (D) oak and hickory trees
    (E) pine, oak, and hickory trees

74. Which best describes the change that takes place when pines become the dominant vegetation?

    (A) The pine trees increase the amount of nutrients available in the soil.
    (B) The pine trees increase the soil moisture.
    (C) The pine trees decrease the amount of sunlight reaching the forest floor.
    (D) The pine trees change the character of the soil from loam to sandy loam.
    (E) The pine trees increase the amount of soil erosion.

75. Which of the following factors would be LEAST likely to restart succession?

    (A) forest fire
    (B) volcanic eruption
    (C) clear-cut logging
    (D) glaciation
    (E) drought

76. Pine beetles are a type of insect that burrow into the bark of mature and over-mature pine trees. The pine trees die as a result of the infestations. If pine beetles attacked a mature pine forest, which of the following events would most likely occur?

    (A) Succession would start over.
    (B) The rate of transition to a hardwood forest would be increased.
    (C) The succession will stall at being a young pine forest.
    (D) The succession will stall at being a mature pine forest while young pines mature.
    (E) The pine beetles will not affect the rate of succession in the forest.

GO ON TO THE NEXT PAGE

PRACTICE TEST—*Continued*

77. Which of the following statements about succession is true?

   (A) Succession is a natural progression that takes place at a constant rate.
   (B) Succession only takes place on freshly cleared or new land such as islands.
   (C) The rate of succession can be changed by factors such as fire, clear cutting, and lava flows.
   (D) Succession is a natural progression of plant types that cannot be reversed.
   (E) Succession always occurs over a short period of time.

Questions 78–80

Number of Hares per square kilometer   Number of Lynx per 100 square kilometers

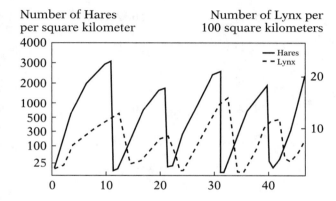

78. If lynxes depend mainly on hares for food, which best describes the relationship between hares and lynxes?

   (A) As the hare population decreases, the lynx population increases.
   (B) As the hare population decreases, the lynx population stays the same.
   (C) As the hare population increases, the lynx population increases.
   (D) As the hare population increases, the lynx population stays the same.
   (E) There is no relationship between the populations of lynxes and hares.

79. Based on this chart, which of the following statements is true?

   (A) Lynxes and hares depend on each other for survival.
   (B) Hares become better at hiding from lynxes over time.
   (C) Hares are capable of reproducing quickly.
   (D) Lynxes only prey on hares in certain seasons.
   (E) Lynxes migrate into and out of areas on a regular basis.

80. What would happen to the hare population if the lynxes were removed from the habitat?

   (A) The hare population would continue on a boom and bust cycle.
   (B) The hare population would dwindle.
   (C) The hare population would grow exponentially and not stop.
   (D) The hare population would quickly reach the carrying capacity and stabilize.
   (E) The hare population would slowly increase over time.

S T O P

IF YOU FINISH BEFORE TIME RUNS OUT, GO BACK AND CHECK YOUR WORK.

PRACTICE TEST 2
BIOLOGY-E

ANSWER KEY

Part A

1. C	11. C	21. B	31. A	41. C	51. D
2. A	12. D	22. A	32. B	42. D	52. B
3. D	13. D	23. D	33. C	43. E	53. B
4. D	14. B	24. B	34. D	44. B	54. C
5. A	15. E	25. D	35. B	45. E	55. C
6. B	16. B	26. D	36. A	46. A	56. A
7. C	17. E	27. A	37. C	47. D	57. C
8. E	18. B	28. E	38. C	48. D	58. B
9. B	19. B	29. C	39. C	49. A	59. E
10. A	20. B	30. B	40. B	50. D	60. B

Part B

61. A	71. C
62. B	72. B
63. C	73. E
64. C	74. C
65. E	75. E
66. D	76. B
67. C	77. C
68. A	78. C
69. D	79. C
70. D	80. D

■ SCORE SHEET

Number of questions correct: _____

Less: 0.25 × number of questions wrong: _____

(Remember that omitted questions are not counted as wrong.)

Raw score: _____

Raw Score	Scaled Score	Raw Score	Scaled Score	Raw Score	Scaled Score	Raw Score	Scaled Score	Raw Score	Scaled Score
80	800	57	690	34	520	11	380	−12	250
79	800	56	680	33	520	10	370	−13	240
78	800	55	670	32	510	9	370	−14	240
77	800	54	670	31	510	8	360	−15	230
76	800	53	660	30	500	7	350	−16	230
75	800	52	650	29	500	6	350	−17	230
74	800	51	650	28	490	5	340	−18	220
73	790	50	640	27	490	4	330	−19	220
72	790	49	630	26	480	3	330	−20	220
71	780	48	620	25	480	2	320		
70	780	47	620	24	470	1	320		
69	770	46	610	23	470	0	310		
68	760	45	600	22	460	−1	310		
67	760	44	600	21	450	−2	300		
66	750	43	590	20	440	−3	300		
65	740	42	580	19	440	−4	290		
64	740	41	580	18	430	−5	290		
63	730	40	570	17	420	−6	280		
62	720	39	560	16	420	−7	270		
61	710	38	560	15	410	−8	270		
60	710	37	550	14	400	−9	260		
59	700	36	540	13	400	−10	260		
58	700	35	530	12	390	−11	250		

Note: This is only a sample scoring scale. Scoring scales differ from exam to exam.

ANSWERS AND EXPLANATIONS

Part A

1. **C** Fermentation is the cellular respiration process that takes place in the absence of oxygen. Fermentation converts glucose to either lactic acid or ethyl alcohol.

2. **A** The Krebs cycle is a cyclic biochemical pathway of respiration. It takes in pyruvate and produces ATP, NADH, and $FADH_2$.

3. **D** Glycolysis is the biochemical pathway that breaks down glucose to pyruvate. Glycolysis produces a net gain of 2 ATP molecules.

4. **D** Earthworms are decomposers because they break down organic matter and return nutrients to the soil. The returned nutrients are ready for use by plants.

5. **A** Cows are primary consumers because they eat plants, which are producers. Primary consumers are on the next trophic level above producers.

6. **B** Lions are secondary consumers because they eat animals, other consumers.

7. **C** Buzzards are scavengers because they find and eat already dead animals rather than killing them.

8. **E** Behavioral isolation occurs when two groups diverge and have different courtship rituals.

9. **B** Mechanical isolation occurs when two groups evolve differences in their genitalia.

10. **A** Geographical isolation occurs when groups are physically separated, such as by a mountain range or large body of water.

11. **C** Temporal isolation occurs when two groups diverge and have different mating seasons.

12. **D** Hybrid sterility occurs when nonfertile offspring are produced. This is a dead end as far as passing genes on is concerned.

13. **D** Imprinting is a learned behavior that occurs at a certain time of an animals life, such as just after birth.

14. **B** A reflex is an automatic and uncontrollable response. This is a direct stimulus–response scenario.

15. **E** Habituation is learned behavior that occurs as a result of doing some repeatedly.

16. **B** All monocots have parallel veins in their leaves.

17. **E** Populations grow as a result of multiple births through the lifespan of an organism. If each organism in a population only reproduced once, the population would not grow.

18. **B** Jellyfish are primitive, multicellular organisms. An opening to the digestive tract serves as both the mouth and anus for jellyfish.

19. **B** Motivation is needed for learning. If an animal lacks motivation, there will be no learning.

20. **B** Plant cells have a cell wall composed of cellulose. The cellulose is rigid and gives the plant cell a defined shape.

21. **B** Cnidarians have two distinct body plans during their lives. A jellyfish is an example of a medusa, and a sea anemone is an example of a polyp.

22. **A** Sometimes during meiosis, a pair of chromosomes fails to separate. This causes an extra chromosome in one daughter cell and a missing chromosome in the other.

23. **D** Fungi have many different forms, but the shape of their spores classifies them all.

24. **B** When a pasture exceeds the carrying capacity, it lacks the food to support that number of animals. A pasture in this condition will have all its available food eaten and will appear barren.

25. **D** The only mutation that can be passed to offspring is one that occurs in the sex cells. These are the only cells that undergo meiosis and take part in reproduction.

26. **D** A dihybrid cross has two factors in the cross. This results in a total of four potential phenotypes with a ratio of 9:3:3:1.

27. **A** Uracil does not occur in DNA but is in RNA. In RNA, uracil replaces thymine and attaches to adenine.

28. **E** Bacteria usually reproduce through binary fission but they sometimes get together, exchange genetic information, and reproduce by a process known a conjugation.

29. **C** During meiosis, the chromosome pairs separate and go to different daughter cells. This means that each daughter cells acquires one allele for a specific trait.

30. **B** The complementary strand of DNA will have the opposite nucleotide bases as the original strand.

31. **A** The mRNA strand will have the opposite nucleotides as the DNA with uracil substituted for thymine.

32. **B** When Linneaus proposed a method for classifying organisms, he based his system on structural similarities. This system has worked fairly well but many refinements are now done using genetic analysis.

33. **C** An ecosystem is all interactions among the organisms in the environment as well as the abiotic features.

34. **D** The diploid number refers to the number of pairs of chromosomes. In humans, the normal diploid number is 23 so that means that a cell has 23 pairs or 46 chromosomes.

35. **B** Plants are made up of many different types of tissues. The tissues that are part of the transport system for plants are vascular tissues such as xylem and phloem.

36. **A** This is the most basic statement of the cell theory.

37. **C** A bird that probes flowers for nectar would need a long, thin beak to reach inside the flower. A hummingbird is an example of a bird that feeds on nectar from flowers.

38. **C** Distilled water is hypotonic compared to a cell. As a result, water moves from an area of higher concentration (outside the cell) to the area of lower concentration (inside the cell).

39. **C** Because of genetic variations, some of the bacteria were able to survive the antibiotics. They passed this genetic advantage to their offspring and soon repopulated the petri dish with antibiotic-resistant bacteria.

40. **B** This scenario is an example of microevolution. Microevolution is a small change in a population but not enough to create a new species.

41. **C** Biogeochemical cycles are cycles where minerals move between the biotic and abiotic part of the environment. Energy is not a mineral.

42. **D** Incomplete dominance occurs when neither of two traits is dominant. When both alleles appear, the phenotype is expressed as a blend.

43. **E** The haploid number for chromosomes is the actual number of chromosomes in a gamete. The total number of chromosomes in an organism would be double the haploid number.

44. **B** Analogous structures are those that serve a similar function but have structural differences and are not linked through evolution.

45. **E** The small intestine is lined with villi that increase the surface area and aid in the absorption of nutrients from digested food. The large intestine carries out the absorption of water, and the large intestines are also the site of some vitamin synthesis by bacteria living there symbiotically.

46. **A** The genetic code is based on sets of three nucleotides called codons.

47. **D** The shape of a virus allows it to attach to a host cell. Once this is accomplished, the virus can inject DNA or RNA into the host cell.

48. **D** Evolution results in changes to proteins. For cytochrome-c, the fewer the changes, the more closely related the organisms.

49. **A** A and B are dominant over O. O can only be expressed if paired with another O. The only way the offspring could have two O alleles is if the parents were AO and BO.

50. **D** The embryo of the corn plant is made up of the embryonic shoot (A), the embryonic root (B), and the cotyledon (E).

51. **D** The endosperm is energy stored for the plant embryo.

52. **B** An enzyme is a catalyst. Catalysts facilitate reactions by lowering the activation energy of the reaction pathway. They cannot change the initial or final energy level of the participating molecules.

53. **B** An insect with incomplete metamorphosis has a nymph stage that looks similar to the adult stage. Unlike complete metamorphosis, there is no pupa stage.

54. **C** Potential energy is the amount of energy for the next trophic level. Each trophic level only passes on about 10% of its total energy to the next higher level.

55. **C** The law of independent assortment states that traits are inherited independently of other traits. This only applies to alleles that are on separate chromosomes.

56. **A** Cells spend most of their time in the G_1 phase. After that comes the S phase, the G_2 phase, mitosis, and finally cytokinesis.

Part B

61. **A** A winter storm will not cause density-dependent deaths. It can be a density-independent cause of deaths.

62. **B** A maple seed has wings that allow it to be carried by the wind to a more distant location.

63. **C** Reptiles were the first animals with internal fertilization. This ended the dependence on water to carry sperm to the egg.

64. **C** Nitrogen-fixing bacteria are found in the ground. They often live in a symbiotic relationship with plants on their roots. Legumes or beans are a common example.

65. **E** Earthworms have both male and female reproductive organs.

66. **D** Random mating does not give any reproductive advantage to a trait. As a result, it does not change allele frequencies in a population.

67. **C** Frog and sunfish both rely on the same food source so they are in direct competition.

68. **A** Energy flows from the producer (algae) through consumers before it reaches the bass.

69. **D** The loss of the secondary consumer would remove pressure from primary consumers and allow their populations to grow until they reach the carrying capacity.

70. **D** It is necessary to read the chart from bottom to top. At the end of the Permian, Crinoids became reduced in diversity, and Blastoids became extinct.

57. **C** Organisms must already have traits for variation before natural selection occurs. Under most conditions, the variation in traits does not provide any particular advantage, so there is no natural selection. The variation only becomes important for natural selection when there is pressure that gives one trait an advantage over another.

58. **B** All of the plants in the first generation will be heterozygous so they exhibit the dominant trait.

59. **E** Individuals have traits that make them more successful, which gives them a reproductive advantage.

60. **B** Hawks are secondary consumers because they eat other consumers.

71. **C** During the Mississippian, all the echinoderm groups increased in diversity.

72. **B** The Echinoids have been increasing in diversity. It is unlikely that they will have a collapse unless there is significant global change.

73. **E** At 80 years, the forest is in a transition with large numbers of pines, oaks, and hickories.

74. **C** The pines are the first plants that grow tall. They shade the soil and reduce the populations of plants that depend on full sunlight.

75. **E** A drought will not likely last long enough to kill off all the trees.

76. **B** If the mature pines are removed, the rate of transition to a climax oak–hickory forest will be increased.

77. **C** Succession is a process that does not follow a distinct timeline. Many factors can affect rate of succession or even restart it.

78. **C** The hares are a food source for lynxes. As the population of hares increases, more food is available for lynxes so their population increases, too.

79. **C** There is a short lag time between the boom and bust cycle on hares so they must have a quick reproduction time.

80. **D** Without the lynxes, the hare will quickly reproduce and reach the carrying capacity.

PRACTICE TEST 3

BIOLOGY-M

The following Practice Test is designed to be just like the real SAT Biology-M test. It matches the actual test in content coverage and level of difficulty. The test is in two parts. Part A (Questions 1–60) is for everyone taking Biology-E or Biology-M. Part C (Questions 81–100) is ONLY for students taking Biology-M. (On the real test, Questions 61–80 are ONLY for students taking Biology-E.)

When you are finished with the test, determine your score and carefully read the answer explanations for the questions you answered incorrectly. Identify any weak areas by determining the areas in which you made the most errors. Review these chapters of the book first. Then, as time permits, go back and review your stronger areas.

Allow 1 hour to take the test. Time yourself and work uninterrupted. If you run out of time, take note of where you ended when time ran out. Remember that you lose $\frac{1}{4}$ of a point for each incorrect answer. Because of this penalty, do not guess on a question unless you can eliminate one or more of the answers. Your score is calculated using the following formula:

Number of correct answers $- \frac{1}{4}$ (Number of incorrect answers)

This Practice Test will be an accurate reflection of how you'll do on test day if you treat it as the real examination. Here are some hints on how to take the test under conditions similar to those of the actual exam.

- Complete the test in one sitting.
- Time yourself.
- Tear out your Answer Sheet and fill in the ovals just as you would on the actual test day.
- Become familiar with the directions to the test and the reference information provided. You'll save time on the actual test day by already being familiar with this information.

PRACTICE TEST 3

BIOLOGY-M

ANSWER SHEET

Part A

1. Ⓐ Ⓑ Ⓒ Ⓓ Ⓔ	21. Ⓐ Ⓑ Ⓒ Ⓓ Ⓔ	41. Ⓐ Ⓑ Ⓒ Ⓓ Ⓔ
2. Ⓐ Ⓑ Ⓒ Ⓓ Ⓔ	22. Ⓐ Ⓑ Ⓒ Ⓓ Ⓔ	42. Ⓐ Ⓑ Ⓒ Ⓓ Ⓔ
3. Ⓐ Ⓑ Ⓒ Ⓓ Ⓔ	23. Ⓐ Ⓑ Ⓒ Ⓓ Ⓔ	43. Ⓐ Ⓑ Ⓒ Ⓓ Ⓔ
4. Ⓐ Ⓑ Ⓒ Ⓓ Ⓔ	24. Ⓐ Ⓑ Ⓒ Ⓓ Ⓔ	44. Ⓐ Ⓑ Ⓒ Ⓓ Ⓔ
5. Ⓐ Ⓑ Ⓒ Ⓓ Ⓔ	25. Ⓐ Ⓑ Ⓒ Ⓓ Ⓔ	45. Ⓐ Ⓑ Ⓒ Ⓓ Ⓔ
6. Ⓐ Ⓑ Ⓒ Ⓓ Ⓔ	26. Ⓐ Ⓑ Ⓒ Ⓓ Ⓔ	46. Ⓐ Ⓑ Ⓒ Ⓓ Ⓔ
7. Ⓐ Ⓑ Ⓒ Ⓓ Ⓔ	27. Ⓐ Ⓑ Ⓒ Ⓓ Ⓔ	47. Ⓐ Ⓑ Ⓒ Ⓓ Ⓔ
8. Ⓐ Ⓑ Ⓒ Ⓓ Ⓔ	28. Ⓐ Ⓑ Ⓒ Ⓓ Ⓔ	48. Ⓐ Ⓑ Ⓒ Ⓓ Ⓔ
9. Ⓐ Ⓑ Ⓒ Ⓓ Ⓔ	29. Ⓐ Ⓑ Ⓒ Ⓓ Ⓔ	49. Ⓐ Ⓑ Ⓒ Ⓓ Ⓔ
10. Ⓐ Ⓑ Ⓒ Ⓓ Ⓔ	30. Ⓐ Ⓑ Ⓒ Ⓓ Ⓔ	50. Ⓐ Ⓑ Ⓒ Ⓓ Ⓔ
11. Ⓐ Ⓑ Ⓒ Ⓓ Ⓔ	31. Ⓐ Ⓑ Ⓒ Ⓓ Ⓔ	51. Ⓐ Ⓑ Ⓒ Ⓓ Ⓔ
12. Ⓐ Ⓑ Ⓒ Ⓓ Ⓔ	32. Ⓐ Ⓑ Ⓒ Ⓓ Ⓔ	52. Ⓐ Ⓑ Ⓒ Ⓓ Ⓔ
13. Ⓐ Ⓑ Ⓒ Ⓓ Ⓔ	33. Ⓐ Ⓑ Ⓒ Ⓓ Ⓔ	53. Ⓐ Ⓑ Ⓒ Ⓓ Ⓔ
14. Ⓐ Ⓑ Ⓒ Ⓓ Ⓔ	34. Ⓐ Ⓑ Ⓒ Ⓓ Ⓔ	54. Ⓐ Ⓑ Ⓒ Ⓓ Ⓔ
15. Ⓐ Ⓑ Ⓒ Ⓓ Ⓔ	35. Ⓐ Ⓑ Ⓒ Ⓓ Ⓔ	55. Ⓐ Ⓑ Ⓒ Ⓓ Ⓔ
16. Ⓐ Ⓑ Ⓒ Ⓓ Ⓔ	36. Ⓐ Ⓑ Ⓒ Ⓓ Ⓔ	56. Ⓐ Ⓑ Ⓒ Ⓓ Ⓔ
17. Ⓐ Ⓑ Ⓒ Ⓓ Ⓔ	37. Ⓐ Ⓑ Ⓒ Ⓓ Ⓔ	57. Ⓐ Ⓑ Ⓒ Ⓓ Ⓔ
18. Ⓐ Ⓑ Ⓒ Ⓓ Ⓔ	38. Ⓐ Ⓑ Ⓒ Ⓓ Ⓔ	58. Ⓐ Ⓑ Ⓒ Ⓓ Ⓔ
19. Ⓐ Ⓑ Ⓒ Ⓓ Ⓔ	39. Ⓐ Ⓑ Ⓒ Ⓓ Ⓔ	59. Ⓐ Ⓑ Ⓒ Ⓓ Ⓔ
20. Ⓐ Ⓑ Ⓒ Ⓓ Ⓔ	40. Ⓐ Ⓑ Ⓒ Ⓓ Ⓔ	60. Ⓐ Ⓑ Ⓒ Ⓓ Ⓔ

Part B

61. Ⓐ Ⓑ Ⓒ Ⓓ Ⓔ
62. Ⓐ Ⓑ Ⓒ Ⓓ Ⓔ
63. Ⓐ Ⓑ Ⓒ Ⓓ Ⓔ
64. Ⓐ Ⓑ Ⓒ Ⓓ Ⓔ
65. Ⓐ Ⓑ Ⓒ Ⓓ Ⓔ
66. Ⓐ Ⓑ Ⓒ Ⓓ Ⓔ
67. Ⓐ Ⓑ Ⓒ Ⓓ Ⓔ
68. Ⓐ Ⓑ Ⓒ Ⓓ Ⓔ
69. Ⓐ Ⓑ Ⓒ Ⓓ Ⓔ
70. Ⓐ Ⓑ Ⓒ Ⓓ Ⓔ
71. Ⓐ Ⓑ Ⓒ Ⓓ Ⓔ
72. Ⓐ Ⓑ Ⓒ Ⓓ Ⓔ
73. Ⓐ Ⓑ Ⓒ Ⓓ Ⓔ
74. Ⓐ Ⓑ Ⓒ Ⓓ Ⓔ
75. Ⓐ Ⓑ Ⓒ Ⓓ Ⓔ
76. Ⓐ Ⓑ Ⓒ Ⓓ Ⓔ
77. Ⓐ Ⓑ Ⓒ Ⓓ Ⓔ
78. Ⓐ Ⓑ Ⓒ Ⓓ Ⓔ
79. Ⓐ Ⓑ Ⓒ Ⓓ Ⓔ
80. Ⓐ Ⓑ Ⓒ Ⓓ Ⓔ

Part C

81. Ⓐ Ⓑ Ⓒ Ⓓ Ⓔ
82. Ⓐ Ⓑ Ⓒ Ⓓ Ⓔ
83. Ⓐ Ⓑ Ⓒ Ⓓ Ⓔ
84. Ⓐ Ⓑ Ⓒ Ⓓ Ⓔ
85. Ⓐ Ⓑ Ⓒ Ⓓ Ⓔ
86. Ⓐ Ⓑ Ⓒ Ⓓ Ⓔ
87. Ⓐ Ⓑ Ⓒ Ⓓ Ⓔ
88. Ⓐ Ⓑ Ⓒ Ⓓ Ⓔ
89. Ⓐ Ⓑ Ⓒ Ⓓ Ⓔ
90. Ⓐ Ⓑ Ⓒ Ⓓ Ⓔ
91. Ⓐ Ⓑ Ⓒ Ⓓ Ⓔ
92. Ⓐ Ⓑ Ⓒ Ⓓ Ⓔ
93. Ⓐ Ⓑ Ⓒ Ⓓ Ⓔ
94. Ⓐ Ⓑ Ⓒ Ⓓ Ⓔ
95. Ⓐ Ⓑ Ⓒ Ⓓ Ⓔ
96. Ⓐ Ⓑ Ⓒ Ⓓ Ⓔ
97. Ⓐ Ⓑ Ⓒ Ⓓ Ⓔ
98. Ⓐ Ⓑ Ⓒ Ⓓ Ⓔ
99. Ⓐ Ⓑ Ⓒ Ⓓ Ⓔ
100. Ⓐ Ⓑ Ⓒ Ⓓ Ⓔ

PRACTICE TEST 3

Time: 60 Minutes

PART A (Core Questions 1–60—for Both Biology-E and Biology-M)

Directions: Determine the BEST answer for each question. Then fill in the corresponding oval on the Answer Sheet.

Questions 1–4

   (A) ribosome
   (B) mitochondria
   (C) chloroplast
   (D) endoplasmic reticulum
   (E) Golgi apparatus

1. Site where photosynthesis takes place

2. Extensive series of membranes throughout the cell

3. Powerhouse of the cell

4. Packaging and distribution system of a cell

Questions 5–7

   (A) lipids
   (B) proteins
   (C) carbohydrates
   (D) nucleic acids

5. long chains of amino acids

6. composed of only carbon, hydrogen, and oxygen

7. also known as fats

Questions 8–11

   (A) commensalism
   (B) mutualism
   (C) parasitism
   (D) symbiosis

8. Two or more organisms in a close, long-term association

9. One organism benefits, while the other suffers from the relationship.

10. Both organisms benefit from the relationship.

11. One organism benefits, and the other does not benefit nor is harmed from the relationship.

Questions 12–15

   (A) organ
   (B) cell
   (C) tissue
   (D) organ system

12. Group of cells with a similar function

13. Smallest unit of organization in living things

14. Many different groups of cells working together

15. The highest level of organization that carries out important body functions

16. Protists are classified by their
   (A) method of feeding
   (B) method of moving
   (C) method of reproducing
   (D) size
   (E) habitat

17. The part of the human brain that controls balance, posture, and coordination is the
   (A) cerebrum
   (B) cerebellum
   (C) medulla oblongata
   (D) thalamus
   (E) hypothalamus

18. The characteristics that gymnosperms and angiosperms share are
   (A) leaves, rhizomes, and spore
   (B) leaves, stems, roots, and seeds
   (C) flat leaves, trunks, and naked seeds
   (D) lack of vascular tissue and small leaflets
   (E) needle-like leaves, stems, roots, and fleshy fruits

GO ON TO THE NEXT PAGE

PRACTICE TEST—*Continued*

19. All of the following are characteristics of living things EXCEPT for the ability to

    (A) perform cellular respiration
    (B) regulate their internal environment
    (C) reproduce
    (D) change their external environment
    (E) pass traits to offspring

20. What happens to an enzyme during a biochemical reaction?

    (A) It becomes part of the product.
    (B) It is unchanged.
    (C) It is broken down into amino acids.
    (D) It reacts with fatty acids.
    (E) It becomes a polypeptide.

21.

    I.   monera
    II.   plants
    III. protists

    Which kingdom(s) contain(s) chemotrophs as members?

    (A) I only
    (B) II only
    (C) III only
    (D) I and III only
    (E) I, II, and III

22. Which bird has feet that are modified for grasping prey?

    (A)

    (B)

    (C)

    (D)

    (E)

23. In RNA molecules, uracil is complementary to

    (A) thymine
    (B) guanine
    (C) cytosine
    (D) adenine
    (E) uracil

24. Most mutations result from

    (A) certain chemicals
    (B) ionizing radiation
    (C) infrared radiation
    (D) ultraviolet radiation
    (E) random events

25. The first vertebrates to evolve a three-chambered heart that ensured all cells in the body received the proper amount of oxygen are the

    (A) fishes
    (B) reptiles
    (C) amphibians
    (D) birds
    (E) mammals

26. Which is the correct order of stages for an insect that undergoes complete metamorphosis?

    (A) egg→larva→adult
    (B) egg→nymph→adult
    (C) egg→nymph→larva→adult
    (D) egg→larva→pupa→adult
    (E) egg→nymph→pupa→adult

27. Which process brings carbon into the living portion of its cycle?

    (A) photosynthesis
    (B) cellular respiration
    (C) combustion
    (D) decomposition
    (E) fixation

28. Microspores of gymnosperms eventually develop into

    (A) seeds
    (B) cotyledons
    (C) female gametophytes
    (D) pollen grains
    (E) archegonia

GO ON TO THE NEXT PAGE

PRACTICE TEST—*Continued*

29. Bacteria are an important part of most food chains because they serve as

    (A) primary consumers
    (B) secondary consumers
    (C) scavengers
    (D) decomposers
    (E) producers

30. Ground tissue provides all of the following functions in plants EXCEPT

    (A) protection of other tissues
    (B) supporting the plant
    (C) storage of water and carbohydrates
    (D) transport of materials
    (E) photosynthesis

31. Which of the following scientific names is written in the correct form to identify a species?

    (A) *meleagris gallopavo*
    (B) *Meleagris Gallopavo*
    (C) Meleagris Gallopavo
    (D) Meleagris gallopavo
    (E) *Meleagris gallopavo*

32. Which best describes the source of genes in an offspring resulting from sexual reproduction?

    (A) The offspring gets a full set of genes from the mother and from the father.
    (B) The offspring gets half the genes from the mother and half the genes from the father.
    (C) The offspring gets all of its genes from the father.
    (D) The offspring gets a random mixture of genes from the mother and father.
    (E) The offspring gets all of its genes from the mother.

33. Which best describes how the following ecosystem will change over time?

```
           ┌─────────────┐
           │  Secondary  │
           │  Consumers  │
           └─────────────┘

┌─────────────────────────────────────┐
│             Herbivores               │
└─────────────────────────────────────┘

      ┌───────────────────────┐
      │      Producers         │
      └───────────────────────┘
```

    (A) The herbivores will decline because there is not enough food to support them.
    (B) The herbivores will increase, and the secondary consumers will increase.
    (C) The populations of producers, herbivores, and carnivores will remain the same.
    (D) The secondary consumers will decline, and the producers will increase.
    (E) The producers will increase to support the herbivores.

34. If an organism has a haploid number of 28, how many chromosomes does it have?

    (A) 7
    (B) 14
    (C) 28
    (D) 42
    (E) 56

35. A pea plant with a genotype of YY produces yellow seeds. A pea plant with a genotype of yy produces green seeds. If the pea plants are crossed, which describes the possible genotypes of the offspring?

    (A) all are YY
    (B) all are Yy
    (C) all are yy
    (D) half YY and half yy
    (E) half YY and half Yy

GO ON TO THE NEXT PAGE ➤

PRACTICE TEST—*Continued*

36. Which set of offspring would result from a cross that was controlled by the law of independent assortment?

    (A) Half the offspring are tall with white flowers and half are short with white flowers.
    (B) All the offspring are tall or short and have white or purple flowers.
    (C) All the offspring are short and have purple flowers.
    (D) All the offspring are tall and have white flowers.
    (E) All the offspring are tall and have purple flowers.

37. Which of the following statements about evolution is accurate?

    (A) Populations evolve, while individuals do not evolve.
    (B) Populations do not evolve, while individuals evolve.
    (C) Populations evolve only when individuals evolve.
    (D) Populations evolve only when isolated individuals evolve.
    (E) Populations evolve only through mutations.

38. On the human skeletal system, which type of joint allows rotational movement?

    (A) slightly moveable joint
    (B) ball-and-socket joint
    (C) pivot joint
    (D) plane joint
    (E) saddle joint

39. Which of the following best describes what will happen if cells are placed in a very salty solution?

    (A) The cells remain unchanged.
    (B) Water moves from inside of the cell to the outside.
    (C) Water moves from outside of the cell to the inside.
    (D) The cells burst.
    (E) The cells dissolve.

40. The color red and the color white are codominant in horses. What would you expect if you crossed a homozygous red horse with a homozygous white horse?

    (A) The offspring is white.
    (B) The offspring is red.
    (C) The offspring has both red and white hairs.
    (D) The offspring is brown.
    (E) The offspring is black.

41. The DNA of two closely related species would likely be

    (A) completely different
    (B) somewhat different
    (C) very different
    (D) very similar
    (E) identical

42. All of the following are mechanisms of reproductive isolation EXCEPT

    (A) geographical isolation
    (B) ecological isolation
    (C) temporal isolation
    (D) reproductive failure
    (E) niche overlap

43. The process of photosynthesis produces many products. Which of these products are used for starting cellular respiration?

    (A) oxygen and ATP
    (B) water and carbon dioxide
    (C) NADP and hydrogen
    (D) glucose and oxygen
    (E) carbohydrates and NADP

Questions 44 and 45

This diagram is a cross section through the primary stem of a woody plant.

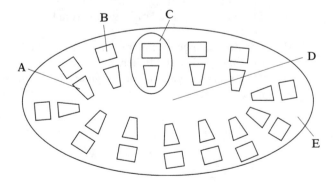

44. Which part of this stem is the vascular tissue?

    (A) A
    (B) B
    (C) C
    (D) D
    (E) E

GO ON TO THE NEXT PAGE

PRACTICE TEST—*Continued*

45. Which part of this stem will develop into the bark of the woody plant?

    (A) A
    (B) B
    (C) C
    (D) D
    (E) E

46. Sequences of DNA that are easily and naturally copied from one location in the genome and inserted elsewhere are called

    (A) duplication genes
    (B) jumping genes
    (C) crossing over genes
    (D) recessive genes
    (E) deletion genes

47. A bat wing and a human's arm are examples of

    (A) homologous structures
    (B) analogous characters
    (C) vestigial structures
    (D) adaptive structures
    (E) derived traits

48. A type of mutation that occurs when part of a chromatid breaks off and attaches to its sister chromatid resulting in the duplication of a gene on a chromosome is called

    (A) deleting
    (B) inserting
    (C) separating
    (D) substituting
    (E) inverting

49. Cellular respiration in the absence of oxygen is called fermentation. What is the product of fermentation in animal cells?

    (A) Acetyl-CoA
    (B) alcohol
    (C) carbon dioxide
    (D) pyruvic acid
    (E) lactic acid

50. Natural selection is an evolutionary force that can affect an entire population. One species can evolve into two species when only the extreme forms of a trait are favored and intermediate forms are selected against. This is known as

    (A) artificial selection
    (B) directional selection
    (C) targeted selection
    (D) disruptive selection
    (E) stabilizing selection

51. An example of a density-dependent factor is

    (A) weather
    (B) climate
    (C) air
    (D) food
    (E) drought

52. Which best describes the advantage of crossing over during meiosis?

    (A) makes for healthy offspring
    (B) provides a source of genetic variation
    (C) creates a random mix of chromosomes
    (D) allows gametes to have half the number of chromosomes
    (E) increases the number of gametes

53. A segment of a DNA molecule that carries instructions for a specific trait is called a

    (A) gene
    (B) chromosome
    (C) nucleotide
    (D) codon
    (E) chromatid

54. Small, round bacteria that grow in a chain are called

    (A) streptococci
    (B) staphylobacilli
    (C) spirillium
    (D) diplococci
    (E) bacillus

55. According to Darwin, organisms best suited to their environment

    (A) are most likely to evolve
    (B) are more likely to survive and reproduce
    (C) are most likely to live the longest
    (D) are the fastest organisms
    (E) have the same chance of survival as other organisms

56. When lions and hyenas fight over a dead zebra, their interaction is called

    (A) mutualism
    (B) competition
    (C) commensalism
    (D) parasitism
    (E) predation

GO ON TO THE NEXT PAGE

PRACTICE TEST—*Continued*

57. Which is the best method for preserving the bio-diversity of an ecosystem?

    (A) creating a preserve in an urban area
    (B) building botanical gardens based on the ecosystem
    (C) preserving a few very large areas on an ecosystem
    (D) preserving many small areas of an ecosystem
    (E) creating greenbelts along creeks and roadways in urban areas

58. Gregor Mendel found that the inheritance of one trait had no affect on the inheritance of different trait. He described this observation as the

    (A) law of dominance
    (B) law of universal inheritance
    (C) law of segregation
    (D) law of independent assortment
    (E) law of separate chromosomes

59. Meiosis is the process of making sex cells or gametes. In humans, how many mature egg cells result from meiosis?

    (A) 1
    (B) 2
    (C) 3
    (D) 4
    (E) 6

60. Which of the following are considered prokaryotes?

    (A) animals
    (B) plants
    (C) fungi
    (D) protists
    (E) bacteria

GO ON TO THE NEXT PAGE

PRACTICE TEST—*Continued*

(Note: On the real SAT Biology test, Part B, questions 61–80, is ONLY for students taking Biology-E. For Biology-M, continue with Part C, questions 81–100. On the Answer Sheet, be sure to start marking your answers on the line for Question 81.)

PART C (Biology-M Questions 81–100)

81. Genetic engineering allows scientists to insert DNA fragments from one organism into an organism of the same or different species. An organism that contains functional recombinant DNA is called

    (A) mutated
    (B) transmorphic
    (C) transgenic
    (D) recombinant
    (E) cloned

82. Hemoglobin is the molecule in red blood cells that carries oxygen. Hemoglobin has a metal in its structure that binds to oxygen. This metal is

    (A) zinc
    (B) phosphorus
    (C) magnesium
    (D) copper
    (E) iron

83. In the process of gel electrophoresis, negatively charged DNA molecules are placed in a gel. The gel has positive and negative electrodes. When a current is applied to the gel, which way will the DNA molecules move?

    (A) The DNA molecules will move toward both the positive and negative electrodes.
    (B) The DNA molecules move to a position equal distance from the electrodes.
    (C) The DNA molecules will move perpendicular to the electrodes.
    (D) The DNA molecules will move toward the positive electrode.
    (E) The DNA molecules will move toward the negative electrode.

84. The electron transport chain in photosynthesis produces

    (A) ADP
    (B) ATP
    (C) NADP⁺
    (D) water
    (E) glucose

85. Antibiotics are not effective against viral infections because

    (A) viruses lack a cell wall that antibiotics can weaken
    (B) viruses have evolved a resistance to antibiotics
    (C) the viral envelope breaks down antibiotics
    (D) the viral envelope does not have a receptor for antibiotics
    (E) viruses only contain RNA which isn't affected by antibiotics

86. During translation, a codon pairs with a

    (A) complementary strand of messenger (mRNA) sequence
    (B) specific amino acid unit
    (C) complementary strand of ribosomal (rRNA) sequence
    (D) specific segment of the DNA sequence
    (E) complementary transfer RNA (tRNA) sequence

87. All of the following are types of asexual reproduction EXCEPT

    (A) fragmentation
    (B) fission
    (C) cloning
    (D) fertilization
    (E) budding

GO ON TO THE NEXT PAGE

PRACTICE TEST—*Continued*

Questions 88–90

Jill notices that in the morning at certain times of the year there are many dead fish at the surface of the pond. She is interested in finding what is causing the fish to die. She notes that this mainly occurs in the summer. The pond has many plants so she thinks this might be the cause. She measures the dissolved oxygen levels in the pond at several different times of the day. She records her data in the following table.

Time	Dissolved Oxygen (ppm)
0800	2.2
1100	5.7
1500	7.6
1800	9.8
2000	7.1

88. Which graph best represents Jill's dissolved oxygen data?

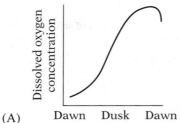

(A)

(B)

(C)

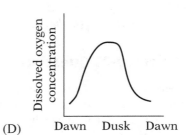

(D)

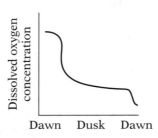

(E)

89. What is the most likely reason for the low dissolved oxygen during the night?

(A) The plants use up all the oxygen at night for the dark reaction.

(B) The fish and the plants both consume oxygen in order to carry out respiration at night.

(C) The plants die off at night and the decay uses oxygen.

(D) The fish become more active at night and use more oxygen.

(E) The temperature of the pond drops so less oxygen can stay dissolved.

90. Which of the following best explains why this takes place during the summer?

(A) The fish are more active in the summer and use more oxygen.

(B) The fish die off during the winter.

(C) The water warms up during the day but cools off quickly at night so the dissolved oxygen levels drop quickly.

(D) The water is warmer so it holds less dissolved oxygen and more sunlight means more photosynthesis.

(E) The plants die during the winter.

GO ON TO THE NEXT PAGE

PRACTICE TEST—*Continued*

Questions 91–94

A student wanted to perform an experiment similar to Gregor Mendel. She gathered a large number of seeds for pea plants and began growing them. Her first part of the experiment was to find homozygous plants.
After finding homozygous plants for both dominant and recessive traits, she used these plants for more crosses.

91. Which best describes how she determined whether plants were homozygous or heterozygous?

    (A) She assumed that each plant showed either the dominant or recessive trait.
    (B) She crossed plants with similar traits. Then she grew the seeds to see what traits the offspring had.
    (C) She crossed plants with other plants with similar traits and different traits. She then grew the seeds from the crosses to look at the ratios.
    (D) She crossed plants with other plants that had similar traits. If the seeds were viable, both parent plants were homozygous.
    (E) She self-pollinated the plants, and then grew the seeds to see if the offspring had the same traits as the parent.

92. What is the phenotypic ratio of the cross between two heterozygous tall plants (Tt)?

    (A) 1 TT, 2 Tt, 1 tt
    (B) 3 TT, 1 tt
    (C) all tall
    (D) 3 tall, 1 short
    (E) 1 tall, 2 medium, 1 short

93. In this experiment, it was found that traits could disappear and reappear in a certain pattern from generation to generation. This occurs because of the

    (A) law of segregation
    (B) law of dominance
    (C) law of phenotypic ratios
    (D) law of independent assortment
    (E) law of reappearance

94. A plant with a genotype of TT produces tall plants. A plant with a genotype of tt produces dwarf plants. If the plants are crossed, what height are the offspring?

    (A) all tall
    (B) half tall, half dwarf
    (C) all dwarf
    (D) 75% tall, 25% dwarf
    (E) 25% tall, 75% dwarf

Questions 95–100

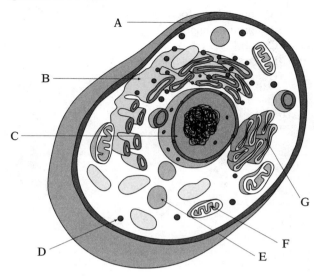

95. Which structure best identifies this cell as a eukaryote?

    (A) A
    (B) B
    (C) C
    (D) D
    (E) E

96. In eukaryotes, the chromosomes are found in structure

    (A) A
    (B) B
    (C) C
    (D) D
    (E) E

97. Structure G is the

    (A) ribosome
    (B) mitochondria
    (C) chloroplast
    (D) endoplasmic reticulum
    (E) Golgi apparatus

98. Structure E contains digestive enzymes used by the cell. This structure is a

    (A) ribosome
    (B) vacuole
    (C) nucleolus
    (D) lysosome
    (E) mitochondria

GO ON TO THE NEXT PAGE

PRACTICE TEST—*Continued*

99. Structure F in this cell functions to

    (A) breakdown food molecules
    (B) produce energy
    (C) replicate DNA
    (D) assemble proteins
    (E) remove waste products

100. This cell is most likely an animal cell because it

    (A) has a cell membrane
    (B) lacks a cell wall
    (C) has mitochondria
    (D) lacks a nucleus
    (E) has a plasmid

STOP

IF YOU FINISH BEFORE TIME RUNS OUT, GO BACK AND CHECK YOUR WORK.

PRACTICE TEST 3
BIOLOGY-M

ANSWER KEY

Part A

1. C	11. A	21. A	31. E	41. D	51. D
2. D	12. C	22. A	32. B	42. E	52. B
3. B	13. B	23. D	33. A	43. D	53. A
4. E	14. A	24. E	34. E	44. C	54. A
5. B	15. D	25. C	35. B	45. B	55. B
6. C	16. B	26. D	36. B	46. B	56. B
7. A	17. B	27. A	37. A	47. A	57. C
8. D	18. B	28. D	38. B	48. B	58. D
9. C	19. D	29. D	39. B	49. E	59. A
10. B	20. B	30. A	40. C	50. D	60. E

Part C

81. C	91. E
82. E	92. D
83. D	93. A
84. B	94. A
85. A	95. C
86. E	96. C
87. D	97. E
88. A	98. D
89. B	99. B
90. D	100. B

SCORE SHEET

Number of questions correct: _____

Less: 0.25 × number of questions wrong: _____

(Remember that omitted questions are not counted as wrong.)

Raw score: _____

Raw Score	Scaled Score	Raw Score	Scaled Score	Raw Score	Scaled Score	Raw Score	Scaled Score	Raw Score	Scaled Score
80	800	57	690	34	520	11	380	−12	250
79	800	56	680	33	520	10	370	−13	240
78	800	55	670	32	510	9	370	−14	240
77	800	54	670	31	510	8	360	−15	230
76	800	53	660	30	500	7	350	−16	230
75	800	52	650	29	500	6	350	−17	230
74	800	51	650	28	490	5	340	−18	220
73	790	50	640	27	490	4	330	−19	220
72	790	49	630	26	480	3	330	−20	220
71	780	48	620	25	480	2	320		
70	780	47	620	24	470	1	320		
69	770	46	610	23	470	0	310		
68	760	45	600	22	460	−1	310		
67	760	44	600	21	450	−2	300		
66	750	43	590	20	440	−3	300		
65	740	42	580	19	440	−4	290		
64	740	41	580	18	430	−5	290		
63	730	40	570	17	420	−6	280		
62	720	39	560	16	420	−7	270		
61	710	38	560	15	410	−8	270		
60	710	37	550	14	400	−9	260		
59	700	36	540	13	400	−10	260		
58	700	35	530	12	390	−11	250		

Note: This is only a sample scoring scale. Scoring scales differ from exam to exam.

ANSWERS AND EXPLANATIONS

Part A

1. **C** Chloroplasts are the organelles that contain chlorophyll and other photopigments used during photosynthesis.

2. **D** The endoplasmic reticulum is an extensive network of membranes that are in the cytoplasm. The endoplasmic reticulum is a transportation network to move molecules around the cell.

3. **B** The mitochondria are the site where ATP is produced, providing energy for cellular functions.

4. **E** The Golgi apparatus consists of flattened sacs that collect and distribute molecules produced by cellular functions.

5. **B** Proteins are long chains of amino acids linked together. Proteins serve many different functions in cells.

6. **C** Carbohydrates are used by the body for energy. Carbohydrates range from such simple sugars as glucose to complex polysaccharides such as starch.

7. **A** Lipids are a diverse class of organic compounds that include olive oil, vegetable oil, and even beeswax. Lipids do not dissolve in water.

8. **D** Symbiosis is two or more organisms that live together in a long-term association. Symbiosis has different forms depending on whether organisms benefit from the relationship or not.

9. **C** Parasitism is a type of symbiotic relationship where one organism benefits at the expense of the other organism. Tapeworms are an example. Tapeworms get food from the digestive system of their host.

10. **B** Mutualism is a type of symbiotic relationship where both organisms benefit from the relationship. Some ants and aphids are an example. The ants care for and protect the aphids. In return, the aphids provide the ants with a sweet liquid.

11. **A** Commensalism is a type of symbiotic relationship where one organism benefits, while the other neither benefits nor is harmed. Barnacles growing on a whale is an example of commensalism. The barnacles are carried across the oceans, while the whale is not affected.

12. **C** A tissue is a group of cells that are serve a similar function.

13. **B** A cell is the smallest unit of life capable of carrying out all functions.

14. **A** Organs are composed of a group of tissues. The tissues collectively work to perform different functions within the organ.

15. **D** Organ systems are groups of organs that work together to make up a system.

16. **B** Protists are classified by the way they move or method of locomotion. The methods are pseudopods, cilia, flagella, or nonmotile.

17. **B** The cerebellum is a small region at the back of the brain. The cerebellum controls smooth, coordinated movements, helps maintain muscle tone, posture, and balance.

18. **B** Gymnosperms and angiosperms are advanced plants. They have many similarities including their leaves, stems, roots, and reproduction with seeds.

19. **D** Most organisms do not have the ability to change their external environments.

20. **B** An enzyme acts as a catalyst for the biochemical reaction. Catalysts lower the activation energy required for a reaction but they are not changed in any way during the reaction.

21. **A** Chemotrophs are able to breakdown inorganic chemical molecules to obtain energy. This has only been found in the Kingdom Monera. Some members of this kingdom are able to break down hydrogen sulfide to obtain energy. Chemotrophs do not depend on sunlight for energy.

22. **A** Birds such a hawks and falcons have strong feet with long talons for grasping prey.

23. **D** In RNA, uracil replaces thymine and is complimentary to adenine.

24. **E** There are many causes of mutations in cells. The most common are the random processes that take place in cells.

25. **C** Amphibians were the first to have a three-chambered heart. This advancement allowed the circulatory system to include lungs.

26. **D** Complete metamorphosis occurs when an organism has a different body shape at different stages of its life cycle. For example, in butterflies, the larva state, called a caterpillar, is very different from the adult butterfly.

27. **A** Photosynthesis is the fixing of atmospheric carbon into molecules that can be used by organisms.

28. **D** Microspores result from meiosis that takes place in the pollen cone of a gymnosperm. The microspores develop into pollen grains, or more correctly, microgametophytes.

29. **D** Bacteria break down or decompose organic matter. Because of their actions, they are considered decomposers in an ecosystem.

30. **A** Ground tissues in plants serve many different functions. Ground tissues do not protect other tissues.

31. **E** The proper way of writing a species name is with the genus capitalized and the specific epithet lower case. The entire name is written in italics or, in older texts, underlined.

32. **B** When gametes are formed in parents; each gamete has half the genetic material of the parent. When the gametes unite, the resulting offspring will receive half the genetic material of each parent.

33. **A** An ecosystem only has so much energy available to pass up to each level of the trophic pyramid. Only about 10% of the energy is actually passed up to the next higher level. When one level of the pyramid is larger than the level below it, there must be a shift to reduce the energy demands.

34. **E** The haploid number of chromosomes is the number of pairs found in an organism. In this case a haploid number of 28 translates to 28 pairs or 56 chromosomes.

35. **B** In this type of cross, the offspring get one allele from each parent. The result is that all offspring will by Yy.

36. **B** The law of independent assortment only applies to traits that are on different chromosomes. The common traits in pea plants all happen to be on different chromosomes so this law applies.

37. **A** Evolution affects populations, not individuals. Individuals can have traits that give them an advantage, and they may pass the traits on, but they do not evolve.

38. **B** The ball-and-socket joint is the type of joint found in the shoulder. The joint allows rotational movement.

39. **B** When a cell is placed in a very salty solution, water moves from the area of higher concentration, inside the cell, to the area of lower concentration, outside the cell.

40. **C** Both codominant traits are always expressed. In horses, the offspring has both red and white hairs.

41. **D** Species that are very closely related have very similar DNA with only minor differences. They are related through a common ancestor.

42. **E** Niche overlap is a form of competition instead of reproductive isolation.

43. **D** Glucose and oxygen are products of photosynthesis. They enter the cellular respiration pathway where they are used to release energy.

44. **C** The vascular tissue in plants moves water up the plant from the roots and moves sugars from the leave, throughout the plant, and down to the roots.

45. **B** The phloem becomes the bark in woody plants.

46. **B** Jumping genes are genes that easily jump or move from one location on a chromosome to another. Jumping genes are what cause some corn to have multicolored kernels.

47. **A** Homologous structures are structures that are similar in two different species. In this case, the bones in the human arm are similar to those in a bat. The finger bones in a human are similar to the thin bones in the bat wing.

48. **B** Inserting is a type of mutation. As the name implies, a repeat of a sequence is inserted into a different chromosome.

49. **E** In animal cells, when fermentation takes place, lactic acid is formed.

50. **D** Disruptive selection takes place when some environmental pressure works to make the extremes in variation the most successful organisms. These organisms are those that reproduce and pass their traits to their offspring.

51. **D** Density-dependent factors are those that affect a population differently depending on its size and density.

52. **B** Crossing over is a process where genetic material is exchanged by two different chromosomes during meiosis. This is similar to shuffling a deck of cards and increasing variation in the genes.

53. **A** Genes are segments on DNA that on a chromosome that have a specific function.

54. **A** Streptococci means long chain of small round bacteria. *Strepto* refers to a chain and *cocci* refers to round.

55. **B** The concept of the survival of the fittest states that those best able to survive are the ones most likely to reproduce and pass on their genes.

56. **B** The ecological concept of competition is when two species try for a limited resource. The species best suited to exploit the resource gets the larger share of the resource.

57. **C** Preserves usually work better as larger areas. The same amount that is fragmented does not have the same healthy exchange of genetic material as one large area.

58. **D** Mendel explained that different traits are inherited independently if they are found on different chromosomes.

59. **A** During meiosis, three of the resulting cells are called polar bodies and are discarded. Only one of the cells becomes an egg.

60. **E** Bacteria are prokaryotes because they lack a true nucleus and membrane bound organelles.

Part C

81. **C** Organisms that have DNA from a different organism are transgenic organisms. They are also called genetically modified organisms.

82. **E** Iron is the metal in the hemoglobin biomolecule.

83. **D** DNA has a slightly negative charge so it moves toward the positive electrode because opposite charges attract.

84. **B** The energy gained through the electron transport chain is used to attach a phosphate onto an ADP molecule to make ATP.

85. **A** Viruses are not living organisms and do not have a cell wall. Antibiotics work by attacking and weakening the cell wall in bacteria but they are ineffective against viruses.

86. **E** Transfer RNA delivers specific amino acids to the ribosomes for protein synthesis.

87. **D** Fertilization is a type of sexual reproduction where two haploid gametes fuse to form a diploid zygote.

88. **A** The dissolved oxygen steadily increases during the day and then falls off after sunset.

89. **B** Oxygen levels drop during the night because respiration, carried out by plants and animals including fish, consumes oxygen. During the day, photosynthesis produces excess oxygen, but at night it is used up by the respiration of plants.

90. **D** The warm water and abundant light cause plants to grow and photosynthesize. During the summer, the conditions are well suited to photosynthesis.

91. **E** Using self-pollinating the plants is the surest way to find which alleles a plant has because the parents of the cross will both have the same alleles for each trait.

92. **D** All the plants that have a dominant allele will be tall. In this particular type of cross, the tall plants have a 3:1 ratio over the short plants.

93. **A** The law of segregation explains why traits skip the F_1 generation only to reappear in the F_2 generation. This occurs because heterozygous plants express the dominant phenotype even though they carry a recessive trait.

94. **A** The cross will produce all tall plants because the genotype is Tt.

95. **C** All eukaryotes have a nucleus surrounded by a nuclear membrane.

96. **C** Chromosomes are always found in the nucleus of eukaryotes.

97. **E** The Golgi apparatus consists of flattened sacs that collect and distribute molecules produced by cellular functions.

98. **D** Lysosomes store digestive enzymes that are used for various tasks such as breaking down old organelles.

99. **B** The mitochondria is the powerhouse of the cell. They produce energy by bonding phosphates to ADP in order to form ATP.

100. **B** Plant cells have a rigid cell wall. Animal cells lack a cell wall and only have a cell membrane surrounding them.

PRACTICE TEST 4

BIOLOGY-M

The following Practice Test is designed to be just like the real SAT Biology-M test. It matches the actual test in content coverage and level of difficulty. The test is in two parts. Part A (Questions 1–60) is for everyone taking Biology-E or Biology-M. Part C (Questions 81–100) is ONLY for students taking Biology-M. (On the real test, Questions 61–80 are ONLY for students taking Biology-E.)

When you are finished with the test, determine your score and carefully read the answer explanations for the questions you answered incorrectly. Identify any weak areas by determining the areas in which you made the most errors. Review these chapters of the book first. Then, as time permits, go back and review your stronger areas.

Allow 1 hour to take the test. Time yourself and work uninterrupted. If you run out of time, take note of where you ended when time ran out. Remember that you lose $\frac{1}{4}$ of a point for each incorrect answer. Because of this penalty, do not guess on a question unless you can eliminate one or more of the answers. Your score is calculated using the following formula:

Number of correct answers $- \frac{1}{4}$ (Number of incorrect answers)

This Practice Test will be an accurate reflection of how you'll do on test day if you treat it as the real examination. Here are some hints on how to take the test under conditions similar to those of the actual exam.

- Complete the test in one sitting.
- Time yourself.
- Tear out your Answer Sheet and fill in the ovals just as you would on the actual test day.
- Become familiar with the directions to the test and the reference information provided. You'll save time on the actual test day by already being familiar with this information.

PRACTICE TEST 4
BIOLOGY-M

ANSWER SHEET

Part A

1. A B C D E	21. A B C D E	41. A B C D E
2. A B C D E	22. A B C D E	42. A B C D E
3. A B C D E	23. A B C D E	43. A B C D E
4. A B C D E	24. A B C D E	44. A B C D E
5. A B C D E	25. A B C D E	45. A B C D E
6. A B C D E	26. A B C D E	46. A B C D E
7. A B C D E	27. A B C D E	47. A B C D E
8. A B C D E	28. A B C D E	48. A B C D E
9. A B C D E	29. A B C D E	49. A B C D E
10. A B C D E	30. A B C D E	50. A B C D E
11. A B C D E	31. A B C D E	51. A B C D E
12. A B C D E	32. A B C D E	52. A B C D E
13. A B C D E	33. A B C D E	53. A B C D E
14. A B C D E	34. A B C D E	54. A B C D E
15. A B C D E	35. A B C D E	55. A B C D E
16. A B C D E	36. A B C D E	56. A B C D E
17. A B C D E	37. A B C D E	57. A B C D E
18. A B C D E	38. A B C D E	58. A B C D E
19. A B C D E	39. A B C D E	59. A B C D E
20. A B C D E	40. A B C D E	60. A B C D E

Part B

| 61. A B C D E |
| 62. A B C D E |
| 63. A B C D E |
| 64. A B C D E |
| 65. A B C D E |
| 66. A B C D E |
| 67. A B C D E |
| 68. A B C D E |
| 69. A B C D E |
| 70. A B C D E |
| 71. A B C D E |
| 72. A B C D E |
| 73. A B C D E |
| 74. A B C D E |
| 75. A B C D E |
| 76. A B C D E |
| 77. A B C D E |
| 78. A B C D E |
| 79. A B C D E |
| 80. A B C D E |

Part C

| 81. A B C D E |
| 82. A B C D E |
| 83. A B C D E |
| 84. A B C D E |
| 85. A B C D E |
| 86. A B C D E |
| 87. A B C D E |
| 88. A B C D E |
| 89. A B C D E |
| 90. A B C D E |
| 91. A B C D E |
| 92. A B C D E |
| 93. A B C D E |
| 94. A B C D E |
| 95. A B C D E |
| 96. A B C D E |
| 97. A B C D E |
| 98. A B C D E |
| 99. A B C D E |
| 100. A B C D E |

PRACTICE TEST 4

Time: 60 Minutes

PART A (Core Questions 1–60–for Both Biology-E and Biology-M)

Directions: Determine the BEST answer for each question. Then fill in the corresponding oval on the Answer Sheet.

Questions 1–3

   (A) Krebs cycle
   (B) electron transport chain
   (C) fermentation
   (D) glycolysis
   (E) Calvin cycle

1. Cellular respiration in the absence of oxygen

2. A biochemical pathway that utilizes pyruvate to produce ATP, NADH, and $FADH_2$

3. A biochemical pathway that breaks down glucose into pyruvate

Questions 4–7

   (A) primary consumers
   (B) secondary consumers
   (C) scavengers
   (D) decomposers
   (E) producers

4. Earthworms eat organic matter and return nutrients to the soil.

5. Cows eat grass.

6. Lions are hunters on the African plains.

7. Buzzards soar in the sky looking for dead animals.

Questions 8–12

   (A) geographic isolation
   (B) ecologic isolation
   (C) temporal isolation
   (D) hybrid sterility
   (E) behavioral isolation
   (F) mechanical isolation

8. Groups are not attracted to each other for mating.

9. Structural differences prevent mating between individuals of different groups.

10. Groups are physically separated.

11. Groups reproduce at different times of the year.

12. Matings between groups do not produce fertile offspring.

Questions 13–15

   (A) dominance
   (B) reflex
   (C) instinct
   (D) imprinting
   (E) habituation

13. Learned behavior that occurs only at a certain, critical time in an animal's life

14. Automatic, unconscious reaction

15. Simple form of learned behavior

16. You are trying to identify a plant. If you look closely at the leaves, you see the veins are all parallel. What does this tell you about the plant?

   (A) The plant is a dicot.
   (B) The plant is a monocot.
   (C) The plant is a gymnosperm.
   (D) The plant is an angiosperm.
   (E) The plant is a bryophyte.

17. Populations tend to grow because

   (A) the large number of individuals reduces the number of predators
   (B) the more individuals there are, the more likely they will survive
   (C) random events or natural disturbances are rare
   (D) there are always plentiful resources in every environment
   (E) individuals tend to have multiple offspring over their lifetime

GO ON TO THE NEXT PAGE

PRACTICE TEST—*Continued*

18.
I.   jellyfish
II.   mollusk
III. earthworm

Which of the above organisms lacks a complete digestive tract?

(A) I, II, and III
(B) I only
(C) II only
(D) III only
(E) I and III only

19. The internal need that causes an animal to act and is necessary for learning is called

(A) trail-and-error
(B) motivation
(C) habituation
(D) conditioning
(E) imprinting

20. The rigid shape of plant cells is due to the

(A) cell membrane
(B) cell wall
(C) cytoskeleton
(D) chloroplasts
(E) centrioles

21. An invertebrate that displays two distinct body forms, medusa and polyp, at different stages in its lifecycle belong to the phylum

(A) Porifera
(B) Cnidaria
(C) Nemotoda
(D) Mollusca
(E) Echinodermata

22. The failure of homologous chromosomes to separate during meiosis is called

(A) nondisjunction
(B) translocation
(C) mutation
(D) crossing over
(E) disjunction

23. Which characteristic of fungi is used to classify them into different phyla?

(A) the type of food they grow on
(B) the type of hyphae they have
(C) the type of mushroom they produce
(D) the way they produce spores
(E) the material that makes up their cell wall

24. A rancher moved his herd of cattle to a different pasture. Which example below indicates that the carrying capacity of that pasture was exceeded?

(A) The herd increased in size.
(B) The pasture became overgrazed and barren.
(C) The pasture had more grasses.
(D) The cows gained weight.
(E) The cows had more calves.

25. Some mutations are a source of genetic variation. Which type of cell is mostly likely to cause a genetic variation that could lead to evolution?

(A) skin cells
(B) body cells
(C) brain cells
(D) sex cells
(E) embryo cells

26. What is the expected phenotypic ratio of a dihybrid cross between two heterozygous individuals?

(A) 3:1
(B) 1:2:1
(C) 3:3:1
(D) 9:3:3:1
(E) 6:4:4:2

27. Which of the following nucleotide bases is found in RNA but not in DNA?

(A) uracil
(B) adenine
(C) cytosine
(D) thymine
(E) guanine

28. Some bacteria are able to reproduce with a simple form of sexual reproduction called

(A) binary fission
(B) fragmentation
(C) meiosis
(D) replication
(E) conjugation

GO ON TO THE NEXT PAGE

PRACTICE TEST—*Continued*

29. Mendel's law of segregation states that
    (A) genes are separated on different chromosomes
    (B) pairs of alleles separate during mitosis
    (C) pairs of alleles separate during meiosis
    (D) pairs of alleles exchange material during crossing over
    (E) genes are passed from parents to offspring

Questions 30 and 31

This is a segment of DNA.

    CGATGGCTA

30. Which represents the complimentary strand of DNA for the segment?
    (A) CGATGGCTA
    (B) GCTACCGAT
    (C) UAGCCAUCG
    (D) CGTAGGCAT
    (E) ATCGGTAGC

31. What is the messenger RNA strand for the DNA segment?
    (A) GCUACCGAU
    (B) UCTACCGUA
    (C) GUTAUUGAT
    (D) CGATGGCTA
    (E) ATCGGTAGC

32. The classification system set forth by Linneaus grouped organisms based on their
    (A) similar coloring
    (B) similar structures
    (C) similar habitats
    (D) genetic similarities
    (E) evolutionary relationships

33. Which of the following best describes an ecosystem?
    (A) a group of individuals of the same species that live together in the same area at the same time
    (B) all populations of different species that live and interact in the same area
    (C) all populations of different species that live and interact in the same area and the abiotic environment
    (D) all the organisms that depend on the resources in a specific region
    (E) the part of Earth where life exists

34. The diploid number of a human cell is 23. How many actual chromosomes are in a normal body cell?
    (A) 22
    (B) 23
    (C) 44
    (D) 46
    (E) n

35. Which tissue transports carbohydrates and water through plants?
    (A) epidermal tissue
    (B) vascular tissue
    (C) ground tissue
    (D) epithelial tissue
    (E) endodermal tissue

36. According to the cell theory, which of the following statements is correct?
    (A) All organisms are made up of one or more cells.
    (B) All organisms must be able to reproduce.
    (C) Cells have organelles to carry on their functions.
    (D) Cells evolved from a primordial soup on early Earth.
    (E) Cells are able to regulate their external environment.

37. Which bird uses its beak to probe flowers for nectar?

    (A)

    (B)

    (C)

    (D)

    (E)

GO ON TO THE NEXT PAGE

PRACTICE TEST—*Continued*

38. Which of the following best describes what will happen if cells are placed in distilled water?

    (A) The cells remain unchanged.
    (B) Water moves from inside of the cell to the outside.
    (C) Water moves from outside of the cell to the inside.
    (D) The cells shrink.
    (E) The cells dissolve.

Questions 39 and 40

In an experiment in a laboratory, a population of bacteria in a Petri dish is exposed to an antibiotic. The antibiotic kills most of the population. However, a few bacteria survive and soon repopulate the Petri dish with antibiotic-resistant bacteria.

39. According to modern evolutionary theory, which of the following explanations is correct for this experiment?

    (A) Some of the bacteria tried and successfully adapted to the new conditions in the Petri dish.
    (B) Some members of the bacteria population developed a resistance to the antibiotic immediately after exposure.
    (C) Some members of the bacteria population already had a resistance to the antibiotic so they were not killed.
    (D) Some of the bacteria quickly evolve into a new species that resists the antibiotic.
    (E) Some of the bacteria protected themselves from the antibiotic long enough to develop a resistance.

40. Which best describes what happened in the petri dish?

    (A) macroevolution
    (B) microevolution
    (C) adaptive radiation
    (D) divergent evolution
    (E) speciation

41. All of the following are cycled though biogeochemical cycles EXCEPT

    (A) water
    (B) carbon
    (C) energy
    (D) phosphorus
    (E) nitrogen

42. You cross a red flowered plant with a white flowered plant, and all of the offspring have pink flowers. What is the most probable explanation?

    (A) Red is dominant.
    (B) White is dominant.
    (C) Pink is dominant.
    (D) Red and white exhibit incomplete dominance.
    (E) Red and white exhibit codominance.

43. If an organism has a haploid number of 24, how many chromosomes does it have?

    (A) 6
    (B) 12
    (C) 24
    (D) 36
    (E) 48

44. Bats and insects both have wings. The wings of bats and insects are examples of

    (A) homologous structures
    (B) analogous characters
    (C) vestigial structures
    (D) adaptive structures
    (E) derived traits

45.
    I.   vitamin synthesis
    II. absorb water
    III. absorb nutrients

    In humans, what function does the small intestine serve?

    (A) I and II only
    (B) II and III only
    (C) II only
    (D) I only
    (E) III only

46. A codon is

    (A) a group of three nucleotide sequences
    (B) the nucleotide units between the start and stop codes
    (C) the nucleotide sequence that serves as the instructions for a protein
    (D) a single nucleotide in an mRNA sequence
    (E) the sequence of nucleotides that signals the start or stop of protein synthesis

GO ON TO THE NEXT PAGE

PRACTICE TEST—*Continued*

47. Which of the following conditions is necessary for a virus to attack a host cell?

    (A) The virus must have the DNA or RNA key sequence to enter the host cell.

    (B) The virus must have the enzymes to cause the host cell to burst so that the host cell may be used as raw materials.

    (C) The virus must have the proper enzyme to puncture the membrane of the host cell.

    (D) The virus must have a particular shape that will match up with the proteins on the surface of the host cell.

    (E) The viral DNA or RNA must have a sequence that is recognized by the ribosomes of the host cell.

48. Cytochrome–c is a protein that scientists often use to compare the evolutionary relationships among species. There is one difference in the cytochrome–c sequence between humans and rhesus monkeys. There are ten differences between humans and kangaroos. What can you infer about the relationship between these species?

    (A) Humans and kangaroos have the same proteins coded in their genes.

    (B) Humans and kangaroos share a more recent ancestor than humans and rhesus monkeys.

    (C) Humans are not closely related to either kangaroos or rhesus monkeys.

    (D) Humans and rhesus monkeys share a more recent ancestor than humans and kangaroos.

    (E) Rhesus monkeys and kangaroos share a more recent ancestor than humans and rhesus monkeys.

49. A man with type A blood marries a woman with type B blood. Their child is blood type O. What are the genotypes of the parents?

    (A) AO and BO

    (B) OO and AB

    (C) Aa and BO

    (D) AO and Bb

    (E) Aa and Bb

Questions 50 and 51

Each corn kernel in an ear of corn is ready to grow into a new plant.

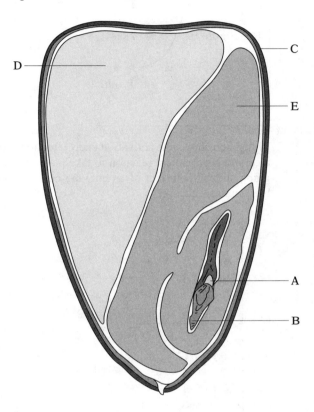

50. Which part of this seed makes up the plant embryo?

    (A) A, B

    (B) A, D

    (C) B, C

    (D) A, B, E

    (E) B, C, D

51. Which part of the seed stores the energy for the plant embryo?

    (A) A

    (B) B

    (C) C

    (D) D

    (E) E

GO ON TO THE NEXT PAGE

PRACTICE TEST—*Continued*

52.

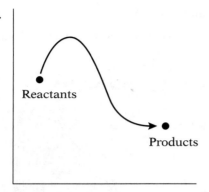

This graph shows the activation energy required for a certain biochemical reaction to take place. Which graph shows the effect of an enzyme on the same biochemical reaction?

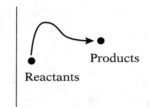

(A)

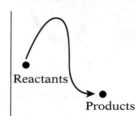

(B)

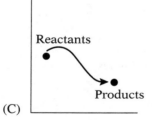

(C)

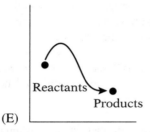

(D)

(E)

53. Which is the correct order of stages for an insect that undergoes incomplete metamorphosis?
(A) egg→larva→adult
(B) egg→nymph→adult
(C) egg→nymph→larva→adult
(D) egg→larva→pupa→adult
(E) egg→nymph→pupa→adult

54. The number of trophic levels that are maintained in an ecosystem is limited by
(A) the number of species
(B) the population size
(C) the loss of potential energy
(D) the number of individuals
(E) the hours of sunshine

55. The law of independent assortment applies to
(A) two genes on different chromosomes
(B) two genes on the same chromosome
(C) two alleles on different chromosomes
(D) two alleles on the same chromosome
(E) two chromosome strands

GO ON TO THE NEXT PAGE

PRACTICE TEST—*Continued*

56. Which is the correct order for the cell cycle beginning with the phase that most cells spend the majority of their time?

    I. G_2 Phase—growth and preparation for mitosis
    II.   Mitosis
    III. G_1 Phase—cell growth
    IV.   S Phase—DNA copied
    V.   Cytokinesis

    (A) III, IV, I, II, V
    (B) III, I, IV, V, II
    (C) II, III, I, IV, V
    (D) IV, III, I, II, V
    (E) V, III, IV, I, II

57. For natural selection to occur, which of the following must be true?

    (A) Individuals must evolve.
    (B) The environment must be constant.
    (C) Variation among organisms must exist.
    (D) Traits must be acquired.
    (E) Many species must be present.

58. What is the phenotypic ratio for a cross between a pea plant with purple flowers (PP) and a pea plant with white flowers (pp)?

    (A) all white
    (B) all purple
    (C) half purple, half white
    (D) 1PP, 2Pp, 1pp
    (E) all Pp

59. Natural selection is a part of evolution of a species. Which of the following best describes the driving force that leads to evolution within a species?

    (A) Individuals within a population change their behavior to accommodate changes in the environment and pass these to offspring.
    (B) Individuals within a population develop new adaptations as selective pressures force change.
    (C) Individuals within a population find new ways to adapt to environmental pressures.
    (D) Individuals within a population use different parts of their body as conditions change and pass those changes to offspring.
    (E) Individuals within a population have variations that give those individuals a better chance of survival.

60. Which of the following organisms is INCORRECTLY paired with its trophic level?

    (A) tree–producer
    (B) hawk–primary consumer
    (C) fungi–detritivore
    (D) fox–secondary consumer
    (E) grasshopper–primary consumer

GO ON TO THE NEXT PAGE

PRACTICE TEST—*Continued*

(Note: On the real SAT Biology test, Part B, questions 61–80, is ONLY for students taking Biology-E. For Biology-M, continue with Part C, questions 81–100. On the Answer Sheet, be sure to start marking your answers on the line for Question 81.)

▬▬ PART C (Biology-M Questions 81–100)

81. During crossing over, chromosomes

    (A) reduce in number
    (B) increase in number
    (C) undergo mutation
    (D) produce new genes
    (E) exchange corresponding genetic information

82. The process of photosynthesis is divided into two main groups of reactions. The light reaction is the process where light energy is converted into chemical energy. What are the products of the light reaction of photosynthesis?

    (A) $NADP^+$, H_2O, and ADP
    (B) CO_2 and H_2O
    (C) O_2 and H_2O
    (D) ADP and ATP
    (E) NADPH, O_2, and ATP

83.

    I.   bryophyte
    II. moss
    III. fern

    Which of the above plants contain vascular tissue?

    (A) III only
    (B) I and III only
    (C) I and II only
    (D) I only
    (E) I, II, and III

84. Spore-producing plants such as mosses depend on

    (A) conjugation for an exchange of genetic material
    (B) a thin film of water for the sperm to swim through to reach the egg
    (C) insects to carry pollen to the egg in the female plant
    (D) wind to carry pollen to the egg in the female plant
    (E) fire to cause the spores to release from the plant

85. The amount of guanine in an organism's DNA always equals the amount of

    (A) uracil
    (B) thymine
    (C) adenine
    (D) cytosine
    (E) thymine and adenine

86. Most cells in an animal are surrounded by

    (A) air
    (B) water
    (C) blood
    (D) synovial fluid
    (E) interstitial fluid

87. The most common carbon-fixing biochemical pathway is the Calvin cycle. How many carbon dioxide molecules must enter the Calvin cycle to yield one glucose molecule?

    (A) 2
    (B) 3
    (C) 4
    (D) 6
    (E) 12

GO ON TO THE NEXT PAGE ➤

PRACTICE TEST—*Continued*

Questions 88–92

The following diagram represents the events of aerobic cellular respiration:

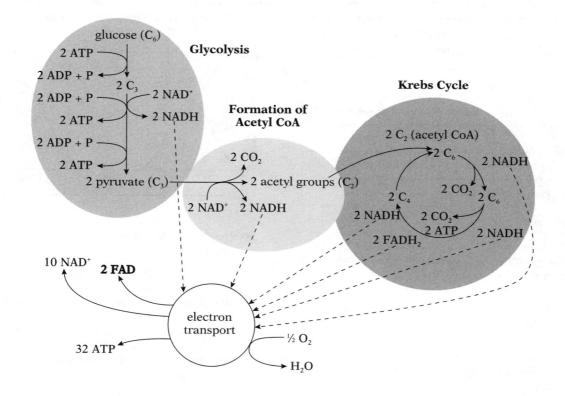

88. The electron transport chain produces

    (A) ADP
    (B) ATP
    (C) NADP$^+$
    (D) oxygen
    (E) glucose

89. Four ATP are produced during glycolysis but the net yield is

    (A) 1 ATP
    (B) 2 ATP
    (C) 3 ATP
    (D) 4 ATP
    (E) 6 ATP

90. The cellular respiration pathway in which glucose is broken down to form pyruvate is called

    (A) aerobic respiration
    (B) the Krebs cycle
    (C) formation of Acetyl CoA
    (D) glycolysis
    (E) electron transport

91. The most ATP in cellular respiration results from the

    (A) Krebs cycle
    (B) glycolysis
    (C) cycling of FAD
    (D) electron transport chain
    (E) formation of Acetyl CoA

92. What happens to the excess carbon atoms during the Krebs cycle?

    (A) They return to glycolysis.
    (B) They are attached to the pyruvate.
    (C) They become carbon dioxide.
    (D) They pass through the electron transport chain.
    (E) They become acetyl groups.

GO ON TO THE NEXT PAGE

PRACTICE TEST—*Continued*

Questions 93–95

A student wanted to cross a true-breeding tall pea plant with a true-breeding short pea plant. The student performed the cross and recorded the phenotypes of the offspring in the F_1 generation. The student then crossed two plants from the F_1 generation and recorded the phenotypes of the offspring as the F_2 generation. The results are in the data table.

	Tall	**Short**
Parents	1	1
F_1 generation	27	0
F_2 generation	17	20

T = tall, t = short.

93. What is (are) the genotype(s) for the F_1 generation?
    (A) TT
    (B) Tt
    (C) tt
    (D) TT and Tt
    (E) Tt and tt

94. What is (are) the genotype(s) for the F_2 generation?
    (A) TT
    (B) TT and Tt
    (C) TT and tt
    (D) Tt and tt
    (E) TT, Tt, and tt

95. If a tall plant from the F_2 generation were to be crossed with a short plant, which of the following statements would be true?
    (A) All the offspring would be short.
    (B) All the offspring would be tall.
    (C) The ratio would be 1:1 tall to short.
    (D) The ratio would be 3:1 tall to short.
    (E) The ratio would be either 1:1 tall to short, or all tall.

Questions 96–100

The graph shows the relationship between pH and the activity of two digestive enzymes pepsin and trypsin. These enzymes work in two different parts of the human digestive system, the stomach and the small intestine.

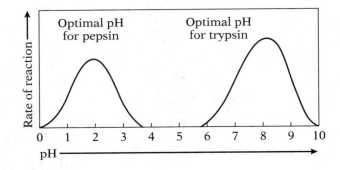

96. How would taking an antacid affect the activity of pepsin?
    (A) The activity would decrease because the pH would increase.
    (B) The activity would decrease because the pH would decrease.
    (C) The activity would increase because the pH would increase.
    (D) The activity would increase because the pH would decrease.
    (E) Taking an antacid would have no affect on the activity of pepsin.

97. Where in the digestive tract would trypsin most likely be found?
    (A) mouth
    (B) stomach
    (C) small intestine
    (D) large intestine
    (E) rectum

GO ON TO THE NEXT PAGE ➤

PRACTICE TEST—*Continued*

98. What is the pH at which trypsin works best?

  (A) 5.5
  (B) 6
  (C) 7
  (D) 8
  (E) 10

99. What is the pH at which pepsin works best?

  (A) 0
  (B) 2
  (C) 4
  (D) 6
  (E) 8

100. Which of the following statements is true about the digestive enzymes pepsin and trypsin?

  (A) Pepsin works best in a basic environment, and trypsin works best in an acidic environment.
  (B) Pepsin and trypsin work best in acidic environments.
  (C) Pepsin and trypsin are both found in the stomach.
  (D) Pepsin works best in an acidic environment, and tyrypsin works best in a basic environment.
  (E) Pepsin and trypsin both work well in acidic and basic environments.

S T O P

IF YOU FINISH BEFORE TIME RUNS OUT, GO BACK AND CHECK YOUR WORK.

PRACTICE TEST 4
BIOLOGY-M

ANSWER KEY

Part A

1. C	11. C	21. B	31. A	41. C	51. D
2. A	12. D	22. A	32. B	42. D	52. B
3. D	13. D	23. D	33. C	43. E	53. B
4. D	14. B	24. B	34. D	44. B	54. C
5. A	15. E	25. D	35. B	45. E	55. C
6. B	16. B	26. D	36. A	46. A	56. A
7. C	17. E	27. A	37. C	47. D	57. C
8. E	18. B	28. E	38. C	48. D	58. B
9. B	19. B	29. C	39. C	49. A	59. E
10. A	20. B	30. B	40. B	50. D	60. B

Part C

81. E	91. D
82. E	92. C
83. A	93. B
84. B	94. E
85. D	95. E
86. E	96. A
87. D	97. C
88. B	98. D
89. B	99. B
90. D	100. D

SCORE SHEET

Number of questions correct: _____

Less: 0.25 × number of questions wrong: _____

(Remember that omitted questions are not counted as wrong.)

Raw score: _____

Raw Score	Scaled Score	Raw Score	Scaled Score	Raw Score	Scaled Score	Raw Score	Scaled Score	Raw Score	Scaled Score
80	800	57	690	34	520	11	380	−12	250
79	800	56	680	33	520	10	370	−13	240
78	800	55	670	32	510	9	370	−14	240
77	800	54	670	31	510	8	360	−15	230
76	800	53	660	30	500	7	350	−16	230
75	800	52	650	29	500	6	350	−17	230
74	800	51	650	28	490	5	340	−18	220
73	790	50	640	27	490	4	330	−19	220
72	790	49	630	26	480	3	330	−20	220
71	780	48	620	25	480	2	320		
70	780	47	620	24	470	1	320		
69	770	46	610	23	470	0	310		
68	760	45	600	22	460	−1	310		
67	760	44	600	21	450	−2	300		
66	750	43	590	20	440	−3	300		
65	740	42	580	19	440	−4	290		
64	740	41	580	18	430	−5	290		
63	730	40	570	17	420	−6	280		
62	720	39	560	16	420	−7	270		
61	710	38	560	15	410	−8	270		
60	710	37	550	14	400	−9	260		
59	700	36	540	13	400	−10	260		
58	700	35	530	12	390	−11	250		

Note: This is only a sample scoring scale. Scoring scales differ from exam to exam.

ANSWERS AND EXPLANATIONS

Part A

1. **C** Fermentation is the cellular respiration process that takes place in the absence of oxygen. Fermentation converts glucose to either lactic acid or ethyl alcohol.

2. **A** The Krebs cycle is a cyclic biochemical pathway of respiration. It takes in pyruvate and produces ATP, NADH, and $FADH_2$.

3. **D** Glycolysis is the biochemical pathway that breaks down glucose to pyruvate. Glycolysis produces a net gain of 2 ATP molecules.

4. **D** Earthworms are decomposers because they break down organic matter and return nutrients to the soil. The returned nutrients are ready for use by plants.

5. **A** Cows are primary consumers because they eat plants, which are producers. Primary consumers are on the next trophic level above producers.

6. **B** Lions are secondary consumers because they eat animals, other consumers.

7. **C** Buzzards are scavengers because they find and eat already dead animals rather then killing them.

8. **E** Behavioral isolation occurs when two groups diverge and have different courtship rituals.

9. **B** Mechanical isolation occurs when two groups evolve differences in their genitalia.

10. **A** Geographic isolation occurs when groups are physically separated, such as by a mountain range or large body of water.

11. **C** Temporal isolation occurs when two groups diverge and have different mating seasons.

12. **D** Hybrid sterility occurs when nonfertile offspring are produced. This is a dead end as far as passing genes on is concerned.

13. **D** Imprinting is a learned behavior that occurs at a certain time of an animal's life, such as just after birth.

14. **B** A reflex is an automatic and uncontrollable response. This is a direct stimulus–response scenario.

15. **E** Habituation is learned behavior that occurs as a result of doing some repeatedly.

16. **B** All monocots have parallel veins in their leaves.

17. **E** Populations grow as a result of multiple births through the lifespan of an organism. If each organism in a population only reproduced once, the population would not grow.

18. **B** Jellyfish are primitive, multicellular organisms. An opening to the digestive tract serves as both the mouth and anus for jellyfish.

19. **B** Motivation is needed for learning. If an animal lacks motivation, there will be no learning.

20. **B** Plant cells have a cell wall composed of cellulose. The cellulose is rigid and gives the plant cell a defined shape.

21. **B** Cnidarians have two distinct body plans during their lives. A jellyfish is an example of a medusa, and a sea anemone is an example of a polyp.

22. **A** Sometimes during meiosis, a pair of chromosomes fails to separate. This causes an extra chromosome in one daughter cell and a missing chromosome in the other.

23. **D** Fungi have many different forms, but the shape of their spores classifies them all.

24. **B** When a pasture exceeds the carrying capacity, it lacks the food to support that number of animals. A pasture in this condition will have all its available food eaten and will appear barren.

25. **D** The only mutation that can be passed to offspring is one that occurs in the sex cells. These are the only cells that undergo meiosis and take part in reproduction.

26. **D** A dihybrid cross has two factors in the cross. This results in a total of four potential phenotypes with a ratio of 9:3:3:1.

27. **A** Uracil does not occur in DNA but is in RNA. In RNA, uracil replaces thymine and attaches to adenine.

28. **E** Bacteria usually reproduce through binary fission but they sometimes get together, exchange genetic information, and reproduce by a process known a conjugation.

29. **C** During meiosis, the chromosome pairs separate and go to different daughter cells. This means that each daughter cells acquires one allele for a specific trait.

30. **B** The complementary strand of DNA will have the opposite nucleotide bases as the original strand.

31. **A** The mRNA strand will have the opposite nucleotides as the DNA with uracil substituted for thymine.

32. **B** When Linneaus proposed a method for classifying organisms, he based his system on structural similarities. This system has worked fairly well but many refinements are now done using genetic analysis.

33. **C** An ecosystem is all interactions among the organisms in the environment as well as the abiotic features.

34. **D** The diploid number refers to the number of pairs of chromosomes. In humans, the normal diploid number is 23 so that means that a cell has 23 pairs or 46 chromosomes.

35. **B** Plants are made up of many different types of tissues. The tissues that are part of the transport system for plants are vascular tissues such as xylem and phloem.

36. **A** This is the most basic statement of the cell theory.

37. **C** A bird that probes flowers for nectar would need a long, thin beak to reach inside the flower. A hummingbird is an example of a bird that feeds on nectar from flowers.

38. **C** Distilled water is hypotonic compared to a cell. As a result, water moves from an area of higher concentration (outside the cell) to the area of lower concentration (inside the cell).

39. **C** Because of genetic variations, some of the bacteria were able to survive the antibiotics. They passed this genetic advantage to their offspring and soon repopulated the petri dish with antibiotic-resistant bacteria.

40. **B** This scenario is an example of microevolution. Microevolution is a small change in a population but not enough to create a new species.

41. **C** Biogeochemical cycles are cycles where minerals move between the biotic and abiotic part of the environment. Energy is not a mineral.

42. **D** Incomplete dominance occurs when neither of two traits is dominant. When both alleles appear, the phenotype is expressed as a blend.

43. **E** The haploid number for chromosomes is the actual number of chromosomes in a gamete. The total number of chromosomes in an organism would be double the haploid number.

44. **B** Analogous structures are those that serve a similar function but have structural differences and are not linked through evolution.

45. **E** The small intestine is lined with villi that increase the surface area and aid in the absorption of nutrients from digested food. The large intestine carries out the absorption of water, and the large intestines are also the site of some vitamin synthesis by bacteria living there symbiotically.

46. **A** The genetic code is based on sets of three nucleotides called codons.

47. **D** The shape of a virus allows it to attach to a host cell. Once this is accomplished, the virus can inject DNA or RNA into the host cell.

48. **D** Evolution results in changes to proteins. For cytochrome-c, the fewer the changes, the more closely related the organisms.

49. **A** A and B are dominant over O. O can only be expressed if paired with another O. The only way the offspring could have two O alleles is if the parents were AO and BO.

50. **D** The embryo of the corn plant is made up of the embryonic shoot (A), the embryonic root (B), and the cotyledon (E).

51. **D** The endosperm is energy stored for the plant embryo.

52. **B** An enzyme is a catalyst. Catalysts facilitate reactions by lowering the activation energy of the reaction pathway. They cannot change the initial or final energy level of the participating molecules.

53. **B** An insect with incomplete metamorphosis has a nymph stage that looks similar to the adult stage. Unlike complete metamorphosis, there is no pupa stage.

54. **C** Potential energy is the amount of energy for the next trophic level. Each trophic level only passes on about 10% of its total energy to the next higher level.

55. **C** The law of independent assortment states that traits are inherited independently of other traits. This only applies to alleles that are on separate chromosomes.

56. **A** Cells spend most of their time in the G_1 phase. After that comes the S phase, the G_2 phase, mitosis, and finally cytokinesis.

57. **C** Organisms must already have traits for variation before natural selection occurs. Under most conditions, the variation in traits does not provide any particular advantage so there is no natural selection. The variation only becomes important for natural selection when there is pressure that gives one trait an advantage over another.

58. **B** All of the plants in the first generation will be heterozygous so they exhibit the dominant trait.

59. **E** Individuals have traits that make them more successful, which gives them a reproductive advantage.

60. **B** Hawks are secondary consumers because they eat other consumers.

Part C

81. **E** Crossing over exchanges genetic material between chromatids and increases genetic variability.

82. **E** The light reaction of photosynthesis depends on light as an energy source. The NADPH and ATP are used to run the dark reaction, while oxygen gas gets released from the plant.

83. **A** Ferns are the most primitive plants to have actual vascular tissue. The presence of vascular tissue allowed these plants to become large.

84. **B** Spore-producing plants need a film of water for the sperm to swim through. This is a limitation on the types of environment in which these plants can live.

85. **D** In DNA, guanine always links to cytosine; therefore, the amount of both must be equal.

86. **E** Most cells in organisms are surrounded by interstitial fluid. Interstitial fluid is made up of water, food molecules, nutrients, and wastes.

87. **D** The Calvin cycle requires six carbon dioxide molecules to produce a single six carbon glucose molecule.

88. **B** The electron transport chain produces 32 ATP molecules, which is the bulk of ATP produced by cellular respiration.

89. **B** Glycolysis produces four ATP molecules, but two are required to run the reaction leaving a net gain of two ATP molecules.

90. **D** Glycolysis is the biochemical pathway that breaks down glucose into pyruvate. Other biochemical pathways can then use the pyruvate.

91. **D** The most ATP is produced in the electron transport chain. The rest of cellular respiration feeds products into the electron transport chain.

92. **C** Carbon dioxide is a waste product of cellular respiration. The carbon dioxide is released to the atmosphere.

93. **B** This results from a cross between two homozygous plants in the parent generation. One is homozygous dominant and other is homozygous recessive. The offspring (F_1 generation) are heterozygous.

94. **E** This is a cross between two heterozygous plants. The result is that the offspring can be homozygous dominant, heterozygous, or recessive.

95. **E** The offspring can be either all tall or half tall, half short because it is uncertain whether the plant from the F_2 generation is homozygous or heterozygous.

96. **A** An antacid would increase the pH in the stomach and decrease the activity of pepsin.

97. **C** The small intestine neutralizes the acid from the stomach and creates a basic environment. Trypsin works best in a basic environment.

98. **D** Trypsin has a peak performance at a pH of 8.

99. **B** Pepsin has a peak performance at a pH of 2.

100. **D** The enzymes each have a peak performance based on the pH of where they are found.

E N D